Gautam Buddha

Gautam Buddha

Series Editor
Dr. M.H. Syed

Editor
R.K. Singh **P.K. Choudhry**

Himalaya Books Pvt. Ltd.

'Ramdoot', Dr. Bhalerao Marg, Girgaon, Mumbai - 400 004
Tel : (022) 23863863. Fax : (022) 23877178
Email : himpub@vsnl.com

First Edition : 2011
Edition : 2016

Published by : **H.B.P.L.**
"Pooja Apartment", 4-B, Murari Lal Street, Ansari Road,
Darya Ganj, New Delhi - 110 002.
Phones: 011-23270392, 23278631; Fax: 011-23256286
Email: hphdel@vsnl.com

Sole Distributors : **Himalaya Publishing House Pvt. Ltd.**

Branch Offices :

Mumbai : "Ramdoot", Dr. Bhalerao Marg, Girgaon, Mumbai - 400 004.
Phone: 022-23860170/23863863, Fax: 022-23877178
E-mail: himpub@vsnl.com; Website: www.himpub.com

Nagpur : Kundanlal Chandak Industrial Estate, Ghat Road,
Nagpur - 440 018. Phone: 0712-2738731, 3296733;
Telefax: 0712-2721216

Bengaluru : Plot No. 91-33, 2nd Main Road Seshadripuram,
Behind Nataraja Theatre, Bengaluru-560020.
Phone: 08041138821, 9379847017, 9379847005

Hyderabad : No. 3-4-184, Lingampally, Besides Raghavendra Swamy
Matham, Kachiguda, Hyderabad - 500 027.
Phone: 040-27560041, 27550139

Chennai : New-20, Old-59, Thirumalai Pillai Road, T. Nagar,
Chennai - 600 017. Mobile: 9380460419

Pune : First Floor, "Laksha" Apartment, No. 527, Mehunpura,
Shaniwarpeth (Near Prabhat Theatre), Pune - 411 030.
Phone: 020-24496323/24496333;
Mobile: 09370579333

Lucknow : House No 731, Shekhupura Colony, Near B.D. Convent School,
Aliganj, Lucknow - 226 022. Phone: 0522-4012353;
Mobile: 09307501549

Ahmedabad : 114, "SHAIL", 1st Floor, Opp. Madhu Sudan House, C.G. Road,
Navrang Pura, Ahmedabad - 380 009. Phone: 079-26560126;
Mobile: 09377088847

Ernakulam : 39/176 (New No: 60/251) 1st Floor, Karikkamuri Road, Ernakulam,
Kochi – 682011. Phone: 0484-2378012, 2378016;
Mobile: 09387122121

Bhubaneswar : 5 Station Square, Bhubaneswar - 751 001 (Odisha).
Phone: 0674-2532129, Mobile: 09338746007

Kolkata : 108/4, Beliaghata Main Road, Near ID Hospital, Opp. SBI Bank,
Kolkata - 700 010, Phone: 033-32449649, Mobile: 7439040301

Printed at : M/s. Aditya Offset Process (I) Pvt. Ltd., Hyderabad. On behalf of HPH.

Preface

Biography, is now a form of literature, very much in vogue. In fact, biography is a description or account of someone's life and the times, which is usually published in the form of a book. A biography is more than a mention of personal facts (life, education, work, relationships and death), it also portrays the subject's experience of events. Technically speaking, a work is biographical, if it covers, all of a person's life. Biography writing has a long history. A biography is real. Ancient Greeks developed the biographical tradition, which we have inherited, although until the 5th century AD, when the word 'biographia' first appeared, in Damascius' "Life of Isodorus," biographical pieces were called simply "lives". It is quite likely that the Greeks were drawing on a pre-existing eastern tradition. Certainly Herodotus' "Histories" contains more detailed biographical information on Persian kings and subjects. The earliest surviving pieces, which we would identify as biographical are Isocrates' "Life of Evagoras" and Xenophon's "Life of Agesilaos," both from the fifth century BC. "Parallel Lives" by Plutarch, a Greek writing under the Roman empire, is a series of short biographies of eminent men.

The Golden Age of English biography emerged in late eighteenth century, the century in which the terms "biography" and "autobiography" entered English lexicon. The classic works of the period were Samuel Johnson's "Critical Lives of the Poets" and James Boswell's "Massive Life of Johnson". Generally American biography followed English model. By World War I, cheap hardcover reprints had become popular. The decade of the 1920s witnessed a biographical 'boom'. Later, biographical writings developed a lot and today biographies are written and compiled in the finest form of the genre. In India too, biography, as a form of literature has been evolved, cultivated and polished over the years. Here is an effort to promote this tradition further.

This series of biographies of great men, great women and celebrities in all walks of life is an adventurous academic endeavour, in its own right. A team of researchers and compilers has worked for a good period of time to accomplish the project. For this purpose, hundreds of books by eminent authors and editors have been consulted and referred to. We have benefited from various works, liberally, in order to illustrate and enrich this effort of ours. Present book is devoted to the great personality of Gautam Buddha.

Gautam Buddha was a spiritual teacher in ancient India, who founded Buddhism. In most Buddhist traditions, he is regarded as "the Supreme Buddha of Our Age, "Buddha", meaning, "awakened one" or "the enlightened one." Gautama, also known as Sakyamuni (Sage of the Sakyas), is the primary figure in Buddhism, and accounts of his life, discourses, and monastic rules are believed by Buddhists to have been summarised after his death and memorised by his followers. Various collections of teachings, attributed to him, were passed down by oral tradition, and first committed to writing about 400 years later. He is also regarded as a god or prophet in other religions, such as Hinduism, the Ahmadiyya sect and the Baha'i faith. He is also called the Tathagata [he, who has come thus], Bhagavat [the Lord], and Sugata [well-gone]. The story of his life is overlaid with legends.

This is a compact and comprehensive account of the above mentioned great life, which is bound to attract the attention of scholars, researchers, students and the general readers, alike. Let's hope this humble effort would receive a warm welcome and due applause.

— ***Editors***

Contents

1

The Holy Life

The Backdrop

The society in which Gautam Buddha was to be born was simple, peaceful ancient society, where, neither politics nor the dispensation of justice, except on rare and sensational occasions, were of any very great interest to the ordinary citizens. Indeed, they were glad to leave the conduct of government to their betters and to be left in peace to pursue their proper occupations. For excitement, there were all sorts of amusements available. There were the temples where the contrite and conscientious congregated daily at fixed hours to pray and offer sacrifices for the redemption and elevation of their souls. Gamblers flocked into the public gambling hall, and in the oracular rattle of the dice, and the tense expectancy of the game, found a satisfying substitute for the Good, the True, and the Beautiful.

There were the opportunities for venal love, with its promise of pulsating bliss for those whose inclinations were of a less abstract nature. In the evenings, usually after a much-needed hygienic treatment at the hot-baths, mystics desirous of curing the ills of the soul through ministrations of the body made their way to the quarters inhabited by the priestesses of Venus. There, in the tortuous friction of flesh against flesh, the separate entities of a four-dimensional universe struggled to cast off the burden of their solitude; forgetting in their momentary abandonment the distinctions between *Prakriti* and *Purusha,* between Being and Non-Being, between the Casual and the Accidental, between the Eternal and the Transient.

Ancestors of Buddha

Sujata, the chief of the Shakyn chan used to rule in Saketa, the present Ayodhya; because the Shakyas used to rule from this place for generations, it was known as Saketa. Due possibly to the conquest of their territory by the Ikashakus, who renamed Saketa as Ayodhya, the Shakyas were driven northwards to Kasi-Kosala. But there too they could not settle long in peace. They were pushed further north in Saketavana, and there on the sloping hills of the Hymalayas they occupied a track of land about 2500 square miles in extent. And they had as their neighbours the Koli clan who were also pushed north like them. The Rohini river which used to supply water to the rice fields of these clans for irrigational purposes, was their boundary. The Shakyas selected the hermitage of the sage Kapila as the centre of their capital and they built a town and called it Kapilavastu. The Kolis had Devadha as their capital, and these towns were 11 miles distant from each other.

The Shakyas used to select one of them as their a and they called him *Raja.* It depended on the choice of the electors of the clan whether it would be for a few years, life time or hereditary. Any way it was revokable if the clan chose it. Sujata's son was Opur who settled with the clan in Kapalivastu. Opur's son was Nipur, and Nipur's son was Ulkamukha. And Ulkamukha's son was Jayasena. Jayasena, had a son Sinhahanu and a daughter Yashodhara who was married to Anjana, son of Devadaha of Koli, and Anjana's sister Kanchana was married to Sinhahanu. Sinhahanu by Kanchana had four sons,—Suddhodana, Dhantadan, Suklodan and Amritodan, and had two daughters, Amita and Piamita. Anjana by Yashodhara had two sons—Suparbuddha and Dandapani, and two daughters—Maya and Gautami Prajapati. Both the sisters—Maya and Gautami Prajapati—daughters of Anjana, were married to Suddhodhana. Suddhodhana through Maya had his son Siddhartha Gautam—the Baddha, and though

Gautami Prajapati—Nanda. Amita, sister of Suddhodana was married to Suprabuddha, and they had a son Devadatta. Dandapani had a daughter known by three names—Yashodhara, Subhadhara Kanchana and Gopa 'Siddhartha, Gautam the Buddha was married to Yashodhara, and had a son Rahula. Suddhodana's brother Suklodana, had two sons—Ananda and Davadatta. Another brother Amritadana had two sons—Mahanama and Anuruddha—and a daughter Rohini. Dhotodana's son was Bhadraka who became the head of the Shakyas after Mahanama. Mahanama became the head after Sudhodhana's death.

Raja Suddhodana was the elected chief of the Shakya leaders who were 80 thousand in number and all of them were called Rajas. *Raja* was the title of any of the clan leaders, who was associated with the management of the state affairs. When there was a dispute over the water supply of the Rohini river between the Shakyas and the Kolis, while trying to settle it amiably, Buddha addressed all the assembled leaders as Mahara. Vaishali had 7777 chiefs and all of them were called *Ganaraja, and* each one had a hand in the management of the state administration, and before he could be consecrated in his office, he had to take a bath in the auspicious tank. *Vaishali* was prosperous for 7777 Rajas were always united and devoted to their duties. Vaishali was surrounded by three ram parts and three water towers. When Kosala King desiring to marry a Shakya Princess sent an emissary to Kapilavastu, all the Shakya leaders were assembled in Hall (Santagar) for consultation. According Lichchhirika, Yrijika, Mallaka, Mudroka, Kukura, Kuru, Panchala and others had the title of a Raja.

Buddha's Parentage

Suddhodana was a very popular president of the Shakya clan. He was loved, esteemed and respected by all for his sense of duty, virtue and honesty. His Queen consorts—Maya and Gautami Prajapati—were not only very beautiful, they were also very noble-hearted and generous. Though they were co-wives, they had no rivalry, but worked together in harmony and cooperation. But they had one regret in their hears, They were: childless. Maya Devi was now 45 years old, and her sister was only younger to her by one year. In the mid-summer festival of Ashari Purnima, there used to be a great carnival in Kapalavastu, commencing seven days previous to the full-moon day. It was the Rain-festival, for on rain depended the prosperity and happiness of the people; so the spontaneous public rejoicings. In the merriments the rich and the poor, men and women, all joined. There used to be dancings, singings, sports, athletic displays and amusements, feasts and drinkings. There used to be illuminations at night. The city was decorated. Even the poorest couples wearing safflower-coloured garments and covering their upper parts with another, wearing garlands, used to go together to the festivities, putting arms round each other shoulders. Professional athletes used to show their wonderful feats. There used to be tricky dances on ropes hung on bamboo poles and on bamboos. Spectators gazed with surprise and wonder at the magicians who apparently swallowed sharp swords. Itinerant traders used to display various kinds of tempting wares. But the most attractive part of the was that of drinking like- that of Greek Dionysia or Roman Bacchanlia. And with hard drinking, there was gaiety, hilarity and voluptuous origies.

The multitude were enjoying the feast And Queen Maha-Maya abstaining from strong drinks and brilliant with garlands and perfumes, took part in the festivities for the six days previous to the full-moon in 625 BC. And when it came to the full-moon, she rose early, bathed in perfumed water. And decked in gala attires, she ate of the choicest foods. After nightfall, when the crowd dispersed with a drizzling shower, Maya Devi after the day's fatigue was in her retiring room and reposing on her couch and singing in rapturous heart in her sweet melody—O how pretty the heavenly nectar is falling! Suddhodana who was also nearby listening to her charming tune, came and laying near her, stroke her locks and was caressing her. As if from ecstasy she awoke, outstretched her arms round her husband's neck in a voluptuous abandon. And for long they were interlocked in lover's embrace. Never before Maya Devi experienced such intense libidinous pleasure. And soon she relaxed and slumbered.

The Dream

Maha Maya awoke in the morning with a dream that a white elephant, plucking a white lotus with his silvery trunk, was striking on her right side and seemed to enter her womb, and she told about this dream to her husband. Suddhodana caused sixty-four eminent Brahmins to be summoned, and spread costly seats on ground, festively prepared with green leaves, Dalbergia flowers and so forth. The Brahmins being seated, he filled gold and silver dishes with the best milk porridge compounded with ghee, honey and treacle, and covering these dishes with others, made likewise of gold and silver, he gave the Brahmins to eat. But not only with food but with other gifts, such as new garments, tawny cows and so forth, he satisfied them completely. And when their every desire was satisfied, he told them the dream, and asked them what would come of it. "Be not anxious, great King," said the Brahmins. "A child has planted itself in the womb of the Queen, and it is a male child and not a female. You will have a son".

Great was the rejoicing in the household. And the court physician frequently visited her to give her advice on her food and toilet. And during the Kartik Purnima festival, Prajapati also conceived. And consequently Suddhodana was in good humour. In the tenth month of Maya's pregnancy, Maya Devi did not; feel well, and she was restless she said to Suddhodana: "I should like to visit my kinsfolk in their city, Devadaha": "So be it", said the King, and from Kapilavastu to the city of Devadaha, he had the road made even, and garnished it with, plantain trees, set in pots, and with banners and streamers; and seating the Queen in a palanquin borne by a number of men, he sent her away in a great pomp. Now between the two cities and belonging to the inhabitants of both, there was a pleasure-grove of Sala trees, called Lumbini grove. And at this particular time (Vaishaki Purnima), this grove was one mass of flowers from the ground to the topmost branches, while amongst the branches and flowers hummed, swarms of bees, and flocks of various kinds of birds flew warbling sweetly.

Birth of a Great Son

The Queen became desirous of disporting herself therein, and the courtiers therefore took her there into. And going to the foot of a Sala tree she seized hold of a flowering branch, and immediately her pains came upon her. Thereupon the people hung a curtain about her and retired. Soon after the attending nurse announced that a son had been born, but the Queen was semiconscious. Then one of Maya's maids rushed to Suddhodana and joyously shouted to him: "Lord, a son has been born to you, who will bring glory to your house". Suddhodana did not say anything but his face brightened with joy, indicating his happiness. And after receiving further details, he had the birth of the sou announced in the city. Then he accompanied by many Shakyas and Brahmins went to the Lumbini grove. There he found assembled many inhabitants of both the cities rejoicing. And the King inclining towards the child, said, "as he has fulfilled my desire, I shall call him Siddhartha." Then in a palanquin accompanied by many inhabitants of both the cities, the mother and the child were brought to Kapilavastu.

Now it came to pass at that time Asita (Kala) Devala, who was an intimate friend of Suddhodhana, practised in the eight stages of meditation, went after his daily meal, and in his rounds, heard that a son had been born to his friend, and in haste entered the dwelling, and having seated himself on the seat assigned to him, he said—"Great King, I hear that a son has been born to you. I would see him." Then the King had the Prince magnificently dressed and brought in.: "Marvellously glorious will be this child; he has all the marks of greatness of a great King or a great Buddha.

Early Childhood

On the fifth day they bathed the baby's head, sayings. "We will perform the choosing a name for him." And they prepared the royal palace by annointing it with 4 kinds of perfumes and by scattering Dalbergia blossoms and other flowers—five sorts in all. And making some porridge of whole rice grains boiled in milk, they invited one hundred and eight Brahmins— men who had mastered the three Vedas. And having seated these Brahmins in the royal palace, and fed them with delicate food and showed them every attention, they asked them to observe the marks and characteristics of the Prince and to' prophesy his future. Among the hundred and eight, Kama, Dhaja, Laksmana, Mamtri, Kondanna, Bhoja, Suama and Sudatta were the same Brahmin fortune-tellers who had interpreted the dream of the night of conception. Seven of these raised two fingers each and gave a double interpretation, saying if a man possessing such marks continue in the household, he becomes a universal monarch; if he retire from the world, he becomes it Buddha.

The Prince was named Siddhartha with auspicious ceremonies. But in the midst of all rejoicings, one event saddened everybody. High fever was burning in Maya Devi, and no medicine could cure her. And she had often delirious ecstatic exclamations about the future of her baby. On the seventh day, clasping her baby and pointing it to her sister, her restless feverish body reposed in eternal slumber. Prajapati nursed her step-son with more love, affection and tender care than her own son Nanda who was born six months after him. And even Siddartha grew up into a brilliant youth, without knowing that Prajapati was not his own mother, and Nanda was not his own brother. And both of them used to grow together in playful merriments. They were very fond of dolls made of wood, but with such dexterity they were made that they appeared to be natural objects. They had small doll elephants, gazelles, horses, cows and chariots for their playthings.

Education and Training

At the age of eight Siddhartha and Nanda were sent to Upadaya (preceptor) Vishvamitra with adequate fees. There Siddhartha quickly learnt the art of writing. Then be studied the Vedas, astronomy, grammar, etymology, metre, prosody, *Sankhya, Yoga, Vaisesik,* antiquities, history, economics, logic and the *Vrihaspati,* system of philosophy (atheistic); from astronomer Shakya Arjuna, he studied mathematics until he attained the age of 19. Now on a certain day the King celebrated the Sowing Festival. On that day they used to decorate the whole city, and all the slaves and other servant would put on new tunica; and perfumed and garlanded, they would assemble together at the King's palace where a thousand ploughs were assembled. On this occasion, there were one hundred and eight ploughs, all save one, ornamented with silver, as were also the reins for the oxen and the crossbars of the ploughs. But the plough that was held by the King was ornamented with red gold as also the horns, the reins and the goad of the oxen. And the King issued forth with a large retinue, taking his sons with him. In this the King, the ministers, patriarchs and cultivators—all joined with great jubilations. But

Siddhartha felt it was a cruel sight. In the burning sun the farmers were goading the innocent oxen with lashes. Instead of joining the festival he was sitting pensively under the dense shade and foliage of a solitary rose-apple tree. The Shakyas began to complain, and there was a discussion about him: "Siddhartha is wholly given over to ease, and is not training himself in any manly arts. What would he do if war were to occur!" The King sent for Siddhartha and said: "My child, your relatives are saying that you are not training yourself, but are wholly given over to ease. Now what do you think we had best to do?" "Father, let the crier go about the City, beating the drum to announce that I will show my proficiency to my relatives in the tournament on the seventh day from now."

Proficiency Proved

Dandapani also announced by beats of drums that his daughter Yashodhara aged 16, a girl renowned for her beauty and would select, as her husband the victor of the contests, whether he is Kshatriya or not. There was a big tournament on the parade ground which lasted for 5 days, and debating for two days in the Assembly Hall, in which all the Shakya and Koli youths participated, and all the patriarchs assembled to cheer, encourage and to criticise as well as the matrons and maidens to cheer their respective heroes,— all dressed in coloured garments, and garlanded and perfumed, in their finest embellishments. It was a jolly crowd, vociferous and merry-making.

The first day was devoted to archery. Three gold figurines of girls were suspended through silvern threads behind an iron plate with three corresponding holes not larger than a beak of a duck, The iron plate was nailed on *sala* poles about 64 hands from the platform. There were 480 contestants. They had leather knapsacks suspended on their backs containing:. horned bows and iron-tipped arrows. The arrow heads that could not hit the marks fell down on the ground, with a bang, being deflected by the iron plate, and the crowd jeered, Three at a time tried. But all failed, at last Devadatta succeeded to snapping a silvern thread and win a prize, and loud was the cheer. Then Siddhartha rose and tried, and snapped another silver thread, and he received a gold figurine of a dream-beauty, and louder still was the resounding cheer. The crowd dispersed for the day talking and gesticulating. Next day was the wrestling match. The parade ground was crowded to overflowing. The public took keener interests than on the previous day. There were 160 contestants. Finally Siddhartha and Devadatta remained good rivals. The issue remained undecided. The trophy of the day was a gold statuette of two wrestlers, and it remained the state possession. The third day was devoted to Fencing with both swords and clubs, the contestants wearing their iron armours and hanging swords in the sheathes on their left side. Siddhartha did not take any part in it, thinking it was a barbarous inhuman sport. Many were wounded.

But Devadatta was the victor of the day and entertained every one with his marvellous skill and dexterity. The fourth day was the day of the Horse-Race for seven miles (Yoyanas), and there were 80 contestants. Siddhartha's marvellous speed and his skill in managing his horse received the praise even of the veteran horsemen, and he got the trophy of a gold statuette of a rider. The fifth day was the last day of the sports, and it was devoted to chariot race. There were 64 contestants. In this as in horse race, Siddhartha outdistanced all his rivals, and for his surprising dexterity, he was declared the best charioteer, and he received the thundering applause of the spectators and a small gold chariot as his trophy. On the sixth, day the Assembly Hall was full with the elite of the two The subject was music and poetry.

There were 96 contestants. Many youths and maidens recited the poems of their compositions to melodious tunes, but Siddhartha's poems were judged to be the best; and he received a gold statuette of Shravasthi as his prize. The next day was the last, but the most important day. For on this day Yashodhara would choose the Victor as her husband in her Svayambara – marriage. Actually there were two formidable claimants for her hand and heart—valiant and daring Devadatta, her first cousin, her father's brother Suprabuddha's son and possible successor to the throne of the Kolis of Deyadaha; and the charming and eloquent Siddhartha, possible successor to the throne of Kapalivastu. Other youths also came with throbbing hearts, for in love hope is seldom lost, and is like an intoxicating beverage where the appetite increases with drinking. Youths came with brilliant headdresses and grey-coloured apparels, perfumed and garlanded. Matrons and maidens came in their finest attires. Patriarchs came in neat and clean dress, dignified serious, but cheerful and talkative. Many Brahmins came, including some distinguished scholars. In the first sessions there were discussions on logic, in which Devadatta seemed to have excelled. In handwriting Siddhartha was the best, and Vishvamitra was the judge. In mathematics Shakya Arjuna was the judge, and Siddhartha stood first. In the session when Devadatta focused on Ethics and Morals, there, was very little apprecintion; but when Siddhartha made remarks by saying that Sympathy and Love are really the essence of Ethics and Morals, they are more than virtues; they are the perennial fountains which not only quench the thurst of the restless seekers after divinity, do also promote the individual as will as the collective happiness, welfare and prosperity; there was loud burst of thundering applause, and Siddhartha received a gold statuette of a preceptor from the hands of Vishvamitra.

Marriage

Yashodhara attired in two safflower coloured flowing garments, her wavy black hair dressed in the form of a bow with white flowers, from her right hand hanging a garland of well scented flowers strung thorough a thin gold thread and heart-shaped knobs, rushed to, accompanied by some or her friends, where Devadatta, Siddhartha and others were sitting, when Devadatta thinking that it was for him, rose to receive it, but to his discomfiture, she put it round the neck of Siddhartha. Siddhartha with a happy smile, his face radiating with joy, clasped Yashodhara's hands, pulled out a precious ring from his own finger, and gave it to her. She hesitated to accept it. "Should I take it?". "Why not, it belongs to me." "But you are depriving yourself to give it to me." "What of that!" "And there was excellent rejoicing. Gautami Prajapati was the first to bless them. Then Suddhodhan, and after him Dandapani, and they embraced each other. Many others followed them, including Amrita, mother of Devadatta and sister of Suddhadana, who in her heart of hearts—longed to have Yashodhara to be his son's. Soon after, marriage took place with a great pomp and show. Siddhartha became cheerful and gay. He lost his habitual pensive mood and his introspective habits. He found Yashodhara infinitely more interesting than his studies. He was 19 and she was 16. Love shrouded their lives with a sweet aroma and intoxicating charms.:. Nature became with them more lovely than ever before. Flowers, birds, trees, running waters, even the passing clouds had a romantic meaning for them now which they did not feel before. It was a beautiful spring morning. There was zephyr — soothing and refreshing. Under a wooden pavilion on the lake in the park upon polished stone pavements, Siddhartha was sitting, Yoshodhara, laying her head on his lap, was reclining herself. The sun was rising in the east, flashing the surrounding sky with radiant colours. The snowy peaks of the Himalayas catching the morning rays of the rising, sun looked like heaps of molten gold in the western sky—resplendent and luminous. Siddhartha and Yoshodhara were gasing at the sight as if it was a feast for their eyes. Their attention was diverted by the chirping noise of a flock of wild duck that was flying on the horizon.

Suddenly a duck fell on the bank of the lake with an agonising sound, not far off from where Siddhartha was sitting. Siddhartha let loose the fingers of the left hand of Yashodhara he was holding with his right hand, and gently laying aside her head on a soft cushion made of his upper garment, he rushed to the place where the bird was lying. He found the white breast of the bird tinged red with blood, and there was an arrow head stuck in it. He pulled but the arrow head, washed the wound with the cold water, and with his careful nursing the bird revived. He even struck the arrow head into the tip of his own finger to find out how he would feel, and few drops of gentle tears like liquid pearl rolled down his cheeks for the suffering bird. Yashodhara was also helping Siddhartha in his nursing, though she remonstrated against hurting his own finger, Devadatta soon after appeared on the scone, and demanded the bird as the shot of his unerring mark. Siddhartha said: "I will not surrender this bird to you, because by my nursing I have saved its life; I have thereby acquired right over it. If your arrow-shot would have killed it outright, then certainly it would have been yours." Devadatta retorted: "You are given over to ease and pleasures of life. You know nothing of Kshatriya's Mrigaya (hunting) code of honour. A Kshatriya can not give up his own kill to others without losing self-respect and public esteem which is more than his life". "But you want to eat it; there will be plenty of fowls and venison for your dinner. After it is strong enough I shall allow it to fly away to its nest to enjoy its freedom". "But you are talking sentimental stuff like a female. After your marriage you have become like your wife." Yashodhara's face became crimson. But she did not say anything. Devadatta hurried away threatening that he would bring it to the notice of the Assembly for its decision. Siddhartha smilingly took Yasodhora's hands, led her to their residence with the duck. Next Thursday evening there was a discussion in the Assembly as to the ownership of the bird. Both Devadatta and Siddhartha explained their positions. The elders decided after, deliverations: "A creature belongs to one who saves its life. Siddhartha has saved its life, so he is entitled to it."

Siddhartha and Yashodhara used to go to the park every day in their chariot. There they enjoyed the lotus blooming in the rippled lake, birds singing from trees to trees, butterflies and insects sauntering from flowers to flowers, rambling in the wooded glens, and gasing steadfastly in clear sun-lit day at the silvery white snow-clad peaks after peaks of the vast and stupendous Himalyan ranges, and the interplay of light and shade of them. They took their picnics there. Now it was an autumn evening. There was a little melancholy sadness in the air at the parting of the summer. Many trees were shedding their leaves, looking like weeping widows bereft of their ornaments. Yashodhara too did not feel well, for she was pregnant. But she kept her usual habits in order to keep her husband's company, so that she could forget her own physical discomforts. This evening she felt tired. Siddhartha too had been drinking the cups of pleasures to the dregs, and with the satiation there was depression and ennui. Enchantment of novelty wears off with familiarity. This is the natural psychological reaction. And it brings introspection of the soul. They were driving back home in the evening. Darkness was gradually thickening. There was a little cold crispness in the air. It was being intensified by a slight shower and wind. Siddhartha was observing that many poor, sick, crippled and old were hurriedly seeking shelter from the inclement weather. Siddhartha asked his charioteer Chhandaka if there was any remedy for these ills. The charioteer said: "No, with wealth there will be poverty;

with organic life there will be sickness, old age and death. This is inevitable. Therefore it is wise to ignore them." "No, by ignoring them, you do not eliminate them. If everyone has equal right and opportunity to acquire and enjoy wealth, there will be no rich and the poor. There will be health. With care and attention to the body and the functioning of its organs, no sickness or senility needs to be corollary to health." "But pleasure and pain, health and sickness go together. We cannot understand one without the other. We only know them by contrasts." "Not necessarily so.. Pleasure is the physiological sensation of the well-being of the body, and mind find their proper functionings. Sickness is due to accidental factors, which can be cured or removed by good physicians, It is simply a question of knowing things in their true perspective and applying the principles in practical life". Yashodhara said little, but was listening to the arguments of her husband and his comrade. They have frequented this road so often. They have seen the poor, the sick, the old from their childhood. It is such a common occurrence. It never before intruded on their mind like an arrow-thrust with such an uneasy feeling. While riding together Siddhartha and Yashodhara were absorbed in each other's look and thoughts like a seductive intoxication, and they ignored the universe outside.

Process of Thinking

Siddhartha returned home, but the thought was still brewing in his mind how to conquer disease, sickness and old age, the scourge of all human beings. After taking his refreshments he retired, but he could not enjoy the refreshing sleep. The thought was agitating his mind like a fever that rages from within. Nest morning after the usual salutation, Yashodhara, seeing her husband brooding and depressed, said to him: "Beloved, why do you look so sad today?" "Dear, you are the source of my joy and pleasures; you delight and enliven me. But behind it is the cancerous tormenting pain that this sensuous joy is but temporary. Disease, senility and death stand in the way of our everlasting union and happiness." "But did not our charioteer wisely say that it is better to overlook the concomitant evils of life. Why not let us enjoy life as long as we can!" "But man is a thinking being, and not an animal. He wants to avoid evils if he can." "Every human being is subject to disease, old age and death; only Gods can avoid them." "Then I shall be a God." Yashodhara became anxious about the demeanour of her husband, and said: "Shall we not go to the park today?" And soon they started. Yashodhara tried to divert her husband's mind from those ugly corroding thoughts with all her feminine arts of coquetry. But Siddhartha was never again the same gay singing bird as before. He did many things almost mechanically as his customary habit so that Yashodhara would not take any offence, but he began to loose interests in them. Siddhartha was engrossed with the problems of human deliverance, from the painful bondage of poverty, sickness, senility and death. If he could only find its solution, then all human miseries would be over. As Yashodhara's pregnancy advanced, she could not accompany Siddhartha in his daily drive to and walks in the Park. Yashodhara's soulful love and winning smiles acted as an antidote to Siddhartha's brooding melancholy thoughts. But without this sobering influence, the solution of the deliverance of man from his bonds of misery became his all-consuming passion.

Thus, days, weeks and months passed. Instead of time giving a brake to the momentum, it rather became more accelerated. Passion became almost a frenzy. One evening Siddhartha was in the park. At that time news was brought to Suddhodana that Yashodhara had given birth to a son. He at once sent a messenger to his son with this happy announcement. Siddhartha was very glad to know that Yashodhara had given birth to a son without any mishap, but uttered with a sigh: "An impediment *(Rakuta)* has been born, a fetter has been born." While Siddhartha was driving back to his residence, accompanied by a joyous multitude in a procession, one Kisa Gautami, a Kshatria maiden, ascended the roof of her dwelling to ' find out what the noise was about, and seeing the splendid body and happy face of Siddhartha, burst forth into the song of joy:—"Full happy now mother is, full happy now that father is, full happy now that woman is who owns this lord so glorious." Siddhartha thought: "Am I really happy? It behoves me to quit the household life and to retire from this world in quest of the true happiness. I will send this lady a teacher's fee." And loosing from his neck a pearl necklace he sent it to Kisa Gautami. And great was her satisfaction at this, for she thought:

"Prince Siddhartha has fallen in love with me, and has sent me a present." When Siddhartha reached home, a beautiful baby was there.

Change of Path

After a few days, when Yashodhara was still convalescent. Siddhartha saw his father, and with usual salutation told him: "Consent to the proposal I shall make; please do not oppose it. I want to follow religious life, — the path of deliverance. I have made this decision, father." Suddhodhana became pensive, and after a minute's hesitation said: "Son, give up the idea. Time has not yet come for you to take to a religious life. Youth is a period of colourful imaginations and volatile thoughts. Its restless yearnings without the background of, practical experience and wisdom lack maturity of judgement. To load an austere ascetic life during youth would be a great error. You have not yet experienced the pleasures of life; before they have been fully enjoyed, your soul would restlessly yearn for them consciously or subconciously. And your firm resolutions would frustrate themselves before the privations and hardships for which your body and mind are unaccustomed. I have grown old. It is for me to lead a religious life. I abdicate my position to your favour. You have got a family. They need you. Enjoy the pleasures of life as long as you can. Then you can be a hermit which is; natural". "But father, how can we enjoy life while sickness, senility and death mock at our face?" "But do we not eat rice, because it is covered within husks? Do we not take the juice of the sugar cane for it is enclosed in fibres? Do we not enjoy the lotus-buds though the roots of them are covered with slime? Sickness and senility can be overcome by rational living. Man dies but once in his life, but he lives years which he can enjoy. My son, do not talk like a child. They are not problems at all. They have been in existence since creation. Be a man. Assert your right in this world, and learn to enjoy it". Siddhartha remained silent, but was not convinced.

Next day was a rainy day. Siddhartha did not stir out. Yashodhara was sitting near her husband, having the baby on her lap. Siddhartha hesitatingly broached out the subject to his wife: "Now you have got a boy, I hope you would not mind if I become a recluse". "But how can I live without you"? "Why, you have said that you could sacrifice your life for my happiness." "If I were a crystal you could see through whether what I said was true or not. But when a mother opposes her child's whims which might cause him harm, does she love him less or more? You are not accustomed to a life of privations. How would you stand it? Beloved have I offended you any way? Are you angry with me? Do not say any more about the religious life. It hurts me." And she began to sob. Tears rolled down, her cheeks like molten pearls. Her tears moved Siddhartha more than her arguments. And he remained silent.

Then one day Siddhartha approached Prajapati Gautami saying: "Mother, I want to be a recluse." "Why, what madness has overtaken you, my son I heard it also from your father, and I thought his arguments had convinced you of its futility. How can I your old mother, your old father, Yashodhara and her newborn babe live without you?" "But you will have everybody else. Nanda will look after you, father, Yashodhara and Rahula". She began sobbing, and clasping his head with her arms, and folding him into her bosom, said: "Before I saw you, the world was meaningless and empty for me; I did not know how to kill my time.

But when I held your tiny body within my arms, gazed at your transparent eyes, looked at your smiling face, when your velvety hands and face touched my face, and I heard prattlings from your twittering lips, the world has become full of interests and colourful for me. You have given me a new life. With your meaningless cruel heartless action, now will you snap it away?"

The Renunciation

It was a dark and gloomy night, though it was the *Ashari-Purnima* (Full-moon night in July); the sky was overcast with clouds. Already there were a couple of showers in the evening. Everything was wet, as if Nature was weeping and shedding its tears. Siddhartha sat pensive. Some *Solution* of poverty, sickness, old age and death must be found. He should try to find it out. But was he sure that by simply leaving his comfortable home, influencial position, beloved wife and son, affectionate parents and dear relatives and friends, in the quest of the unknown, he would find out the elixir of life by which Humanity could be redeemed? But would it not be cowardly not to try it? Was he not heroic enough to sacrifice his personal comforts for the sake of suffering man? Was it a good policy to feed the body, but to starve the soul? No, he would not die every beat of his pulse like a coward; but in his daring attempt to find out a solution for all, he would die but once like a hero on the battlefield. Conquest over *Mara* (*Kama:* Desire) is a better achievement than a victory in a battlefield. No, he was determined to achieve his aim or to perish in the attempt. Thus, resolved he got up, went to Yashodhara's apartment, opened the door of her chamber. Within the chamber was burning a lamp fed with sweet smelling oil, and Yashodhara lay sleeping on a couch strewn deep with jasmine and other flowers, her hand resting on the head of her son. If Yashodhara is awakened, she would rather die than allow him to leave her. But would he sneak away like a thief from his own home Would he not embrace his baby before he would go? "No, if I were to raise my wife's hand from the child's head, she would awake." At that time Rahula was seven days old. He stood there for a moment indecisive, gasing at them. "No, I cannot stand it any longer. Their looks make me dizzy and irresolute like a strong drink". Thus, in a hurry he crossed the corridor and shouted, "Chhandak, Chhandak, saddle a horse for me." "But it is a cloudy night and the weather is inclement."' "What of that, the business is imperative." Thus, saying he went back to where Yashodhara was, to have a last look at them. When he, came back to see whether the horse was saddled and briddled, the full-moon was shining in the middle of azure blue sky spreading soft silvery radiance in all directions. Siddhartha mounted the horse and Chhandaka drove it as fast as the favourite horse Kanthaka could carry him.

Siddhartha rode a distance of about 30 miles, not stopping till the morning dawned, and reached the bank of the river *Anoma* (illustrious), thus crossing in six hours' ride the territories of 4 states—Shakya, Kola, Malla, and Maineya. And stopping on the "river bank, Siddhartha asked Chhandaka: "What is the name of the river?" "Its name is Anoma (illustrious)." "And my retirement from the world shall be from here," thus saying, he gave the signal to his horse with his heels, and the horse crossed the shallow river bed of 146 hands, and landed on the opposite bank. Siddhartha, dismounting and standing on the sandy beach that stretched away like a sheet of silver, said to Chhandaka after taking off his ornaments: "My good Chandaka, take these ornaments and Kanthaka, and go home; I am about to retire from the world." Chhandaka replied: "I will also retire from the world, and keep your company". "But how then will my father and my relations know what has become of me unless you go back and tell them? It is not for you now to be a recluse, go now," and made him take the ornaments and the headdress. Then he thought: "These locks of mine are not suited to a monk. But there is no one to cut the hair. Therefore, I will cut them off myself with my sword." And grasping a scimitar with his right hand, he seized his locks and cut them off to two-finger breadth in length. And again thinking, "these garments of mine made of Varanasi cloth are not suited to a monk" exchanged them with those of a hunter who was passing the river bank. Then he said to Chhandaka:

> "Go and tell my father and my mother that I am well'. When Chhandaka after much weeping was to mount the horse, he found that after some snorings the horse that was lying was dying, and died soon. Chhandaka, being deserted by his most intimate friend and loosing his favourite horse, returned to Kapilavastu, weeping and wailing.

When Suddhodana and Prajapati heard everything from Chhandaka on his return, they were overwhelmed with sorrow. When Yashodhara heard it she fell unconscious. When she gained her consciousness she cut her beautiful looks of which she was proud, threw all her ornaments away, saying as her dearest thing had left her she had no use for those decorations which she only wore to be pleasing to her beloved. When Prajapati met Yashodhara in such a miserable condition, they wept together.

The Wanderings

Gautam, then became the guest in the hermitage of two Brahmin nuns—Shakya and Padma—one after the other. Then he went to the retreat of a Brahmin recluse—Raivata. Thence he reached the Vaishali— the Licchhavi capital—, where he met the famous teacher Arara Kalama, who had 300 disciples and Gautam joined his school on the Hiranyavati." Gautam assiduously learnt all that Arara Kalama taught him. After his learning was finished, Arara Kalama, being satisfied that Gautam had a vast store of knowledge, was really earnest, of genuine ascetic tendency with stoic indifference to pleasures, said to Gautam: "I have taught you all that I know-You know now as much as I do. I therefore propose to you that you remain here as my assistant in the school". But as Arara Kalama used to teach that personal salvation or liberation can only be obtained through the acquirements of virtue, and virtue can be acquired through physical hardships, privations and sufferings, and then alone the liberated soul enters into Heaven where he perpetually enjoys all its attendant pleasures, and as Gautam did not agree with this doctrine, known as *Akincha Nyatana Dharma,* he politely declined the tempting offer, and proceeded towards Magadha.

Gautam settled near the city of Rajagriha on the other side of the hill. And his fame spread far and wide as a Kshatriya, learned ascetic, Bimbisara (344-491 BC) hearing of this, one evening mounted his chariot, started off from the city for the hill, and reaching it, he walked up to the shade of the tree under which Gautam was sitting, and addressed him:— "O Recluse, what is your country, who is your father, who is your mother, and what is your caste? You appear to be of high birth and learned." Gautam replied: "Perhaps, O King, you have heard the name of Kapilavastu, one of the fine cities. There my father Suddhodhana is the chief of the Shakya clan. For travelling and leading a religious life. I have left my parents." "Blessed be you. An ancient bond of amity binds both of our families. It is a great pleasure for me to have seen you. Do not stay in this lonely hill. Nor is it necessary that you should sleep on this hard ground. You have youth and beauty. You are not accustomed to this hard life. Come to the city. There I shall find a place for you where you will be comfortable, and all your necessities would be cared for". "But Sir, I have left my beloved parents and Kapilavastu, not for personal comforts, nor for pleasures of life; only to find a solution of poverty, sickness, old age and death, and for that I am leading an ascetic wandering life." "Body needs nourishment, and senses are insistent, in their demands". "I do not seek the gratification of my senses or of my passions, but have retired from the world for the sake of supreme and absolute enlightenments, great King." "If you find the solution of, those great problems, do not forget to give me their benefit — a friend of the Shakyas". After saluting Gautam, and wishing him well, Bimbisara came back to his chariot with his retinue, ascended his chariot, and returned to Rajagriha.

In a nearby place there was a renowned metaphysical school having 700 pupils conducted by Rudraka, son of Rama. Gautam joined it. The cardinal principle of Rudraka's doctrine was that Faith, Energy, Good Memory, Concentration of mind and special knowledge were essential for salvation. It was known as *Naiva Sangana Asangayatam*. The liberated soul is beyond the reach of wisdom or folly. Gautam realised after attending the school for sometime that mere philosophical discussions were not sufficient, but personal efforts through ascetic practices and contentment of mind were imperative to come to a solution of his problems. He therefore decided to leave the place.

Admiring Gautam's self-control, spiritual earnestness and universal brotherly sympathy, Kaundilya, Ashvajita, Bhadriya, Vashpa and Mahanama, five pupils of Rudraka, followed Gautam, and became his disciples. Wandering for a while they reached Gaya Sir (Hill of Gayal) near the place where the Nairanjana and the Phalgu rivers meet. There he thought: "Unless one has learnt perfect self-control and is free from all yearnings and longings, he cannot secure physical and mental contentment, free from agonising anxiety. As one can not ignite or produce sparks by frictions of wet woods, but only of dry woods, so one, whose soul is sunk in anger and malice, greed and envy, can not enkindle light of can only be produced by one who is free from them." While one day Gautam, sitting down with his face to the east in the shade of the Pandava rock, attempted to eat his meal which he obtained by begging, his stomach turned, and he felt as if his inwards were on the point of coming out by his mouth (violent vomiting). Thereupon in the midst of his distress at that repulsive food, for he had never before so much as seen such a fare,—he began to admonish himself, saying: "Siddhartha, although you were born into a family having plenty to eat and to drink, into a station in life where you lived on fragrant third season's rice with various dishes of the finest taste and flavours, yet when you saw a monk clad in garments taken from the rubbish-heap, you exclaimed, "Oh when shall I be like: him and eat food which I have begged?" And then you retired from the world, and now that you have your wish, and have renounced all, what, pray is this you are doing?" When he had thus-admonished himself, his disgust subsided, and he ate his meal with his companions.

Then following the bank of the river Nairanjana, Gautam and his followers reached Uruvilva village. Seeing its sylvan charms and panorama on the Nairanjana whose water was clear like crystals (near present Buddha Gaya), they selected this place for their austere ascetic practices and devotion in which six years were spent. For six years under the shade of a tree he exposed himself to the sun, the rain and the wind, and practised austerities and self-mortitications and privations to such an extent that his robust health vanished, and his body became simply a skeleton, in which only his eyes glowed undiminished lustre. He ate only slight portions of fruits, rice, milk, curds or sweetened mixed barley and sesame cakes that were left to him by passers-by.

The fame of his austerities and fasting habits, and living on almost practically nothing spread round Uruvilva like the sound of a great bell hung in the canopy of the skies. Now, one day, as he was deep in a trance of suppressed breathing, he was attacked by violent pains, and he fell senseless to the ground. Now the five followers who attended on Gautam like servants and did all manner of service for him, and kept constantly at his beck and call, thought that their master had died a saint's death, and when his death was announced,, large numbers of surrounding villagers gathered round him to do him the last honour.

But Gautam within a few hours regained his consciousness. He was extremely emaciated and exhausted. The six girls of the chief of the village came to this place with milk and rice as an offering to the dead saint. Finding that he was alive they offered it to him. Gautam ate the plate of rice and the bowl of milk with great relish and refreshment to the satisfaction and astonishment of the spectators. Finding that the saint ate what was given to him, for six days, these girls brought him different dishes of food. Gautam gained strength and vitality. And the realisation dawned on him now that the six years spent in austerities were like time spent in endeavour ring to tie the air into knots. And coming to the decision, "These austerities are not the way to enlightenment," he went begging through the village for food and raiment and lived upon it. Gautam's 5 disciples who were devoted to him and at his service thought: "It is now six years that this man has been performing austerities without being able to attain to omniscience. And how much less can be expected to do so in future, now that he has again taken to ordinary material food begged from the villagers. He has became luxurious and given up the struggle.

For us to look for any benefit to come from that quarter would be as reasonable as if a man were to imagine he could bathe his head in a dewdrop. We will have nothing more to do with him." With that they took their bowls and robes, and left Gautam, and going 120 miles north east entered Rishipattana (Varanasi). When Gautam's faith was wavering, when he was questioning within himself whether he was not chasing after the mirage of hope, and all his efforts and sacrifices were not in vain, and instead of getting perfect enlightenment and mental harmony, he was suffering now more mental anguishes, than physical decrepitude, knowing not what path now to follow, and finding no illuminating ray to dispel the gloom of his despair, and showing the true direction which would lead to the solution of his problems for which he has sacrificed every thing; man holds dear,—power, position, comforts, devoted charming wife, lovely son, affectionate parents and faithful relatives — and when he needed most the personal care and sympathy of his followers to enkindle in him the dying embers of his faith, he was cruelly deserted by them, which depressed him very much. Mentally weary, physically exhausted, hungry and thirsty. Gautam was sitting pensively facing the rising sun under a banyan tree, waiting for the hour to go begging. Now at that time there lived in Senari village close to Uruvilva a girl name Sujata born in a merchant's family. On reaching maturity she made a prayer to a certain banyan tree, saying: "If I get a husband of my choice of equal rank with myself, and my first-born is a son, I will make a yearly offering to you." And wishing to make her offering on the full-moon day of the month of Visakha, Sujata was preparing milk-rice pudding. When the cooking was finished, Sujata told her slave-girl Purna to go quickly and to get everything ready at the holy place. To the surprise of Purna when she went near the banyan tree, she saw Gautam sitting under its shade, and she became greatly excited, and exclaimed to Sujata: "Our deity methinks has come down from the tree today, and has seated himself ready to receive our offering in person." Sujata filled a dish with thickly cooked milk-rice and covered it with another and wrapping it in a cloth, she adorned herself in all her ornaments, and with the dish on her head she proceeded to the foot of the banyan tree. As soon as, she caught sight of Gautam, she was exceedingly overjoyed, supposing him to be a tree-god, and she kept constantly bowing. And taking the pot from her' head, she uncovered it and placed the dish of milkrice in the hand of Gautam and a vase of flower-scented water near him. Then Gautam looked at Sujata, and she perceived that he was a holy man and with obeisance addressed him: "O Saint, accept my offering, and go withersover it seems to you good". And adding: "May your wishes prosper like mine own", she departed.

Gautam then rose from his seat and with the dish and water in his hands he proceeded to the banks of the Nairanjana and depositing the dish on the bank, descended into its water. After bathing he dressed himself and sitting down with his face to the east, he made the whole of the thick sweet milk-rice into 49 pellets and ate it with great relish. Then Gautam took his noonday rest on the bank of the river in a grove of Sal-tree in full bloom. And at nightfall, at the time the flowers droop on their stalks, he rose up and went towards the Bo-tree along the road. Just then there came from the opposite direction a grass-cutter named Sollhiya and he was carrying grass and seeing there was a holy man on the road, he gave him eight handfuls of the grass. Then Gautam facing the east from the trunk of the Bo-tree spread the grass at its foot and made a cushion out of it.

Gautam was reclining on the spread cushion of the grass. Then he saw the full-moon was rising in the east like a silvery orb. It reminded' him unconsciously the evenings spent with Yashodhara. How romantic, delightful and heavenly were they? Yet the same soothing moonbeams, the same gentle fragrance wafting wind! But how different? Instead of the' soft couch, tender like the plucked feathers of birds, loose silk-cotton fibres, lotus-petals, baby's touch, or the kiss of the beloved, he was resting on the newly cut grass, not much softer than the stone, on which it was laid. Yet Yashodhara's presence as if by magic could have transformed everything into thrilling beatitude, earth into a paradise. Still certainly she, can be his if he wills. Not only she,—position, power, influence, comforts, affection, sympathy and good will of all—were available to him if he so desires, for he knows he will be eagerly welcomed. Notwithstanding he was being tantalised by the lure of an illusory paradise which is vanishing into the air like the mirage of hope. How palatable and energising tasted the rice-pudding in the morning? Yet how much more savoury were the dishes and intoxicating charms of the home! He almost killed himself with fasting and asceticism. Yet desire was springing within his subconscious mind like a perennial fountain. By his eccentric acts he has not only ruined his health and made himself miserable, he has wrecked the happiness of his tenderly loving Yashodhara, newly born innocent son, devoted mother Prajapati and fond old father Suddhodana and other faithful relatives and friends. Yet he was groping in the dark. That is more agonising than the physical sufferings. Had he any certitude of gaining the mental contentment and the enlightenment for which he longed for the solution of his problems, surely he would not have minded the cost he has been paying for it. But if he now return home, sweet home, to enjoy all its charms and pleasures, would it give him mental satisfaction? Would it not be a confession of failure? Would it not been life of cowardly existence and ignoble life of living death? Gautam jumped up as if in a frenzy and sat cross-legged, determined and resolute. "I must have-enlightenment. And unless Desires *(Mara-Smara)*. are entirely killed and uprooted, enlightenment remains obscure like a crystal covered with dust."

Conquest of Desire

With this conquest of desire, Gautam became calm and serene. And all his doubts and despair vanished. Idyllic surrounding invited contemplation. The moon was shining splendidly a soft radiance of light and hope. The zephyr from the Niranjana was wafting fragrance,—soothing and refreshing. The longings for sensual delights and earthly pleasures, which like passionate waves in the stormy sea toss the frail boats of life being vanquished, there was undisturbed mental harmony and equipoise, congenial for the concentration of thoughts. Gautam realised that ignorance (Abidhya) was the root cause of all miseries. Out of ignorance of physical and psychic laws, we crave and do things in a way which provoke bodily and mental disharmony, hence pains. This can only be remedied by proper (i) food, (ii) exercise, (ii) education, (iv) outlook of life, (v) will, (vi) discipline or self-control, (vii) thoughts and speech, (viii) actions with concentration of mind. With this enlightenment Gautam became the Buddha at the age of 35 in 529 B. C, and experienced the supreme joy and exalted serenity of mind. Divorced from all religious ceremonies and observances, all mystic ascetic austerites and self-mortifications, man can enjoy the supreme harmony and bliss of life just by proper living. That man is the architect of his own fate was the greatest inspired revelation of the Buddha for the right progress and welfare of mankind.

Preaching Dharma

Now, Buddha to preach his new Dharma for the benefit of mankind, yielded to their entreaties and proceeded to Rsipattana Mrgadava (Sarnath) near Varanasi to preach his new gospel. Here he delivered his First Sermon known as the "Turning of the Wheel of Law" *(Dbarmacakrapravartana)* to five Brahmin ascetics *(Bhadravargiyas)* who had earlier deserted him at Gaya for giving up the practice of austerities A Gandhara relief shows Buddha seated under a tree surrounded by a number of devotees among whom may be recognised his first five disciples with their shaven heads.

Some time later Buddha again proceeded to Uruvilva near Gaya to convert Kashyapa and his brothers who were fire-worshipping Jatilas In Kashyapa's fire-temple lived a fierce serpent. Buddha spent a night in this temple and subdued the serpent with his own effulgence. A relief panel on the Eastern Gateway of the Great Stupa at Sanchi shows the scene of this Miracle of the Fire Temple The temple is shown with an altar in front, a throne indicating the presence of Buddha, the five-hooded serpent the Brahmin ascetic Kashyapa and his brothers, as also the Niranjana river. After the miracle at the fire-temple Kashyapa and his brothers arranged a sacrifice. But Buddha spread a spell over them so that wood could not be split, fire could not be lit, and sacrifice could not be offered until Buddha consented Another relief panel from the Eastern Gateway of the same Stupa at Sanchi illustrates this second miracle. When news of Gautam's attainment of Buddhahood had reached King Suddhodana he sent repeated messages to his son to return to Kapilavastu Buddha finally consented to visit his *home town* But the proud Shakyas were at first unwilling to show due respect to him. Buddha won them over by walking miraculously through mid-air and performing many other wonders A relief panel the Eastern Gateway of the Great Stupa at *Sanchi shows* at the bottom the aerial pathway, while the scene of Maya's dream incised at the top indicates that the scene is the Miracle of Kapilavastu.

Anathapindika, a rich merchant of Shravasti, became a follower of Buddha and presented Prince Jeta's Park at Shravasti to the Lord for constructing a monastery Punce Jeta agreed to sell the park for as many gold Karsapana coins as would cover the ground A relief medallion on the Bharhut railings shows a bullock-cart bringing the coins to the garden and two persons engaged in spreading them Anathapindika is shown as carrying a waterpot for consecrating the gift by pouring water.

While at Shravasti King Prasenajit of Kosala visited Buddha, and the latter performed one of his great miracles to convince people of his superiority over the heretical teachers, Puma Kashyapa and others. At his bidding an immense pathway appeared in the sky from east to west, and there were many wondrous lights He made water and fire issue from his body, then seated on a lotus he multiplied himself in all directions A Gandhara sculpture shows the pavilion of the Miracle at Shravasti where the contest was held Buddha is seated in the centre on a lotus flanked by Sakra and Brahma on either side, while women peep from windows above.

It is said that Buddha went up to the heaven of" the Thirty-three gods *(Trayastrimsa)* to expound his *Dharma* to his mother, who was reborn there When he was about to descend a triple ladder appeared in the sky at Sakra's command, and accompanied by Brahma and Sakra, Buddha came down it near Sankasya A relief panel on the *stupa* railings from Bharhut shows the triple ladder, a throne under a tree, two flying deities and devotees waiting A footprint on the top and lowermost rungs of the middle ladder indicates the descent.

Once when Buddha was at Kaushambi a monkey offered him honey in a bowl and then drowned itself in a nearby tank. A relief panel from the Northern Gateway of the Great Stupa at Sanchi shows this scene.

In the course of his journeys in Magadha, Buddha lived for some time in the Indrasala cave on Vediyaka hill near Rajagriha where Sakra visited him to discuss some philosophical problems He was accompanied by his Gandharva musician Pancasikha.

Devadatta, the jealous cousin of Buddha, made several attempts to destroy him. Once he hired some assassins and waylaid Buddha But eventually the assassins confessed their guilt and were converted A relief panel from Gandhara shows the assassins assembled behind a wall, while one of them bows down at the feet of Buddha.

Last Days

From Gridhrakut (Rajagriha) the Buddha with a number of his disciples went to Ambalattika where he stayed as the guest of the King. This was the last rains the Buddha spent at Gridhrakut. He was now 79 years old. From Ambalattika they reached Nalanda where they stayed at Pavarika mango-grove. Here Sariputra met him. Nalanda was the birthplace of Sariputra, and Nalanda became the great seat of learning. From Nalanda, they reached Pataligama (Pataliputra), then a small village, but was being fortified by Sunidha and Varsakara, the chief ministers of Ajatashatru, ostensively as a defensive measure against the Vajjiatis, but really to attack them. The Magadha ministers invited the Buddha and his disciples to dine them, and they were fed with sweet dishes of boiled rice and cakes. Only Sariputra did not eat the cakes.

The Buddha and his party crossed the Ganga, some by boats, some by rafts of wood and others by rafts of basketwork, and reached Kotigrama. Kotigrama was the Kundagrama or Kundapura, a caravan halting place in the suburb of Vaishali, the birth place of Mahavira. From Kotigrama the Buddha went to where the Natikas lived; there he resided in the Natika brick-hall. The Natikas were the Gnatri Kshatrias, the kinsmen of Mahavira. Here Ambapali paid the Buddha a visit, and asked the Buddha and the Sangha to stay in her park—Arabapalivana which was in its neighbourhood.

From Ambapali's mango grove the Buddha went to Beluva, another suburb of Vaishali, wherein dwelt the general-in-chief of the Licchhavis and who was a follower of Nigrantha, and he became a lay disciple of the Buddha. Here he addressed his disciples: "O Bhikshus, do you take up your abode round about Vaishali, each according to the place where his friends, intimates and close companions *may live* for the rains. I shall enter upon the rainy season here at Beluva."

Now when the Blessed One had thus spending the rainy season, there fall upon him a dire sickness, and sharp pains came upon him, even unto death. But the Blessed One, mindful and self-possessed, bore them without complaint. Now very soon after the Blessed One began to recover; when he had quite got rid of the sickness,' he went out from the monastery, and sat down behind the monastery on a seat spread out there. And the venerable Ananda went to the place where the Blessed One was, and saluted him, and took a seat respectfully on one side, and addressed him: "I have beheld how the Blessed One was in health, and I have beheld how he had to suffer. And though at the sight of the sickness of the Blessed One my body became weak as a creeper, and the horizon became dim to me, and my faculties were no longer clear, yet notwithstanding I took some little comfort that the Blessed One would not pass away from existence until at least he had left instructions as touching the Sangha."

"What, then, Ananda, does the *Sangha* expect from me? I have preached the truth without making any distinction between esoteric and exoteric doctrine: for in respect of the truths, Ananda, the Tathagata has no such thing as the closed fist of a teacher, who keeps something back. Surely, Ananda, should there be any one who harbours the thought, "It is I who will lead the brotherhood," or "the Sangha is dependent on me," it is he who should lay down instructions in any matter concerning the Sangha. Now the Tathagata, Ananda, thinks not that it is he who should lead the brotherhood, or that the Sangha is dependent upon him. Why then should he leave instructions in any matter concerning the Sangha. I, too, O Ananda, am now grown old, and full of years; my journey is drawing to its close: I have reached my sum of days; I am turning eighty years of age: and just as a worn-out cart, Ananda, can only with much additional care be made to move along, so me thinks, the body of the Tathagata can only be kept going with much additional care.

The Buddha loved both Rajagriha and Vaishali. From Chapala Chetaya, he went to the Kutagara Hall in the Mahavana, where all the monks were assembled, to whom he addressed: "O brethren, ye to whom the truths I have perceived have been made known by me: having thoroughly made yourselves masters of them, practise them, meditate upon them and spread them abroad—in order that pure religion may last long and be perpetuated, in order that it may continue to be for the good and happiness of the great multitudes, out of pity for the world, to the good and the gain and weal of men."

From Vaishali the Buddha went to Bhandagama, where he taught the four noble truths of deliverance: (i) The noble conduct of life; (ii) the noble earnestness in life; (iii) the noble kind of wisdom; (iv) the noble salvation in wisdom. Then the Buddha addressed the brethren: "Great is the fruit, great the advantage of earnest contemplation when set round with upright conduct. Great is the fruit, great the advantage of intellect set round with earnest contemplation.' The mind sot round with intelligence is free from the great evils— that is to say from sensuality, from egoism, from delusion and from ignorance."

From Bhandagama the Buddha proceeded to Hathigama; from Hathigama to Anibagama; from Ambagama to Jambagama: from Jambagama to Bhojanagara where he stayed at the Ananda Chetiya. From Bhojanagara the Buddha came to Pava where he stayed at the Mango Grove of Chunda, who was by family a smith.

And Chunda the worker in matals went to the place whore the Blessted One was, and saluting him took his seat respectfully on one side and said: "May the Blessed One do me the honour of taking his meal together with the brethren at my house tomorrow." The Buddha gave his consent to it by silence, and at the end of the night Chunda made ready in his dwelling place sweet rice and cakes and a quantity of *Sukara maddasam.* And he announced the hour to the Blessed One, saying, "The hour.. Lord, has come, and the meal is ready." And the Blessed One robed himself early in the morning, and taking his bowl, went with the brethren to the dwelling place of Chunda. When he had come thither he seated himself on the seat prepared for him. And when he was seated he addressed Chunda: "As to the *Sukara-maddhavam,* you have made ready, serve me with it, Chunda; as to the other food the sweet rice and cakes, serve the brethren with it." "Even so Lord." Now when the Blessed One had eaten the food prepared by Chunda, there fell upon him a dire sickness—the disease of dysentery and sharp pain came upon him. But the Blessed One, mindful and self-possessed, bore it without complaint and said to Ananda: "Come Ananda lot us go on to Kushinara."

But the Buddha could not proceed far. Hew as weak, debilitated and fatigued. He went aside from the path to the foot of a certain tree and said to Ananda: "Fold, I pray you, Ananda, the robe and spread it for me. I am weary; Ananda, I must rest a while." Ananda spread out the robe fourfold, and the Buddha seating himself on it, said: "Fetch me, I pray you, Ananda, some water. I am thirsty Ananda, and would drink". "The river Kakustha, Lord, not far of, is clear and pleasant, cool and transparent, easy to get down into and delightful. There the Blessed One may both drink the water and cool his limbs." "Fetch me, I pray you, Ananda, some water. I am thirsty and would drink." Ananda taking a bowl went down the streamlet, filling it up into its clear water free from turbidity, brought it to the Buddha, and the Buddha drank of the water. Now at that time a man named Pukkusa, a young Mallian, a disciple of Alara Kalama, was passing along the high road from Kushinara him, saluted him and took his rest respectfully on one side. Pũkkusa was impressed by the unruffled calm of Buddha's face though he was suffering from acute agonising pains, Such a self-control was marvellous and superhuman. And though examples of self-discipline. Pukkusa supplicated the Buddha: "May the Blessed One accept me as a disciple, as a true believer, from this day forth as long as life endures", and he presented a pair of robes of cloth of gold, furnished and ready for wear: "May the Blessed One show me favour by hands." In accepting it in my hands". "In that case, Pukkusa, robe me in one, and Ananda another". "Even so, Lord", said Pukkusa.

Now the Blessed One with a great company of the brethren went on to the river Kakustha, went down into the water, and bathed and drank. And coming up out again on the other side he went on to the Mango Grove, where he addressed Chundaka: "Fold, I pray you, Chundaka, a robe in four and spread it out, I am weary, and would lie down". And the Blessed One laid himself down on his right side, with one font calm and self-possessed, and Chundaka seated himself in front of him. Then the compassionate heart of the Buddha, even in the midst of his exhausting agonising pains, thought of the mental anguishes it might cause to Chunda if he knows that the food taken in his house had been causing him pains and might hasten his death, and in that case he wanted Andanda to give consolation to Chanda.

Now the Blessed One said: "Come, Ananda, let us go on to the Sala Grove of the Mallas, the Upavattana of Kushinara on the further side of the river Hiranyavati. And when they reached the place the Buddha said: "Spread over for me, I pray you, Ananda, the couch with its head of the north, between the twin Sala trees. I am weary and would lie down." Ananda spread a covering over the couch, and the Buddha laid himself on his right side, and Upavana was fanning him standing in his front. As the Buddha wanted the unobstructed view he said to Upavana, "Stand aside O brother; stand not in front of me."

Ananda felt that the Buddha's vitality was ebbing away, and it might take a serious turn, and he was weeping and murmuring: "Alas! I remain still but a learner, one who has yet to work out his own perfection. And the master is to pass away from me—he who is so kind." When the weeping and sobbing of Ananda was brought to the Buddha's notice, he called Ananda in his presence and addressed him: "Enough, Ananda, do not let yourself be troubled; do not weep I Have I not already, on former occasions, told you that it is in the very nature of all things most near and dear unto us that we must divide ourselves from them, leave them, saver ourselves from them;? How then, Ananda, can this be possible—whereas anything whatever born, brought into being and organised, contains within itself the inherent necessity of dissolution—how then, can this be possible, that such a thing should not he dissolved? No such condition can exist! For a long time, Ananda, have you been very near to me by acts of love, kind and good, that never varies, and is beyond all measure. You have done well, Ananda. Be earnest in effort, and you too shall soon be free." "But let not the Blessed One die in this little wattle and daub town, in this town in the midst of jungle, in this petty town.

For there are other great cities, such as Champa, Rajagriha, Shravasthi, Saketa, Kaushambi and Varanasi. Let the Blessed One die in one of them. There are many wealthy nobles and Brahmins and heads of houses, believers in the Tathagata, who will pay due honour to the remains of the Tathagata." "Say, not so, Ananda, say not so".

And the Buddha sent Ananda to announce to the Mallas of Kushinara that the Buddha was very sick the Sala grove in the Upavattana of their own village. Then the Mallas, with their young men and maidens and their wives, being grieved and sad and afflicted at heart, went to see the Buddha. Ananda caused the Mallas of Kushinara to stand in groups, each family in a group, and so presented them to the Blessed One in the first part of night: "Lord, a Malla of such and such a name, with his children, his wives, his retinue and his friends, humbly bows down at the foot of the Blessed One." A learned Brahmin by the name of Subhadra was living there at that time. Hearing that the Buddha was sick, he came to see him to clear off some of his doubts, and he said to Ananda: "Now a certain feeling of uncertainty has sprung up in my mind; and this faith have in Sramana Gautam, that he, methinks, is able to present the truth that I may get rid of this feeling of uncertainty. O that I, even I, Ananda might be allowed to see the Sramana Gautam." "Enough, friend Subhadra! Trouble not the Tathagata. The Blessed One is weary". Thus, thrice Subhadra made requests to Ananda to interview the Buddha, and thrice he was refused. The Buddha overheard it, and called Ananda forth and said to him: "Do not keep out Subhadra. He may be allowed to see me. Whatever Subhadra may ask of me, he will ask from a desire for knowledge and not to annoy me. And whatever I may say in answer to his question, that he will quickly understand." Then Ananda said to Subhadra: "Enter in, friend Subhadra; for the Blessed One gives you leave." Then Subhadra, went to the place where the Blessed One was, saluted him courteously, and after exchanging with him the compliments of esteem and of civility, he took his seat cm one side, and said to him: "The Brahmins by saintliness of life, Gautam, who are heads of companies of disciples and students, teachers of students, of schools of doctrine, esteemed as good men by the multitude, to wit, Purana Kashyapa, Maskari Gosala, Ajita of the garment of hair, SANJAYA, THE SON OF BELLASTHA, KAKUDHA Katyana and the Nigrantha of the Gnatri elan — have they all, "according to their own assertion, thoroughly understood things, or have they not, or some of them have understood and some have not?" "Enough Subhadra! Let this matter Test where they are.

Only those who adopt and practise the noble eightfold paths which is to be but found in my doctrine, will receive proper understanding." Subhadra was satisfied with the reply and he wanted to be the disciple of the Buddha. Buddha said to Ananda: "As it is, Ananda, receive Subhadra into the Sangha." Then the Buddha addressed the assembled brethren: "It may be, brethren, that there may be doubt or misgiving in the mind of some brother, as to the truth or the path and way. Enquire, brethren, freely. Do not have to reproach yourselves afterwards with the thought, our teacher was face to face with us and we could not bring ourselves to enquire of him when we were face to face with him.' All the brethren remained silent. Then the Buddha said, "It may be, brethren, that you put no questions out of reverence for the teacher. Let one friend communicate to another." All the brethren remained silent as before. Then Ananda said to the Buddha; "How wonderful a thing, is it, Lord, and how marvellous! Verily I believe, that in this whole assembly of brethren there is not one brother who has any doubt of misgiving as to the Buddha, or the truth, or the path or the way."

The Passing Away

Then the Blessed One addressed the Brethren: "Behold now, brethren, I exhort you. Decay is inherent in all component things! Work out your salivation with diligence!" These were the last words of the Buddha. Then there was a deep silence. Ananda became anxious and said: "O venerable Anuruddha, the Blessed One is dead." "Nay brother, Ananda the Blessed One is not dead.

He has entered into that the in which both sensations and ideas have ceased to be" and went to the Upavattama, to the Sala Grove of the Mallas which was in bloom, and where the body of the Blessed One lay. There they past the day in paying honour, reverence, respect and homage to the remains of the Blessed One with dancing, hymns and music, and with garlands and perfumes; and in making canopies of their garments, and preparing decoration wreaths to hang there on. This way six days passed. On the seventh day some of the Mallas of Kushinara said: "Let us carry the body of the Blessed One to a spot on the south and outside of the city to perform the cremation ceremony." Others said: 'Let us carry it to the shrine of the Mallas called Mukuta-bandhana to the east of the city and there let us perform the cremation ceremony." The later suggestion became popular. Thereupon eight chieftains among the Mallas bathed their heads and clad themselves in new garments to carry the body of the Blessed One and entering the city by the north gate they carried it through the midst of the city to the shrine—Mukuta-bandhana, and there they laid down the body of the Blessed One. Now at that time the venerable Mahakashyapa was journeying along the high road from Pava to Kushinara with a great company of brethren. He met a nude Ajivaka ascetic who was travelling in the opposite direction. Kashyapa asked the nude ascetic: "O friend, surely you know our Master." Yes friend. I know him. This day the Sramana Gautama has been dead.

Then they rushed to the cremation ground to salute the last remains of the Tathagata. The Mallas were about to set fire to the funeral pile when Kashyapa reached the place. And out of reverence for him they waited a while for his instructions. Then Kashyapa with his other companions bowing down with clasped hands thrice walked reverently round the pile; and then uncovering the feet, they bowed down in reverence at the feet of the Blessed One. Then fire was set to the funeral pile. And when the body of the Blessed One had been burnt up, there came down a heavy shower which extinguished the funeral pile of the Blessed One. The Mallaa of Kushinara who also brought jars of water scented with all kinds of perfume poured it upon the funeral pile.

Then the Mallas of Kushinara surrounded the bones of the Blessed One in their council hall with a lattice work of spears, and with a rampart of bows; and there for seven days they paid honour, reverence, and respect and homage to them with dance and songs and with garlands and music.

The Aftermath

Soon the news of the death of the Buddha spread out. And the King of Magadha, Videhaputra Ajatashatru, sent an ambassador with the message to the Mallas of Kushinara: "The Blessed one was a Kshatriya. I am also a Kshatriya. I am worthy to receive a portion of the relics of the Blessed one. Over the remains of the Blessed One will I put up a sacred Cairn, and in their honour will I celebrate a feast". The Licchhavis of Vaishali, the Mallas of Pava, the Kaliyas of Ramagama and the Bulis of Allakappa sent also ambassadors with the similar message: "The Blessed One was Kshatriya. We are also Kshatriyas. We are worthy to receive a portion of the relics of the Blessed One. Over the remains of the Blessed One will be put up a sacred Cairn and in their honour will we celebrate a feast". The Shakyas of Kupilavastu sent the ambassador with the following message: "The Blessed one was the pride of our race. We are worthy to receive a portion of the relics of the Biassed One. Over the remains of the Blessed one we will put up a sacred cairn, and in their honour will we celebrate a feast. And the Brahmin of Vethadvipa sent a messenger, saying that us a Brahmin, he deserves a portion of the relic of the Blessed One over which he would build up a sacred.

When they heard these things the Hallos of Kushinara spoke to the assembled brethren: "The Blessed One died in our domain. We will not give away any part of the remains of the Blessed One." Then Drona, an influential Brahmin, intervened and said: "Forbearance was the cardinal doctrine of the Buddha. And it is unbecoming that over division of the remains of that superman, there should be strife, wounds and war. Let us in one accord and friendly harmony make eight portions of it so that the *Stupas may* rise in every land and the religion of the Buddha might spread". "Do you then O Brahmin, divide the remains of the Blessed One yourself equally into eight parts which is a fair division." "Be it so," said Drona, and he divided the remains of the Blessed One into eight parts, and he said to thorn: "*Give me*, sirs, this vessel, and I will set up over it a sacred Cairn and in its honour will I establish a feast. And they gave the vessel to Drona the Brahmin. After the remains were distributed, the Moriyas of Pipphalivana sent a messenger to the Mollas of Kushinara for a portion of the relics of the remains of the Blessed one, claiming on the ground of being Kshatriyas.

But when they heard the answer: "There is no portion of the remains of the Blessed One left over, which have been all distributed on the 21st day of Parinirvana," then they took away the The King of Magadha, the Videhaputra Ajatashatru, the Licchhavis of Vaishali, the Bulis of Alla-kappa, the Koliyas of Ramagana, the Mallas of Pava, the Mallas of Kushinara, the Vethadipika Brahmin' and Drona made mounds at Rajagriha, Vaishali, Allakappa, Ramagama, Pava, Kushinara, Vethadipa respectibly and held feasts. There were eight mounds (stupas) for the remains, one for the vessel and one for the embers.

2

Age of Buddha

The sixth century before Christ was an era of great spiritual upsurge throughout the ancient East in India it was marked by the birth of Gautam Buddha.

The epic story of the Master's life,—his miraculous birth under a *Sal* tree, his carely mental snuggles and renunciation of the world, his sojourn in search of True Knowledge and its attainment, his preachings among men, and demise after a fruitful life of eighty years devoted to the cause of deliverance of all sentient beings, have been told in great detail in the *Buddha-carid,* the *Lalilavistra* and other Buddhist texts. Here it is proposed to place before the reader the life-story of the Master as narrated in sculptures by ancient Indian craftsmen during the first *two* hundred years or so before and after Christ These come mainly from places like Bharhut, Sanchi, Gandhara, Mathura, Nagarjunakonda and Amaravati, and have a charmingly simple narrative quality.

It is said that after performing the ten virtues *(Paramitas) in* innumerable previous births, recounted in the *Jataka* stories, Bodhiattva, destined to be an omniscient Buddha, had been born in Tusita heaven when the gods besought him to be reborn *on* earth to deliver mankind Bodhisattva then decided to be born of King Suddhodana of Kapilavastu and his Queen Mahamaya Maya had a dream in which she saw the divine Bodhisattva enter her body in the form of a white elephant. This story is narrated in three successive panels in a relief sculpture from the asucle is based on an illustrated talk delivered by the author at the Lalen Mreum Jul., 1956. The illustrations are of exhibits in the Lalen Mreum. Copyright reserved by the Department of Archaeology. Government of Amaravati of are 2nd century AD. The scenes from life to right show the divine Bodhisattva seated on a throne in Tusuta heaven while entreated by the gods to be reborn on earth, his descent from heaven in the form of a white elephant carried in a palanquin by the gods with music and dancing, and the Queen's dream. The last scene only is depicted in a circular bus relief on the Bharhut railings of *circa* 2nd century BC.

When the Queen spoke of her dream to the King, he summoned the soothsayers to interpret it. They declared that she had conceived a son, destined to be either a Cakravarti Raja or a Buddha. The gods guarded the mother and child during gestation. When her confinement approached, Maya wished to see her parents at Devahrada, but at Lumbini Park on the way she was delivered of the child while she stood under a *Sal tree* holding its branch. The child was received by the attending Dikpalas, but he immediately descended on the ground and taking seven lotus steps in all directions exclaimed triumphantly that he was the foremost of the world. A Gandhara relief reproduced here shows the divine child coming out of the light side of the lady of Queen Maya who stands under a *Sal* tree holding its banding branch. The god Sakra (India) receives the child on a pure of cloth while Brahma looks on from behind, and above, a heavenly being whistles to indicate the rejoicings in heaven. The flywhisk in the panel, a symbol of loyalty, suggests the future greatness of the newborn child who is shown as having descended on the ground and standing with his right hand raised in Abhaya, about to take the first seven steps.

The child Bodhisattva was then given his first bath, and mother and child were brought back to Kapilavastu amidst great rejoicings. These scenes are depicted in a Gandhara relief divided into three panels. The story runs from right to left. The first scene on the right shows the bath, the second in the middle the return of Queen Maya from Lumbini in a bullock-cart with the child in her arms, and the third on the left, musicians outside the city-gates of Kapilavastu welcoming mother and child.

Shortly after, the sage Asita visited King Suddhodana and wished to see the newborn child. When he was brought, the sage bowed respectfully to him for he recognised that the child was a Buddha to be. He was named Siddhartha. The King then called the astrologers to cast his son's horoscope. They discerned in his body the thirty-two infallible marks of greatness and declared that he was a Tathagata who would forsake the world when he had seen four ominous sights.

Maya having died shortly after childbirth, Siddhartha was brought up by his aunt and stepmother Mahaprajapati Gautami. Like other Shakya Princes he was admitted into a school where he showed himself superior to all others. A relief from Gandhara shows young Siddhartha seated on a stool writing on a tablet.

At nineteen Siddhartha was married to Yashodhara, daughter of his uncle Suprabuddha. Time passed on and Bodhisattva lived in luxury befitting a Prince. His father took great care that none of the ominous sights predicted by the soothsayers should meet his eye, but to no avail. The day came when Siddhartha driving in his chariot to the pleasure gardens saw the first of the ominous sights — a decrepit old man. He returned home with a heavy heart. On another day he saw a sick man on the road, and on a third, a corpse. His mind was greatly agitated. Then on a fourth occasion he saw a monk whose serene bearing made a deep impression on him, and he longed to be an ascetic. The birth of his son Rahula at this moment made him decide on renunciation, for he saw that his worldly ties were multiplying. His father redoubled his efforts to keep him away from such thoughts, and arranged for his nightlong entertainment by the palace dancers and singers. About midnight they became tired and' fell asleep. The sight of sleeping women, boring and in dishabille, made Siddhartha realise the deceptives of appearances and the futility of worldly pleasures. Gandhara relief represents the scene in two panels, he upper one shows Siddhartha reclining on a couch with Yashodhara seated beside, and female musicians entertaining him. The lower one shows Yashodhara asleep on a couch and the tired musicians dozing in unseemly attitudes. Bodhisattva's mind was illed with disgust arid he decided to leave the place at once. He asked his groom Chandaka to bring his horse Kanthaka. Mounted on his favourite horse and accompanied by his groom, Siddhartha then left the palace in quest of True Knowledge amidst rejoicings in heaven. The *Mahabhiniskramana* or Great Renunciation is illustrated by another Gandhara relief sculpture which shows the Prince passing through the city-gates of Kapilavastu on his horse while his groom holds a parasol over his head and two Yakshas lift up the hoofs of the horse lest there be noise. Mara, the Evil One, stands in front urging Bodhisattva to abandon his quest.

Travelling far Siddhartha arrived on the bank of the Anoma where he alighted from his horse and gave up his jewels and ornaments to Chandaka bidding him return to Kapilavastu with Kanthaka. Cutting off his long hair he then flung it to the sky where it was received in a golden casket by Sakra for worship in heaven. A bas-relief on the Bharhut railings of *circa 2nd* century BC depicts the scene of the worship of Buddha's hair-lock in heaven. The three-storied building is the Vaijayanti Palace of god Sakra and the building with a domed-roof Sudharma, the Assembly Hall of the gods. The panel shows Buddha's hair-lock placed on a throne and nymphs dancing around to the accompaniment of music.

In Search of True Knowledge

Wandering from place to place in search of True Knowledge Siddhartha Gautam came upon Alara Kalama of Vaishali and Rudraka Ramaputra of Rajagriha, and became their disciple. But their teachings did not satisfy him, and he resolved to apply himself to the severest austerities *(Mabapadhana* or the Great Effort) at Uruvilva near Gaya. For six years he performed the most severe penance and became as thin as a skeleton. But the Truth still eluded him. He realised that self-mortification was not the way to Enlightenment and gave up the practice of austerities. At daybreak on the full-moon, day of Vaisakha Bodhisattva took his seat under a big pipal tree on the bank of the Niranjana, when Sujata the village headman's daughter came to make her offering to the holy tree. Seeing Bodhisattva seated under the tree shining in his own effulgence she took him to be the tree-god come to life, and offered him the food. Nourished by her food Bodhisattva resumed his meditation resolved on attaining *samyaksambodhi.* He obtained from a grass-cutter a bundle of soft green grass, spread it at the foot of the pipal tree and thereon took his seat. A Gandhara relief shows Gautam approaching the seat under the Bodhi tree on which grass has been spread. Behind him is Mara carrying a sword.

Mara thought that his authority over the temporal world would end if Bodhisattva attained supreme knowledge. He was, therefore, determined to use all his powers to prevent Bodhisattva from attaining *samyaksambodbi.* He tempted, threatened and entreated Bodhisattva, but when all his efforts failed Mara attacked him with his hosts. But Bodhisattva remained unmoved in his seat and overcame Mara and passed on to Buddhahood. A fragmentary relief sculpture from Gandhara shows below seated Buddha (broken) two of Mara's soldiers with sword and shield tumbling down in defeat.

When the venerable Mahakashyapa of Uruvilva, accompanied by a number of the monks proceeding to Kushinagar, on the way heard from a nude Ajivaka that the Buddha had his Parinirvana there some Bhikshus led by Subhadra felt relieved that there would be no one now to enforce Sangha regulations. This made Maha-Kashyapa thinking and feeling anxious about the future of the Sangha, he suggested to the Bhikshus: "Friends we shall recite together and collect the *Dharma* (Precepts) and *Vinaya* (Rules of the Sangha, expounded by the Buddha) and collect them". "In that case you select the representatives for the Sangiti (Council)."

First Council

On the twenty first day of the Buddhis Maha Parinirvana when his relics were being distributed among the claimants by Drona, Maha-Kashyapa annuonced the names of 500 representatives for the Council that would be held at Rajagriha daring the rainy season, to which all the assembled Bhikshus agreed.

Ajatashatru, the King of Magadha, built for the purpose on the side of the Verbhana Hill, in front of the Saptaparni Cave near Rajagriha, a magnificent Council Hall with pillars and stairs and decorated with flowering plants. Within four months of the Mahaparinirvana, on the Sukla-Panchami day in the month of

Sravana 482 BC commenced the session of the Council, known as the *First Sangiti* of 500 hundred Bhikshu representative, under the presidency of the venerable Maha-Kashyapa, and of them the following wore prominent: attentive learner Ananda, Upali versed in Vinaya; the metaphysician Anurudha, the poet Vangis, eloquent Purna, the marvellous orator Kumara Kashyapa, versatile Daksha, keen-witted Katyana and clear — thinker Kosthitha. Mahakashyapa, addressed the assembly: "Friends, which shall we recite first—Dharma or the Vinaya." "Venerable Maha Kasya pa, *Vinaya* is the regulating force of our *Sangha*. As long *Vinaya will* remain uncorrupted, so long the Sangha will last. Let us therefore recite the *Vinaya* first.' "But who will lead us?" asked the president. "Upali, was the answer. "Why, is not Ananda capable of doing that?" "No that he is incapable. But even the Blessed One during his life time used to say that of all those versed in Vinaya, Upali was the best. Therefore we shall follow his lead.' Then the president said: "Friend Upali, whore was the first Parajika promulgated?" "In Vaishali, Sir." "Concerning whom was it spoken?" Concerning Sudinna, the son of Kalanda." "In regard to what matter?" "Sexual intercourse." Thus, did the venerable Mahakashyapa question Upali as to the matter, as to the occasion, as to the individual concerned, as to the (main) rule, as to the sub-rule, as to who would be guilty as to who would be innocent through both the Vinayas (Ubhato-Vinaye), that is relating to Bhikshu and Bhikshunis, except Sutra Vibhanga and Khandakas). Then Mahakashyapa asked the Sangha: "Who shall lead us now in reciting and chanting Dhamma." "Ananda" was the unanimous answer of the Bhikshus. Like that of Upali, in like manner did Mahakashyapa question Ananda through the five *Nikayas,* and as he was successively asked, so did Ananda make reply.

Then the five hundred assembled Thera Bhikshus chanted over together Vinaya and Dhamma. Because they chanted together it was called Sangiti, and the first Sangiti lasted for seven mouths. After the Dhamma recitations were fixed, the Sangha for their correctness, study, recitation and dissemination appointed Ananda for Diga Nikaya or Agama (Dirgha, that is, collection of large Sutras about 34); disciples of Sariputra for Majjim N (Madhama: 152 Sutras of medium length); Sanjukta N (Mixed: Mahakashyapa for 56 groups of Sutras); Anuruddha for Anguttar N (Sutras in II

Nipatas or sections). But no name is mentioned for Khuddaka N (Kshudraka collection, containing 12 books by some, 15 books by others: (i) Jataka; (ii) Mahaniddesa (Sayings of Sariputra); (iii) Chullaniddesa (Sayings of Sariputra): (iv) Pati Sambhidba marga (Prati Samboda marga; (v) Sutra Nipata (70 Sutras); (vi) Dharmapada (Moral Sayings); (vii) Udana (82 Prayers); (viii) Itibuttaka (thus said the Buddha); (ix) Vimana Battu (about heaven); (x) Peta Battu (Spirit world); (xi) Thera Gatha (poems of the monks); (xii) Theri Gatha (Poems of the nuns.). These twelve Books are common to both parties. Majjimas add following three; (xiii) Chariya Pithaka (the life of the Buddha); (xiv) Buddha Vansa (the previous Buddhas 24); (xv) Apadana (the lives of saints).

Vinaya consisted of (i) Parajikas, (on sins involving expulsion); (ii) Pachitriyas (on sins requiring forgiveness), both known together as Sutra Vibhanga, (iii) Maha Vagga, (iv) Chulla Vagga, known together as Khandaka, (v) Parivara Patha, (vi) Bhikhsus Patimokkha, (vii) Bhikhsuni Patimokkha, known together as Ubhayani Patimokkhani of the three Pitakas (baskets). Only two— Vinaya (Rules of the Sangha), Dhamma or Sutra (Religious discourses) are found mentioned in the First Council of Rajagriha, and not the remaining *Abhidhamma*, the metaphysical portion. Perhaps it was not compiled before the Second Council that took place at Vaishali about 100 years later. Devout Buddhists believe that Abhidhamma was included in the Kuddaka, the last of the five Nikeyas Ananda recited. Abhidhamma consisted of seven books:— (i) Dhamma Sangani, (ii) Vibhanga, (iii) Katha Vatthu of Tissa Moggaliputra of Ashoka Sangiti, (iv) Pugggla Pannati (about realisation), (v) Dhatukatha (human character), (vi) Yamaka (opposite sayings), (vii) Patthana (actions). It is said that Pali Tripitakas consisted 84 thousand verses or sayings, of which 82 thousands were the utterances of the Buddha himself and remaining two thousands by his disciples.

Second Council

The Second Sangiti took place at Vaishali in 384 BC in the tenth year of the reign of Ajaya Udayan, known also as Kalashoka, who removed the capital from Rajagriha to Pataliputra in 391 BC to decide 10.

A Bhikhsu Yasa, son of Kakandaka, came at that time to sojourn at Vaishali. He objected to the offering and receipt of coins in the Sangha. This the Vaishali Vajjian monks did not like and as a protest and disciplinary measure they suspended Yasa. Yasa wont to Kaushambhi. And from that place he sent messengers to the Sanghas of Avanti and other western and southern states to decide those ten important Vinaya rules. Seven hundred delegates joined this Second Council from the east, west, north and south to decide under the presidency of Revata of Sorayya at the beautiful Balikaram where Ajita arranged the seats to decide the issue. But as they could not come to any final decision they appointed the following eight: 4 from the east and 4 from the west to settle it. Eastern: Sabhakami who was of a hundred and twenty years standing from the date of his Upasampada and who had been a pupil of Ananda and was living at Vaishali; Khujja-sobhita; Salha; Vasabhaganika. Western: Revata of Soreyya;. Sambhuta Sanavasi of the Ahoganga Hill; Yasa; Sumana. Their unanimous verdict was against the Vajjians. Not satisfied with this decision the Vajjians made a grand assembly known as Maha Sangiti, for 10,000 monks joined it at Mahavana, Kutagara with the help of Kalasoka after two years, in 382 BC. They introduced new ideas and compositions in the five Nikayas. They discarded many rules of Vinaya and introduced many new rules regarding name, dress, manners and necessities of the monastic life. They discarded Abhidarma Prakarana, Patasambhida and some portions of the Jatakas.

Thus, the Buddha Sanga was split up into Sthavirbadi or *Theravadi,* known later as *Hinayana,* and Maha Sanghik or *Mahayana.* Again Mahayana subdivided into five sections before the time of Ashoka (272-232 BC). The following books were added by these five sects. (i) Mahasangika.—Bhikshu Vinaya; Bhikshuni, Vinaya; Mahavastu, (ii) Sarvastibad.—*Dharma* Madyamagama; Sanjuktagama, Ekottaragama and Kshudrakagama including Sutra-Nipata, Udana, Dharmapada, Sthaviragatha, Vimanavastu and Buddhavansa. *Vinaya:* Pratimoksha Sutra; Vinaya Sanjukta Vastu; Vinaya Sangha Vedaka Vastu; Bhikshuni Pratimoksha; Ekasata Karma; Nidana; Matrika; Pravrajaya Upasampada Karmavakya; Vinaya Nidana-Matrika *Gatha;* Vinaya Sanjukta Vastu Gatha; Vinaya Gatha; Dasadhya

Vinaya; Vinaya Vibhasha. *Abhidharma:* Satapada Sastra; Sangita-Paryaya Pada Sastra; Prakarana Pada Sastra; Vignana Kaya-Pada Sastra; Dhatnkaya-Pada Sastra; Dharma Skanda-Pada Sastra; Pragnapti Pada Sastra. *Buddhas Life:* Lalita Vistara, (iii) Kasyapiya— *Vinaya:* Prati Moksha Sutra; Virati Vishayaka Vinaya Sastra. *Buddha's life:* Buddhavadana, (iv) Dharmagupta— *Vinaya*: Bhikshuni Karma; Chaturvarga Bhikshu Pratimoksha; Dvavinsati Prosanartha Sastra. *Buddha's life*: Bhuddha Charita, (v) Mahisasaka.— *Vinaya:* Pancha varga Vinaya; Vinaya Karma; Bhikshu Pratimoksha; Bhikshuni Pratimoksha. *Buddha's life:* Vinaya Pitaka Mula.

Ashokan Council

Ashoka Sangiti took place at Pataliputra in 265 BC in the fifteenth year of Ashoka's coronation or the eighteenth year of his reign, in the 219th years of Mahaparinirana of the Buddha under the presidency of Tishya son of Maudgali in the Asokarama in which one thousand delegates were present and the session lasted for nine months. Here the rules of the Sangha and the doctrines of the Dharma were rehearsed and settled. In the gathering the metaphysical aspects of Sthaviravad and Sasvatavada were thoroughly discussed and their five hundred arguments have been embodied in the Kathavatthu of the Abhidarma Pitaka. About this Sangiti Ashoka had an edict inscribed at Bhavra near Joypur. "King Piyadasi (Beloved of the gods) of Magadha, greeting the Council wishes it success and glory. You know, venerables, how great is my respect for the Buddha, Dharma and Sangha. All those things which were spoken by the Blessed Buddha were well-spoken, and by looking upon authority true Law will long endure. I honour, O Venerables, the following books of the Law:— The substance of the Vinaya, the state of the just (Arya vasani), the fears of the future (Aranyaka anagata bhaya of the Angutara Nikaya), Munigatha (the 12th Sutra of Sutra Nipata), Moneya Sutra, the questions of Upatessa (Sariputra Prasna of the Mahavagga), the exhortations to Rahula regarding falsehood (61st Sutra Rahulabad in Majjima Nikaya) spoken by the Blessed Buddha. These Books of Law, venerables, I hope that the honourable monks and nuns may constantly learn and reflect upon; so also the laity of the either sex".

From this edict it is evident that Ashoka did not mention about the complete text of the Tripitakas. Perhaps they were not even known in his time and have been later compilations. Ashoka had the relics of the Buddha dug out from all the eight places except Ramagram, and had them distributed throughout his vast domain, and memorial *Stupas* were erected on them. And under the guidance of Tishya he sent for the spread of the Noble Religion of the Buddha the following: Madhyantika to Kashmir and Gandhara; (i) Mahadeva to Mahisha (South of Godhavari; Mysore); (ii) Rakshita to Vanavasi (Aravali Hills); (iii) Yavana (Bactrian) Dharma Rakshita to Aparanataka (the Borderland); (iv) Maha Dharma Rakshita to Maharastra; (v) Maha Rakshita to Yonaloka (Bactria, Syria); (vi) Madhama to Himavanta (Tibet and Nepal); (vii) Sona or Uttara to Suvarnabhumi (Malay Peninsula); (viii) Mahendra to Lanka (Ceylon 247 BC). Sangamitra, Sister of Mahendra, daughter of Ashoka, accompanied her brother to Ceylon and took with her a branch of the Boddhi tree of Gaya and placed it at Anuradhapur which is still living; the tree must be now 245 + 1938-2188 years old. He also sent missionaries to Autiochus of Syria (260-247 BC), son of Selleucos; Ptolemy Philadelphus of Egypt (285-247 BC) Antigonus Gonatus of brother of Olympus and maternal uncle of Alexander. According to the Nigliva inscription Ashoka, in the fourteenth year of his coronation (256 BC).

He enlarged the Buddha Stupa of Konagamana. In the twentieth year of his coronation (249 BC) he made 'is" preceptor Upagupta to Lumbini, the birth place of the Buddha, eroded there a pillar, and made a gift of the village to the Sangha according to Pareyar inscription.

Mahadeva Council

Mahadeva Sangiti was Mahasanghic Council that took place 242 BC under the presidency or Mahaneva a very able organiser and popular figure. Nearly 500 delegates attended it under the patronage of Ashoka, who like ancient rulers was without any bigotry, was tolerant towards the cardinal principles of all sects and religions. Here some Vinaya texts were revised.

Tisya Sangiti took place in 245 BC under the presidency of Mahendra a disciple of Mahadeva at Stuparama of Anuradapur in the reign of Tisya. Arista, the companion of Mahendra, recited the entire Vinaya Pitaka. Dhamma Pitakas were also recited. In this assembly came Indragupta from Rajagriha, Dharmasena from Rishipattan, Priyadarsi from Jetavana Vihara of Vaishali, Uru Bhuddha Rakshita from Mahavana Vihara of Vaishali, Uru Dharma from Goshitarama of Kaushambhi, Rakshita Urusanga Rakshita from Dakshina Giri Vihara of Ujjaini, Mitirna from Asokarama of Pataliputra. Uttirna from Kashmir, Mahadeva from the Pallava Kingdom, Yavana Maha Dharma Rakshita from the Yavana Alexander (Alsanda, Uttara from Vindhachal, Chitra Gupta from Buddhimanda Vihara of the Buddha Gaya, Chandra Gupta from Vanavasa and Surya Gupta from the famous Kailash Vihara with numerous followers. *Parivarapata* in the Vinaya seems to have been added by the monks of Lanka.

Vattagamani Council

Vattagamani Sangiti took place about 29-25 BC at Abhaya Giri Vihara under the presidency of Mahatisya. A few thousand Ceylonese monks attended it. The Vinaya, Nikayas, Anga and Dharmaskanda were recited and sung together and then texts were written into books for the first time.

Kaniksha Council

Kaniksha Sangiti took place at Jalandhara in the middle of the first century AD Kaniksha became a jealous convert under the guidance of Parsvika, and inspired by him he held a council of five hundred monks under the presidency of Vasumitra. Kaniksha had the Dharma, Viniya and Abhidharma written into books, commentaries written on them—Upadesa, Vinaya Vibasha Sastra, Abhidharma Vibasha Sastra—each containing 100,000 couplets in Sanskrit, possibly, 6600,000 words in all, and they were revised by Ashvaghosh and then engraved on copper plates, which were enclosed in stone boxes on which a towering mound was built. Kaniksha's dominions extended over a vast territory, Madura in the south and as far as Bokhara in Central Asia. Over Central Asia spread the glorious message of equality, fraternity and service to humanity, preached and propagated by the Blessed Buddha.

Emperor Ming-Ti in 62 AD sent emissaries to Takshasila to obtain the holy writings, and from this time not only Chinese and

Indian monks began to cross the Central Asian deserts to set and spread the Buddhist enlightenments which were diligently translated into Chinese, and the New Religion began to spread in China. Korea took up Buddhism in 372 AD, and from Korea it was introduced into Japan in 552 AD. From Kalinga Buddhism was introduced in Java and Bali in sixth century AD.

Buddha's Language

In what language did the Buddha preach? He was born in Kapilavastu, under the suzerainty of Kosala. So possibly Sauraseni was his native language. He spent much of his ministry in Magadha, and so possibly spoke Magadhi with the people of the province. Mahendra who introduced the Buddhist sacred books to Ceylon from which they have been introduced to Burma and Siam, spent much of his time at Ujjaini and there spoke *Saurasini*. Pali in the earliest texts is a mixed dialect of both Saurasent and Magadhi. Only in Bhattagamini Sangiti (20-25 BC), the texts were put into writing. In the meantime during oral transmissions both the language and substance might have undergone transformations. It is therefore doubtful whether the Pali texts contain really the utterances of the Buddha in his spoken language or represent the true doctrines he preached.

Two Main Sects

At Vaishali at 382 BC the Buddha Sangha split up into two main sections — Mahasangre or universal love, sympathy, service and wisdom. The Hinayana eared for personal salvation through Ahratship. None of the schools believed in God or immortality of the soul. Their *Atman* was the self and not the soul. Personality was composed of the proper adjustment of the component parts of the body as a chariot is the assemblage of all its portions fitted in their proper places which Nagasena explained to Hollander (120-80 BC), the Indo-Greco-Bactrian King. The Buddhism insisted on following the eightfold paths by which, physical, mental and moral excellence could be attained, as an ideal of human perfection. It denounced asceticism on the one hand, hedonism in the opposite direction, and advocated the middle course of eudemonism, avoiding both the extremes. It did not believe in rituals, priesthood or incantations of magic formulas. Though its main votaries were the aristocrats of the day, it did not believe in caste distinctions. Its *Sangha* was open to all alike. This had a popular appeal, and necessarily therefore in course of time its high ideal had to be lowered in order to approach the credulous and superstitious mass mind. Buddhism was a practical ethical application to life for its betterment and happiness with the object of obtaining social justice and harmony. It had hardly any metaphysics or philosophy Of its own. What it had approximated the principles of Sankhya. Everything is impermanent. Life is in constant flux and new adjustments. The universe is subject to external change and transformations. This impermanence of things *(anitta)* became later the *Maya,* and the eternal changes and transformations became the *ananta or asima Brahmin* of the Vedanta. Buddhi (enlightenment) and Pragna (wisdom) especially of the Pragna Paramita of the Mayayana (Sophia of gnosticism) is practically identical with Sat-chit-ananda of the Brahmasutra.

Before Kaniksha's time, the Buddha was simply an ideal and a model. But by this time his images begun to be created and worshipped. Of course before his time the Nandas encouraged it as a state policy, as they wanted to lower the arrogance and pretensions of the superiority of the Brahmins.

But likewise for the similar purpose they patronised all the heretic sects—the Ajivakas and the Jainas. Pushyamitra no doubt persecuted the Buddhists, being a *strict adherent of Vedic rites.* "But this did not affect the Buddhists, for they had already endeared themselves in the public estimation by their acts of public service, particularly rendering medical help to the sick and charitable deeds by their excellent Sangha organisation, containing many selfless monks and nuns whose heart always throbbed for relieving the distress of the people. Medical study and the practice of medicine became the principal occupations of the monks. In the splendid Universities of Takshashila, Banasi and Nalanda, medical research had the foremost place in the educational system. The famous Charaka was the court physician of Kaniksha. Though Kaniksha did much to popularise and spread Buddhism, he paved the path of its degeneration. For Sakas wore not only superstitious, they also introduced T*antrieism* into India and Jalandhara, Puna, Sriparvata Odiana and Kamakhya, in the outskirts of Aryan culture, became the centres of its propagation, and this new seductive cult with its sensuous appeals corroded slowly but surely the moral fabric of both Buddhism and Brumanism, which gradually introduced the Shakti Cult into their own systems. Of course there was corruption before. It could not be otherwise when so many youths and maidens under momentary impulses became monks and nuns. Many of them were of robust health and of romantic disposition and they led carefree lives. So if to some of them biotic impulse proved too irresistible, it was regarded as an unworthy episode in their lives, due to lack of self-control which should have been exercised.

But they had not yet any philosophy to sublimate sexual indulgences and orgies into a mode of their salvation. This is what the Shakti cult of Tantra did for both Brahminism and particularly for Buddhism, and made it fall from its pinnacle of purity, nobility and idealism into filthy degradation of mystic sensualism, thus leading to social corruption. No society can succeed and prosper without an ideal which can only be sustained by moral strength. Self-discipline is the basis of moral strength. Self-discipline is not possible without sexual purity in life. Marriage, by regulating sexual cravings which are as natural as hunger for food and thirst for drinks, conduces to the purity of homo life.

Buddhism snatching away valiant Kshatriya youths from the arms of their wives not only blew away of the strongest rampart of national defence and laid it open to the aggression of the Yavanas, Shakas, Hunas and others, but also forced corruption in social life. Brahminism enjoined play during childhood, studies and discipline during youth, gainful occupations and marriage during the adult life, and after the children have been born and grown up, retirement into social service. It had no system of celibate monks and nuns, which were the peculiarities of the Buddhist and Jaina monastic life. The Buddhists an the Jainas regarded sexual union as impure, and as a corollary, sexual continence as a moral virtue. It may be good for a few who are devoted to a noble ideal, intense intellectual research or to social service, service and not for hundreds of thousands. If the strong, valiant and the elites leave their home and useful occupations and lead a vagrant unproductive life, it is bound to have dire consequences. It can not be expected that their youthful wives once accustomed to sexual delights, would give them up as a mockery of life; rather they would solicit illegitimate and irregular connections, thereby spreading venereal diseases and wrecking the peace and contentment of home life.

The procreating left to the lower classes who lack discipline, character, ideal and education, would lead to racial degeneration. To feed such a huge army of unproductive vagrants, many of whom rendered very little service, would have tasked the gainful labour and productive resources of the country. No doubt the Buddhist period from sixth century BC to 8th century AD, was the moat glorious epoch of our history. With its magic touch of enlightenment and inexpensive simplification of religious practices, arts and sciences flourished; peace and contentment prevailed. Simplicity of living with a refined spiritual outlook of life became the national ideal. Hospitals for men, even for animals, were in every educational centre. But these activities were fed not on the recreative interests, but on the main capital of the vitality of the nation which soon became exhausted and lay prostrate.

Mahayama introduced the Buddha worship. And with Buddha, Boddhisattvas (Buddha elects) were worshipped. And they conceived too past, present and future Buddhas (Manusi Buddha), and their etherial bodies were known as Dhyani Buddha. Above them all was the *Adi Buddha* (the primal Buddha) who was shapeless, formless, eternal, infinite, the source of Justice, Love and Wisdom, almost like the *Satchit Ananda Brahmin* of the *Verlunta,* The later Mahayanists, even (Vajrayanists), conceived for this *Adi Buddha a* consort *(Shakti), Niratana Devi,* a formless goddess who dwells in the infinite void (expanse) and in whose embrace *Adi Buddha* reposes and disappears, as in water salt is dissolved. And like *Adi Buddha* other Buddhas had their own consorts or *Shaktis.*

The Trinity

'Like the trinity of the Hindus, *(Brahma, Vishnu Shiva),* the *Vajrayanists* also conceived *Amitava; Avali-Ketasvara and Gautam as Triratra.* Their original trinity *(Trirotna)* Buddha, Dharma and Sangha, pure ideological conceptions, were formed into images. Dharma as a female by the left side and Sangha as a male by the rightside of the Buddha began to the worshipped. This is the image of the Jagganath temple at Puri which was a Buddhist centre. Dharmaraja was also worshipped like the Hindu Yama. Mahakala with his consort Mahakali was also worshipped as the gate keeper (Dvarapala) of the Buddha, and later identified with him. Vajrapani, the thunder wearer (Indra) was also first conceived as a bodyguard of the Buddha, and later he was made a Buddhisattva.

Kuvera, the god of wealth became his body guard and began to be worshipped. Practically with the compromises, Vedicism divorced of its rituals became identical with Buddhism which was later known as Hinduism. As Nagarjuna's (1st Century AD) *Pragna Paramita* (Sophia of the gnosticism) which formulates Buddha as an infinite eternal formless vast expanse (Maha-sunya), full of justice, kindness, love, charity (karuna) and wisdom, was beyond the comprehension of the masses, the above-mentioned gods were conceived to satisfy popular demand. And to explain them about si hundred *Dharanis* or treatises were written.

But as it also proved too obstruse for the masses, these gods began to be worshipped with some syllables (*Mantras)* extracted from these *Dharanis.* And these Mantras were regarded to have magic power to bestow health, wealth, prosperity, progeny and happiness. And these *Mantra* reciters were highly respected as on their *Mantras* depended their welfare, and they wore called Mantruyanists. Later these mantra reciters (gurus) began to be worshipped to get the same benefit. Upto this time these *Gurus* were celibate monks.

But now arose a sect among them who began to take *Shaktis* (female companions) for the attainment of their perfection. They argued that as in the union of *Purusa* (matter) with *Prakrita* (energy) there is the evolution of the universe, and the existence depends out the sexual congress of the males and the females; so highest wisdom, immeasurable strength and beatitude of mind could be obtained by the union of a real searcher after truth *(sadhaka)* with his female counterpart *(aku).*

They were known as *Vajrayanists*— (thunder-bearers). But as public opinion was against them, a secret sect rose among them, known as *Kala-chakrayanists,* who practised sensual orgies in a group (chakra) *in* the dead of night, and as a stimulus to their debauchery, they added liquor, fish) meat and dancing. It was gross sensuality tinged with mysticism. From them arose the *Sahajiyas* (Simple Methodists) who believed that in the sexual union of the select partners, there is not only promotion to health, exhilaration of the spirit, mental contentment would naturally lead to infinite beatitude and liberation.

Thus, a sublime philosophy gradually descended into degraded superstitious sensuality which the Blessed One preached to avoid and has created legions of useless vagrants who are infesting the country.

3

Preaching and Converts

From Varanasi the Buddha had proceeded on his journey to Uruvilva. On his way feeling tired, he was resting at the foot of a tree. At that time 30 young men running on the road, seeing the Buddha resting, asked him: "Have you seen a girl pass by this road?" "No" answered the Buddha. "But who are you?" "We are musicians. We go from town to town for the entertainment of aristocracies. Today we brought a girl with us for our pleasures. While we were napping, she fled away, taking with her as much of our valuables us she could." "That is the consequence of wreckless pleasure-hunting. Instead of hunting the girl for your merriments if you rather search within to find out how to conquer your evil passions, you would rather be happy." They answered the Buddha with loud jeers. "Do you play flate?' asked the Buddha to one who was the most boisterous in his hilarity. "Certainly", he answered:. "I am one of the finest players. The Kings praise my art very much". "Give me your flute", the Buddha said. A flute was handed over to the Buddha out of curiosity, thinking it would be a great joke. But when the Buddha began to play the flute, they were simply astonished. They never heard such a symphony before. Their mirth was subdued, and they begged the Buddha to teach them the art. "No, you can not learn it before you give up your evil passions." "Master, we shall do that," they said. "After you have done that, come to me."

Jatila impressed by the august personality of the Buddha, asked the Buddha to stay with him a few days longer." The irrefutable logic and rationalism of the Buddha, his bright and cheerful countenance, his genial and loving temperament, free from passions and prejudices; convinced Kashyapa of the worthlessness of *Fire-warship,* and he throwing away his fire-worshipping implements into the Nirajana, became an ardent follower of the Buddha.

Halt at Gaya

The Buddha, Kashyapa and a few Jatila Brahmins on their way to Rajagriha halted at the Elephant Rook of Gaya. At that time two younger brothers of Kashyapa— Nadi Kashyapa and Gaya Kashyapa — were staying at Gaya. They, being perplexed by the sight of fire-worshipping implements of his brother floating down the river, came to see him as to the reasons of his strange behaviour. While they were talking a fire broke out in a neighbouring forest. Then Buddha pointing it out said: "You see the flames of fire shooting up, and the smoke spreading: and you hear its roaring and cracking sound. The eyes only perceive the object; this perception stimulates internal sensation. If there has been previous experience, then mind compares it with that, and knows it is fire. If it were not so, then a lunatic or one who has never seen fire could be cognizant of it. As with the eyes, so with other senses.

The perception of external things excite mental sensation; mind then compares it with previous experiences, and calls it pleasure or pain. Mind is therefore the central focus of sensations of pleasure and pain. Our desires and passions of anger, greed, jealousy and envy are the internal fires that burn within us and consume us. External objects like a fair seductive damsel, gold or jewelleries fan the flake. If fire or lamp burns when we are asleep or when our eyes are closed, we do not perceive or feel any sensation; so if we have self-control and our desires and passions are under a strict discipline, external sensuous charms can no longer excite our internal cravings or produce sensations of pleasure and pain. We rise above them. We are not excited by pleasure and pain, both external and internal. We are in a state of ecstatic bliss."

At Rajagriha

The Buddha remembering that he had promised Srenika Bimbisara (54-1-492 BC) that in case he received enlightenment, he would communicate it to him, came to Rajagriha, accompanied by the venerable Kashyapa and a few other Jatila disciples and stayed at Yastivana in the suburb. When the Magadha King heard of it, he, with followers came to Yaṣtivana, and saluted the Buddha. Kashyapa" was a well-known figure in Rajagriha, and was highly venerated by all classes of people for his austerities.

The crowd therefore was uncertain which was the teacher and which the disciple. The Buddha perceived this confusion of the visitors. And he therefore asked Kashyapa why he had given up Fire-worship. Kashyapa understood the motive of the question, and he answered: The sacrificer, according to the Vedas, is supposed to get all his desires fulfilled—desires for wealth, power, women and progeny. Through your teaching I have realised that Desires are the root-cause of all our miseries. And unless we have self-control we can not get the bliss and contentment of mind. That is why I have given up sacrifices." And Kashyapa saluted the Buddha as his teacher.

Bimbisara professed to follow the Dharma, and invited the Buddha and his followers to go to the palace for the meal. When next day the Buddha and his disciples went to the palace, the Buddha was received with great veneration and enthusiasm; and Bimbisara said to the Buddha: "Your presence, O great teachers give me a great pleasure. And it is desirable that I should see you as often as possible, so that I can hear your blissful words. Receive from me this present. Nearer to the city than where are you staying, there is a lovely extensive park, known as Bamboo Grove (*Venu Vana)* where you and your disciples can live comfortably. I give you this Venu Vana, and by your acceptance of this, you will afford me a great joy." The Buddha smiled indicating his acceptance Then one -courtier brought a gold vase to the King filled with perfumed water, and the King poured water from it into the hands of the Buddha, saying: "As from my hands, O great teacher, the water is poured into your hands, so from my hands, o great teacher, the Venu Vana goes into your hands." There was great rejoicing of the multitude at the news of the dedication of the Venu Vana to the Buddha Sangha. And the Buddha spent many rainy seasons in the Venu Vana, and there delivered many of his famous discourses.

At that time Sanjay Vairatiputra, one of the six Tirthikas, was the head of a monastery at Rajagriha, having 250 inmates of which Sariputra and Maud-galyana were two important members. It happened that Ashvajit, one of the first five members of the Deerpark and when he had been practising austerities at Uruvilva, in the course of his missionary wanderings, reached' Rajagriha, and while out for begging his noonday meal, was met by Sariputra who was struck by his appearance of calm dignity, robust health and cheerful disposition, and Sariputra asked him what philosophy he following. Ashvajit answered that he was but an humble follower of the Buddha's Dharma. Asked again to explain it, he expounded the fundamental principles of the Buddhist tenets, and thinking that Sariputra was amply going to make an argumentative debate with him, he told him that if he was desirous of further-discussions on the subject, he could see the Buddha himself. Charmed with the new philosophy, Sariputra accompanied by his intimate friend Maudgalayana went to Vena Vana to interview the Buddha. So much were they impressed by the Buddha's discourses, that they not only became his ardent converts but also his right hand men in the Buddhist Sangha. Sariputra was called the Commander-in-Chief of the Dharma (*Dharma* Senapati), for he was one of the finest debaters of that time.

Sons of many noble families of Rajagriha became the disciples of the Buddha, and leaving their homes, joined the Sangha, and Venu Vana became crowded with their activities. And there was serious discontent in the city. They used to say: "Why has the Shakya scion come in to our midst? Have not we enough of monks already who preach virtue? Do they not seduce our children! But by this Shakya scion our homes are being depleted and women are being made widows in their conjugal relation. He is creating tension between the husband and wife. A plague would have been less harmful to us and would have made fewer widows. As he has captured the principal disciples of Sanjaya, for whom has he spread the net mow?" When it was brought to the notice of the Buddha, he said to his disciples: "Do not be anxious. This discontentment would not last long. I teach people only to be self-reliant through self-control, practice of virtue and purity of the mind." Suddhodana, coming to know that his son was the head of a great Sangha, and was staying at Rajagriha, said to Udayin: "I am very unhappy Udayin; I have become old. I might die any time. Before I die I would like to see my son. Udayin, in other days, you were his best friend. I do not know anybody else who could influence him better than you could do. Tell him all about my sadness, my earnest longing to see him, and I hope he would not be insensible to my distress."

Visit to Kapilavastu

Before the winter was over, Udayin brought the message of Suddhodana to the Buddha. The Buddha decided to go to Kapilavastu to see his old father and other relations. On hearing of this Bimbisara went to Venu Vana with his sou Ajatshatru and asked the Buddha for some personal tokens. Early in the spring when the trees were putting on new foliage, the Buddha with Sariputra Maudgalayana and a few other disciples started for Kapilavastu. *At* last the Buddha reached Kapilavastu with his followers. The Shakya and the Koli chiefs assembled at the Banyan tree rest house *(Nayagradharama)* in the outskirt of the city which was meant as the guest house for the visiting: *Paribraiakas.* Many of the elders thought as they were senior to Siddhartha, they should not salute him; but those who were junior saluted him. Suddhodana, moved by the sight of his beloved son after seven years, clasped him in his arms, smelt the apex of his head, and said: "My son" with a faltering and choked voice, happy tears trickling his eyes and cheeks, "You have come home. Make now your old father, old mother, Yashodhara, your son and other relations happy by staying will us, and taking the responsibility of home and the state". The old man could not say more, but sa down with the Buddha's hand in his arms. Suprabuddha, brother of Dandapani whose daughter Yashodhara the Buddha married and deserted, remonstrated with the Buddha for his folly of leading a mendicant's life, and having a following of homeless beggars in rags, causing mental anguish to his old father and mother, and particularly deserting such a devoted wife like Yashodhara. Yashodhara, with her unrivalled beauty and charms, could have married much worthier person but by selecting a crank, has made her whole life-miserable. Now he hoped that he had had enough of that silly monkish nonsense, and would enjoy the comforts of home. Not only he would be happy by that, but he would also make others happy. The Buddha and Sariputra expressed displeasure at such remarks, and after unseemly scenes, the Buddha with his disciples remained at the Rest House, and the Shakya and the Kolis returned to their respective homes, nobody thinking of inviting the Buddha and the other monks for dinner as generally was the custom. The Buddha politely answered his father: "I know you have tender affection and solicitude for me. But if you extend even a part of the infinite love and affection which you have for me and with which you are embracing me to all mankind, you will gain a bigger Siddhartha than a smaller one you have lost; and you would realty enjoy the blissful contentment of mind."

The next day the Buddha with his disciples had set out from the *rest house* to beg in the city for their midday meals. After crossing the city gate the Buddha hesitated for a while whether they should go to the palace for their dinner, but finally decided that they would adhere to the monastic rule of the Sangha of begging their food from house to house. But as soon as they began to beg, they were followed by a crowd, and the citizens began to peer through the windows and ascend the roofs of their houses to see this great spectacle that Prince Siddhartha, who once rode the streets of Kapilavastu in magnificent chariots in stately splendour dressed in costliest garments, was now begging his food, clad in beggarly mendicant's clothes. A maid servant of Yashodhara brought to her notice that her husband Prince Siddhartha was begging his meals in the streets of Kapilavastu, followed by a crowd. Yashodhara trembled when she heard it, but rushed frantically to her father-in-law, and announced the news to him. Suddhodana being startled at such a happening rose up, and holding his outer robe with his hand, hurried to the place of occurrence, and removing the crowd, faced his son, and asked him: "My son, why are you putting all of us into shame! Why are you begging meals? Do you think I am unable to provide you and your companions with your necessities!" "But father, this is the custom with us." "Custom with us, what do you mean by it? Are we not descended from, the race of illustrious Shakya Kshatriyas, and has any of them ever begged?" "You and your family may proudly claim Sakhya descent", said the Buddha "But I am a monk and I have to follow the monastic custom of begging my food and living on alms. But father when one has found a hidden treasure, it is his duty first to present his father with the most precious of the jewels. Permit me to present to you the boat jewels of the cardinal tenets of the doctrine of enlightenment I have found after many painful efforts". Suddhodhana without answering it simply look his son's bowl, led him to his house where the members of the family and other relatives assembled. Suddhodana asked about Yashodhara. Prajapati answered: "I asked her to come with me. But she said: "I would not acompany you. If I am of any value in his eyes and if by my life I have lived, I deserve to see my husband, then he will himself come. Then I can welcome him better here; I can show him all the respect due to him." The Buddha then made a discourse.

Then dinner was served. After dinner the Buddha and his companions took their usual siesta. In the afternoon when the sun was reclining in the west, the Buddha asked the permission of Suddhodana to see Yashodhara. Suddhodana said: "When Yashodhara heard that you had become a monk, she discarded her fine and cosily garments. She threw away her necklace and bracelets. She began to sleep on mats instead of bed. She gave up using perfumes and garlands. She takes only one meal a day. She is so devoted to you that when other Kings, thinking by your becoming a monk she became a widow, sent her valuable presents in order to win her favour and her hands, she sent them all back with remonstrance". The Buddha took with him Sariputra and Maudga-layan, and keeping them outside the door, guided by a maidservant, entered into her chamber, leaving directions to his two followers that even in case Yashodhara tried to embrace him, they should not prevent her from doing so, though it was against the monastic rule that any one of them should be touched by a woman.

When Yashodhara saw the Buddha entering into her room, a monk in a coarse yellowish garment, with shaven head and shaven beard, though she knew it would be so, but in her mental picture she always beheld her beloved Siddhartha with raven-black curly flowing locks, bejwelled turban, embroidered silken robe, she was so terribly shocked that she could not restrain herself, though she had preconceived so many things to say to one who was dearer to her than her own life, and when she found him near her again after the lapse of seven long weary years, in order to reclaim him again to her alone, she simply wept, sobbed, fell at his feet, holding them fast. Yashodhara could not and did not utter a single word; only the Buddha's feet were wet with her tears. The Buddha felt compassionate and sympathetic. He tried to console her by praising her virtue and devotion; but she remained disconsolate, and the Buddha left her to her tears. "While returning to the *rest house,* the Buddha was followed by his younger brother Nanda. Nanda was of a gay and cheerful nature. He was devoted to his elder brother. He was in high glee, in the company of one for whom he had deep affection and high respect and whom he met again after seven years. The Buddha asked Nanda: "Nanda, are you happy?" "Yes, brother,, Jam happy; I am happy that you have come, and to-be in your company. I have missed you so much these: years. Father tried his utmost to persuade you to stay in Kapilavastu, and to take the responsibility of the State. So also uncle Suprabuddha exhausted in vain his eloquence on you. When you have categorically declined to have anything with the worldly affairs and will devote your, entire life to the mission of your Dharma, father and other Shakhya chiefs and relatives have decided to consecrate me tomorrow with your permission to the chief's office of the Shakyas after father's demise. And day after tomorrow I shall be married to Sundarika (Janapada Kalyani). She is so lovely. She loves me and I love her. Oh, how happy I shall be, and he danced in joy. The Buddha asked: "Are you sure, Nanda, you will be very happy?" "Yes, brother, why not". "Now Nanda return home". The Buddha went to the *rest house and* Nanda returned home.

Next day when the Buddha came to the cousecration ceremony (Yuvaraja avisekha), all the Shakya elders, Suprabuddha, and particularly Prajapati, earnestly appealed to the Buddha to reconsider the matter, and not to hurt their feelings. They said that he was learned, clever, and had acquired vast experience with the affairs of men through his wide travels, and he was the fittest man to lead the Sakhyas to honour and glory. But as the Buddha remained obdurate to all of their appeals and entreaties, the ceremony of anointing and consecrating Nanda as the Yuvaraja by all the Shakya Chiefs was gone through mechanically in an atmosphere of subdued melancholy depression. Before the feast the Buddha expounded he merits of the doctrine of enlightenment in the midst of solemn silence-In the afternoon when the Buddha left the palace for the *rest house,* he was again followed by Nanda. The Buddha said: "Tell me Nanda frankly how you, feel. Reveal your secret thoughts to me," "'Brother", Nanda replied: "I doubt whether you would understand *me.* You have disdainfully kicked away comforts, power and affluence. You have abandoned your tenderly loving Yashodhara." "And you are rapturous for one day you expect to be the chief of the Sakhyas." "Yes, and more than that, I love pretty Sundarika, and tomorrow she shall be my wife." "Nanda, I have pity for your naivete; you do not know that with the desires are enchained endless sorrows. And sensual gratifications have their depressing reactions, and they can not give you everlasting happiness. After light comes the darkness. Pleasures change into pain."

For some time Nanda remained silent as the subject was of very little interest to him. But the Buddha's words had a hypnotic influence over him. The Buddha asked him whether he had understood him. "No, I do not thoroughly understand it;" but as he did not want to appear to look foolish before his learned brother, he said: "Brother you are wiser than me. Your trend of thought is interesting me." The Buddha said: "I am glad to know that, brother; only with the conquest of the desires, through self-control one can enjoy the tranquillity of the mind. Do you follow me? Yes, I shall follow you in your path" Then after reflection, Nanda thought that he was too foolish to say that he would follow the footsteps of his brother. Will he give up power and position, particularly the pretty Sundarika? And he sighed sadly, accompanied the Buddha, but did not say anything to the Buddha for the fear of being reproached by him. But at the corner of a street Sundarika smilingly approached Nandi and asked him:

"Where are you going, Nanda." Nanda remained silent.. Then she addressed the Buddha: "Are you taking: him?" "Yes," answered the Buddha. "But he will come soon." Nanda wanted to say, "Yes, Sundarika, I shall be back soon to you," but did not dare to say that in the Buddha's presence, and he followed the Buddha. Sundarika understood by the silence that Nanda was lost to her, and she wept.

Son in Order

About a week afterwards Yashodhara dressed Rahula, her seven years old son in his best garments, and patting him on his forehead with infinite mother's tender love, said to him: "My Rahula is a lovely nice boy, is it not." "Yes, mother, I am a nice boy," answered Rahula in his soft modulated voice which was to Yashodhara like the divine music. "Can you do what I shall tell you?" "Certainly I can, mother." "Can you ask from your father something?' "But the father is now sleeping," meaning Suddhodana. Yashodhara, holding Rahula up to the window, pointed out to him the -Buddha, "That good looking monk is your father. And he has great wealth which we have not seen since he left us; go to him and ask for your rights: say," "I am your son; I shall like to be the head of the Shakya clan, and I want my ancestral inheritance. Give it to me." Rahula went up to the Buddha and with artless touching affection said to him: "Father, how happy I am to be near you. I am your son Rahula. I know you possess enormous treasures. I shall like to be the head of the Shakya Clan. I want my ancestral inheritance." The Buddha kept silent. But Rahula followed him to the rest house. And the boy used to repeat every now and then: "Give me my inheritance, Father." The Buddha used to change places, but the boy used to follow him like a shadow, repeating his demand for his inheritance. 'Though disturbed, the Buddha did not stop him from following him, nor his followers did. Finally the Buddha said to Rahula: "My child you do not know" what treasure you are demanding from me as your inheritance. The treasure you are demanding will grow less and less with time and uses, and will bring vexations in consequence. But you have the right to the inheritance of the real treasure of enlightenment I have found which has brought me bliss and it would be blissful to you." The Buddha asked Sariputra to admit Rahula into Order, and take charge of his instructions. "When Yashodhara heard of Rahula's conversion, she was prostrate at this unexpected happening. Suddhodana rushed into the Rest House to ascertain it, and then addressed the

Buddha: "You are my son; when you renounced the world I was overwhelmed with sorrow. When you converted Nanda I was sorely grieved. But with the conversion of Rahula, I have almost lost my sanity. I know personally how father feels at the separation from his son. I therefore request you that you will not in future convert any body without the consent of his parents." The Buddha readily approved of it and made this the rule in his Order. After a few more interviews with his father arid other Shakya and Koli Chiefs the Buddha returned to Rajagriha.

King Sudatta used to feed the poor and the distressed (anatha), he was known as Anathapindatha (giver of food to the poor). Anathapindatha, hearing the reputation of the Buddha and of his novel doctrine, paid him a visit, and was moved and charmed by the personality and conversation with the teacher. Anathapindatha frankly said to the Buddha: "I have to look after large financial transactions. Consequently I have to watch tirelessly their manifold operations so that I sustain no loss. For I have many employees, and on my success depend their livelihood. I Know, Mahatma (Great soul) your disciples blame the worldly life full of anxieties and cares, the source of all miseries, and praise the carefree monk's life. I know you have personally renounced power and position. And you have established a Sangha of simplicity of living, and service, and known the path of true Great teacher, though I am very much occupied with my business and trade, my mind always yearns to do good to others. I always try to help the poor and distressed. Now my question is, whether I shall renounce the world so that I can with my whole heart devote myself to the service of mankind, or I shall give my surplus profits to others so that they can relieve the sick, poor and the distressed." The Buddha replied: "Only the pure in heart can enjoy the tranquillity of wealth and position should renounce it. But there is no need of denouncing wealth for one who is not attached to it, and who liberally gives for the good and welfare of many. You rather with enthusiasm and energy develop your business, and increase your wealth. My Dharma does not teach any one to renounce, the world unnecessarily. My Dharma only inculcates people to lead an honest and pure life, giving up pride, luxury and impurity of the mind. Even a monk who is lazy, addicted to comforts and luxury, lacks in energy and enthusiasm in relieving the distress of his fellow men, cannot get the lasting bliss. Whoever is pure in mind, tireless and indomitable in the discharge of his duties, and like lotus bloom which thrives in water but water not adhering to it, he manages his mundane affairs, whether a monk or a householder, he will enjoy peace and contentment." Anathapindatha was highly gratified with these convincing words of the Buddha. And he respectfully addressed the Buddha: "O Great Soul, for the residence of the monks of your Sangha I desire to build a rest house (Vihara) at Shravasti, and I shall be highly gratified if it is acceptable to you". The Buddha appreciated the generosity of Anathapindatha, and giving his consent to it said: "The friendship of a liberal and charitably disposed person is always valuable. Anger, hatred, greed and jealousy can not flourish in the heart of one is saturated with charity and kindness.

The of charity are the stepping stones to the givers' own salvation. The tree of discriminate charity he plants will give refreshing shade, charming flowers and fruits to him and others in future". Anathapindatha took Sariputra for the selection of the site for the Vihara at Shravasti. Anathapindatha found the Jetavana (Park) in the suburb of Shravasthi very charming. It belonged to Prince Jeta. But he would sell it only at a very high price. As Anathapindatha liked the place, and Sariputra also approved of it the great merchant covered the whole ground with coins, which was demanded as the sale price. But when Prince Jeta learnt that it was meant for the Buddha Sangha, he later built with parts of the sale proceeds four high gate-towers on the four sides of the park.

Rainy Season

The Buddha spent his first rainy season (529 BC) at Varanasi Deer Park. The second and third rainy seasons (527-528 BC) were spent at Rajagriha Veun Vana. But before the rains were over, the Buddha was suffering from dysentery. Jivaka the great physician cured him of the disease. Jivaka became so much charmed and devoted to the Buddha, in order to him often, donated his Mango-grove *(Amra Vana)* in Rajagriha to the Buddha Sangha, where the Buddha often stayed.

When the Jeta Vana was ready Anathapindatha sent one of his faithful assistants to the Buddha at the Venuvana. The messenger said to the Buddha: "My master prostrates himself at your feet, and he hopes you have enjoyed good health; and he reminds you by the promise you made that you would visit Shravasti." The Buddha replied: "I will go", and after a few days he started for Shravasti with a number of disciples. When Anathapindatha heard that the Buddha with his disciples was reaching Shravasti, he accompanied by his wife Purna Lakshami, his sous, daughters and other rich merchants and citizens, met them near the city gate with flowers and incense, and conducted them in a big procession to the Jeta Vana. Anathpindatha asked the Buddha: "Venerable, what shall I do with this park?" "Donate it in perpetuity to the Sangha." The Anathpindatha had a gold vase brought to him filled with water which he poured into the hands of Buddha, saying: "I present the Jeta Vana to the Sangha of which the Buddha is the head for now and for ever." "This is well done," said the Buddha. "I accept this gift. This will be for us a happy asylum. We shall live here in peace, protected from heat and cold. Ferocious animals would not be able to enter here, nor there would be much buzzing of the mosquitoes. This place is also free from violent storms and scorching sun. This will be a fine place for meditation." Anathpindatha one day thought that all the people of Shravasti should take pride in the Buddha Vihara of the place, and which therefore should be built with public subscription in Jetavana.

The King approved of it, and made a proclamation by beat of drums: "Listen, O, inhabitants of Shravasthi. For seven days the merchant Anathpindatha, mounted on an elephant will ride through the streets of the city, begging alms for the construction of a Buddha Vihara. Each one should subscribe whatever he can". The Buddha began his ministry at the age of 35. He died at the ago of 80'. He preached his Dharma indefatigably for 45 years, of which he spent 22 rains in Jetavana where many discourses were made. Kala, brother of Prasenjit became the first convert. Then Prasenjit became also an ardent follower of Buddhism through his wife Mallika. Vishakha also erected a Vihara in the eastern suburb of Shravasthi, known as Purvarama. The Buddha spent 3 rains in it.

The Buddha did not stay long in Shravasti. He returned soon to Rajagriha. There he converted Ugrasena, son of the treasurer of Bimbisara. At that the plague was raging at Vaishali, the capital of Licchhavi Republic. The Buddha with his band of selfless workers reduced virulence and the suffering caused by the disease. For this reason out of gratitude Gosringha presented the Buddha Sangha the Kutagara Vihara in Salavana. At this time the Buddha heard that there was severe tension between the Shakyas and the Kolis over the supply of the irrigating water from the Rohini river. The Buddha went to the place, via Shravasti and brought out the compromise. The Buddha stayed a few days at Kapilavastu at the rest house and then returned to Kutagar in Mahavana of Vaishali. While staying there during the fifth rains, the Buddha heard that his 97 years old father Suddhodana was seriously ill; The Buddha with Nanda came to Kapilavastu. Suddhodana at the sight of his sons rallied a little. But he died with full consciousness on the Ashvini full-moon day. The Buddha cremated him and gave consolation to his relatives. Prajapati, the step mother of the Buddha and mother of Nanda, wanted to be a nun, as she said she had no interest in worldly affairs, but the Buddha persuaded her not to do so. Nanda too was very restless for Sundarika. But when the Buddha pointed out to Nanda during their stay at Kapilavastu that Sundarika did no longer care for him, and she had married another man, and after marriage and with a number of children, she had lost her beauty and charms, Nanda was reconciled to a certain extent to his monastic life. From Kapilavastu the Buddha returned to Kutagara Vihara in Mahavana of Vaishali. There Gautami Prajapati with a number of Shakya and Koli ladies went for the admission into the Buddhist Sangha. Buddha at first declined. Then Ananda, the cousin of the Buddha, intervened. Ananda said that if Maya Devi was alive, his own mother, her desire certainly could not be so easily brushed aside as that of his stepmother. But Prajapati loved him and nursed him just like a mother without feeling any difference. The reference was touching. Women were now admitted under certain restrictions. But the Buddha warned that if women 'were not admitted into the Sangha, the purity of the Sangha would have lasted longer.

From Vaishali the Buddha returned to Rajagriha. The seventh rains the Buddha spent at Shravasti Jetavana, coming there via

Sanaksa. Prasenjit began to take serious interest in Buddhism and invited him to his place.

The eighth rains the Buddha spent on the Sansumara Hill near Kapilavastu, and there he converted the father and mother of Nakula and Moggali (Mandgali). The ninth rains was spent at Ghositarama in the suburb of Kausambhi. There. Moggali stirred up dissension in the Sangha. The Buddha advised both the parties to be patient, sympathetic and charitable to each other; but failing to bring out a compromise he went alone to Parileshyaka village where the villagers built for him Rakshitarana under the Bhadrasala tree. The tenth rains the Buddha spent alone at Rakshilarama where the repentant Bhikshus came for forgiveness and he pardoned them. He returned with them to Jetavana. Prasenjit had an ugly daughter, nicknamed by the public as Virupa. Prasenjit invited Ganga, a rich merchant to his palace, and offered him the hand of his daughter, thinking, Ganga once married to her, would not dare to illtreat or desert her for her unattractive appearance. Ganga was highly gratified at such a grand proposal and he thankfully agreed to it. But after marriage when he saw the face of his-newly married wife, he felt himself unhappy and miserable. The Buddha coming to know of this told Ganga that more than passing beauty the virtuous-character and good manners are to be appreciated, and was raconciled.

The eleventh rains the Buddha spent at Rajagriha. But on his way from Shravasti he passing through a village—Eknala not far from Rajagriha where a Brahmin named Bharadvaja was celebrating the harvest festival with feasts, songs and merriments, the Buddha presented his alms bowl, whereupon Bharadvaja said to the Buddha: "Do not stay in our midst, O, monk, for your life is not a good example to us. We have to work hard for our living. With open eyes we have to watch the seasonal changes. In proper time we send our servants to till the soil with the plough in the scorching sun with the sweat on their brow. Then we have to sow seeds with our servants. When the plant grows, we have to take out the weeds. In the harvest time we collect them, thrash out the grains, and put the corn into the granary. Then we have to spread it to the sun to kill the insects. We have to pound them in a mortar to shell out the grains. After all these laborious works, we now enjoy it. But you simply run the streets or the highways, and at dinner time present your begging bowl. It would be better for your body and soul, instead of begging, to work out your living like us." The Buddha smiled and said: "Yes, friends, like you, I also plough and sow; and when the work is finished, I take my meal." "You plough and sow? "Where are your ploughing bulls and the sowing seeds?" "True knowledge is the seed I sow. The pious works I perform are the rains that fecoudate the soil of my conscience. My energy is my bulls, Dharma is my plough, mind is my handle and lash, love and sympathy are the furrows. Purity of heart is my plant, and desire is the weed I take out. Nirvana or contentment of mind is my harvest I gather". Bharadvaja moved by this simile followed the Buddha to be his disciple. And entering Rajagriha they saw a number of danseuses dancing surrounded by a crowd. And one of the prettiest girl among them—Kuvalaya—shouting:—"Look at me O lords! Have you got in the whole of Rajagriha so enticing a beauty like me!" And she began to dance, in rapid rotations. She was dressed in a number of silken gowns and with her rapid whirling movements, they began to be puffed up like the plumage of peacocks. And the more rapidly she began to dance her whirling dances, one by one her gowns fell down, and she was standing still like a statue completely nude to the amazing admiration of the crowd. And then the Buddha remarked to Bharadvaja that beauty without character is a seductive evil.

The twelfth rains he spent at Vairanti and returned to Shravasti by Prayag and Kanyakubja. The thirteenth rains the Buddha spent at Chalika near Shravasti. The fourteenth rains the Buddha spent at Jetavana in Shravasti and where he ordained his son Rahula, then eight years old, preaching on that occasion the Rahual. He then proceeded to Kapilavastu. The fifteenth rains the Buddha spent at Nigradarama at Kapilavastu where he devlivered a lesson to his cousin Mahanama, who succeeded Suddhodana in the headship of the Shakya' clan.

Suprabuddha, the head of the Koli Clan, reproached and condemned the Buddha for deserting Yashodhara, Dandapani.

The sixteenth rains the Buddha spent at Alavi, where he went at the request of its King to remove by his preachings the superstitious fears of the populace.

The seventeenth rains the Buddha spent at Rajagriha and made a speech on the occasion of the death of the courtesan Srimati. During the autumn the Buddha came to Alavi via Shravasti and refused to preach until a hungry man was well-fed. The eighteenth brains the Buddha spent at Chalika near Shravasti, and while there gave consolations to a weaver who accidentally killed his own daughter. The nineteenth rains he spent at Venuvana. And during the autumn and winter he made a lecturing tour throughout the whole of Magadha. While travelling, once finding a deer caught in a snare, he released it, at which the hunter became enraged at him and wanted to kill him.

Bat the Buddha pacified his wrath by his soothing words, and the hunter become the lay disciple of the Buddha and gave up the cruel profession of hunting used to feed regie the dinner, though the food was excellent. When asked the reason of this distaste, they said that nothing was so appetising as love, which was lacking in his place. This made him thinking.

Thinking perhaps that it was unsafe to keep Mahanama any longer as the head of the Shakya Clan, as the deception practised on Prasenjit might be disclosed, the Shakyas chose Bhadraka son of Dhotodana, brother of Suddhadana, as their leader. But Mahanama still feeling himself nervous persuaded his brother Anuruddha, his cousin Ananda, son of Sukhodana, Bhadraka, the ruling head, Devadatta son of Suprabuddha, the chieftain of Koli, Kimbila, and their barber Upali to take to monastic life; and while the Buddha was staying at Anupia, a Malla town, they presented them-solves before the Buddha, and the Buddha thinking they were good acquisitions made them enter the Sansha.

From Anupia the Buddha journeyed forth to Devadatta felt slighted, and he came at Rajagriha and spent the twentieth rains.

The Buddha addressed the monks thus: "O Bhikahns I am now 55 years old. Though decrepitade has not yet set in, still I need a personal attendant (*Opasthayaka*). So long Nagasamal, Nagita, Upavana, Sunakshatri, of an attendant I suffer much inconveniences. Therefore appoint for me an attendant." Sariputa, Maudgalyana, Ananda and others coveted this position; but the Buddha selected Ananda for this work. And Ananda accepted it under certain conditions. Seeing the popularity of the Buddha, the

Tirthikas induced the courtesan Sundari to spread scandals about him, but they where discomforted.

At Chalika

From Shravasti the Buddha went to Chalika. Anuruddha went to Anga with the newly married daughter of Anathapindatha. At Chalika the notorious Angulimala who plundered and harassed the public was converted. The Buddha returned to Rajagriha. There Devadatta approached the Buddha to give him the lead in the Sangha Buddha did not entertain the idea. Then he proposed to amend some of the Sangha rules, which was ruled out. Enraged at this Devadatta secured the patronage of the Prince. Ajatashatru and with his help he created a split in the Sangha to Ajatashatru the Prince and said to him". In former days, Prince, people were long-lived; but now their term of life is short. It is quite possible therefore that you may complete your time while you are still a Prince. So do you, Prince, kill your father and became the Raja, and I will kill" Sramana Gautam, and become the Buddha.

The Princes Abhaya, Silavat and Vimala, sons of Bimbisara, became Buddhist monks, for otherwise they were afraid they might have been put to death, as their father met his end by their brother Ajatashatru. In *Thera Gatha* Silavat says that Ajatashatru was anxious to kill him. We find Vaihalva, took the help of his grandfather Chetaka, the head of the Licchhavi clan, ever some spoils of war when Ajatashatru was ruling in Anga as Viceroy.

Wife in Nunnery

While the Buddha was staying at Shravasti, Yashodhara thought: "My husband is a monk and a Buddha. The son also leads a monastic life with him. What is the use of my staying at home. I shall go to Shravasti and enter into a nunnery so that I can always see my husband and my son". With this decision she went to Shravasti and entered into a nunnery, and *thus got* opportunities to see her husband and her beloved son. Rahula that time was a Sramana and he very often used to go to see his mother. One day Rahul a went to see his mother. But he could not as usual find her at the porch. A nun informed him that Yashodhara (Bimba Devi) was suffering from constipation. Then

Rahula went to his mother's bed side and asked her: "What should you eat with this ailment?" Yashodhara answered: "When I was at home I used to get my constipation relieved if I took mango juice mixed with sugar. But now we live upon begging; where shall I get sugar-mixed mango-juice?" Rahula said: "I am going to get it. And as soon as I get it, I shall come back. Rahula had as his preceptor Dharma Senapati Sariputra as his preceptor, Maudgalyana as his "teacher, Ananda as his uncle, and the Buddha himself as his father, Rahula indeed was very fortunate. But instead of going to any body else, he went to his preceptor and saluting him, stood there sad and dejected. Sariputra asked him: "Child, why are looking so sad today?" Rahula answered: "Venerable, my mother is suffering from constipation; she believes that if she can drink sugar-mixed mango juice it would relieve her." "All right I shall get it for her. Do not be anxious on that account". Sariputra took Rahula with him to Shravasti, and making him sit on a stone he entered into the palace. At this time the gardener brought a bucketful of ripe sweet mangoes. The King himself skinned out the mangoes, spread sugar on them and squeezed the juice into the bowl to its full. Sariputra handed it over to Rahula, saying: "Take it to your mother." Rahula did it, and Yashodhara partaking of it was cured of her constipation. Another time Yashodhara was suffering from hyperacidity and when Rahula informed Sariputra of it, Sariputra secured for her fresh buttered rice and carpfish curry which she wanted to relieve her (492-480 BC), surrounded the beauties of the nocturnal sky. Then the autumnal full-moon was radiating its soothing and serene beams; charmed by it the King said: "Friends, how delightful is this full-moon night! *What* a lovely spectacle!. And how relaxing Yet I find no peace of mind Can I go to Sramanas or Brahmins who can tranquillise One minister said, "Let us go to veteran versatile Puran Kashya a, leader of a big sect and respected by all the people and his words might give you the contentment of mind." The King remained silent. Then other ministers began to praise in the similar terms.

The King saluted the Buddhha, took his seat and said to the Buddha. "If you will permit me, I shall ask you a few questions." "Maharaja, you can ask me any question you please." "Venerable, men are engaged in various trades and occupations and with their earnings and profits, they with their family members enjoy life. So their benefits are apparent. But what is the benefit or reward of the monastic life?" "Maharaja, have you put this question to any monk or Brahmin ever before?" "Yes I did." "If you have no objection, you can tell me the answers they gave you." After usual courtesy I asked Puranakasyapa the benefits and merits of monastic life. According to him, he who oppresses people, steals, robs others, speaks untruths, is tainted with adultery or even murders people, commits no sin. And neither he who with liberal hand distributes charity, performs worship and sacrifices at every shrine, does good of others, practices self-control, acquires thereby any virtue. Then I went to Maskariputra Gosala. He answered: There is no sin or virtue. Man has no control over his life. There is no will as an independent motive power. Every organic (animals and plants) and inorganic substance is subject to the immutable law, and automatically follows its evolutionary course. The wise might think that he would be acquiring virtue.

The fool acts according to his intelligence. Bat man is happy or unhappy, according to the laws os physical harmony he has observed. Nature's balancing is impartial and knows no favouritism. If you shoot an there is a certain limit beyond which it cannot go. So there is a limit to the power of physical resistance. Whether he is learned or ignorant wise or do that, I shall ask you one. Maharaja, your slaves, work for your comforts from early in the morning till midnight. If one of them thinks: "What is the use of taking HE much trouble. If he puts on the yellow garb, and it comes to your notice that one of your former slaves has became a monk, and is practising self-control and austerities in solitude, would you compel him to be your slave again?" "Never, on the otherhand, I shall honour him if I happen to meet him." "Then it is apparent, Maharaja, one gets certain benefits of a monastic in this very life." "Admitted. But besides these, can you mention other advantages?" "If the monk by his self-control and discipline has conquered his passions, greed and envy, is healthy in mind and body, and with enlightenment and purity of mind enjoys contentment of mind, and is happy and cheerful, he also radiates cheerfulness and tranquillity all round like the lotus or moonbeams. So a man tossed with passions, remorsed with guilty conscience, restless with greed and envy, sleepless with disturbed mind, feeling life as a cruel drag and mockery, seeing that tranquil, happy and:, healthy monk, is inspired with a new outlook of life, breathes freely and refreshingly like an energised and invigorated man, like a sick man cured of his disease, like the thirsty wanderer in a desert brought to an "Excellent, very excellent," said the Videhaputra Ajatashatru, King of Magadha. "You have shown me the right way, by showing me what was hidden, by illuminating the dark spaces as if by a lamp. I have done a great wrong, a wicked thing, by robbing my father—a noble and just King of his life just for the sake of kingdom. For my past, and as warning to my future, let me take recourse to you, your Dharma and Sangha". "We accept your repentance and confession, O Great King, for one, who is remorseful of his past wicked deed, would never commit it again." "If you will permit us, we shall go, now. We have got so many duties and obligations to perform," spoke Videhaputra Ajatashatru, King of Magadha. Ajatashatru was a materialist, which he taught to Dipta. His real object of befriending the powerful and growing Sangha of the Buddha was rather diplomatic than that of religious conviction or repentance. Ajatashatru encouraged the schism in the Sangha, by encouraging and helping Devadatta as long as Bimbisara was alive who was a patron of the Buddha.

But as soon as Ajatashatru usurped the throne, especially when the aged Bimbisara was starved to death in the prison, and his brothers in fear of death entered into Sangha, Ajatashatru had no longer any need of Devadatta, and consequently he was unceremoniously driven off. Magadha and Kosala were struggling for supremacy for the paramount power in Aryavartha. And over the dowry of Khasi, both powers tried their strength. The aged and enfeebled Prasenjit was no match for the active and ambitions Ajatashatru. Though Ajatashatru was taken as a prisoner, Prasenjit was compelled or thought it prudent to make truce by ceding the same Khasi territory with his daughter Bajra Kumari in marriage with hint. Devadatta rushed to Shravasti to win favour of Prasenjit; but as possibly truce was concluded and of the influence of the Buddha Sangha, he got an unfriendly reception in Kosala court.

But whatever that may be, the trial of a strength between Magadha and Kosala whetted the ambitions appetite of Ajatashatru for further aggrandisement of his kingdom: he was already planning an attack against the Licchhavis of Vaishali. When the

Blessed One was dwelling in Rajagriha on the hill called the Vulture's Peak, the Videhaputra Ajatashatru King of Magadha was desirous of attacking the Vajjians. He spoke to the Brahmin Varsakara, the Prime Minister of Magadha: "Go to the Blessed One and bow down in adoration at his feet on my behalf and enquire in my name whether he is free from illness and suffering and in the enjoyment of ease and comfort and vigorous health. Then tell him that Ajatashatru, the Magadha King in his eagerness to attack the Vajjians has resolved, I will root out these Vajjians, mighty and powerful though they be; I will destroy these Vajjians; I will being these Vaggians to utter ruin." 'So long, Ananda, rejoined the Blessed One, the Vajjians hold their full and frequent public assemblies, so long they may be expected not to decline bat to prosper.

So long as the Vajjians meet together in concord, and rise in concord and carry out their undertakings in concord —so long as they enact nothing not already established, abrogate nothing that has already been enacted and act in accordance with the ancient institutions of the Vajjians as established in former days—so long as they honour and esteem and revere and support the Vajjian ciders and hold it a point of duty to hearken their words—so long as no women or girls belonging to their clans are detained among them by force or abduction—so long as the rightful protection, defence and support shall be fully provided for Arhats among them so that the Arhats from distance may enter the realm—30 long may the Vajjians be expected not to decline but to prosper". Then the Blessed One addressed Varsakar the Brahmin and said, "When I was once staying, O Brahmin, at Vaishali at the Sarandada Temple, I taught the Vajjiana these conditions of welfare, and so long as those conditions shall continue to exist among the Vajjians, so long may we expect them not to decline, but to prosper." "We may expect then, answered the Brahmin, the welfare and not the decline of the Vajjians when they are possessed of these conditions of welfare, how much more so when they are possessed of all the seven. So, Gautam, the Vijjians can not be overcome by the King of Magadha, that is, not in battle, without diplomacy or breaking up their alliance. And now, Gautam, we must go; we are busy and have much to do." And when the Buddha was passing through Pataligama (Pataliputra), Sinidha and Varsakara, the chief ministers of Magadha, were building a fortress to keep back the Vajjians, and they invited the Buddha and his disciples to dine with them. This happened one year before the Buddha's death.

Centre of Jainism

Vaishali was the important centre of Jainism. For Mahavir the founder of the Jainas was related to the chief of the Licchhavis, and he was born in its suburb. Vardauiana (548-476 BC) was born at Kundapara, a caravan halting place in the suburb of Vaishali at 588 BC (according to orthodox tradition at 599 BC). His father was a petty chief— Siddhartha of the Gnatri clan. And his mother was Trishula or Videhidatta a sister of Chetaka, the head of the Licchhavi confederacy. Chetaka's daughter—Chellana was married to Srenika Bimbisara, the King of Magadha, and their son for that reason was called Videhiputra Ajatashatru. As Ajatashatru waged war against his aged grandfather Chetaka, and conquering it, he laid the foundation of later day Empires of Nandas and Mauryas, he befriended the Buddha Sangha which he once persecuted as friendly to his father. Though closely related, Ajatashatru could not expect friendly attitude patronised the Licchhavis. And not only for imperial purposes, but also to feed his old grudge against the Viceroy of Anga, they helped his brother Vaihalva to wage war against him over some spoils of elephant *Sreyonaga* and other jewels.

Prasenjit's son Virudak grew up. When he was seven years old, seeing the dolls and other presents boys receive from the parents of their mothers, he asked his mother Vasava Kshatriya one day: "Mother, other children receive a good deal of presents from their maternal house. Have not you father and mother?" "Child, the Shakya Raja is your grandfather. Because they live very far, they cannot send you anything." But when Virudak was sixteen years old (493 BC), he expressed his desire to go to Kapilavastu. Vasavakshatria said: "What is the use of going so far?" But on his insistence, she gave her consent. Virudak with the permission of his father started with a large retinue. Vasana Kashtria in the meantime informed Mahanama through a letter. "I am pretty happy. Lot not the elders or any body tell Virudak any of the secrets." When the Shakyas learnt that Virudak was coming, they sent all the youngsters to the country places, as they would not "salute Virudak. Virudak was received cordially by the Shakyas at the assembly hall, and he was introduced to the elders, whom he saluted respectfully. But us none saluted him, he was a little surprised; but he was told that all younger than him were in the country places. After a few days, Virudak left Kapilavastu. A maid servant was washing the chair on which Virudak sat with milk and water, saying that the son of the slave-maid Vasava Kshatria spoilt it. An officer of Virudak who had left his sword there by mistake heard this remark and it rapidly spread among the army. When Virudak heard it, he said: "'Let them purify the seat now with milk, but when I am a King I wi'l wash it with the blood of the Shakyas." When Prasenjit heard of it, he became angry, humiliated Vasava Kshatriya and disinherited Virudak (493 BC). Presenjit said to the Buddha: "Your kinsmen have given me a slave girl.

So I have been compelled to dispossess Vasava Kshatriya and her son of the ranks given to them." The Buddha answered: "Maharaja, the Shakyas have committed a wrong. If they had to give a daughter, they ought to have given a daughter of their own. But only this can be said in their favour. Vasava Kshatriya had a Shakya as her father and she has been crowned as a Queen. Virudak's father is a King. Aristocracy is traced through father's lineage and not through maternal line (7 Kastinarar J.).

The Commander-in-chief of Prasenjit was Bandula. Bandula was an honest and upright man. He was against corruption and bribery. That made him very popular. But it also antagonised many whose selfish interests were jeopardised. They brought it to the notice of the King that Bandula was planning to dethrone. The Raja sent Bandula to the frontier to subdue an insurrection there. But he secretly instructed some army officers to kill Bandula on his way back. Bandula was assassinated When Prasenjit came to learn that Bandula was really innocent and had no evil motive, he became very repentant. Then he appointed Dhirga Carayana as the chief of his army. Dhirga (K) Charayna was a shewed intriguer. He brought the whole army under his control and then devised a plan, revenging the murder of his uncle Bandula and his sons. Once the Buddha was halting at Ulumpa, a border town on the Shakya territory.

Prasenjit went there to visit him, and in order to show humility, he handed over crown and other insignia of loyalty in the upkeep of Dirga-Karayana before he entered into the chamber of the Buddha Dirga-Karayana with the support of the array proclaimed Virudak as the King of Kosala and left for Shravasti, leaving only a horse and a maid servant for Prasenjit. Prasenjit hearing of the treachery of his commander-in-chief and the army, rode on the horseback to Rajagriha to beg military help from his son-in-law, Ajatashatru. But when he reached Rajagriha, it was already night, and the city gate was closed. He stayed in an out-house; but due to fatigue and exhaustion of the journey, he died the same night (486 BC) Ajatashatru with due honour and ceremony cremated his father-in-law. Once Virudak was seated on the throne of Shravasti, he thought of avenging his insult at Kapilavastu. He marched his powerful army against the Shakyas. The. Buddha intervened, but it was of no avail. The Shakyas defended their territory and independence with desperate heroism. But at last their resistance was overcome, and the Shakyas were massacred up to the infants in their mothers wombs (405 Bhadrasala J). This melancholy event and the destruction of Kapilavastu took place just one year before Buddha's death in 485 BC. But while returning from his victory, in a drunken orgy Virudak got drowned by a fall from his riding elephant.

dissolution—how then, can this be possible, that such a thing should not be dissolved? No such condition can exist! For a long time, Ananda, have you been very near to me by acts of love, kind and good, that never varies, and is beyond all measure. You have done well, Ananda, be earnest in effort, and you too shall soon be free." "But let not the Blessed One die in this little wattle and daub town, in this town in the midst of jungle, in this petty town.

For there are other great cities, such as Champa, Rajagriha, Shravasthi, Saketa, Kaushambi and Varanasi. Let the Blessed One die in one of them. There are many wealthy nobles and Brahmins and heads of houses, believers in the Tathagata, who will pay due honour to the remains of the Tathagata." "Say, not so, Ananda, say not so!"

And the Buddha sent Ananda to announce to the Mallas of Kushinara that the Buddha was very sick the Sala grove in the Upavattana of their own village. Then the Mallas, with their young men and maidens and their wives, being grieved and sad and afflicted at heart, went to see the Buddha. Ananda caused the Mallas of Kushinara to stand in groups, each family in a group, and so presented them to the Blessed One in the first part of night: "Lord, a Malla of such and such a name, with his children, his wives, his retinue and his friends, humbly bows down at the foot of the Blessed One." A learned Brahmin by the name of Subhadra was living there at that time. Hearing that the Buddha was sick, he came to see him to clear off some of his doubts, and he said to Ananda: "Now a certain feeling of uncertainty has sprung up in my mind; and this faith have in Sramana Gautam, that he, methinks, is able to present the truth that I may get rid of this feeling of uncertainty. So that I, even I, Ananda might be allowed to see the Sramana Gautam." "Enough, friend Subhadra! Trouble not the Tathagata. The Blessed One is weary". Thus, thrice Subhadra made requests to Ananda to interview the Buddha, and thrice he was refused. The Buddha overheard it, and called Ananda forth and said to him: 'Do not keep out Subhadra. He may be allowed to see me. Whatever Subhadra may ask of me, he will ask from a desire for knowledge and not to annoy me. And whatever I may say in answer to his question, that he will quickly understand." Then Ananda said to Subhadra: "Enter in, friend Subhadra; for the Blessed One gives you leave." Then Subhadra,

4

Buddha's Mission

The Enlightenment

The enlightenment came to Gautam while sitting cross-legged under the bodhi-tree on eight handfuls of grass which a grass-cutter, Sotthiya, had given him, and which, when he had shaken it out, had assumed the shape of a comfortable seat 'fourteen hands long.' The incidental circumstances attending the enlightenment are, of course, quite extrinsic to the real issue; for in any case it matters little how and where Gautam received his initiation of wisdom. Even if we did know that the event took place under a bodhi-tree, a rose-apple tree, or a bamboo tree, we should be none the wiser as to its real meaning. However, in passing it may be pointed out that one of the very early accounts does not mention the famous bodhi-tree *(Ficus religiosa)* at all, and completely ignores the obliging grass-cutter and the folding grass-seat.

Two Views

As far as can be seen, from the earliest times, biographers have been inclined to interpret Gautam's enlightenment in two distinct ways. On the lower level there is the melodramatic and miraculous view. It represents the process through which the enlightenment was reached as an almost physical process of conquest of supernatural power; the dramatic effect being realised by staging a full-blooded battle between Gautam and the forces of evil. This view finds its crudest and most exciting expression in the legend of Gautam's combat with Mara, the tempter. The legend is to be found both in the Pali and Sanskrit sources, though there are a number of variants of the temptation-theme which differ from one another in minor details. The whole story of the assault of Mara is too fantastic to bear repetition; but to show some idea of the lines on which the experience is resolved we might give the description of these cosmic upheavals which apparently preceded the actual combat between the Bodhisattva and the 'Evil One':

> 'When the conflict began between the Saviour of the world and the Prince of Evil a thousand appalling meteors fell; clouds and darkness prevailed. Even this earth, with the oceans and mountains it contains, though it is unconscious, quaked like a conscious being—like a fond bride when forcibly torn from her bridegroom—like the festoons of a vine shaking under the blasts of a whirlwind. The ocean rose under the vibration of a whirlwind. The ocean rose under the vibration of this earthquake; rivers flowed back towards their sources; peaks of lofty mountains, where countless trees had grown for ages, rolled crumbling to the earth; a fierce storm howled all around; the roar of concussion became terrific; the very sun enveloped itself in awful darkness, and a host of headless spirits filled the air.'

Rhys Davids saw in the story of 'a visible Tempter an attempt to objectify Gautam's inner conflict after he had given up the penance, and all his old temptations had come back upon him with renewed force. 'In the legend,' he wrote, 'the very thoughts passing through the mind of Gautam appear in gorgeous descriptions as angels of darkness or of light... but they have still a depth of meaning to those who strive to read between the lines of these, the first half-inarticulate efforts the Indian mind had made to describe the feelings of a strong man torn by contending impulses.' He also emphasised curious points of resemblance between Milton and the Buddhist poets; and, indeed, the resemblance is unmistakable. There is a great deal in the surcharged imagery of the Buddhist poets—an imagery which often borders on the grotesque—which reminds one of Milton's grandiloquent outbursts. The description of the cosmic convulsion given above, and several passages in Ashvaghosha's version of the assault of Mara, for instance, might well be paralleled by passages from *Paradise Regained)* like the following:

> ... And either tropic now
> Can thunder, and both ends of heaven; the clouds
> From many a horrid rift abortive poured
> Fierce rain with lightning mixed, water with fire
> In ruin reconciled; nor slept the winds
> Within their stony caves, but rushed abroad
> From the four hinges of the world, and fell
> On the vexed wilderness, whose tallest pines
> Tho' rooted deep as high, and sturdiest oaks.
>
> Bow'd their stiff necks, loaden with stormy blasts,
> Or torn up sheer. Ill wast thou shrouded then,
> O patient Son of God, yet only stood'st
>
> Unshaken! Nor yet staid the terror there:
> Infernal ghosts and hellish furies round
> Environed thee; some howled, some yelled,
> some shirked,
> Some bent at thee their fiery darts, while thou Sat'st
> unappalled in calm and sinless peace.

But it is very doubtful whether the Buddhist poets had any conscious intention of communicating 'spiritual truths' by means of an imagery drawn from tangible things. On the contrary, it would seem that their main reason for resorting to this uncouth symbolism was, that they were unable to understand Gautam's crucial experience in any other terms. Rhys Davids himself admitted as much when he said: 'It may be questioned how far the later Buddhists have been able to realise the spiritual truth hidden under these material images; most of them have doubtless believed in a real material combat, and a real material earthquake.' And in this respect there is no reason to suppose that the early Buddhist possessed any greater capacity for psychological subtlety than the later ones.

Of course, both in the early and late periods, there were individual Buddhists to whom Gautam's enlightenment signified something totally different from a physical feat. And because they saw it as something of a 'spiritual' order, they tried to convey its meaning in a totally different langauge. What they give us is not a man fighting with demons of darkness, but a mystic struggling to realise in himself that inner vision which can penetrate the veil of temporal relationships and see what is behind and beyond.

Spiritual Process

They have actually described the whole process through which Gautam discovered the right mode of meditation, and attained the mystical *elan*—a state of continuous Present, of poise and harmony, which has no place in it for the contrarieties and distinctions which are the lot of ordinary mortals. With an almost scientific precision they outline the curve of Gautam's experience, and show him gradually eliminating all the avenues of mental and sensory knowledge in order to rise to that condition of super-consciousness where knowledge is immediate, intuitive, and final.

The account of it is given in the *Mahasaccaka-sutta*. It is written in the first person singular, but that is no guarantee that it is an accurate report of Gautam's own words:

"Now having taken solid food and gained strength, without sensual desires, without evil ideas I attained and abode in the first trance of joy and pleasure, arising from seclusion and combined with reasoning and investigation. Nevertheless such pleasant feelings as arose did not overpower my mind. With the ceasing of reasoning and investigation I attained and abode in the second trance of joy and pleasure arising from concentration, with internal serenity and fixing of the mind on one point without reasoning and investigation. Nevertheless such pleasant feeling as arose did not overpower my mind. With equanimity towards joy and aversion I abode mindful and conscious, and experienced bodily pleasure, what the noble ones describe as "dwelling with equanimity, mindful, and happily," and attained and abode in the third trance. Nevertheless such pleasant feeling as arose did not overpower my mind. Abandoning pleasure and abandoning pain, even before the disappearance of elation and depression, I attained and abode in the fourth trance, which is without pleasure and pain, and with purity of mindfulness and equanimity. Nevertheless such pleasant feeling as arose did not overpower my mind.

'Thus with mind concentrated, purified, cleansed, spotless, with the defilements gone, supple, dexterous, firm, and impassible, I directed my mind to the knowledge of the remembrance of my former existences. I remembered many former existences, such as, one birth, two births, three, four, five, ten, twenty, thirty, forty, fifty, a hundred, a thousand, a hundred thousand births; many cycles of dissolution of the universe, many cycles of its evolution, many of its dissolution and evolution; there I was of such and such a name, clan, colour, livelihood, such pleasure and pain did I suffer, and such was the end of my life. Passing away thence I was born elsewhere. There too I was of such a name, clan, colour, livelihood, such pleasure and pain did I suffer, and such was the end of my life. Passing away thence I was born here. Thus, do I remember my many former existences with their special modes and details. This was the first knowledge that I gained in the first watch of the night. Ignorance was dispelled, knowledge arose. Darkness was dispelled, light arose. So is it with him who abides vigilant, strenuous, and resolute.

'Thus with mind concentrated, purified, cleansed, spotless, with defilements gone, supple, dexterous, firm, and impassible, I directed my mind to the passing away and rebirth of beings. With divine, purified, superhuman vision I saw beings passing away and being reborn, low and high, of good and bad colour, in happy or miserable existences according to their Karma. Those beings who led evil lives in deed, word, or thought, who speak evil of the noble ones, of false views, who acquire Karma through their false views, at the dissolution of the body after death are reborn in a state of misery and suffering in hell But those beings who lead good lives, in deed, word, and thought, who speak no evil of the noble ones, of right views, who acquire Karma through their right views, at the dissolution of the body after death are reborn in a happy state in the world of heaven... This was the second knowledge that I gained in the second watch of the night...

"Thus with mind concentrated, purified, cleansed, spotless, with the defilements gone, supple, dexterous, firm, and impassible, I directed my mind to the knowledge of the destruction of *asavas* [cankers]. I duly realised [the truth] "this is pain," I duly realised [the truth] "this is the cause of pain," I duly realised [the truth] "this is the way that leads to the destruction of pain." I duly realised "these are the *asavas*"... "this is the cause of *asavas*"... "this is the way that leads to the destruction of *asavas.*" As I thus knew and thus perceived, my mind was emancipated from the *asava* of sensual desire, from the *asava* of desire for existence, and from the *asava* of ignorance. And in me emancipated arose the knowledge of my emancipation. I realised that destroyed is rebirth, the religious life has been led, done is what was to be done, there is nought (for me) beyond this world. This was the third knowledge that I gained in the last watch of the night. Ignorance was dispelled, knowledge arose. Darkness was dispelled, light arose. So is it with him who abides vigilant, strenuous, and resolute."

There is no need to emphasise the metaphysical and mystical character of this analysis. As it is presented here, the interpretation is comparatively simple and even naive. However, it was from such humble beginnings that there was to spring up the vast and impressive edifice of Mahayana Metaphysics. The theory of a causal chain and the scheme of 'dependent origination,' which is dimly anticipated here, when followed to its logical conclusion was to lead to the Madhyamika doctrine of Sunyata—the *ne plus ultra* of all Critiques of Pure Reason. Certain quite innocent hints dropped in this interpretation were to encourage audacious metaphysicians like Nagarjuna to venture on a most hazardous flight through the limitless realms of 'absolute vacuity.' M. Rene Grousset has described this flight in words which cannot be improved upon. "The sage,' he says, 'has gone down into the depths of his heart. He has seen there... the external world, in the phenomenon of representation, taking shape and vanishing there. He has seen the dissolution of all that we call ego, of the substantial soul... and of the phenomenal ego... In place of this world of moral suffering and material obstacles, of internal egotism and objective adversity, an apparently bottomless gulf opens in the heart—a luminous and as it were submarine gulf, unfathomable, full of ineffable beauties, of fleeting depths and infinite transparencies. On the surface of this vacuity into which the eye plunges dazzled, the mirage of things plays in changing colours, but these things, as we know, "exist only as such"—*tathata*—and therefore are as if they were not. And once this mirage is dispelled, behold— in the intimate contemplation of that bottomless and limitless depth, in that unrivalled purity of the absolute vacuity— behold all virtualities arising, all powers emerging.'

This is the other, more refined, interpretation of Gautam's enlightenment.

Both these interpretations have their modern exponents; and some typical instances have been anatomised elsewhere. There are even today, on the one hand, those who champion the concept of a 'fight' and on the other, those who repose their faith in the idea of a mystico-metaphysical flight through the boundless void. The first view has a powerful appeal for the mythic imagination. In fact, it is the mythological view; and writers like H. Kern are probably quite justified in suggesting that most of the legends of Buddha, and in particular the legend of his combat with Mara, the spirit of darkness, have their basis in the ancient astronomical lore, and personify the sun-myth. The latter view, because of its mystical implications, serves to furnish the spiritual elite with a sanction for their Credo. Taken together the two views supplement each other.

And yet both views fail to be convincing. They fail to be convincing because if either of them were accepted Gautam's whole behaviour after his enlightenment becomes incomprehensible. The first view is in any case too infantile to be taken seriously. The second view cannot be rejected so easily. It has behind it the sanction of most eminent and capable authorities, modern as well as ancient. Nevertheless, in the ultimate analysis, it turns out to be as unsatisfying as the more popular interpretation. There is, in fact, sufficient warrant for rejecting it; and this warrant is furnished by the actual life led by Gautam from the time of his enlightenment right up to the day of his death.

"By their deeds shall ye know them. Wherever there is doubt, a man's deeds must be regarded as the acid test. This is the criterion that must be applied to Gautam. He was thirty-five when he received enlightenment; he died when he was past eighty. What was he doing during the long period which separates these two events? The question is well worth considering. One thing is certain: he did not devote the rest of his life to 'an intimate contemplation of that bottomless and limitless depth' from which 'all virtualities arise, all powers emerge.' A preoccupation of this nature is not without certain fascination. The fact that a great many Mahayanist metaphysicians were positively enamoured of 'the unrivalled purity of the absolute vacuity' proves that it must have powerful attractions. Gautam, however, seems to have resisted its temptations quite as successfully as those of his dancing girls. He had apparently no use for 'the unrivalled purity of absolute vacuity.' His tastes were altogether more solid and less abstract. He was a matter-of-fact person, and after his visit to Alara and Uddaka he had been confirmed in his conviction that it was a sterile occupation to spend all one's time in trying *to* attain the state of Nothingness, or the state of Neither-consciousness-nor-nonconsciousness.

The years of his ministry he spent instead in attempting an alleviation of the lot of his fellow men, often at the cost of considerable inconvenience to himself. He travelled many a weary distance, and travelling in those days was anything but a pleasurable pastime. For more than forty years he wandered from village to village preaching a doctrine which was not at all esoteric, but as the late Sir Charles Eliot observed, 'essentially practical, human, business-like.' The people to whom he preached were frequently obstinate and stupid; in reasoning with them he had to have infinite patience and forbearance. He had often to suffer fools gladly. He was misunderstood, misrepresented—in some instances, openly maligned. His struggle against the respectable prejudices and superstitions of his age brought on him the abuse of vested interests—an abuse, which, says a Buddhist dialogue, 'was copious, not at all stinted.' What was the motive which induced him to return from the shores of the Great Beyond to undertake a thankless, and often hopeless, mission? Having reached the verge of 'the submarine gulf of the Madhyamika school, he could easily have remained there to enjoy the beatific vision of its 'ineffable beauties, fleeting depths and infinite transparencies.' But as far as can be judged from his behaviour, he preferred attending to mundane affairs to the contemplation of mystic beatitudes. It is true, he insisted upon an objective view of reality, and a clear understanding of man and his place in the universe. But such a view and understanding were not for him ends in themselves; they were only means to an end. He advocated them because he regarded them as the indispensable perquisites of a reasonable and decent way of living. And it was on this way of living that he placed the whole emphasis throughout the years of his ministry.

In another discourse, which is significantly entitled *Of The Irrelevant,* he made his position in this matter still more clear. One of his disciples, Malunkya, it is said, had been feeling very much worried about some metaphysical problems. Unable to keep his doubts to himself any longer, he made up his mind one day to question Gautam point-blank on these issues. So, going up to him, he asked disarmingly: 'If the lord knows that the world is eternal, let him tell me so. If the lord knows this world is not eternal, let him tell me so. If the lord does not know whether the world is eternal or not, then the only straightforward thing for one who knows not, nor discerns, is to avow that he knows not nor discerns.'

Faced with this disconcerting enquiry Gautam asked Malunkya whether 'the lord' had made any promise to enlighten him on these abstruse matters as a condition of his joining the Brotherhood. Half-heartedly, Malunkya admitted that no such promise had been given. 'It comes to this then,' said Gautam, 'that I never promised, nor did you stipulate that, as a condition of your following the higher life under me, I should expound these matters to you.' And he went on to explain, by means of a parable, where precisely the emphasis should be and where it should not be. 'If a man were to say...' he argued, 'that he would not follow the higher life under me, until I had answered all the questions you enumerate, he would get no answer from me until death overtook him. It is as if a man were transfixed by an arrow heavily coated with poison, and his friends and kinsfolk were to get a leech-

expert in dealing with arrow-wounds, but the man were to declare he would not have the arrow taken out until he knew whether the archer who had shot him was noble, or a Brahmin, or a middle-class man or a peasant—what the archer's name was—whether he was tall or short or of a medium height— whether he was black or brown or fair—what particular village or township or city he hailed from—what kind of bow he had—whether his bowstring was made from bamboo, or hemp, or leaves of the *Calotropis gigantea*—whether the shaft of the arrow was a wild reed or a planted shoot— whether the shaft was feathered with plumage of a vulture, or a heron, or a falcon, or a peacock, or some other fowl— whether the gut binding that shaft came from an ox, or a buffalo, or a hart, or a monkey—whether his arrow was a plain arrow, or was barbed with horn, or iron, or a calf's tooth, or with an oleander thorn. The man would never get to know this before death overtook him... The higher life,' he added, 'is not contingent on the truth of any thesis that the world is either eternal or non-eternal. In either case, as in each of other theses you adduce, there still abides the fact of birth, decay, and death; there still abide the facts of grief and tribulation, of ill, sorrow, and distraction—and of their extirpation in the here and now... I have not taught that the world is either eternal or not eternal; that it is finite or infinite; that life and the body are either identical or distinct; that after death a truth-finder passes or does not pass to a further existence, or does both or neither. And why have I left these things untaught?—Because they are unprofitable, not fundamental to the higher life of which I speak...'

Scientific Method

All these factors tend to lead to a radically different interpretation of the nature of Gautam's experience. In the first place, it is quite clear that all along Gautam had followed the strictly scientific method of elimination through 'trial and error.' He had gone as far as it was possible with the metaphysical enquiry only to find that theoretical knowledge did not touch the heart of the matter, and that in fact it led one into a mental wilderness. With utmost scrupulousness he had practised the disciplines enjoined by well-known mystics and ascetics, even subjected himself to such horrible penances as wearing haircloth, and lying among decomposing corpses in the cemetery, but found them fruitless; With the realisation of the futility of these methods there had been born in him an entirely new definition of the problem. The emphasis had shifted from the metaphysical to the moral issue. The question was no longer the attainment of a supra-conscious state of ecstatic bliss, but 'the extirpation of grief and tribulation, of ill, and sorrow, and distraction in the here and now.' This transference of emphasis was one aspect of enlightenment. The other was the working out of a technique of living which would be conducive 'to passionlessness... to tranquillity, to insight... and to Nirvana'—or, in other words, 'to the extirpation of grief and tribulation, of ill, and sorrow, and distraction in the here and now.'

There was thus no mystery attached to Gautam's enlightenment. It was a simple and intelligible experience; or, perhaps, it would be more correct to say that it was neither more nor less mysterious than, for instance, the discovery and formulation of the Laws of Gravitation. Gautam and Newton, it is true, worked in very different fields. Ultimately, however, that difference counts for little. What is more significant is the essential identity of their methods. Gautam's field of investigation was the universe of human mind, the relationships and laws that govern it, and the properties and behaviour of those subtle elements which enter into its structure. It is by no means an easy field to investigate on scientific lines. It is easy enough to be objective about a dead frog, but not so easy to be objective about one's own heart, pulsating with a whole world of desires. Nevertheless, Gautam did succeed in subjecting 'the world within' to some kind of critical scrutiny, and thus managed to introduce a certain measure of objectivity into the subjective chaos. This was his distinctive achievement; this, too, the meaning of his enlightenment.

The discovery of profoundest truths often comes from the recognition of simplest relationships. Consequently, in all such discoveries, there is an element of surprise, of instantaneousness, and even of mystery; that is to say, although one may have followed a long process of intellectual argument and experimental analysis, the final crystallisation of truth seems to be effected in an unexpected and sudden manner—in a flash of revelation, as it were. Gautam's experience appears to have been of this character. As Mr. Wells rightly interprets it: 'When the mind grapples with a great and intricate problem, it makes its advances, it secures its positions step by step, with but little realisation of the gains it has made, until suddenly with an effect of abrupt illumination, it realises its victory. So it would appear to have happened to Gautam.'

The emphasis on 'the way' in *Samyutta-Nikaya* is not altogether without meaning: enlightenment was essentially the working out of a way of life that would bring about 'the extirpation of grief and tribulation, of ill, and sorrow, and distraction in the here and now.' In the very nature of things, this could not but be 'difficult to perceive, hard to realise.' It was a moral way; though 'moral' in a peculiar psychological sense. The rest of his life Gautam devoted to preaching this way. 'By their deeds shall ye know them'— and it is reasonable to assume that he was not so much interested in 'explaining the world' as—to borrow a phrase from Marx's criticism of Feuerbach—in 'changing it.' But Gautam was aware, as no doubt Marx in his own way was aware, that before attempting to change the world one must understand it 'such as it is.' In a later discourse Gautam was to declare: 'So long, monks, as I did not comprehend, as it really is, the satisfaction in the world as such, the misery in the world as such, the escape therefrom as such, so long did I not discern the meaning of being enlightened... But, monks, when I fully comprehended, as it really is, the satisfaction in the world as such, the misery in the world as such, the escape therefrom as such, then did I discern the meaning of being enlightened in the world. Then did knowledge and insight arise in me...'

Enlightenment was the recognition of the world—as it really is: and as it can be, with the use of a little more understanding, through being Vigilant, strenuous, and resolute.'

Before the First Preaching

Gautam did not start 'turning the Wheel of Doctrine immediately after his enlightenment. On the contrary, for a while he hesitated to take this step. According to some accounts he spent about a month in the neighbourhood of the Bodhi-tree, meditating on 'the Chain of Causation in direct and reverse order.' But the probability is that his meditations were not quite so abstract. It is conceivable that he was anxious to be quite clear in his own mind as to the precise implication of certain conclusions. However, he was even more anxious to face the practical issue involved. He was by no means convinced of the wisdom of returning to 'the blinded world to beat the Drum of the Immortal.' Indeed, he entertained serious doubts on the matter; and it took him considerable time and thought to decide what to do next.

His misgivings and hesitancy before undertaking his lifelong mission are unequivocally set forth in the formal statements of the *Majjhima-Nikaya.* 'Then I thought,' he says, 'now I have gained the doctrine, profound, hard to perceive, hard to know, tranquil, transcendent, beyond the sphere of reasoning, subtle, to be known by the wise. Mankind is intent on its attachments, and takes delight and pleasure in them. For mankind intent on its attachments... it is hard to see the principle of Causality, origination by way of cause. Hard to see is the principle of the cessation of all compound things, the renunciation of clinging to rebirth, the extinction of all craving, absence of passion, cessation, Nirvana. But if I were to teach the Doctrine, and others did not understand it, it would be a weariness to me, a vexation...'

These are not Gautam's own words, but they probably represent a fairly faithful picture of the state of his mind after the enlightenment. He was not certain of his capacity for converting people, and, in a way, this uncertainty was characteristic of him. Moreover, in this case, he had a very good reason for his hesitation. Considered from any angle— whether moral, religious, or social— he had arrived at a position, which, though it may not appear startling today, was certainly revolutionary in the sixth century BC. On the moral question, in striking contrast to the arbitrary and empty taboos of conventional moralists, the ethics that he had evolved had their basis in practical psychology. They derived sanction from the concept of certain limits of human experience. He knew that this would give rise to all sorts of misapprehensions. In religious matters, his gospel seemed to deprive the organised hierarchical institutions of their very *raison d'etre* by taking no notice whatever of the priestly paraphernalia of elaborate rituals, ceremonies, sacrifices, and charms. He knew that by denying the priestly mediation, as a condition for salvation, he was asking for trouble. On the social side, he was not willing to recognise any distinctions of class and colour, and he was firmly convinced that 'both bad and good qualities, blamed and praised respectively by the wise, are distributed among each of the four classes.' He was aware that if he were to preach an equalitarian doctrine of this nature, it would mean stirring up the hornet's nest of vested interests. What is more, he felt that the fact that he attached little importance to metaphysics and mysticism would render him extremely unpopular with representatives of various metaphysical and mystical schools. On the other hand, although he could easily have enlisted the wholehearted support of the Lokayatikas, or the Worldly-Wise, he had no keen desire to get involved with that boisterously hilarious tribe. 'The springy step' which usually goes with all uncritical flamboyance and enthusiasm, did not particularly appeal to his rather sober bent of mind. The choice, he knew, did not lie between idealistic pretensions and the self-complacency implicit in aggressive and uncomprehending materialism. Somewhere there was a middle way which avoided both; and, as far as he himself was concerned, he was determined not to compromise himself with either of these two extremes. He wanted to place first things first, and was conscious that such a sane and balanced attitude was unlikely to win the approval of his countrymen.

It is not difficult to imagine the kind of thoughts which must have passed through Gautam's mind while he was deciding whether he should go out into the world to preach his doctrine. Naturally he was bewildered by the vast gulf which seemed intellectually to separate him from his contemporaries. The mission which his own destiny had now proposed to him appeared of an overwhelming magnitude and full of risks. He was not sure he would be equal to the task it would impose. He was alone. He felt helpless and weak in face of the exacting demands of his own vision. Finally, however, he decided to take the risk. The Canon, of course, brings Brahma Sahampati down from Heaven to induce Gautam to undertake turning the Wheel of Doctrine so that 'those beings of little impurity that are falling away through not hearing the Doctrine' might be saved. But it would be altogether more appropriate if we gave the whole credit for this decision to the Tathagata's own private judgement.

Right Way of Life

Gautam had now made up his mind on the crucial question which had been baffling him. He would devote himself to preaching what he considered to be the right way of life. He knew that the task involved risks, though he felt they would be worth while. But before he embarked on this lifelong mission he wanted to discuss things with his former teachers, Alara Kalama and Uddaka Ramaputta. Both were men of ripe wisdom, rich in experience and years, well-versed in the art of preaching. He felt it would be useful to have their advice. Also, perhaps, he entertained some faint hopes of converting them to his own cause. True, they were both interested in metaphysics, but the systems to which they adhered were, in their own way, quite novel, advanced, and distinctly revolutionary—at least by the metaphysical standards of the day. There was just a chance that his earnestness might convince them, that whatever the attractions of abiding in the state of Nothingness, or the state of Neither-consciousness-nor-nonconsciousness, it was far nobler to strive for a more humane and reasonable order in the here and now. In any case, he knew, they could hardly grudge him practical advice as to what to do. He had had no word with them since he left them, nor heard of them in the intervening years. His apprenticeship under them had been brief and had ended abruptly; but in both cases the parting had been quite friendly. So he tried to get in touch with them again. Unfortunately, however, they had both been dead some time.

The Canon says that the knowledge of their death was revealed to him in a flash of vision. But we are justified in suspecting that there was also some earthly source of information. Anyhow, whatever may have been the nature of the source from which the information came, it made him change his plans and decide to go straight to Banaras. He knew that the five mendicants who had been his admiring companions when he was practising austerities, and who had left him in anger because he had given up the penance and taken to 'solid food,' were now in that city. The *Majjhima* suggests that this was his main reason for going there. The idea occurred to him, it says: 'The five monks did much for me, who attended me when I was intent on striving. What if I first teach the doctrine to the five monks?' This idea might have been at the back of Gautam's mind; but doubtless there were other, far weightier reasons which made him decide in favour of Banaras. Since he wanted to preach—and in those days preaching was the only possible way of spreading ideas—there was no better place than Banaras in which to begin.

At that time Banaras had already become the greatest city of India—a position which it was long to retain. When Megasthenes visited India, it was supposed to have a circumference of eighty-six miles—though probably these measurements are exaggerated. Even in Gautam's days it was by far the largest city within the confines of the Hindu world. It was a flourishing metropolis, 'opulent, prosperous, populous, abundant with food, crowded with people,' a famous seat of Brahminical learning, a manufacturing centre of unrivalled importance. It was famous for its gorgeous temples and textile fabrics worked with gold, its shrines and metallurgical factories turning out brassware of all descriptions, its rich priests and workers in ivory. Trade-routes converged upon it from every direction.

Pilgrims journeyed thither from far-off places, anxious to wash away their sins in the celestial stream flowing from the locks of Shiva, the Destroyer and Purifier of the Universe. There were many rich Hindus who looked forward to living therein old age, that they might spend their declining years in an atmosphere congenial to meditation and prayer, and that their funeral rites might be performed on the very banks of the holy Ganges. The vast multitudes who could not afford to die in the City of Felicity tried at least to arrange to have their ashes sent to Banaras.

The prosperity of its citizens owed not a little to the active trade in the holy water, which, of course, was sent to all parts of India in sealed urns. Yet, though a place of pilgrimage, Banaras was by no means dull. It attracted not only penitents, but pleasure-seekers. If it was renowned for its learned exponents of Sacred Lore, it was no less famous for its courtezans, skilled in the art of initiating the pilgrims of pleasure into obscure rites. People came to Banaras not only to repent, but to indulge. Indeed, the proximity of the Celestial Stream tended to make both visitors and inhabitants somewhat lax in their morals. Such easy access to

Absolution made people bold. After bathing in the 'fountain of sin,' men went for a dip in the Sacred Stream and were pure again. It was all very simple. There was an equal demand for the services of priests and prostitutes. Banaras was a gay and lively city.

Practical Considerations

There were many practical considerations which induced Gautam to journey to the City of Felicity 'to beat the Drum of the Immortal. The journey itself was quite uneventful, except that Gautam had an amusing encounter with Upaka, an Ajivika ascetic. Upaka, who met Gautam on the road near Gaya, asked him: 'Your faculties, friend, are clear, the colour of your skin is pure and clean. Whom do you follow, friend, in leaving the world? Who is your teacher, and whose doctrine do you approve?'

This was quite a natural question from one mendicant to another. Gautam, on his part, was willing to explain to Upaka, what his purpose and intentions were. Probably he told him that he had discovered what lay at the root of human suffering, and a way to the attainment of happiness in the here and now. It is hardly likely that Gautam's answer to Upaka was given in the formal verses which the *Majjhima* attributes to him; but a claim of this sort, even when couched in the most modest terms, is apt to sound a little presumptuous—especially to an experienced ascetic.

Upaka was not a credulous child who could easily be taken in. He had been an ascetic long enough to have learnt to temper with cynicism his Salvationist ardour. He had doubtless heard many upstart mendicants make similar claims. He had every reason to think that Gautam was yet another lunatic or charlatan of the same species. Suffering or no suffering, he certainly did not care to be duped by a quack or a madman. For himself he entertained no illusions about the possibilities of life, happiness, or 'the extirpation of grief and tribulation in the here and now.' He had long since realised the 'wearisome condition of humanity,' and found a safe anchor in Makkhali Gosala's radical fatalism. He was now quite resigned to his hopelessness, and had no strong wish to try a new 'way,' no matter how rosy its prospects seemed. Death was at least something certain; and he was not prepared to abandon that last certitude of life. He shook his head sceptically at Gautam. As far as Gautam's 'way' was concerned, he was not impressed, and he had little to say. 'Would that it might be so, friend,' was his wise comment. 'Venerable Gautam,' he said, 'your way lies yonder.' He himself significantly turned down a bypath in the opposite direction. Gautam's first serious attempt at conversion had been a failure. But one who wishes to found a 'Kingdom of Happiness' has to take such discouragements philosophically.

Gautam reached Banaras 'by gradual journeying.' Whether by accident or design, the first men he was to meet on reaching the City of Felicity were the five monks who had left him in disgust when he had wisely given up his resolve to starve himself to death in search of the Immortal. They were staying outside the city in a park known as the Deer-park of Isipatana. They had not yet forgiven him his refusal to be a martyr for their sake. As they saw him coming from afar, they said among themselves: 'This, friends, is the ascetic Gautam coming, who lives in abundance, who has given up exertion, and has turned to a life of abundance. We must not greet him, nor rise in respect of him, nor take his bowl and robe, but we will set a seat for him.' However, as he approached and greeted them, they were unable to carry out their decision. They seem to have been moved to remorse.

One of them took his bowl and robe, one prepared a seat, another set water for his feet. After which Gautam told them that at last he had gained the doctrine he had sought; that this doctrine, if properly cultivated, would lead to the realisation and fulfilment of human purpose 'even in this life.' But the five monks would not hear of it. They were as sceptical of his claims as Upaka. They were ready with their taunts about his living in abundance. They said: 'By that exercise, friend Gautam, by that course and practice of self-mortification, you have not gained that superhuman, truly noble knowledge and insight. Will you, when you now live in abundance, have given up exertion, and have turned to a life of abundance, gain that supernatural, truly noble knowledge and insight?' For them the only possible access to the Immortal lay through a torture-chamber, though for themselves they had the sense to be content with a vicarious realisation of 'supernatural, truly noble knowledge and insight.' Gautam tried very patiently to convince them that he had not given up exertion, and that he had not turned to a life of abundance. It was a long and tiresome argument. In the end, however, he persuaded them to accept his good faith and listen to what he had to say. Even then it is doubtful if they were convinced of the underlying truth of his instructions. It seems much more likely that they were impressed by a new note of earnestness and determination in Gautam's manner; and this must have led them to reason thus: 'This man seems fairly resolute and intent on his mission. He has plenty of zeal and enthusiasm. Let us follow him and see how he carries it out. If he succeeds, we shall have the honour of being known as his first disciples. If he fails—as he probably will— we can easily disown him, as we did before.. Our reputation will be none the worse for that. And there is always the chance that he might succeed.'

According to the Vinaya, at this juncture Gautam preached two sermons to the five monks. The account in the *Majjhima* has, however, no place for these pronouncements. It seems certain that, like the Sermon on the Mount, most of Gautam's sermons were never preached in the form in which we find them today. As they now stand, they are doubtless synthetic products compiled by Canonical writers and commentators, who wanted to present the basic tenets of the faith in a tabloid and formal shape for the greater ease and comfort of the laity as well as clergy. At the same time, it stands to reason that, having brought them round to his point of view, Gautam enlightened the monks as to the doctrine which he had worked out so carefully; and that in both the discourses there is, in fact, a nucleus which faithfully represents his beliefs on certain fundamental issues.

In the first sermon Gautam begins by exhorting the monks to avoid the two extremes: 'that conjoined with the passions, low, vulgar, common, ignoble, and useless, and that conjoined with self-torture, painful, ignoble, and useless.' He then passes on to the problem of conduct, and defines the Middle Way as an Eightfold Path—the eight factors being 'right views, right intention, right speech, right action, right livelihood, right effort, right mindfulness, right concentration.'

Foundation of the Order

Gautam had exaggerated his difficulties. His fear that he would not find people willing to listen to 'the Drum of the Immortal' proved entirely groundless. For the first few months after the foundation of the Order, at any rate, everybody appears to have been enchanted by his preaching. There was no repetition of his unhappy encounter with the cynical Upaka. He found many men and women who were prepared to hail him as the new Prophet. The doctrine which he knew was 'hard to perceive, hard to know, tranquil, transcendent, beyond the sphere of reasoning, subtle, to be known by the wise'—the doctrine which, like the salt-sea, had throughout a uniform taste, the taste of Nirvana; the doctrine which he was afraid would not have the slightest appeal for a humanity feverishly intent 'on its attachments'—this doctrine, strangely enough, caught up the popular imagination.

Miracles are rare—but not impossible. The conversion of the five recalcitrant monks was admittedly a rather lukewarm affair. However, several other conversions which followed were full of fervour and spiritual zeal. There was the case of a youth called Yasa. He was the son and heir of a flourishing and worldly-wise guildmaster of Banaras. His youthful years, like those of most rich young men of the day, had been devoted to the pursuit of the Sublime through the avenue of the senses. In a moment of recoil from his life of indulgence and luxury, he decided to take refuge in the new gospel of Renunciation. His father, hearing of his impetuous and foolish resolve, hastened to the Deer-park of Isipatana in order to rescue him from the evil company into which he had fallen. But it was too late. Not only did the guildmaster fail in rescuing his son, but as sometimes happens with those who go to scoff, he himself remained to pray. He found Gautam's instructions so profoundly moving that he begged to be accepted as a lay disciple. Yasa's mother and wife were the next to succumb to the lure of the new Faith. They were the first two women to take refuge in the Buddha. The Wheel of the Excellent Law was now in full swing. More and more citizens of Banaras were drawn into the Tathagata's circle. Before three months after his arrival in the Deer-park of Isipatana, Gautam had sixty full-fledged monks in his Order, apart from a large number of lay followers. These sixty initiates were sent out 'to beat the Drum of the Immortal in the neighbouring countryside. Their mission was prodigiously successful. Soon, so many people were coming forward to take refuge in Gautam's gospel that he was unable personally to attend to all of them. A formula of ordination had to be devised and the monks themselves were allowed to admit newcomers into the Brotherhood.

Seclusion and Peace

The rains had now set in, which meant a suspension of missionary activities for three months. Gautam spent this time in comparative seclusion and peace. But as soon as the monsoons were over, work was resumed with renewed vigour. Gautam now decided to move his headquarters to Uruvela. The journey to Uruvela is said to have been eventful; for it was while on the road that, in a spectacular manner, he won over thirty rich young men, who in some later accounts figure as 'the friends of the series of wealthy ones.' These bright young men had gone to the woods to indulge in pastoral love-making. They had their wives with them; and one of them who was still a bachelor had thoughtfully taken a courtesan with him.

The courtesan was to cause them some embarrassment. Indeed, she was to be responsible for landing them in the arms of the Prophet of Renunciation. For while these would-be 'friends of the series of wealthy ones' were amusing themselves with amorous frolics in a pleasant grove, the courtezan had taken her chance to steal their belongings. When they discovered what had happened they were naturally much distressed, and immediately set out in search of the runaway. On the road they encountered Gautam and his party. They asked him had he *seen* the woman. But Gautam, instead of giving them any information about the courtezan, remarked with a familiar irrelevance: 'What do you think, young men: which is better, for you to go in search of a woman, or to go in search of yourselves?' Whether it was that the thirty young men really received a sudden flash of enlightenment, or merely felt a sense of shame at being found in an embarrassing situation, Gautam's thrust is said to have gone home. They readily agreed that it would be far better to go in search of themselves. Gautam then pronounced a discourse and the men were formally admitted into the Order.

It was an infectious doctrine. And it caught laymen and monks alike. After the conversion of the thirty young 'friends of the series of wealthy ones' came the much more important conversion of three brothers named Kassapa. All three were well-known hermits who believed in some occult and magical fire-cult. One lived in the woods of Uruvela, and was consequently known as Uruvela Kassapa; another on the river nearby, and was called Nadi Kassapa, or Kassapa of the river; the third near Gaya, and was called Gaya Kassapa. Presumably, Gautam was anxious to win over the support of these three brothers since between them they had nearly a thousand followers, and no doubt he expected these disciples to follow in the footsteps of their teachers. He succeeded in realising his purpose, though not without prolonged and tedious argument.

Richest Sermon

It was to the Kassapas that he preached probably the richest in lyrical spirit of all his discourses. Entitled 'the Sermon on the Lessons to be drawn from Burning,' it is much more familiarly known as 'the Sermon on the Conflagration of Senses,' or simply as 'the Fire Sermon.' It is, in fact, more than a sermon: it is a magnificent poem, which, for its formal arabesque beauty of reiteration, deserves to take its place alongside *Ecclesiastes* and the *Song of Songs.* There is music in it; a music lucid and precise in its meaning, ecstatic in its rhythmic repetition—like a Bach fugue.

We possess a vivid account of the circumstances under which this Sermon was delivered. Gautam was staying at the time in a hermitage on the Elephant Rock near Gaya. Beyond lay the verdant and delightful valley of Rajagriha with its encircling chain of emerald hills. One evening Gautam and his new disciples were sitting on a promontory; they saw a vast flame rise from the hill opposite. The forest was on fire. The conflagration spread with a lightning rapidity till the whole earth, the horizon, and the sky itself seemed to be devoured by flames. It was an awe-inspiring spectacle; everybody was visibly moved. Gautam, who had a habit of building parables of a universal application from things which to others appeared to have no more than an incidental and transitory significance, recognised in the flame an image embodying a deep symbolic truth. He took up the theme and developed it in a slow monotonous tone. He wanted his companions to realise that it was not only the distant forest that was ablaze. The fire in truth, was nearer to them than they could realise. There were nearer things which also were being consumed, but by subtle and invisible flames. The human heart, for instance, was perpetually burning. And not the human heart alone. 'For,' said Gautam to his wondering audience, 'Everything, O monks, is in flames. And what everything is in flames? The eye is in flames. The visible is in flames; the knowledge of the visible is in flames; the feeling which arises from contact with the visible, be it pleasure, be it pain, be it neither pleasure nor pain, this also is in flames. By what fire is it kindled? By the fire of desire, by the fire of hate, by the fire of fascination, it is kindled; by birth, old age, death, pain, lamentation, sorrow, grief, distress, it is kindled... This I say... Knowing this, O monks, one who is wise becomes weary of the eye, he becomes weary of the visible, he becomes weary of the knowledge of the visible, he becomes weary of the feeling which arises from contact with the visible, be it pleasure, be it pain, be it neither pleasure nor pain.. This Isay...'

And so, at once vehement and meditative, he spoke on far into the night, like a person drifting with the impulse of an inexorable mood or thought. And those among his fellow 'wayfarers,' who could visualise the processes behind and beyond the veil of appearances, saw not only the elements of human experience, but the infinite universe of sense and succession in all its potentialities, converging into the likeness of a restless and hungry flame endlessly feeding on itself—placed in a void without beginning, and without end.

Growth of Order

The Wheel continued to turn. In the middle of winter, with his now quite numerous contingent of disciples, Gautam decided to move to Rajagriha, capital of Magadha. Apart from missionary reasons, there were a number of practical reasons for this move. The winter in North India is quite severe. No doubt Gautam felt that it would be much more convenient to spend the winter months in some town where certain indispensable amenities of life could be had more easily. The solitudes of Uruvela and Gaya were pleasant to live in. Here it was possible for the Tathagata to abide and meditate in comparative peace. There were no importunate but important householders to pester him with their tales of woe. But for everything and every place under the sun there is a season. And the ill-equipped hermitages in the neighbourhood of Gaya and Uruvela were hardly suitable for residence during the winter months.

The nights were now growing colder. The winds that came from the mountains were as bitter pains. There were frequent frosts. Towards 'the dark half of the month' snow was expected. There was hardly a leaf on the trees. The earth was hard and brittle. The monks shivered in their saffron robes. The problem of the early morning bath was beginning to present increasing difficulties. Gautam was a good psychologist. He was aware that the faith which thinks nothing of moving mountains would often give way under a cold bath. He did not wish to put the faithful to unnecessary trials. Also he was no believer in ascetic or Spartan ideals. If he did not consider 'the higher life' to be contingent on 'nakedness, matted hair, dirt, fasting, lying on the ground, sprinkling the body with ashes, or sitting motionless for long periods,' still less did he think it a matter of cold baths. He had himself no inclination, nor did he demand it of his disciples, to attain Nirvana prematurely by being frozen to death. There have been any number of prophets who have shown great solicitude for their disciples' souls.

But few among them have ever been concerned for their physical well-being. Gautam was one of those rarer prophets who combined an interest for the welfare of people's souls with an equally live interest in that of their bodies. Almost the first thing to which he attended on his arrival in Rajagriha was to arrange for the provision of necessary stoves so that the monks could have hot baths. And so it came to pass that, although many incider as in the life of the Buddha were automatically relegated to oblivion, his grateful disciples never forgot to hand down the tradition about the stoves. Gratitude could hardly have gone further. It should be added that as a result of Gautam's emphasis on personal hygiene, Buddhist monasteries, unlike their Christian counterparts, have always been equipped with adequate arrangements for baths.

The hot baths were an important consideration. But it wasn't merely to provide hot baths for the Brotherhood that Gautam had come all the way to Rajagriha. There were other things calling for attention. There was 'the Drum of the Immortal.' Rajagriha was a flourishing, go-ahead city. It was fast rising in importance and prosperity, thanks to the wise policy of King Bimbisara, who believed in commerce even more than in conquest, and so encouraged all kinds of trade—including, as has earlier been remarked, the 'horizontal trade.' Gautam expected his mission to evoke a favourable response among the citizens. The response which he actually met, however, far transcended his expectations. No less a person than the King himself came to visit him. Bimbisara was a hearty monarch, and, as is the way of Kings, kept a needlessly large harem. But allowing for this pardonable vanity, he was a genuine and intelligent man. He felt immediately drawn to Gautam, and asked to be accepted as a lay disciple. He invited the whole Brotherhood to dinner at the palace next day, when he himself waited on the Buddha. Further, he endowed a park known as the Veluvena, or Bamboo grove, for the use of Gautam and his Order. This was the beginning of a lifelong friendship between the two.

The news that the King had accepted the Buddhist doctrine caused a sensation. So august an example was bound to be enthusiastically followed by his humble subjects. Ever-increasing crowds were now pressing forward to take refuge under the sheltering wings of Gautam's doctrine. The wheel was gathering momentum at a startling rate. Gautam could not have helped feeling somewhat bewildered by the unexpected success of his mission. On the surface it looked nothing short of a miracle that the doctrine 'profound, hard to perceive, hard to know, tranquil, transcendent, beyond the sphere of reasoning, subtle, to be known by the wise' should have so readily been accepted by the popular, mind. Yet the miracle is not altogether incomprehensible. The phenomenal success of the Buddha was due not *to* the merits of his doctrines, but to the things which it seemed to promise. Those who joined the Order as monks or lay followers seldom troubled themselves about the doctrinal implications of Gautam's gospel. What they saw in it was a magical formula leading to the 'extirpation of grief and tribulation in the here and now,' as well as in the hereafter. There were also other attractions. For the rich it was a new and fashionable craze; to the poor it offered real benefits, since within the Brotherhood no distinctions of caste or rank were observed. Moreover, Gautam enjoined no harsh discipline, no course of self-torture, as a condition for the attainment of the Immortal. Nor, unlike the organised Brahminical religion, did he demand costly sacrifices and offerings as his commission for acting as go-between in arranging salvation for mortals. Thus, the doctrine was not without certain obvious advantages. To laymen it seemed to offer all the beatitudes of a religious life without imposing the obligation of tedious formalities and observances. It was, therefore, natural that at first men should have thronged to take refuge in the new teaching.

Doctrinal subtleties are never the decisive factor in conversions. The quick conversions effected by Gautam were no exception to this law. How much appreciation of the doctrine entered into them may be judged from the story of the conversion of Sariputta and Moggallana. These two men, who were to become Gautam's chief disciples in later years, were serving apprenticeship under Sanjaya, an ascetic living in Rajagriha, who himself claimed some two hundred and fifty odd disciples. Early in life they had pledged a mutual bond that whoever first should catch the Absolute was to tell the other. One day, it is said, Sariputta saw Assaji, an elder of Gautam's Order, going through the street early in the morning on the usual alms-begging round.

The elder in question walked with a measured gait. The movements of his arms conformed to the strictest rules of decorum. His eyes were fixed on the ground with becoming modesty. Sariputta was impressed. He was more than impressed. For some inexplicable reason he felt that Assaji was one who had attained the Immortal. Such perfect deportment signified nothing less than 'arahatship.' He followed the elder at a respectable distance, and choosing an opportune moment saluted him, saying: 'Your faculties, friend, are clear, the colour of your skin is pure and clean, whom do you follow, friend, in leaving the world?' Assaji told him that he was a follower of Gautam. Sariputta's next question was naturally about the nature of Gautam's teaching. Here, however, the elder was unable to give Sariputta much information. Decorous behaviour is one thing; the understanding of doctrine quite another. And Assaji, for all his perfect deportment and clear faculties, had never bothered to go into the doctrine which he was supposed to practise. He was blissfully vague as to his master's teaching. Sariputta's awkward question caused him considerable embarrassment. He tried to excuse himself by saying that he was only a novice, and as such it would be a presumption on his part to expound the intricacies of arahatship. Yet far from being put off by Assaji's excuses, Sariputta was charmed. He found the elder's reluctance extremely touching, and interpreted it as a part of the becoming modesty of an arahat. Also, at the back of his mind, there was probably the feeling that Assaji's evasive answer was due to his desire not to share the knowledge of the Absolute.

For himself he had no doubt whatever that Assaji possessed that knowledge. He had seen and believed. It was impossible for a man to walk through the streets with such admirable calm without having the Immortal up his sleeve. Therefore he persisted in his enquiry. He said he understood perfectly the elder's difficulties. For himself, he added, he did not want exhaustive information. He would be content with a brief statement of the doctrine. 'Well, friend, tell little or much, but tell me just the meaning—just the meaning is what I want; why speak many words?, he pleaded earnestly. He did not plead in vain. Assaji felt helpless faced with such earnestness. In his confusion, he murmured something about the Tathagata having told 'the cause of all things that proceed from a cause—and also their cessation.' Assaji's statement would not have convinced a child; but it convinced Sariputta. One step was enough for him; and we are told that 'the spotless eye of the doctrine' arose instantaneously in Sariputta.

True to his promise, Sariputta hastened to tell his friend Moggallana of the happy event. In credulity Moggallana had little to learn from Sariputta; and it did not take long for 'the spotless eye of the doctrine' to arise in him too. And not in him only. The other disciples had only to be told to be persuaded into accepting the new gospel. The spotless eyes of the doctrine were springing up everywhere in alarming fashion. The Wheel was turning.

But it is in the very nature of enthusiasm that it cannot last. Signs that the popular effervescence was dying began to appear even during the two months that Gautam stayed at Rajagriha. There were no spectacular mass-conversions following the conversion of Sariputta, Moggallana, and Sanjaya's two hundred and fifty pupils. Indeed, there had been some trouble over that affair. When his faithless disciples had told him of their intention to transfer their allegiance to Gautam, and had given him friendly advice that he should likewise become a devotee of the Buddha, Sanjaya had been furious. Fortunately the language in which he expressed his opinion of the new Messiah, who had enticed all his pupils away from him, has not been recorded. But it is recorded that hot blood came from his mouth when he saw his disciples leaving him.

Sanjaya was not the man to forget an injury. He took the desertion of his pupils very much to heart, and lost no opportunity of discrediting Gautam and his Order in every possible way. He wrote bitter verses attacking the Tathagata and his monks. He broadcast these throughout the city by word of mouth. Soon they were on the lips of every street urchin. The purport of these verses was that 'the ascetic Gautam is come to bring childlessness; the ascetic Gautam is come to bring subversion of families. Already hath he turned ten thousand hermits into his disciples, and he hath enticed two hundred and fifty mendicant-disciples of Sanjaya into his own Order. And now many distinguished and noble youths of the Magadha kingdom are betaking themselves to the ascetic Gautam to lead a religious life. The ascetic Gautam is intent on depopulating and ruining the country.'

Sanjaya's propaganda achieved its end. An atmosphere of tension was created in which it was impossible even for the Tathagata to escape ridicule and abuse. Though he continued to enjoy the confidence and friendship of the King of Magadha, he lost some of his popularity with the general public. His men began to be coldly received, if not with open hostility. Worldly-wise householders avoided the Buddhist missionaries. When the joys of 'arahatship' were painted to them in glowing colours, they calmly confessed their preference for the simpler pleasures of conjugality and parenthood. When members of Gautam's Order went to beg for alms, they found angry wives shutting doors in their faces. They were not going to feed men who designed to entice away their husbands. Apprehensive hermit-philosophers and mystagogues wondered if their own disciples would next desert to join Gautam's crusade. Sanjaya was getting his own back.

These angry demonstrations were ominous. They marked the beginning of the long polemics between orthodox Brahminism and Buddhism destined to last for several centuries, and indeed until the virtual disappearance of Buddhism from India. The organised dispensers of religious benefits—the Brahmins—had begun to voice their disapproval. Ruling hierarchies—whether of temporal or spiritual order—have at all times considered reformers a nuisance. The Brahminical Dispensation of that day was no exception to this rule. At first the priestly order had not paid much attention to Gautam's missionary activities. They had been inclined to regard him as yet another of those whimsical but harmless mystics with whom they were fairly familiar; no doubt they had hoped that eventually he would settle down with a few kindred spirits in some forest-hermitage.

This they would not have minded at all. They were powerful enough to afford a few heretics who had, moreover, the saving grace of being amusing. But they soon discovered that they had miscalculated. Gautam's challenge went beyond the limits they could safely tolerate. Success for his crusade, they were quick to realise, would mean complete ruin for them and their kind. And already their position was far from secure. There were the sceptics who were constantly causing them embarrassment by demanding that they should produce Brahma in flesh and blood. There were the Lokayatikas who libellously described their ritual and ceremonies as frauds. They could not afford yet another radical, even if indirect, attack on their authority.

They found Sanjaya a godsend. They took up his refrain with alacrity, and accused Gautam of being responsible for mass-desertions by husbands of their wives— and, consequently, being instrumental in causing childlessness. With an unfailing shrewdness, characteristic of the Brahminical genius, they saw at once that this was an issue on which they could make common cause with the whole patriarchal system. At heart no true patriarch had anything but contempt for the effeminate monastic ideal of celibacy. The Brahmins, on their part, did not reject celibacy outright. Indeed, they gave it a definite place in their scheme of things. But they insisted—and the qualification was of paramount importance—that for everything there is a season, a time for every purpose under heaven. There is a time to procreate, and a time to be a celibate. And youth and middle age are not the times for celibacy, from a Brahminical standpoint. By common consent these are the years best suited for procreation. Old age is the proper time and season for undertaking such vows, it was sensibly suggested. When one has done one's duty towards society and produced enough offspring to ensure the continuation of the race, one is fully entitled to do penance, which leads to higher beatitudes. But not before.

Such were the sane views held by the Brahminical hierarchy. And they were not held on arbitrary grounds. The warrant for these opinions was derived straight from Brahma's mouth. Biblical law-givers were not original and unique in commanding the children of Israel to beget and multiply. The Hindu law-givers had forestalled them in this practical wisdom. Manu's Sacred Laws had left no ambiguity on this point. And the Brahmins never forgot to lay special emphasis on the necessity for the systematic, continuous, and resolute prolification of the species. 'Go ye and beget and multiply,' they exhorted the laity. They did more than merely exhort. Example is the best precept, and the Brahmins themselves set the pace. It was eminently desirable that men should beget and multiply.

The intricate, almost endless ceremonies connected with these natural processes, formed the chief source of priestly revenue. 'The Order of Philosophers' was interested in many other things besides philosophy. For instance, it was vitally interested in births, copulations, and deaths. Most of the solemn sacrificial ritual was intimately linked with these cardinal events of human life. A birth meant free meals and various other rich gifts for the priests. When they consecrated a marriage, gold and silver poured into their sacerdotal pockets. At death they arranged for the well-being of the departed soul in the next world—but not without charging adequate fees. It did not need much philosophy to see that a falling birthrate would inevitably be reflected before long by a corresponding decline in the number of marriages and deaths. It was the simplest arithmetic. Gautam had himself admitted that this best of all possible worlds is a world of 'dependent origination.' As such there was no choice. To keep the Wheel of Becoming in motion, every one must beget and multiply. It was essential for the livelihood of priests. For what would become of them were a large number of householders to forsake their homes and take to a monastic life?

It was a matter of the utmost gravity. The finances of the Brahminical Dispensation were at stake. The very foundation of the patriarchal society was threatened. The astute leaders of the priestly and patriarchal interests were in perfect accord on this question. This craze for celibacy must be nipped in the bud. The contagious doctrine must at all costs be prevented from spreading. It was all very well for Gautam's newly-ordained 'arahats' to rhapsodise about the delights of 'Disburdenment.' The priests and patriarchs also desired 'Disburdenment,' though naturally of a different kind. Everybody has his special problems.

The priests and patriarchs had theirs. Most of them had their nubile daughters. This was a heavy responsibility. How could they ever find 'worthy wooers' for the 'ripe unwedded maidens' if all the eligible young men of Magadha were to be lured away into the Buddhist Brotherhood by the charms of 'arahatship'? It was a question well worth some serious reflection. No householder wished to keep a virgin daughter in his house after she had attained puberty. Gods above looked very unfavourably on any attempt to prolong virginity. The Sacred Texts said so explicitly; they made it imperative for parents to find suitable husbands for their daughters when they had reached the crucial age of ten. Failure to conform to this rule entailed very disagreeable consequences, not only for the offending parents, but for all their remote ancestors in heaven. Parolles in *All's Well That Ends Well* remarks: 'It is not politic in the commonwealth of nature to preserve virginity.' This is a belief the Hindu Law-Givers have echoed all through the ages. The ancients, like Vashistha and Yajnavalkya, were still more vehement in their condemnation of the virgin state. They had no use for it whatever. They regarded it as something contrary to the Divine purpose, and maintained that, preserved beyond a certain age, it was not only impolitic, but definitely sinful.

The priests and patriarchs of Rajagriha had reasons to feel alarmed. They had nothing against the Tathagata personally. Those among them who had met him, held him in high esteem. He was gentle and compassionate; he had charming manners; as a man they had nothing but praise for him. When they met him, orthodox Brahmins themselves could not help feeling a measure of admiration. The more advanced and catholic thinkers in the Brahminical hierarchy would probably have confessed, in private at any rate, that there was a great deal of truth and wisdom in what he said. But truth and wisdom are not always expedient. Indeed, expediency often demands the sacrifice of truth and wisdom. Gautam's teaching raised certain practical issues bearing on the general good. Here the priests and patriarchs differed vitally from him. They had their own ideas for the general good. The thorny question of celibacy was a typical instance.

A Misunderstanding

The Tathagata was by no means blind to the practical issue. The opposition to his teaching was the result of misunderstanding. He had never conceived the Middle Way as being fundamentally incompatible with propagation. He did not want to make every one a monk. To avoid misunderstanding he had been careful not to include celibacy among the conditions of his noble Eightfold Path. Further, from the very beginning, he had drawn a clear line of distinction between a discipline to be practised by the many, and a discipline to be followed by the chosen few only. These latter, it is true, were to consider themselves as dedicated men, and were expected to renounce all personal ties. But there was nothing unreasonable or perverse in this demand. To serve a great cause it is often necessary to abandon all longings for personal fulfilment. The cause to which Gautam desired to devote himself and his Order was certainly worthy of such sacrifice. However, he did not expect—and did not even desire—this sacrifice from the multitude. For this reason he had been anxious to emphasise the difficulties of his doctrines, rather than its promises. If, in spite of all these precautions, some householders still seemed to be eager to renounce their attachments, it was not the Tathagata's fault.

Gautam explained all this in his defence; but it was no good protesting. It is difficult to catch up with a lie. In polemics the first shot is often half the battle; Sanjaya and the vested interests who supported him had won the first round. Gautam was unable to counteract the misrepresentations which they had spread. Despite his personal charm and his influential friends, he was subjected to characteristic Brahminical abuse, 'copious, not at all stinted.'

Within two months Gautam had come to the conclusion that a temporary retreat from Rajagriha might best serve to kill the controversy. An opportunity for such retreat had also presented itself. He had received an invitation from his aged father to visit Kapilavastu. Although Gautam had never communicated with his people since he left home, they had heard of him from time to time through various sources. After his enlightenment, he had suddenly achieved celebrity. The news of his success had doubtless reached his family. It was not their notion of success, but they could no longer afford to ignore him. Indeed, they were anxious to take up the broken threads, even to make some kind of public demonstration of their lasting affection and regard for the prodigal. Among his followers the prodigal now counted such exalted personages as the King of Magadha it was obviously time to recognise him.

Gautam went to Kapilavastu. He and his mendicants stayed in a grove outside the town. His father and kinsfolk came to see him, but there was no killing of the fatted calf. It seems that they were chagrined by the sight of a shaven monk in yellow robes; it revived painful memories of all the tribal and paternal hopes he had betrayed; and they left without providing a proper meal for the prodigal and his companions. Gautam, however, was not very much perturbed by this impoliteness. Next morning he set out to beg food from house to house, as was his custom. Suddhodana soon came to hear that his son was asking for alms in the streets like any motley beggar. It is said he was deeply moved. But even more than being moved, he was alarmed perhaps.

He was probably no longer the President of the Republic, but he was still an eminent and highly-honoured citizen of Kapilavastu. He had his own and his family's reputation to consider. He did not want his son to be seen begging in the streets of his native town. What would the people say? He hastened to find Gautam, and after some persuasion, brought him to his house.

All the members of the household were present, with one conspicuous exception—'the ruddy goose parted from her mate.' Suddhodana explained the reason of his daughter-in-law's absence. He said that she had let it be known: 'If I have any value in his eyes, he will come himself to my presence. I can welcome him better here.' Gautam understood the subtle hint. He went to her chamber accompanied by two of his mendicants whom he previously cautioned that should she try to 'do reverence' to the Tathagata in a manner which might not be strictly in conformity with the rules and regulations of the Order, they should not prevent her from so doing, nor show any bewilderment at her conduct. Fortunately, however, the contingency did not arise. The lady did not make any embarrassing demonstration of her affection for her long-lost husband. She was sensible enough to realise the gulf which divided her from Gautam; and even if she had entertained any ardent designs, the spectacle of a recluse in rough garments, with a shaven head and a grave and weather-beaten face, must have been sufficient to make her abandon them. She respectfully clasped his feet and wept.

The reconciliation between the prodigal and his family was now complete. Nevertheless, Gautam's family could not fully approve of his mode of living. There is no real basis of understanding between those who are worldly-wise and those for whom the process of 'wayfaring' through the world is itself the end: the two ways are fundamentally incompatible. Suddhodana, though he was very fond of his son, found his behaviour both strange and shocking. Moreover, during his stay in Kapilavastu Gautam did a number of things which were liable to strain his relations with his family still further. It is recorded, for instance, that he persuaded Nanda, his half-brother, and son of Mahaprajapati, whose coming-of-age ceremony had just been celebrated, 'to leave the world'; also that he conferred 'Disburdenment' on his own son, Rahula, by admitting him to the Order.

The account of this latter incident is at once pathetic and amusing. After Gautam had been about a week in Kapilavastu, his wife had the happy inspiration of dressing up the child in his best clothes and saying to him: 'See, dear, that golden-coloured ascetic... He is your father, and he had four great vases of treasure, but since he left the world we do not see them. Go and ask for your inheritance...' Rahula did as he had been instructed. While Gautam was having his meal the boy walked up to 'the golden-coloured ascetic' and said lovingly: 'Pleasant, ascetic, is your shadow.' He then asked for his inheritance. Gautam, however, did not pay any heed to the child's demand and went on eating. Having finished the meal he rose to go to the Nigrodha park where he was staying. Rahula followed him, still asking for the 'four great vases of treasure' which his mother had told him had been hidden. On his part, Gautam maintained an enigmatic silence with regard to the hidden treasure. When he reached the Nigrodha grove he asked Sariputta to 'disburden' the unsuspecting Rahula,' and bestow upon him the priceless gift of the doctrine. This was done and Rahula had his inheritance, though it was not the kind of treasure for which either the child or his mother could feel very grateful.

Both these acts of Gautam were hardly calculated to promote understanding between his father and himself. Suddhodana was very much upset by the loss both of his second son and grandson. But he was too old to pick new quarrels with his son, and too heart-broken to make angry scenes. All he could do was bemoan: 'When you abandoned the world, it was no small pain to me, so when Nanda did, and especially so in the case of Rahula. The love of a son cuts through the skin, having cut through the skin it cuts through the hide, the flesh, the sinew, the bone, the marrow...' He begged Gautam not to confer ordination 'on a son without the permission of his mother and father. This request Gautam readily granted: he had no intention of enticing sons from their parents. Rahula, being his own son, was a special case.

The prodigal's visit to his parental home came to an end soon after these unfortunate incidents. On his way to Rajagriha he stayed for a time at Anupiya, on the banks of the river Anoma, in the neighbourhood where he had dismissed his charioteer on the historic night of his Renunciation. It was a fruitful sojourn, and there were several additions to the Brotherhood. The most important among them were Ananda, Devadatta, Anuruddha, and Upali. The first two were Gautam's cousins. The former was to become the Tathagata's most intimate and faithful companion; the latter was to achieve notoriety as his most insidious rival. Anuruddha afterwards distinguished himself by his mastery of the Buddhist metaphysics. And the last, Upali, a barber by birth and profession, was later on to display the same skill in intellectual hair-splitting which he had hitherto shown in hairdressing, shaving, and other kindred crafts.

The situation in Rajagriha had eased considerably. Gautam spent the rainy season—the second after his enlightenment—at Rajagriha, where he found the people once again sympathetic to the doctrine.

Preaching Over Half a Century

Gautam's ministry lasted for nearly half a century. No connected chronicle of this long stretch of time is available, and perhaps none is needed. In the accounts of his life as a wandering preacher, we may agree with Oldenberg, 'unquestionable truth is mixed up with just as much unquestionable romance.' To separate one from the other is in itself a difficult task; to attempt to construct anything like a definite and reliable chronology is attempting the impossible. However, the more credible episodes connected with the first twenty years of his wandering can be seen to form some kind of a vague sequence.

After spending the rainy season at Rajagriha, Gautam visited Savatthi. This visit was highly opportune. For Savatthi was at the time one of the most flourishing cities in India, being the capital of King Pasenadi of Kosala, who shared with King Bimbisara of Magadha the balance of political power in the valley of the Ganges. Gautam's visit to Savatthi was made possible through the mediacy of Sudatta, a rich and highly-honoured householder. Sudatta had come to transact some business in Rajagriha, and to see his sister who was married to a guildmaster in that city. The latter happened to be a lay follower of the Tathagata, and it was through her that Sudatta met the Buddha. Sudatta was quickly converted to the new faith, and before leaving Rajagriha he invited Gautam to his native city, offering to make all arrangements for the journey as well as for his stay there. Gautam, who was above all a practical man, readily accepted the offer. His next Retreat, consequently, was spent at Savatthi. Sudatta left no stone unturned to make this stay a success. He even bought a very beautiful.

This discourse—the intentions of which are clear enough—is evidently a happy invention of the commentators themselves. But it is certain that Gautam spent many a Retreat in the monastery at Jatavana, and that Sudatta figures in the list of the eighty chief disciples under the well-merited title of 'chief of almsgivers.'

The fourth year of Gautam's ministry is noteworthy for two events. One, that Gautam was called in to settle an irrigation dispute between the Koliyans (his mother's clan) and the Shakyas. His arbitration succeeded in reconciling the two clans. The other was the conversion of Ugrasena, the son of a rich guildmaster of Rajagriha who had abandoned his worldly estate and turned rope-dancer for the love of an acrobat's daughter.

Next year Gautam had to pay a hurried visit to Kapilavastu to see his dying father. After performing the obsequies of Suddhodana, he returned to Mahavana in the neighbourhood of Vaishali, the capital of the powerful confederation of the Licchhavis. Mahaprajapati, his aunt and stepmother, as also his own wife and some other distinguished ladies from Kapilavastu, are said to have followed him to Vaishali. So far Gautam had allowed women to become his lay disciples, but he had withheld from them the privilege of complete 'Disburdenment' Mahaprajapati and her companions, however, begged to be allowed 'to leave the world,' to take full refuge in the Tathagata's doctrine and discipline. This naturally would have involved the founding of an Order of female mendicants; and Gautam, for various reasons which are not difficult to understand, was rather reluctant to take such a step. Eventually he granted Mahaprajapati's request, but only on certain strict conditions. He is even reported having remarked to Ananda, whose advocacy was principally responsible for the founding of the Order for women: 'If women had not received the going forth in the doctrine and discipline, the religious system would have lasted long, the good doctrine would have stayed for a thousand years; but as women have gone forth, now the religious system will not last long, now, Ananda, the good doctrine will last only five hundred years. Just as houses, where there are many women and few men, are easily broken into by robbers, even so in the doctrine and disciple in which a woman goes forth the religious system will not last long...' The cynicism implied in this remark probably voices the sentiments of some latter-day Buddhist anchorite rather than of Gautam himself; for it is completely incongruous with an earlier statement of Gautam apropos the same incident, where he admits to Ananda that a woman is in everyway 'capable' of realising 'the fruit of Entering-the-stream, of the Once-returner, of the Non-returner, and even of the Arahatship.'

No doubt Gautam had cause to hesitate before admitting women into the Order, but his hesitation was not actuated by any contempt for them as such. And although the prophecy contained in the above lament came remarkably near being true—and, indeed, one might say that the dissolution of the doctrine and discipline started even earlier than the prophet had predicted—it is only fair to state that the blame for this unhappy contingency must be apportioned equally among the male and female mendicants.

Sixth Retreat

Gautam spent his sixth Retreat at Makula hill, near Kaushambi (modern Allahabad). When the rains were over, he returned to Rajagriha and admitted Bimbisara's wife, Kshema, to the Order. Gautam's popularity with people in high places could not fail to excite jealousy. There were frequent attempts by his enemies to discredit both himself and his creed; two serious attempts of this nature are recorded as having been made during the seventh year of his ministry. On one occasion, when Gautam was staying at Jetavana monastery, a rival sect induced a woman named Chincha to visit the Buddha, and afterwards to feign pregnancy and accuse the Tathagata of having been the cause of her undoing. They seem to have forgotten that pregnancy is not a thing that can be feigned, and consequently their conspiracy was quickly exposed. Another story tells of a still more serious attempt to bring Gautam into disrepute. Members of a hostile organisation persuaded a woman known as Sundari to pay frequent visits to Jetavana. They then had her killed and her body thrown in Gautam's monastery. Fortunately, in a drunken brawl, the hired assassins blurted out their crime and were apprehended by the King's spies. It is difficult to determine how much truth there is in these stories, but on the face of it they seem credible. If they are true, then Gautam's life during his Buddahood could not have been quite so Nirvanic as has usually been represented.

The eighth rainy season was spent at Sumsumaragiri, a town near Kapilavastu. It was here that Gautam converted Nakulapita and his wife. The conversion took place under strange circumstances. The couple had the original idea when they saw Gautam of claiming him as their long-lost son, saying to him: 'Son, you have left us for such a long time, where have you been living?' Gautam, though he must have felt embarrassed by this unexpected recognition, is said to have admitted their claim. But, significantly, he explained that he had been their son not in his present, but in some previous birth. This remark is often produced as a proof of Gautam's belief in reincarnation. But it is impossible to examine it objectively without concluding that the Tathagata was merely respecting the feelings of a credulous but well-meaning couple.

Next year a still more curious adventure befell Gautam. He was staying at Kaushambi. Magandiya, an ambitious and opulent Brahmin, had a daughter to marry. She had reached the critical age, and the worthy Brahmin was anxiously on the lookout for a suitable 'wooer.' He happened to see the Buddha, and noting him to be sound in wind and limb decided that he would make an excellent match. He decided to speak to Gautam. Magandiya's wife, who appears to have been rather a sensible person, tried to dissuade him from making a fool of himself, and even told him, that as far as she knew the Tathagata was not interested in women, and therefore it was futile to offer him their daughter's hand in marriage. But the ambitious Brahmin was not to be dissuaded so easily. So he went to Gautam, put his proposal before him with all the vehemence and earnestness of which he was capable; and it was with some difficulty that Gautam at last got rid of this importunate and insistent Brahmin. Magandiya's daughter, when she came to know that Gautam had refused her, was gravely chagrined. She took the refusal as a personal slight, and never forgave him. It is even recorded that later, when she was happily married to Udena, the ruling chief of Kaushambi, she had her revenge. Discovering that another lady in Udena's harem,

Samavati, was a devotee of the Buddha, she conspired against her and brought about her death by having her palace set on fire.

The tenth year of Gautam's ministry was a fateful one in the history of the Order: it saw the first breaking out of serious dissension in the Brotherhood. An unknown monk of Kaushambi is said to have been the cause. He had committed some minor transgression, yet when it was pointed out to him, he refused to admit it. Now according to the existing rules a man could not be regarded as a transgressor unless he himself recognised his offence. In spite of this, however, the monk was excommunicated. A heated controversy followed. Some members of the Order maintained that the excommunication was unjustified; others held that not to have taken some drastic action against the impenitent monk would have been tantamount to putting a premium on evil. Eventually the matter was referred to Gautam. He tried hard to restore peace between the two parties. 'Do not look long,' he said, 'do not look short; for not by hatred are hatreds calmed; by non-hatred are hatreds calmed.' But all his attempts towards peace failed. The dispute rose to such heights that Gautam was forced to retire to the solitudes of Parileyyaka forest, leaving the querulous mendicants to fight out the issue amongst themselves. It was three months before the monks came to their senses and went to Savatthi begging Gautam's forgiveness.

There were only two important conversions in the eleventh and twelfth years—those of Bharadvaja and Veranja. The twelfth year was also marked by the outbreak of a serious famine in the Gangetic valley. This could not help having unhappy repercussions for the Brotherhood whose members were dependent upon the charity of the householders. Food was scarce and the World-Renouncers seem to have had a lean time. It is recorded, for instance, that Veranja had invited the Tathagata to spend the Retreat with him, only to find it impossible to keep his promise; he got out of it by conveniently forgetting all about it till the return of better times, when he sought out the Buddha and apologised for his forgetfulness.

The thirteenth and fourteenth years were both uneventful. The former was spent at Calika hill; the latter at Savatthi. Next year Suppabuddha, Gautam's father-in-law, had a fatal accident trying to stop a runaway horse. It is doubtful if Gautam felt this death as a great personal loss. Ever since the day he had left his house and thus condemned his wife to what was virtually a lifelong widow-hood, relations between himself and his father-in-law had been strained. Gautam, it is true, harboured no ill-feelings against Suppabuddha, but the latter had never forgiven the Tathagata for deserting his daughter. Even time had failed to heal the breach between them; Suppabuddha's bitterness against Gautam had rather become intensified with the years; and only a week before he died Suppabuddha had been drunk and cursed Gautam publicly in the streets of Kapilavastu.

The sixteenth rainy season was spent at Alavi, the seventeenth at Rajagriha, the eighteenth at Calika Hill, and the nineteenth at Rajagriha again. This period was not marked by any important happenings. In the twentieth year of his ministry Gautam converted Angulimala, an infamous robber, the terror of the countryside round Savatthi, who was known to wear 'a garland of his victims' fingers. When King Pasenadi came to hear of this remarkable conversion he is said to have 'complimented Buddha as the tamer of the untamed.'

Personal Companion

It was in the same year that Ananda was appointed Gautam's permanent personal companion. This appointment was made under somewhat curious circumstances. The custom hitherto had been that the mendicants in the Tathagata's entourage attended him each day in turn. The system had worked satisfactorily until one day Gautam was treated contemptuously by the elder Nagasamala. Gautam and the elder were walking down a country road when they came to a cross-road. As though to assert his independence, Nagasamala pointed in one direction and said, 'that is the way, lord, we will go by that.' But as it was not the direction which Gautam wished, he pointed the other way and said: 'No, Nagasamala, this is the way—we will go this way.' Nagasamala was possibly in a churlish mood: he refused to take the Tathagata's gentle hint. In vain Gautam tried to reason with the elder, but his gentleness was wasted, and Nagasamala angrily put down Gautam's bowl and robe. 'Here, lord,' he said, 'is your bowl and robe,' and so saying, departed. Gautam was naturally distressed by this incident; and though at the time he said nothing about it, he explained to the Brotherhood at Savatthi later, that now he was advancing in years, he felt the need of a permanent companion. All the mendicants, including Sariputta and Moggallana, offered their services. Ananda, the last to rise and offer himself, was the one to be accepted. For the rest of the Tathagata's life, the last enjoyed the privilege of being the first.

It was a monotonous journey. Days passed; seasons changed; but there was hardly ever any variation in the normal routine of the Tathagata's life. Years followed each other in a long but unexciting procession. The records of the last twenty-five years of Gautam's ministry are far too vague to form a narrative; all that can be said is that they were spent in wandering from place to place preaching his philosophy of life. It was an age of wandering preachers. The whole country was alive with a spiritual and intellectual restlessness seldom surpassed, and only rarely equalled, in later history. Some idea of the interest in abstract problems shown by the people in general may be formed from the fact that not only men, but women ascetics were in the habit of taking to a wandering mode of life, and we may regard as typical the case of the woman-preacher who 'was in the habit of going from village to village, and setting up at the entrance to the village a broomstick with the announcement, that she was willing to discuss with any one who should overturn it.'

Great Wanderings

Gautam himself wandered a great deal. Even when very old he spent the best part of the year travelling from place to place. His yearly round was confined to the valley of the Ganges, that is to say, the country of the Magadhas, the Shakyas, the Kosalas, the Licchhavis, the Vamsas, and the Vajjians. The rainy season and the mid-winter months were spent in Retreat. These Retreats were kept at either of the monasteries built by Gautam's wealthy patrons at Rajagriha and Savatthi for the use of the Order.

Buddha's Routine

Buddhaghosa has left an account of the Tathagata's daily life, which, when divested of its euphony and supernatural details, gives what is probably a true picture. 'The Blessed One...' he writes, 'used to rise up early (about five in the morning) and, out of consideration for his personal attendant, was wont to wash and dress himself without calling for any assistance. Then, till it was time to go on his round for alms, he would retire to a solitary place and meditate. When that time arrived, he would dress himself completely in the three robes (the dress which every one in the Brotherhood was expected to wear), take his bowl in his hand and, sometimes alone, sometimes attended by his followers, would enter the neighbouring village or town...' The procedure of going out to beg alms, however, was only formal. For the Tathagata had many well-to-do lay followers, and these appear to have vied with each other in feeding him, as well as his mendicants. Buddhaghosa writes: 'Then clad in their best and brightest, and bringing garlands and nosegays with them, they [the rich lay followers] would come forth into the street and, offering their flowers to the Blessed One, would vie with one another saying: "Today, sir, take your meal with us; we will make provision for ten, and we for twenty, and we for a hundred of your followers."' Even a far less compassionate person than the Blessed One would have found it difficult to refuse such warm solicitations, and it is not surprising that Gautam readily accepted the invitation to a meal and let his host 'take his bowl, and spread mats for him.' After the necessary ritual of taking 'some solid food' was over, there followed the inevitable discourse.

In his sermons, we are told, the Blessed One paid due regard to the 'spiritual capacity' of his audience. 'And when he had thus had mercy on the multitude,' continues Buddhaghosa, 'he would arise from his seat and depart to the place where he lodged. And when he had come there, he would sit on the open verandah, awaiting the time when the rest of his followers should also have finished their meal. And when his attendant announced they had done so, he would enter his private apartment. Thus, was he occupied up to the midday meal.'

Eight Fold Path

Afternoons were spent in exhortation to the brethren in the fold to follow the Eightfold Path. Then some among the flock 'would ask him to suggest a subject for meditation suitable to the spiritual capacity of each, and when he had done so, they would retire each to the solitary place he was wont to frequent, and meditate on the subject set. Then would the Blessed One retire within the private chamber, perfumed with flowers; and calm and self-possessed, he would rest awhile during the heat of the day. Then when his body was reposed he would arise from his couch and for a space consider the circumstances of the people near, that he might do them good. And at the fall of the day, folk from the neighbouring villages or town would gather together at the place where he was lodging, bringing with them offerings of flowers. Seated in the lecture-hall, in a manner suitable to the occasion, and suitable to their beliefs, he would discourse to them of the Truth. Then, seeing that the proper time had come, he would dismiss these folk, who, saluting him, would go away. Thus, was he occupied in the afternoon.'

Generally the day ended as peacefully as it began. At sunset 'should the Blessed One feel the need of the refreshment of a bath, he would bathe, while some brother of the Order, attendant on him, would prepare the divan in the chamber, perfumed with flowers. And in the evening he would sit alone, still in all his robes, till the brethren, returned from their meditations, began to assemble. Then some would ask him questions on things that puzzled them, some would speak of their meditations, some would ask for an exposition of the Truth. Thus, would the first watch of the night pass, as the Blessed One satisfied the desire of each, and then they would take their leave. And part of the rest of the night he would spend in meditation, walking up and down outside his chamber; and part he would rest lying down, calm and self-possessed, within...' And before long another day would dawn, and there would be another turn of the Wheel.

Of course, Buddhaghosa has idealised. In actual practice the routine of the Blessed One's life probably did not work out in quite so idyllic a manner. Buddhaghosa has evidently forgotten the daily embarrassments which must beset the head of a quasi-religious Order, and from which Gautam was by no means immune. He has forgotten, too, the prolonged and painful polemical discussions into which Gautam was often drawn, much against his will. And his account obviously takes no cognizance of the misrepresentations to which the Blessed One was frequently subjected by certain rival sects and schools who wished to discredit the man and his philosophy. To ignore these aspects of Gautam's life is to leave the picture incomplete. And yet Buddhaghosa's picture, partial as it is, yields an impression which somehow seems to correspond truly to the inner curve of Gautam's life. Fundamentally his manner of living was absolutely consistent with the 'way' he had postulated: it was peaceful, quiet, profound. Beyond the difficulties and embarrassments which arose from his intercourse with the world of men, beyond the long-drawn polemics in which he was involved, because of the strange simplicity and newness of his doctrine, and beyond the insufferable fools whose misunderstandings he had to suffer so patiently and for so long, there was in him a quietude, a core of serenity which nothing could disturb.

The period of his ministry was no doubt full of incidents; yet it would not be a distortion of facts to suggest that essentially it was an uneventful period. For there is in the life of each individual a decisive moment, a final turning-point which determines one's particular path through this world. After that crucial event, the pattern of one's being admits of no further change. One's awareness, it is true, may become more comprehensive, and one's thought more mature, but there is no qualitative change in the nature of one's awareness and thought; in other words, though one may 'know more, one cannot know *differently*.' In Gautam's psychological development this decisive turning-point came at the time of his enlightenment. The conclusions which he then formed did not undergo any significant change during the rest of his life. The horizon of his vision continued to expand, to become more inclusive and sharply outlined, as the years passed. But it remained, to the end of his days, the same horizon and the same vision.

It was also in some ways a lonely journey. In the very nature of things, it could not have been otherwise. For a person who represents what Professor I. A. Richards describes as 'the most aware point of his age' is inevitably so far in advance of the understanding of his contemporaries, that he cannot help feeling an intimate sense of isolation. A lifelong solitude is the penalty of all genius; and Gautam, too, had some experience of this kind of personal solitude. No man could have been kinder, more considerate and gentle, in his dealings with his fellow-men. But his relationships were nearly always kept on an impersonal plane. During the whole of his life he does not seem to have formed any personal attachments. Even Ananda, who for nearly a quarter of a century was his constant companion, could not break through that ultimate barrier which separated him from his Master.

Fervent Devotion

Gautam was by no means friendless. He commanded not only respect and admiration, but fervent devotion. He had a very wide circle of friends. These were drawn from all quarters, high as well as low. In choosing his friends and acquaintances, Gautam 'ignored completely and absolutely all advantages or disadvantages arising from birth, occupation, and social status. He had no use for snobbery of any kind, and lost no opportunity of discouraging it. Powerful potentates and lowly pariahs were received by him on a basis of absolute equality; he refused to make any distinction between Queens and courtezans when they came to visit him. During his lifetime, at any rate, the Order was a most democratic institution. 'One of the most distinguished members of his Order,' writes Rhys Davids, 'the very one of them who was referred to as the chief authority, after Gautam himself, on the rules of the Order, was Upali, who had formerly been a barber, one of the despised occupations. So Sunita, one of the Brethren whose verses are chosen for insertion in the *Thera Gatha,* was a pukhusa, one of the low tribes. Sati, the propounder of a deadly heresy, was of the sons of the fisherfolk, afterwards a low caste, and even then an occupation, on account of its cruelty, particularly abhorred. Nanda was a cowherd. The two Panthakas were born out of wedlock, to a girl of good family, through intercourse with a slave (and hence were, according to Manu, to be regarded as outcasts). Kapa was the daughter of a deer-stalker. Punna and Punnita had been slave-girls. Sumangalamata was daughter and wife to a worker in rushes, and Subha was the daughter of a slave.' Had Gautam's views been accepted by his countrymen, the Hindu caste system would never have come into existence.

Notable Followers

There were many picturesque and interesting personalities amongst Gautam's friends and followers. In high places, there were the Kings of Magadha and Kosala. Both Bimbisara and Pasenadi were deeply devoted to the Tathagata, and remained so till they met their death in the tragic circumstances which have been mentioned elsewhere. Bimbisara, in particular, held Gautam in very high esteem. He not only gave valuable gifts to the Brotherhood, but actually found time from his varied kingly duties to visit the Buddha frequently and hear the doctrine.

Gautam's other royal benefactor, Pasenadi of Kosala, was a man of sober-minded bent. He does not seem to have been quite so lively and entertaining a figure as King Bimbisara. He was far less effusive and vehement in protesting his abiding regard for the Blessed One. But probably his interest in the Eightfold Path was more genuine. He had been educated at the university of Takhasila (modern Taxila), the capital of Gandhara. This early training had developed in him a seriousness of purpose and intellectual honesty sadly lacking in the inconsequential, though affable, Bimbisara. He showed himself highly efficient in the discharge of his administrative duties, and his serious philosophic nature made him cultivate 'the companionship of the good.' His admiration for Gautam was based on a true understanding of the man's worth.

Besides these royal personages, Gautam counted among his lay followers many gentlemen of noble birth, aristocratic patriarchs, chiefs of clans, wealthy merchants, and guildmasters. The term 'the friends of the series of the wealthy ones' which occurs in the Sanskrit texts is not without significance. Sudatta, alias Anathapindaka, was not the only man who gave alms 'to the unprotected'; doubtless there were many other guildmasters who were equally charitable towards the Brethren. Further, Gautam's circle was not confined only to those who accepted his doctrine. It included intellectuals, dialecticians, mystics, and philosophers holding views widely different from his own. Indeed, he was perhaps better understood by those who disagreed with him than those who avowed adherence to his doctrine. And although he was up in arms against the Brahminical orthodoxy and voiced the most devastating heresies, the Brahmins showed on the whole a surprising tolerance towards him and his followers. The more enlightened among them—men like Pokkharadi and Sona-danda for instance—not only respected his point of view, but sympathised with it, though they were far too deeply committed to orthodoxy to come out into the open with their sympathies.

Prominent Members of the Order

Among the members of the Order itself, Ananda, Sariputta, Moggallana, Upali, and Devadatta enjoyed a certain pre-eminence. Another important personage, though not a member of the Brotherhood, who was on intimate terms with the Tathagata was the physician Givaka Koma-rabhakha. Givaka had risen to fame and wealth in a most remarkable and adventurous manner. He was the son of a courtesan. His mother had abandoned him immediately after his birth, fearing her worth would sink in the eyes of men if they were to know that she had borne a child. After an unhappy childhood spent in dire poverty and misery, Givaka somehow drifted to Takhasila. Here he was lucky enough to attract the attention of a renowned physician, who so took to the youth that he adopted him as his son, and taught him all that there was to teach about human diseases and their cures.

Givaka showed a great aptitude for medicine, and before long was himself an accomplished physician. Then came the chance of his life. 'At that time,' says the Vinaya, 'the Magadha King Seniya Bimbisara suffered from a fistula; his garments were stained with blood.' As though the agony of a fistula were not enough, the ladies of the seraglio took a perverse pleasure in mocking him. When they saw his bloodstained garments, they jeered and said: 'His Majesty is having his courses! His Majesty will bring forth!' Bimbisara was annoyed, but could do nothing to prevent his playful concubines making fun of him, especially as he was already advanced in years. He confessed his misery to the Royal Prince. 'I am suffering, my dear Abhaya,' he moaned, 'from such a disease that my garments are stained with blood; and the Queens when they see it mock me. Pray, my dear Abhaya, find me a physician who can cure me.' Abhaya's choice fell on Givaka; and a better choice could not have been made. Givaka performed a successful operation on Bimbisara. As a token of his gratitude, the merry monarch appointed Givaka to the coveted post of Royal Physician. Later, when Bimbisara discovered the virtues of the Eightfold Path and became a patron of the Buddha, he generously placed Givaka's services at the disposal of the Tathagata.

Gautam had many female admirers. He was far too attractive a personality not to have aroused the maternal instinct. We hear of many charitable ladies who contributed to the general ease and happiness of the Brethren in diverse ways. 'The work of ministering to the Order,' writes Sir Charles Eliot, 'of supplying it with food and raiment, naturally fell largely to pious matrons, and their attentive forethought delighted to provide for the monks those comforts which might be accepted, but not asked for.' A notable figure among these ministering ladies was Vishakha, wife of Punnavaddhana, son of Migara. Domestic unhappiness had led her to take refuge in the Buddha as a lay follower. She is said to have built a monastery at Savatthi in the Pubbarama, or 'the Eastern Park,' for the use of the Brotherhood. On another occasion, it is recounted, she asked eight boons of Gautam. These included permission to provide food for various types of monks, and to furnish them with bathing-costumes—'for,' said she, 'it shocks my sense of propriety to see them bathe naked.' Gautam had enough common sense to grant these boons.

Heartfelt Conviction

Understanding has never been among the conspicuous virtues of the faithful. There is a very touching passage in the Dhammapada which may well represent Gautam's own heartfelt conviction. 'If a traveller,' it says, 'does not meet with one who is his better, or his equal, let him keep to his solitary journey; there is no companionship with a fool.' For Gautam had to make most of his journey in the company of people who were little better than fools. It was not just the cussedness of his uncomprehending enemies from which he had to suffer; in this respect the members of his own fraternity were probably the worst sinners. He had founded the Brotherhood in the hope of creating a nucleus for a new and more humane kind of society; those joining it were expected to propagate, by the example of their strenuous effort and vigilance as much as by their exhortations, a new and more reasonable way of life. Yet, from the stories recounted in the Vinaya, it would appear that the 'worthy Brethren' thought of almost everything except the purpose which the Buddha had so much at heart.

This was inevitable. The composition of the Order was far too heterogeneous for it to be a body of altruistic humanitarians intent on furthering 'the welfare of mankind.' The motives out of which many people had come to 'disburden' themselves were questionable. Some had taken refuge with the Buddha because it was a new craze. Others had attached themselves to the Order thinking 'the precepts which these Sakyaputtiya Samanas keep and the life they live are commodious; they have good meals and lie down on beds protected from the wind.' There were many more who had renounced the world under the stress of necessity; these included runaway slaves and domestic servants, deserters from the army, debtors in distress, criminals fleeing from Justice, youths wishing to break away from the tyranny of family-life, bankrupt business men, and harassed householders. Indeed, at one period these stricken souls were joining the Order in such alarming numbers, that the authorities got so 'vexed and indignant,' and 'murmured' so effectively, that Gautam had to make the rules for 'Disburdenment' much more strict than they were at the beginning. However, in spite of all the caution that was exercised, it was impossible to prevent 'undesirables' from furtively attaching themselves to the Brotherhood.

Not all the 'worthy Brethren' had the perfect deportment of the elder Assaji, whose 'decorous walk and looks and motions of the arms' had made such a deep impression on Sariputta's mind. In fact, most of them were rather uncouth and noisy fellows who paid little heed to the rules of decorum and decency. Innumerable examples of their bad behaviour are recorded. They left doors and lattices in the monastery open. They left bathrooms in a filthy condition. They behaved rudely towards the householders when they went out to beg alms, and 'entered dwellings roughly and left them roughly.' They wrestled, and held boxing bouts, and rubbed their bodies with oil as though they were going to take part in some physical culture championship. They ate their meals noisily and carelessly. They walked on the couches with unwashed and dirty feet. They broke furniture belonging to the Brotherhood to light bonfires. Some rose up in the night towards dawn, 'and putting on wooden shoes, walked up and down in the open air, talking in tones high, loud and harsh...; and in so doing they both trod upon and slew all kinds of insects and disturbed Bhikshus in their meditation.' The dead insects, of course, could not protest; but the Bhikhsus, who were disturbed in their meditation, would get Vexed and indignant.

The world-renouncers often succumbed to the lure of the world. They would get heavily drunk and then lie about the monastery, unmindful, and displaying their nakedness. The number of serious misdemeanours increased vastly when the Order of the Female Mendicants was brought into being. Gautam's reluctance to take this step would seem to have been justified; for bhikhsus and bhikhsunis frequently misconducted themselves together. On one occasion, we read, some of the Brethren had the original idea of wooing some of the bhikhsunis by throwing dirty water at them.

Bhikhsunis, on their part did everything 'to set men's hearts ablaze,' and would bedeck themselves with frills, fringes, and girdles 'as do women who are still enjoying the pleasures of the world.' Besides such cases of misconduct, the living together of men in comparative segregation from women, led to a certain amount of homosexuality.

The 'temperate' bhikhsus had good reasons for being annoyed. Their fellow-mendicants were always doing something or other which brought discredit either on themselves or the Order. Of course, the bhikhsus who caused trouble were not always moved by the spirit of evil; quite often their offence was merely due to an incorrigible naivety of temperament. A majority of the Brethren were simple-minded people who knew little of the ways of the world, and consequently found the Middle Way even harder to follow. Especially, they seem to have been very prone to fits of absent-mindedness. Some of them suffered from this malady so much that, when going out to beg alms, they forgot to put on proper robes and undergarments, and aroused the people's hostility or amusement.

Not much love was lost between individual members of the Brotherhood. Factions, rivalries, petty jealousies and quarrels were rife, and not all the sweet reasonableness of the Tathagata could convince his cantankerous disciples of the futility of trying 'to appease hatred by hatred.' Sometimes the enmity between Brethren broke out in a virulent form; then the contending parties would not scruple to level charges and countercharges of the most serious kind. In particular, there was constant friction between the novices and the elders. The former, we read, 'did not show reverence and confidence towards the Bhikhsus, and did not live in harmony with them. The Bhikhsus were annoyed, murmured, and became angry.' The Bhikhsus, on their part, took every chance to pinprick the novices and impose hardships on them, with the result that novices also were often 'annoyed, murmured, and became angry.'

Quality of Confession

Gautam himself was possessed of a quality of compassion such as has seldom been seen among men. His sympathy was all-embracing and spontaneous; his generosity was equalled only by his profound understanding of human nature. When Panthaka came to him homeless and weary, Gautam tended him with his own hands. It is best to give the description of the incident in Panthaka's own words. 'Then the lord,' he says, 'came and stroked my head and taking my arm led me into the garden of the monastery, and out of his kindness he gave me a towel for my feet.' Another time he refused to preach until a farmer who had come to hear his discourse and had not eaten, had been fed.

But Gautam's example of gentleness and pervasive love appears to have been lost on most of his followers. For instance, when one of the bhikhsus was suffering from an offensive skin disease and lay in his own excreta, none of the Brethren would go near him. Gautam saw him lying untended and was deeply grieved. He had him carried to the monastery, heated water for his bath, and himself bathed him. Then when the diseased mendicant had been clothed in dry and freshly washed garments, Gautam sadly told the Brethren: 'You, monks, have no mother or father. If you do not wait one on the other, who is there who will wait on you? Whosoever, monks, should wait on me, he should wait on the sick.' But such exhortations, though they might have caused a moment's remorse, apparently did not leave any enduring impression on the monks' minds. The gods themselves, says Schiller, struggle in vain against stupidity. The Tathagata's struggle with *Dummheit*—or rather, DUMMHEIT—seems to have been equally fruitless.

On reading the section in the Vinaya which deals with rules concerning footwear, clothing, etc., one is perplexed by the utter incapacity of the Brethren to understand even the most elementary points of discipline. If so many misunderstandings could arise on such minor issues, it is hardly surprising that there should have been gross misinterpretations and distortions of the doctrine. Not all the members of the Order were experienced dialecticians. In fact, their general level of intelligence appears to have been astonishingly low; even the best among them exhibited a distressing half-wittedness.

Gentle and Effective

It was only a strong sense of humour that saved Gautam from frequent heartbreak. His irony was so gentle and effective that a few examples might be quoted. Once, towards the end of his life when Gautam was staying at Nalanda in the Mango grove of Pavarika, Sariputta, who was famous for his understanding of the doctrine, and was even called 'the Spotless Eye of the Doctrine,' came and said to him: 'Lord! Such faith have I in the Exalted One, that methinks there never has been, nor will there be, nor is there now, any other, whether recluse or Brahmin, who is greater and wiser than the Exalted One, that is to say as regards the higher wisdom.' Gautam, who always tried to discourage the tendency to hyperbole, replied: 'Grand and bold are the words of thy mouth, Sariputta. Thou hast roared a veritable lion's roar in this that thou hast said. Of course, then thou has known all the Exalted Ones who in the long ages of the past have been Arahats, Awakened Ones, comprehending their minds with thy mind, and aware what was their conduct, what their doctrine, what their wisdom, what their mode of life, and the liberty to which they attained?' Sariputta, amazed that his praise had not been appreciated, replied: 'Not so, lord.' 'Of course,' continued the Buddha, 'then thou hast perceived all the Exalted Ones who in the long ages of the future will be Arahats, Awakened Ones, comprehending their minds with thy mind, and aware what will be their conduct... doctrine... wisdom... mode of life and... liberty?' 'Not so, lord,' confessed the wondering Spotless Eye of the Doctrine. 'But at least then, Sariputta,' continued the Buddha, 'thou knowest that I now am Arahat, an Awakened One, comprehending my mind with thy mind, and aware that this is the Exalted One's conduct, such is his wisdom, such his doctrine, such his mode of life, and such the liberty to which he has attained?' 'Not so, lord,' blurted out Sariputta in confusion. 'Lo! then, Sariputta,' concluded the Buddha driving his point home, 'no knowledge hast thou concerning Arahats, Awakened Ones, past, future or present. Why then forsooth are thy words so grand and bold? Why hast thou roared this all-comprehensive lion's roar?'

When Ajatashatru, after having starved his father to death and usurped the throne, was stricken with remorse, he came to Gautam and confessed his transgression, saying, 'transgression overcame me, lord, in that in folly, stupidity, and wickedness, for the sake of lordship I deprived my righteous father, the righteous King, of life. May the Lord accept my transgression as transgression that I may be restrained in the future.' The lord, of course, accepted Ajatashatru's transgression—there was no alternative—but he could not refrain from commenting that 'His Majesty had all the makings of a saint in him, if only he had not killed that excellent man, his father.

Gautam was often pestered by people who were desirous of knowing the fate of their departed dead, and hearing stories of the Blessed One's own adventures in his previous births. Out of politeness Gautam is said to have complied with these requests, though, it is added, he always had an enigmatic smile on his face while telling these fairytales. But there were moments when his patience almost gave out.

Thus, when Ananda came to him and said: 'The brother named Salha has died at Nadika, lord. Where has he been born, and what is his destiny? The sister named Nanda has died, lord, at Nadika. Where is she born, and what is her destiny?' and went on to enquire after a dozen other departed souls, Gautam was really rather unhappy. 'Now there is nothing strange in this, Ananda,' he sadly answered his credulous disciple, 'that a human being should die, but that as each one does so, you should come to the Buddha, and enquire about him in this manner, that is wearisome to the Buddha.'

For all his sense of humour, his subtle irony, his patient nature, and his mature wisdom, the Tathagata must have been at heart a sad man.

5

Teachings of Buddha

Gautam Buddha delivered his first sermon in the language, Pali on the banks of the river Ganges at Varanasi. He spoke to a small audience of just five men, who became his first followers as they saw that Buddha glowed with a brilliant inner radiance. Gradually, he drew larger and larger crowds and instructed them to spread his message far and wide.

The core of his teaching consists of the Four Noble Truths, followed by the Eight-Fold Path.

The Four Noble Truths are as follows:

- The world is full of suffering and sorrow.
- The cause of suffering is desire.
- The renunciation of desires will lead to salvation from the world.
- The path to salvation can be achieved by following the Eight-Fold Path.

The Eight Fold Path is as under:

- Right Knowledge means a basic and thorough understanding of the Four Noble Truths.

- Right Attitude means having an unselfish and mentally healthy attitude to life, free from hatred and covetousness.
- Right Speech means speaking words that are good and true. One should not lie or gossip.
- Right Action means always conducting oneself in a way that does not harm, hurt nor displease anyone. Adultery, cheating, stealing and murder are specifically denounced.
- Right Means of Livelihood means that one must always strive to earn one's livelihood by honest means.
- Right Effort means one should conscientiously strive to develop good tendencies and destroy negative inclinations.
- Right Awareness means we should introspect about our inclinations and not give in easily to temptation.
- Right Meditation means working towards training your mind towards intense concentration, which, in turn, will lead to salvation.

Buddhism also advocated the doctrines of Karma and reincarnation. Buddha preached that the soul goes through many incarnations before it finally sheds all its Karma and is reunited to its pure state. He called this state Nirvana. This is a state where all the desires and cravings of the mind become extinct and a state of total, uninterrupted bliss is experienced.

What is notable about Buddhism is the absence of a personal Creator or God in its tenets. While Buddha did not deny the existence of God, he preached that the universe is guided and governed by a Supreme Power that did not possess a name or form. Consequently, all rites and rituals became defunct.

Buddha's Preaching

Lord Gautam Buddha preached: 'We will have to find out the cause of sorrow and the way to escape from it. The desire for sensual enjoyment and clinging to earthly life is the cause of sorrow. If we can eradicate desire, all sorrows and pains will come to an end. We will enjoy Nirvana or eternal peace. Those who follow the Noble Eightfold Path strictly, viz., right opinion, right resolve, right speech, right conduct, right employment, right exertion, right thought and right self-concentration will be free from sorrow. This indeed, O mendicants, is that middle course which the Tathagata has thoroughly comprehended, which produces insight, which produces knowledge, which leads to calmness or serenity, to supernatural knowledge, to perfect Buddhahood, to Nirvana.

'This again, indeed, O mendicants, is the noble truth of suffering. Birth is painful, old age is painful, sickness is painful, association with unloved objects is painful, separation from loved objects is painful, the desire which one does not obtain, this is too painful – in short, the five elements of attachment to existence are painful. The five elements of attachment to earthly existence are form, sensation, perception, components and consciousness.

'This again, indeed, O mendicants, is the truth of the cause of suffering. It is that thirst which leads to renewed existence, connected with joy and passion, finding joy here and there, namely, thirst for sensual pleasure, and the instinctive thirst for existence. This again, indeed, O mendicants, is the noble truth of cessation of suffering, which is the cessation and total absence of desire for that very thirst, its abandonment, surrender, release from it and non-attachment to it. This again, indeed, O mendicants, is the noble truth of the course which leads to the cessation of suffering. This is verily the Noble Eightfold Path, viz., right opinion, etc.'

Source of Buddha's Teachings

The Buddha's teachings have been reconstructed from stories, found mainly in the Sutra Pitaka. Although some stories describe his miraculous powers, others suggest that the Buddha tried to convince people through reason and persuasion rather than through displays of supernatural power. According to Buddhist philosophy, the world is transient (anicca) and constantly changing; it is also soulless (anatta) as there is nothing permanent or eternal in it. Within this transient world, sorrow (dukkha) is intrinsic to human existence. It is by following the path of moderation between severe penance and self-indulgence that human beings can rise above these worldly troubles. In the earliest forms of Buddhism, whether or not god existed was irrelevant.

Teaching of Rebirth

The Buddha regarded the social world as the creation of humans rather than of divine origin. Therefore, he advised Kings and gahapatis to be humane and ethical. Individual effort was expected to transform social relations. The Buddha emphasised individual agency and righteous action as the means to escape from the cycle of rebirth and attain self-realisation and nirvana, literally the extinguishing of the ego and desire — and thus end the cycle of suffering for those who renounced the world. According to Buddhist tradition, his last words to his followers were: "Be lamps unto yourselves as all of you must work out your own liberation."

Way to Salvation

During the course of meditation, Gautam Buddha after attaining the enlightenment came out with the certain principles which have become the pillars of Buddhism. These teachings have also become the guidelines for the followers of Buddha. These principles can broadly be explained under the following categories.

The Panchshila

All the religions of the world are based on the fundamental principles of good conduct and prohibit their followers to indulge in the misconduct and misbehaviour that may harm the society at large. So, the Panchshila of Buddha is comprised of the basic teachings of conduct which are as under:

• No killing	Respect for life
• No stealing	Respect for others' property
• No sexual misconduct	Respect for our pure nature
• No lying	Respect for honesty
• No intoxicants	Respect for a clear mind

Diamond Sutra

Diamond sutra is a short Mahayana sutra of the Perfection of Wisdom (prajna-paramita) genre. The diamond sutra teaches the practice staying in the middle path and avoidance of abiding in extremes of mental attachment. Mind always moves to the extreme of any thing. Abiding in the middle means living in this present moment and the self is revealed in the practice of middle.

Accurate translation of the Diamond Sutra in Sanskrit will be Vajra Cutter Sutra. Vajra is the word in Sanskrit for diamond. Diamond sutra is a conversation between Buddha and His disciple Subhuti and happened in the city of Shravasti.

Section I: The Convocation of the Assembly: Thus, have I heard. Upon a time Buddha sojourned in Anathapindika's Park by Shravasti with a great company of bhikshus, even twelve hundred and fifty. One day, at the time for breaking fast, the World-honoured One enrobed, and carrying His bowl made His way into the great city of Shravasti to beg for His food.

In the midst of the city He begged from door to door according to rule. This done, He returned to His retreat and took His meal. When He had finished He put away His robe and begging bowl, washed His feet, arranged His seat, and sat down.

Section II: Subhuti Makes a Request: Now in the midst of the assembly was the Venerable Subhuti. Forthwith he arose, uncovered his right shoulder, knelt upon his right knee, and, respectfully raising his hands with palms joined, addressed Buddha thus: World-honoured One, if good men and good women seek the Consummation of Incomparable Enlightenment, by what criteria should they abide and how should they control their thoughts? Buddha said: Very good, Subhuti! Just as you say, the Tathagata is ever-mindful of all the Bodhisattvas, protecting and instructing them well.

Now listen and take my words to heart: I will declare to you by what criteria good men and good women seeking the Consummation of Incomparable Enlightenment should abide, and how they should control their thoughts. Said Subhuti: Pray, do, World-honoured One. With joyful anticipation we long to hear.

Section III: The Real Teaching of the Great Way: Buddha said: Subhuti, all the Bodhisattva-Heroes should discipline their thoughts as follows: All living creatures of whatever class, born from eggs, from wombs, from moisture, or by transformation whether with form or without form, whether in a state of thinking or exempt from thought-necessity, or wholly beyond all thought realms all these are caused by Me to attain Unbounded Liberation Nirvana. Yet when vast, uncountable, immeasurable numbers of beings have thus been liberated, verily no being has been liberated. Why is this, Subhuti? It is because no Bodhisattva who is a real Bodhisattva cherishes the idea of an ego-entity, a personality, a being, or a separated individuality.

Section IV: Even the Most Beneficent Practices are Relative: Furthermore, Subhuti, in the practice of charity a Bodhisattva should be detached.

That is to say, he should practice charity without regard to appearances; without regard to sound, odour, touch, flavour or any quality. Subhuti, thus should the Bodhisattva practice charity without attachment. Wherefore? In such a case his merit is incalculable. Subhuti, what do you think? Can you measure all the space extending eastward?

No, World-honoured One, I cannot.

Then can you, Subhuti, measure all the space extending southward, westward, northward, or in any other direction, including nadir and zenith? No, World-honoured One, I cannot. Well, Subhuti, equally incalculable is the merit of the Bodhisattva who practices charity without any attachment to appearances. Subhuti, Bodhisattvas should persevere one-pointedly in this instruction.

Section V: Understanding the Ultimate Principle of Reality: Subhuti, what do you think? Is the Tathagata to be recognised by some material characteristic? No, World-honoured One; the Tathagata cannot be recognised by any material characteristic. Wherefore? Because the Tathagata has said that material characteristics are not, in fact, material characteristics. Buddha said: Subhuti, wheresoever are material characteristics there is delusion; but who so perceives that all characteristics are in fact no-characteristics, perceives the Tathagata.

Section VI: Rare is True Faith: Subhuti said to Buddha: World-honoured One, will there always be men who will truly believe after coming to hear these teachings?

Buddha answered: Subhuti, do not utter such words! At the end of the last five hundred-year period following the passing of the Tathagata, there will be self-controlled men, rooted in merit, coming to hear these teachings, who will be inspired with belief. But you should realise that such men have not strengthened their root of merit under just one Buddha, or two Buddhas, or three, or four, or five Buddhas, but under countless Buddhas; and their merit is of every kind. Such men, coming to hear these teachings, will have an immediate uprising of pure faith, Subhuti; and the Tathagata will recognise them. Yes, He will clearly perceive all these of pure heart, and the magnitude of their moral excellences. Wherefore? It is because such men will not fall back to cherishing the idea of an ego-entity, a personality, a being, or a separated individuality.

They will neither fall back to cherishing the idea of things as having intrinsic qualities, nor even of things as devoid of intrinsic qualities. Wherefore? Because if such men allowed their minds to grasp and hold on to anything they would be cherishing the idea of an ego-entity, a personality, a being, or a separated individuality; and if they grasped and held on to the notion of things as having intrinsic qualities they would be cherishing the idea of an ego-entity, a personality, a being, or a separated individuality.

Likewise, if they grasped and held on to the notion of things as devoid of intrinsic qualities they would be cherishing the idea of an ego-entity, a personality, a being, or a separated individuality. So you should not be attached to things as being possessed of, or devoid of, intrinsic qualities. This is the reason why the Tathagata always teaches this saying: My teaching of the Good Law is to be likened unto a raft. [Does a man who has safely crossed a flood upon a raft continue his journey carrying that raft upon his head?] The Buddha-teaching must be relinquished; how much more so misteaching!

Section VII: Great Ones, Perfect Beyond Learning, Utter no Words of Teaching: Subhuti, what do you think? Has the Tathagata attained the Consummation of Incomparable Enlightenment? Has the Tathagata a teaching to enunciate? Subhuti answered: As I understand Buddha's meaning there is no formulation of truth called Consummation of Incomparable Enlightenment. Moreover, the Tathagata has no formulated teaching to enunciate. Wherefore? Because the Tathagata has said that truth is uncontainable and inexpressible. It neither is nor is it not. Thus it is that this unformulated Principle is the foundation of the different systems of all the sages.

Section VIII: The Fruits of Meritorious Action: Subhuti, what do you think? If anyone filled three thousand galaxies of worlds with the seven treasures and gave all away in gifts of alms, would he gain great merit? Subhuti said: Great indeed, World-honoured One! Wherefore? Because merit partakes of the character of no-merit, the Tathagata characterised the merit as great.

Then Buddha said: On the other hand, if anyone received and retained even only four lines of this Discourse and taught and explained them to others, his merit would be the greater. Wherefore? Because, Subhuti, from this Discourse issue forth all the Buddhas and the Consummation of Incomparable Enlightenment teachings of all the Buddhas. Subhuti, what is called "the Religion given by Buddha" is not, in fact Buddha Religion.

Section IX: Real Designation is Undesignate: Subhuti, what do you think? Does a disciple who has entered the Stream of the Holy Life say within himself: I obtain the fruit of a Stream-entrant?

Subhuti said: No, World-honoured One. Wherefore? Because "Streamentrant" is merely a name. There is no stream-entering. The disciple who pays no regard to form, sound, odour, taste, touch, or any quality, is called a Streamentrant.

Subhuti, what do you think? Does an adept who is subject to only one more rebirth say within himself: I obtain the fruit of a Once-to-be-reborn?

Subhuti said: No, World-honoured One. Wherefore? Because "Once-to-be-reborn" is merely a name. There is no passing away nor coming into existence. [The adept who realises] this is called "Once-to-be-reborn."

Subhuti, what do you think? Does a venerable one who will never more be reborn as a mortal say within himself: I obtain the fruit of a Non-returner?

Subhuti said: No, World-honoured

One. Wherefore? Because "Non-returner" is merely a name. There is no non-returning; hence the designation "Nonreturner." Subhuti, what do you think? Does a holy one say within himself: I have obtained Perfective Enlightenment?

Subhuti said: No, World-honoured One. Wherefore? Because there is no such condition as that called "Perfective Enlightenment." World-honoured one, if a holy one of Perfective Enlightenment said to himself "such am I," he would necessarily partake of the idea of an ego-entity, a personality, a being, or a separated individuality. World-honoured One, when the Buddha declares that I excel amongst holy men in the Yoga of perfect quiescence, in dwelling in seclusion, and in freedom from passions, I do not say within myself:

I am a holy one of Perfective Enlightenment, free from passions. World-honoured One, if I said within myself: Such am I; you would not declare: Subhuti finds happiness abiding in peace, in seclusion in the midst of the forest. This is because Subhuti abides nowhere: therefore he is called, "Subhuti, Joyful Abider-in-Peace, Dweller-in- Seclusion-in-the-Forest."

Section X: Setting Forth Pure Lands: Buddha said: Subhuti, what do you think? In the remote past when the Tathagata was with Dipankara Buddha, did he have any degree of attainment in the Good Law?

No, World-honoured One. When the Tathagata was with Dipankara Buddha he had no degree of attainment in the Good Law.

Subhuti, what do you think? Does a Bodhisattva set forth any majestic Buddhalands?

No, World-honoured One. Wherefore? Because setting forth majestic Buddhalands is not a majestic setting forth; this is merely a name.

[Then Buddha continued:] Therefore, Subhuti, all Bodhisattvas, lesser and great, should develop a pure, lucid mind, not depending upon sound, flavour, touch, odour, or any quality. A Bodhisattva should develop a mind which alights upon no thing whatsoever; and so should he establish it. Subhuti, this may be likened to a human frame as large as the mighty Mount Sumeru. What do you think? Would such a body be great?

Subhuti replied: Great indeed, World-honoured One. This is because Buddha has explained that no body is called a great body.

Section XI: The Superiority of Unformulated Truth: Subhuti, if there were as many Ganges rivers as the sand grains of the Ganges, would the sand-grains of them all be many?

Subhuti said: Many indeed, World-honoured One! Even the Ganges rivers would be innumerable; how much more so would be their sand-grains?

Subhuti, I will declare a truth to you. If a good man or good woman filled three thousand galaxies of worlds with the seven treasures for each sand-grain in all those Ganges rivers, and gave all away in gifts of alms, would he gain great merit?

Subhuti answered: Great indeed, World-honoured One!

Then Buddha declared: Nevertheless, Subhuti, if a good man or good woman studies this Discourse only so far as to receive and retain four lines, and teaches and explains them to others, the consequent merit would be far greater.

Section XII: Veneration of the True Doctrine: Furthermore, Subhuti, you should know that wheresoever this Discourse is proclaimed, by even so little as four lines, that place should be venerated by the whole realms of Gods, Men and Titans as though it were a Buddha-Shrine. How much more is this so in the case of one who is able to receive and retain the whole and read and recite it throughout! Subhuti, you should know that such a one attains the highest and most wonderful truth. Wheresoever this sacred Discourse may be found there should you comport yourself as though in the presence of Buddha and disciples worthy of honour.

Section XIII: How This Teaching should be Received and Retained: At that time Subhuti addressed Buddha, saying: World-honoured One, by what name should this Discourse be known, and how should we receive and retain it?

Buddha answered: Subhuti, this Discourse should be known as "The Diamond of the Perfection of Transcendental Wisdom" — thus should you receive and retain it. Subhuti, what is the reason herein? According to the Buddha-teaching the Perfection of

Transcendental Wisdom is not really such. "Perfection of Transcendental Wisdom" is just the name given to it. Subhuti, what do you think? Has the Tathagata a teaching to enunciate?

Subhuti replied to the Buddha: World-honoured One, the Tathagata has nothing to teach.

Subhuti, what do you think? Would there be many molecules in [the composition of] three thousand galaxies of worlds? Subhuti said: Many indeed, World-honoured One! Subhuti, the Tathagata declares that all these molecules are not really such; they are called "molecules." [Furthermore,] the Tathagata declares that a world is not really a world; it is called "a world."

Subhuti, what do you think? May the Tathagata be perceived by the thirty-two physical peculiarities [of an outstanding sage]? No, World-honoured One, the Tathagata may not be perceived by these thirty-two marks. Wherefore? Because the Tathagata has explained that the thirty-two marks are not really such; they are called "the thirty-two marks."

Subhuti, if on the one hand a good man or a good woman sacrifices as many lives as the sand-grains of the Ganges, and on the other hand anyone receives and retains even only four lines of this Discourse, and teaches and explains them to others, the merit of the latter will be the greater.

Section XIV: Perfect Peace Lies in Freedom from Characteristic Distinctions: Upon the occasion of hearing this Discourse Subhuti had an interior realisation of its meaning and was moved to tears. Whereupon he addressed the Buddha thus: It is a most precious thing, World-honoured One, that you should deliver this supremely profound Discourse. Never have I heard such an exposition since of old my eye of wisdom first opened.

World-honoured One, if anyone listens to this Discourse in faith with a pure, lucid mind, he will thereupon conceive an idea of Fundamental Reality. We should know that such a one establishes the most remarkable virtue. World-honoured One, such an idea of Fundamental Reality is not, in fact, a distinctive idea; therefore the Tathagata teaches: "Idea of Fundamental Reality" is merely a name. World-honoured One, having listened to this Discourse, I receive and retain it with faith and understanding.

This is not difficult for me, but in ages to come — in the last five-hundred years, if there be men coming to hear this Discourse who receive and retain it with faith and understanding, they will be persons of most remarkable achievement. Wherefore? Because they will be free from the idea of an ego-entity, free from the idea of a personality, free from the idea of a being, and free from the idea of a separated individuality. And why? Because the distinguishing of an ego entity is erroneous. Likewise the distinguishing of a personality, or a being, or a separated individuality is erroneous. Consequently those who have left behind every phenomenal distinction are called Buddhas all.

Buddha said to Subhuti: Just as you say! If anyone listens to this Discourse and is neither filled with alarm nor awe nor dread, be it known that such a one is of remarkable achievement. Wherefore? Because, Subhuti, the Tathagata teaches that the First Perfection [the Perfection of Charity] is not, in fact, the First Perfection: such is merely a name. Subhuti, the Tathagata teaches likewise that the Perfection of Patience is not the Perfection of Patience: such is merely a name. Why so?

It is shown thus, Subhuti: When the Rajah of Kalinga mutilated my body, I was at that time free from the idea of an ego-entity, a personality, a being, and a separated individuality. Wherefore? Because then when my limbs were cut away piece by piece, had I been bound by the distinctions aforesaid, feelings of anger and hatred would have been aroused in me.

Subhuti, I remember that long ago, sometime during my past five-hundred mortal lives, I was an ascetic practising patience. Even then was I free from those distinctions of separated selfhood. Therefore, Subhuti, Bodhisattvas should leave behind all phenomenal distinctions and awaken the thought of the Consummation of Incomparable Enlightenment by not allowing the mind to depend upon notions evoked by the sensible world — by not allowing the mind to depend upon notions evoked by sounds, odours, flavours, touch-contacts, or any qualities.

The mind should be kept independent of any thoughts which arise within it. If the mind depends upon anything it has no sure haven. This is why Buddha teaches that the mind of a Bodhisattva should not accept the appearances of things as a basis when exercising charity. Subhuti, as Bodhisattvas practice charity for the welfare of all living beings they should do it in this manner. Just as the Tathagata declares that characteristics are not characteristics, so He declares that all living beings are not, in fact, living beings.

Subhuti, the Tathagata is He who declares that which is true; He who declares that which is fundamental; He who declares that which is ultimate. He does not declare that which is deceitful, nor that which is monstrous. Subhuti, that Truth to which the Tathagata has attained is neither real nor unreal. Subhuti, if a Bodhisattva practices charity with mind attached to formal notions he is like unto a man groping sightless in the gloom; but a Bodhisattva who practices charity with mind detached from any formal notions is like unto a man with open eyes in the radiant glory of the morning, to whom all kinds of objects are clearly visible.

Subhuti, if there be good men and good women in future ages, able to receive, read and recite this Discourse in its entirety, the Tathagata will clearly perceive and recognise them by means of His Buddha-knowledge; and each one of them will bring immeasurable and incalculable merit to fruition.

Section XV: The Incomparable Value of this Teaching: Subhuti, if on one hand, a good man or a good woman performs in the morning as many charitable acts of self-denial as the sand-grains of the Ganges, and performs as many again in the noonday and as many again in the evening, and continues so doing throughout numberless ages, and, on the other hand, anyone listens to this Discourse with heart of faith and without contention, the latter would be the more blessed.

But how can any comparison be made with one who writes it down, receives it, retains it, and explains it to others! Subhuti, we can summarise the matter by saying that the full value of this Discourse can neither be conceived nor estimated, nor can any limit be set to it.

The Tathagata has declared this teaching for the benefit of initiates of the Great Way; He has declared it for the benefit of initiates of the Supreme Way. Whosoever can receive and retain this teaching, study it, recite it and spread it abroad will be clearly perceived and recognised by the Tathagata and will achieve a perfection of merit beyond measurement or calculation — a perfection of merit unlimited and inconceivable.

In every case such a one will exemplify the Tathagata Consummation of the Incomparable Enlightenment. Wherefore? Because, Subhuti, those who find consolation in limited doctrines involving the conception of an egoentity, a personality, a being, or a separated individuality are unable to accept, receive, study, recite and openly explain this Discourse.

Subhuti, in every place where this Discourse is to be found the whole realms of Gods, Men and Titans should offer worship; for you must know that such a place is sanctified like a shrine, and should properly be venerated by all with ceremonial obeisance and circumambulation and with offerings of flowers and incense.

Section XVI: Purgation Through Suffering The Retribution For Past Sins: Furthermore, Subhuti, if it be that good men and good women who receive and retain this Discourse are downtrodden, their evil destiny is the inevitable retributive result of sins committed in their past mortal lives. By virtue of their present misfortunes the reacting effects of their past will be thereby worked out, and they will be in a position to attain the Consummation of Incomparable Enlightenment.

Subhuti, I remember the infinitely remote past before Dipankara Buddha. There were 84,000 myriads of multimillions of Buddhas and to all these I made offerings; yes, all these I served without the least trace of fault. Nevertheless, if anyone is able to receive, retain, study and recite this Discourse at the end of the last (500-year) period, he will gain such a merit that mine in the service of all the Buddhas could not be reckoned as one-hundredth part of it, not even one thousand myriad multi millionth part of it—indeed, no such comparison is possible.

Subhuti, if I fully detailed the merit gained by good men and good women coming to receive, retain, study and recite this Discourse in the last period, my hearers would be filled with doubt and might become disordered in mind, suspicious and unbelieving. You should know, Subhuti, that the significance of this Discourse is beyond conception; likewise the fruit of its rewards is beyond conception.

Section XVII: No One Attains Transcendental Wisdom: At that time Subhuti addressed Buddha, saying: World-honoured One, if good men and good women seek the Consummation of Incomparable Enlightenment, by what criteria should they abide and how should they control their thoughts?

Buddha replied to Subhuti: Good men and good women seeking the Consummation of Incomparable Enlightenment must create this resolved attitude of mind: I must liberate all living beings, yet when all have been liberated, verily not any one is liberated. Wherefore? If a Bodhisattva cherishes the idea of an egoentity, a personality, a being, or a separated individuality, he is consequently not a Bodhisattva, Subhuti. This is because in reality there is no formula which gives rise to the Consummation of Incomparable Enlightenment.

Subhuti, what do you think? When the Tathagata was with Dipankara Buddha was there any formula for the attainment of the Consummation of Incomparable Enlightenment?

No, World-honoured One, as I understand Buddha's meaning, there was no formula by which the Tathagata attained the Consummation of Incomparable Enlightenment.

Buddha said: You are right, Subhuti! Verily there was no formula by which the Tathagata attained the Consummation of Incomparable Enlightenment. Subhuti, had there been any such formula, Dipankara Buddha would not have predicted concerning me: "In the ages of the future you will come to be a Buddha called Shakyamuni"; but Dipankara Buddha made that prediction concerning me because there is actually no formula for the attainment of the Consummation of Incomparable Enlightenment.

The reason herein is that Tathagata is a signification implying all formulas. In case anyone says that the Tathagata attained the Consummation of Incomparable Enlightenment, I tell you truly, Subhuti, that there is no formula by which the Buddha attained it.

Subhuti, the basis of Tathagata's attainment of the Consummation of Incomparable Enlightenment is wholly beyond; it is neither real nor unreal. Hence, I say that the whole realm of formulations is not really such, therefore it is called "Realm of formulations." Subhuti, a comparison may be made with [the idea of] a gigantic human frame.

Then Subhuti said: The World-honoured One has declared that such is not a great body; "a great body" is just the name given to it.

Subhuti, it is the same concerning Bodhisattvas. If a Bodhisattva announces: I will liberate all living creatures, he is not rightly called a Bodhisattva. Wherefore? Because, Subhuti, there is really no such condition as that called Bodhisattvaship, because Buddha teaches that all things are devoid of selfhood, devoid of separate individuality.

Subhuti, if a Bodhisattva announces: I will set forth majestic Buddhalands, one does not call him a Bodhisattva, because the Tathagata has declared that the setting forth of majestic Buddhalands is not really such: "a majestic setting forth" is just the name given to it. Subhuti, Bodhisattvas who are wholly devoid of any conception of separate selfhood are truthfully called Bodhisattvas.

Section XVIII: All Modes of Mind are Really Only Mind: Subhuti, what do you think? Does the Tathagata possess the human eye?

Yes, World-honoured One, He does.

Well, do you think the Tathagata possesses the divine eye?

Yes, World-honoured One, He does.

And do you think the Tathagata possesses the gnostic eye?

Yes, World-honoured One, He does.

And do you think the Tathagata possesses the eye of transcendent wisdom? Yes,

World-honoured One, He does.

And do you think the Tathagata possesses the Buddha-eye of omniscience?

Yes, World-honoured One, He does.

Subhuti, what do you think? Concerning the sand-grains of the Ganges, has the Buddha taught about them?

Yes, World-honoured One, the Tathagata has taught concerning these grains.

Well, Subhuti, if there were as many Ganges rivers as the sand-grains of the Ganges and there was a Buddha-land for each sand-grain in all those Ganges rivers, would those Buddhalands be many?

[Subhuti replied]: Many indeed, World-honoured One!

Then Buddha said: Subhuti, however many living beings there are in all those Buddhalands, though they have manifold modes of mind, the Tathagata understands them all. Wherefore? Because the Tathagata teaches that all these are not Mind; they are merely called "mind".

Subhuti, it is impossible to retain past mind, impossible to hold on to present mind, and impossible to grasp future mind.

Section XIX: Absolute Reality is the Only Foundation: Subhuti, what do you think? If anyone filled three thousand galaxies of worlds with the seven treasures and gave all away in gifts of alms, would he gain great merit?

Yes, indeed, World-honoured One, he would gain great merit!

Subhuti, if such merit was Real, the Tathagata would not have declared it to be great, but because it is without a foundation the Tathagata characterised it as "great."

Section XX: The Unreality of Phenomenal Distinctions: Subhuti, what do you think? Can the Buddha be perceived by His perfectly-formed body? No, World-honoured One, the Tathagata cannot be perceived by His perfectly-formed body, because the Tathagata teaches that a perfectly-formed body is not really such; it is merely called "a perfectly-formed body."

Subhuti, what do you think? Can the Tathagata be perceived by means of any phenomenal characteristic? No, World-honoured One, the Tathagata may not be perceived by any phenomenal characteristic, because the Tathagata teaches that phenomenal characteristics are not really such; they are merely termed "phenomenal characteristics."

Section XXI: Words cannot Express Truth. That Which Words Express is not Truth: Subhuti, do not say that the Tathagata conceives the idea: I must set forth a Teaching. For if anyone says that the Tathagata sets forth a Teaching he really slanders Buddha and is unable to explain what I teach. As to any Truth-declaring system, Truth is undeclarable; so "an enunciation of Truth" is just the name given to it.

Thereupon, Subhuti spoke these words to Buddha: World-honoured One, in the ages of the future will there be men coming to hear a declaration of this Teaching who will be inspired with belief?

And Buddha answered: Subhuti, those to whom you refer are neither living beings nor not-living beings. Wherefore? Because "living beings," Subhuti, these "living beings" are not really such; they are just called by that name.

Section XXII: It cannot be said that Anything is Attainable: Then Subhuti asked Buddha: World-honoured One, in the attainment of the Consummation of Incomparable Enlightenment did Buddha make no acquisition whatsoever?

Buddha replied: Just so, Subhuti. Through the Consummation of Incomparable Enlightenment I acquired not even the least thing; therefore it is called "Consummation of Incomparable Enlightenment."

Section XXIII: The Practice of Good Works Purifies the Mind: Furthermore, Subhuti, This is altogether everywhere, without differentiation or degree; therefore it is called "Consummation of Incomparable Enlightenment." It is straightly attained by freedom from separate personal selfhood and by cultivating all kinds of goodness. Subhuti, though we speak of "goodness", the Tathagata declares that there is no goodness; such is merely a name.

Section XXIV: The Incomparable Merit of this Teaching: Subhuti, if there be one who gives away in gifts of alms a mass of the seven treasures equal in extent to as many mighty Mount Sumerus as there would be in three thousand galaxies of worlds, and if there be another who selects even only four lines from this Discourse upon the Perfection of Transcendental Wisdom, receives and retains them, and clearly expounds them to others, the merit of the latter will be so far greater than that of the former that no conceivable comparison can be made between them.

Section XXV: The Illusion of Ego: Subhuti, what do you think? Let no one say the Tathagata cherishes the idea: I must liberate all living beings. Allow no such thought, Subhuti. Wherefore? Because in reality there are no living beings to be liberated by the Tathagata. If there were living beings for the Tathagata to liberate, He would partake in the idea of selfhood, personality entity, and separate individuality.

Subhuti, though the common people accept egoity as real, the Tathagata declares that ego is not different from non-ego. Subhuti, those whom the Tathagata referred to as "common people" are not really common people; such is merely a name.

Section XXVII: It is Erroneous to Affirm that all Things are Ever Extinguished: Subhuti, if you should conceive the idea that the Tathagata attained the Consummation of Incomparable Enlightenment by reason of His perfect form, do not countenance such thoughts.

The Tathagata's attainment was not by reason of His perfect form. [On the other hand] Subhuti, if you should conceive the idea that anyone in whom dawns the Consummation of Incomparable Enlightenment declares that all manifest standards are ended and extinguished, do not countenance such thoughts. Wherefore? Because the man in whom the Consummation of Incomparable Enlightenment dawns does not affirm concerning any formula that it is finally extinguished.

Section XXVIII: Attachment to Rewards of Merit: Subhuti, if one Bodhisattva bestows in charity sufficient of the seven treasures to fill as many worlds as there are sandgrains in the river Ganges, and another, realising that all things are egoless, attains perfection through patient forbearance, the merit of the latter will far exceed that of the former. Why is this, Subhuti? It is because all Bodhisattvas are insentient as to the rewards of merit.

Then Subhuti said to Buddha: What is this saying, World-honoured One, that Bodhisattvas are insentient as to rewards of merit?

[And Buddha answered]: Subhuti, Bodhisattvas who achieve merit should not be fettered with desire for rewards. Thus, it is said that the rewards of merit are not received.

Section XXIX: Perfect Tranquillity: Subhuti, if anyone should say that the Tathagata comes or goes or sits or reclines, he fails to understand my teaching. Why? Because TATHAGATA has neither whence nor whither, therefore is He called "Tathagata".

Section XXX: The Integral Principle: Subhuti, if a good man or a good woman ground an infinite number of galaxies of worlds to dust, would the resulting minute particles be many?

Subhuti replied: Many indeed, World-honoured One! Wherefore? Because if such were really minute particles Buddha would not have spoken of them as minute particles. For as to this, Buddha has declared that they are not really such. "Minute particles" is just the name given to them. Also, World-honoured One, when the Tathagata speaks of galaxies of worlds, these are not worlds; for if reality could be predicated of a world it would be a self-existent cosmos and the Tathagata teaches that there is really no such thing. "Cosmos" is merely a figure of speech.

[Then Buddha said]: Subhuti, words cannot explain the real nature of a cosmos.

Only common people fettered with desire make use of this arbitrary method.

Section XXXI: Conventional Truth Should be Cut off: Subhuti, if anyone should say that Buddha declares any conception of egoity do you consider he would understand my teaching correctly? No, World-honoured One, such a man would not have any sound understanding of the Tathagata's teaching, because the World-honoured One declares that notions of selfhood, personality, entity and separate individuality, as really existing, are erroneous - these terms are merely figures of speech.

[Thereupon Buddha said]: Subhuti, those who aspire to the Consummation of Incomparable Enlightenment should recognise and understand all varieties of things in the same way and cut off the arising of [views which are mere] aspects.

Subhuti, as regards aspects, the Tathagata declares that in reality they are not such. They are called "aspects".

Section XXXII: The Delusion of Appearances: Subhuti, someone might fill innumerable worlds with the seven treasures and give all away in gifts of alms, but if any good man or any good woman awakens the thought of Enlightenment and takes even only four lines from this Discourse, reciting, using, receiving, retaining and spreading them abroad and explaining them for the benefit of others, it will be far more meritorious.

Now in what manner may he explain them to others? By detachment from appearances — abiding in Real Truth. So I tell you — Thus, shall ye think of all this fleeting world: A star at dawn, a bubble in a stream; A flash of lightning in a summer cloud, A flickering lamp, a phantom, and a dream. When the Buddha finished this Discourse the venerable Subhuti, together with the bhikshus, bhikshunis, lay-brothers and sisters, and the whole realms of Gods, Men and Titans, were filled with joy by His teaching, and, taking it sincerely to heart, they went their ways.

Dhammapada Discourses

The Dhammapada, an anthology of 423 verses, has long been recognised as one of the masterpieces of early Buddhist literature. From ancient times to the present, the Dhammapada has been regarded as the most succinct expression of the Buddha's teaching found in the Theravada Pali Canon of scriptures known as the Khuddaka Nikaya (Minor Collection) of the Sutra Pitaka.

Buddhist tradition has it that shortly after the passing away of the Buddha his disciples met in council at Rajagriha for the purpose of recalling to mind the truths they had received from their beloved Teacher during the forty-five years of his ministry. Their hope was to implant the principles of his message so firmly in memory that they would become a lasting impetus to moral and spiritual conduct, for themselves, their disciples, and for all future disciples who would seek to follow in the footsteps of the Awakened One.

With the Teacher no longer among them, the monks found themselves with the responsibility of handing on the teaching as faithfully as possible. Having no written texts to rely on, they did as their ancestors had before them and prepared their discourses for recitation, that is, basic themes were repeated with variations in order to impress the ideas on their hearers. At that time, according to the Sinhalese, the Dhammapada was orally assembled from the sayings of Gautam given on some three hundred different occasions.

Subsequently, several renditions of the Dhammapada in the Sanskrit and Chinese languages came into circulation. Likewise, a number of stanzas are to be found almost verbatim in other texts of the canonical literature, testifying to the esteem in which its content was anciently held. Since first collated, the Dhammapada has become one of the best loved of Buddhist scriptures, recited daily by millions of devotees who chant its verses in Pali or in their native dialect.

It was inevitable that differences in interpretation of teaching as well as of disciplinary practices would arise, with the result that about a century after the First Council was held a second gathering was called to affirm the purity of the doctrine. It was at this Second Council that the Arhats divided into two main streams, namely, the Mahasanghika or "Great Assembly" and the Theravada or "Doctrine of Elders."

These gradually developed into the Mahayana or Northern School of Buddhism espoused chiefly in India, Tibet, China, and later Japan, and the Hinayana or Southern School whose stronghold is Sri Lanka, Burma, and the countries of Southeast Asia.

Message of Peace

They call it a message of peace and harmonious coexistence from ancient India to the modern world. An exhibition on the Lotus Sutra, believed to be a record of Gautam Buddha's teachings towards the end of his life and been transcribed between the first and second century CE, is on at Ravindra Natya Mandir, Prabhadevi, in the city.

The exhibition — comprising a collection of artefacts, calligraphic and pictorial representations of the transcriptions, including historic originals and reproductions from India, Nepal, China and Japan — has already travelled to Japan, Singapore, Hong Kong, Laos, Delhi, Chennai, Bangalore and Kolkata. This is its first appearance in the city.

The teachings have also been translated into a number of non-Asian languages such as German, Italian and Greek. "When I think about how many Buddhists must have endured tremendous adversities to protect and transmit the Lotus Sutra over countless centuries, I could not help but think that they looked happy to have survived the trials and tribulations and to be able to meet with so many people," says Dr. Daisaku Ikeda, president of exhibition organisers Soka Gakkai International. "The Lotus Sutra is an effort to develop a means for the contemporary society to confront the rampant suffering of our age and to make the social and cultural diversity of our world a source of creativity and joy for all."

One of the exhibition's main sections is devoted to the Chinese Mogao Cave paintings that depict famous scenes in the Lotus Sutra. "Each painting portrays the Lotus Sutra's key messages to humanity such as the sanctity of life, women's rights, the power of the people and the eternity of life, among others."

The inauguration ceremony on Friday was attended by Mumbai Sheriff Indu Shahani and National Gallery of Modern Art director Dr. Saryu V Doshi. Performances by children on some of the parables on display were a highlight of the ceremony. The exhibition, co-hosted by The Institute of Oriental Philosophy, will be on till September 21.

Four Noble Truths

Introduction

The teachings on the four noble truths are among the very first of many teachings that Shakyamuni Buddha gave in Sarnath (near Banaras or Varanasi in North-East India), seven weeks after attaining enlightenment in Bodh Gaya. These teachings are known to contain the essence of the Buddhist path, regardless of the tradition one follows.

The Suffering

According to the Buddha, whatever life we lead, it has the nature of some aspect of suffering. Even if we consider ourselves happy for a while, this happiness is transitory by nature. This mean that at best, we can only find temporary happiness and pleasure in life.

Suffering (or unsatisfactoriness) can be distinguished in three types:

- Suffering of suffering: this refers to the most obvious aspects like pain, fear and mental distress.
- Suffering of change: refers to the problems that change brings, like joy disappears, nothing stays, decay and death.
- All-pervasive suffering: this is the most difficult to understand aspect, it refers to the fact that we always have the potential to suffer or can get into problematic situations. Even death is not a solution in Buddhist philosophy, as we will simply find ourselves being reborn in a different body, which will also experience problems.

To illustrate this with the words of the 7th Dalai Lama (from 'Songs of spiritual change' translated by Glenn Mullin:

"Hundreds of stupid flies gather
On a piece of rotten meat,
Enjoying, they think, a delicious feast.
This image fits with the song
Of the myriads of foolish living beings
Who seek happiness in superficial pleasures;
In countless ways they try,
Yet I have never seen them satisfied."

Note that "suffering" is an inadequate translation of the word "Dukkha", but it is the one most commonly found, lacking a better word in English. "Dukkha" means "intolerable", "unsustainable", "difficult to endure", and can also mean "imperfect", "unsatisfying", or "incapable of providing perfect happiness". Interestingly enough, some people actually translate it as "stress".

"Suffering is a big word in Buddhist thought. It is a key term and it should be thoroughly understood. The Pali word is dukkha, and it does not just mean the agony of the body. It means that deep subtle sense of unsatisfactoriness which is a part of every mind moment and which results directly from the mental treadmill.

The essence of life is suffering, said the Buddha. At first glance this seems exceedingly morbid and pessimistic. It even seems untrue. After all, there are plenty of times when we are happy. Aren't there. No, there are not. It just seems that way. Take any moment when you feel really fulfilled and examine it closely. Down under the joy, you will find that subtle, all-pervasive undercurrent of tension, that no matter how great this moment is, it is going to end. No matter how much you just gained, you are either going to lose some of it or spend the rest of your days guarding what you have got and scheming how to get more. And in the end, you are going to die. In the end, you lose everything. It is all transitory."

Causes of Suffering

The reason that we experience suffering comes ultimately from our mind. According to Buddhism, our main mental problems or root delusions are: attachment, anger and ignorance. Because of these delusions, we engage in actions that cause problems to ourselves and others. With every negative action (karma) we do, we create a potential for negative experiences.

How can attachment bring us suffering?

We just have to think of chocolate and there is the temptation of eating more than is good for us. Or as example, my favourite story: the way people used to catch monkeys in South India:

One takes a coconut and makes a hole in it, just large enough that a monkey can squeeze its hand in. Next, tie the coconut down, and put a sweet inside. What happens next is pure attachment. The monkey smells the sweet, puts his hand into the coconut, grabs the sweet and... the hole is too small to let a fist out of the coconut. The last thing a monkey would consider is to let go of the sweet, so it is literally tied down by its own attachment. Often they only let go when they fall asleep or become unconscious because of exhaustion.

Ultimately, the Buddha explains that our attachment to life keeps us in cyclic existence or samsara, which does not bring us continuous happiness.

How can anger bring us suffering?

As will be explained in the page on karma, all of our actions have consequences. Doing harm to others will return to us as being harmed. Anger is one of the main reasons we create harm to others, so logically it is often the cause of suffering to ourselves.

How can ignorance bring us suffering?

This is explained in two ways:

> "The conventional explanation is that because we are not omniscient, we regularly get ourselves into trouble. We do not realise all the consequences of our actions, we do not understand other beings and we do not understand why the world is exactly the way it is. So we often end up in situations where we do not take the best actions. Just reflect for a moment how often we think: "If only I had known this earlier..."

The more complicated explanation refers to the most profound aspect of Buddhist philosophy: *ultimate truth* or *emptiness.* This is a vast subject, and also after reading the page on wisdom it is still unlikely that it will be completely clear; it takes years of study and meditation to realise the insight into the wisdom of emptiness. To put it very simple: reality is not what it seems to us. As reality is different from our opinions about it, we get ourselves into trouble. As long as we fail to realise the ultimate truth, we will be stuck in cyclic existence. While being in cyclic existence, we will always experience some aspect of suffering (which is at least having the potential for future suffering).

Suffering can End, Nirvana is Peace

This is the most positive message of Buddhism: although suffering is always present in cyclic existence, we can end this cycle of problems and pain, and enter *Nirvana,* which is a state beyond all suffering.

The reasoning behind this Third Noble Truth is the fact that suffering and the causes of suffering are dependent on the state of our own mind, so if we can change our own mind, we can also eliminate suffering. The reasons we do actions that cause ourselves and others harm come from our delusions. When we possess the proper wisdom (conventional and ultimate), we can rid ourselves of delusions, and thus of all our problems and suffering. When this process is complete, we can leave cyclic existence and enjoy the state of Nirvana, free of problems.

The reasoning so far is simple enough, when we are ill, we go to a doctor. He knows (hopefully) what is wrong and prescribes medicines and gives us advice, which we need to take and follow up to get well again. Likewise, when a spiritual teacher prescribes us a practice and the development of wisdom to end our suffering, we still need to follow the instructions, otherwise there will be no effect. That leads us to the last Noble Truth of the Path of the 'medicine'.

True Path or Eightfold Noble Path

If we can control our body and mind in a way that we help others instead of doing them harm, and generating wisdom in our own mind, we can end our suffering and problems.

Buddha and Language

Language is one of the most fundamental features of human culture, some would say the most fundamentally important. The use of language distinguishes man, as a biological genus, from other animals. No other animals have yet been shown to possess articulate speech as we know it in men, no doubt many animals succeed in communicating with each other in limited ways by the use of vocal sounds, but in spite of the efforts of many able biologists, no one has yet proved that such communication approaches the elaborate conventionalised systems which characterise all known human speech. And conversely, no human group has ever been found which lacked a language in this sense.

In one way, then, language may be said to be a unitary feature characterising all men. But in another sense, which is socially much more important, language divides man from man. For no two languages, no two dialects of the same language even, are exactly alike. And language differences are very noticeable. The most naive human being quickly becomes aware of them, though it usually does not occur to him to formulate them, and if pressed, he would often find it hard to do so. If he hears speech in a language so remote from his experience that he cannot understand it, his first reaction may be that the alien speaker cannot really talk at all. The Russian word for Germans means literally "dumb, people who can't talk" — that is, can't talk Russian. There are many similar instances. If the alien speaker uses a dialect closely related to the hearer's own, then, while the hearer may understand perfectly or nearly so, he may be more or less surprised, and his surprise may be tinged with amusement or scorn; the speaker may seem to him to be strangely ignorant of the "proper" way of talking. There are countries where only one language is spoken, but where in the course of time strikingly different dialects of that language have developed. It often happens then that one such dialect acquires superior social prestige, most commonly for political reasons, it is often the language of the capital. This becomes the "standard" language of the country, like standard Southern British, or standard French (originally local to Pans), and all members of the politically or culturally dominant class speak it; but often many of them can also speak the dialects of their original homes.

A peculiar variant of this situation occurs when the "upper" classes adopt a language of culture which is not the same as any dialect actually spoken (by the uneducated) in the country. It may be a language quite unrelated to any of the country's living dialects, Latin occupied this position in Hungary for centuries, until 1825 Latin was the only language allowed to be spoken in the Hungarian Parliament. In the Roman Catholic Church, wherever it flourishes, Latin even now has a certain vogue, in writing and speech. It is thus used especially when Roman Catholic priests need to communicate with each other but cannot speak or understand each other's vernaculars, for example, when a German and a Spanish priest have occasion to write or speak to one another. A very similar situation exists in India. Most Indians know that when a South Indian pandit, whose native language is Dravidran, communicates with a North Indian pandit, both will naturally write or speak in Sanskrit, which is ordinarily the only language known to both. With this we draw near to the main topic of this paper. The general historic position in India of Sanskrit as a literary and religious language is so well known to Indian readers, and to most others who are likely to see this article, that I shall not discuss it. What interests me litre is its relation, and the relation of linguistic usage in general, to Buddhism, and to the Buddha himself.

Two monks, brothers, of fine (cultivated)· language and fine (eloquent) speech, came to the Buddha and said. Lord, here monks of miscellaneous origin (literally, of various names, clan-names, races or castes, and families) are corrupting the Buddha's words by (repeating them in) their own dialects, let us put them into Vedic *(chandaso aropema).*

The Lord Buddha rebuked them: Deluded men, how can you say this? This will not lead to the conversion of the unconverted. And he delivered a sermon and commanded (all) the monks. *You ate* not *to* put the Buddha's words into Vedic. Who does so would commit a sin. I authorise you, monks, to learn the Buddha's words each in his own dialect.

This incident is certainly a part of the oldest Buddhist tradition, for very similar accounts are found in a number of Chinese translations of the Buddhist canonical works. They are fully presented in French translations by Lin Li-kouang, L'*aide-memoire de la vraie loi.*

Several facts of considerable interest emerge from a study of the various forms of this ancient passage.

First: Dialect differences were clearly and easily preceptible in the speech of the monks who attended the Buddha. It is said, in a Chinese translation, that "their pronunciations are not the same."

Second: Many, doubtless most of these monks spoke Middle Indic dialects. There were some, particularly born Brahmins, who knew and could use the sacred language of Brahminism; but it may perhaps be assumed that even they, when not speaking to one another, made use of Middle Indic. In one of the Chinese translations the two originally Brahmin monks complain that their fellow-monks "do not know masculine and feminine gender, nor singular and plural, nor present, past, and future, nor long and shore vowels, nor metrically light and heavy syllables." Such traits of language, which seemed errors to the Brahmins, characterise some Middle Indic dialects as they would appear from the standpoint of Sanskrit, when compared with it'.

Third: When proposing to codify the Buddha's teachings in their own "cultured" language, the two Brahmin monks say *chandaso aropema,* which certainly means "let us put (them) into Vedic." Some have understood, "into verse". But this makes no sense in the context; it is clearly not verse as contrasted with prose, but a different *language,* which they wish to use. The word *chandas* is regularly used by Panini when he notes a Vedic usage that differs from his own Sanskrit; he always says *chandasi,* "in the Veda" (such and such a form is used). This use of *chandas is* also familiar in epic and classical Sanskrit literature. Here *chandas* need not refer to the poetic parts of the Veda alone, and it is not at all likely that it was so intended. The Brahmins and Upanishads, which are mainly prose, are classed is parts of the Veda, that is *chandas.* The language of the Upanishads, even the oldest of them like *Brhar-nyaka* and *Chandogya, is* fairly close to classical Sanskrit; but it could still be called linguistically *chandas* "Vedic". It was probably something like this language that the Brahmin monks wanted to use. It may, of course, have been even closer to Paninean Sanskrit;. We have no way of telling. But no such term as "Sanskrit" is used in the Pali text, nor even in the commentaries on it, indeed, the Pall equivalent (Samkhata) of the word Samskrta seems never to be used in a linguistic sense Nor do the Chinese translators use any word which proves that their Indic originals used that word. Panini's date is still uncertain, and it is at least possible that he was later than the Buddha. In any event, the use of the word Samskrta of the Sanskrit language seems to be relatively late. The high, cultivated language of Brahmins, into which the two monks wanted to translate the Buddha's teachings was known to them as "Vedic" *(chandas), in* contrast with the Middle Indic dialects which were used by most of their brother-monks, some Middle Indic dialect was doubtless used by the Buddha himself.

Fourth: The Buddha emphatically rejected the proposal of the Brahmin monks, and gave orders that all monks should learn and repeat his teachings in their own several dialects. This clearly implies that when the Buddhist gospel was carried by missionaries into new regions, the converses were to exercise the same privilege. They were to learn and recite the teachings in their own local dialects. This is very definitely stated in several of the Chinese translations, which command use of "the popular language" of the various regions or countries. And all versions of this passage, northern and southern, make very clear the Buddha's reason for this injunction. He was preaching a gospel for all men, not for a select elite. He wanted to be sure that every human being could understand his message. He felt that his aim would be defeated if his words were codified in a learned, literary language (Vedic) which only the upper classes could understand.

At first, it seems clear that Buddhist monks and missionaries obeyed this injunction. Early Buddhist inscriptions, like those of Bharhut, give evidence of this. Wherever Buddhist communities were established, versions of the sacred texts, or some of them, were recited in the local vernaculars. In one or two cases, extensive local canons of this sort, or parts of them, in Middle Indic vernaculars, have survived to this day. The best known is the Pali canon; it originated somewhere in west-central India. We may be certain that there were many others, but most of them have been lost.

As long as Buddhism spread only in the northern parts of India the use of local vernaculars can hardly have involved mulling like what we should call "translation". In the Buddha's time, the popular dialects of those regions were almost exclusively Indo-Aryan, and chiefly in the Middle Indic stage. They must also at that time have been so close to each other as to be mutually intelligible. A Buddhist missionary could recite the texts in his own vernacular, and his hearers would repeat them in theirs, perhaps without even clearly apprehending the linguistic differences. (But it is quite possible, also, that the dialect of the missionary may at times have been imitated, to some extent, by the local converts, consciously or unconsciously) Translation cannot has become a serious problem until Buddhism spread to Dravidian-speaking regions in the south, and to extra-Indian countries like Chinese Turkestan, Tibet and China. However, after a few centuries the Buddha's followers in India, and in some adjoining countries, began to ignore his injunction to clothe his teachings only in genuine, popular vernaculars. Instead they began to make use of canons composed in learned languages, which were not, or no longer, the native dialects of any people. Pali itself was originally based on a north Indian vernacular, but after But must monks carried the Pali canon to Ceylon, Burma, Siam, and Cambodia, it came to be a church language, like Latin in Europe. It had to be learned in school, and is still so learned in southern Buddhist careatries. In India itself, or in some puts of it, what happened was different.

The great social prestige of Sanskrit, as a language of literature and culture among brahminical Hindus, began to influence their Buddhist neighbours and associates. Like the two learned monks in the old Vimya story, later Buddhists felt that it would be more dignified if they imitated the Brahmins and Sanskritised their compositions. Some of them—the poet Ashvaghosha is an example—frankly abandoned the use of vernaculars in literary works, and used standard Sanskrit as a vehicle Ashvaghosha is believed to have been a Brahmin himself originally, and to have undergone the usual brahminical Sanskrit education in his youth.

A different and a very curious course was adopted by one group of Buddhists. Instead of completely giving up the literary use of vetnaculars, they took an old Middle Indic dialect (its original locale is unknown to us) in which Buddhist texts existed, and partially Sanskritised it, but so imperfectly that the underlying Middle Indic still showed through the half-veneer of Sanskrit.

It has often been described as a corrupt or bad Sanskrit, but this distorts the truth. It is a blend of Middle India with Sanskrit, but its basis, or substratum, is Middle India, the Sanskrit features are secondarily and superficially laid on.

To be sure, as time went on, this Sanskritising process was carried further and further. In the oldest texts preserved to us, notably the *M. hastan*, middle India or hybridised phonology and grammatical forms are still very abundant, though genuine Sanskrit forms are perhaps equally so In later times, more and more regular Sanskrit forms appear. Often these replace original Middle Indic or hybrid forms in later versions of the same passages, so that we can see the presses of Sanskritisation going on before our eyes. The latest works of this tradition came to look superficially like almost standard Sanskrit, though careful study will always reveal some Middle India forms. But even the latest Buddhist Hybrid Sanskrit texts still retain numerous words, lexical items, which show their vernacular origin. Though they may be made to look like Sanskrit, though their phonetic shape and grammatical formations may be perfectly standard Sanskrit, these items of vocabulary never occur in Sanskrit, or never in" the same meanings, whereas they do occur (for the most part) in Middle Indic dialects, especially Pali. They thus prove that they belong to the Hybrid tradition, going back ultimately to Middle Indic, in spite of their seeming Sanskrit guise.

Thus the Buddha's desire that his teachings be couched in the native dialects of all peoples was frustrated, at least in his native land. It would not have consoled him to know it, but there ensued one result of interest to linguists—the development of a strange, artificial, literary language, perhaps unique in its nature—Buddhist Hybrid Sanskrit.

Pali 'Maraji': Sanskrit 'Smarajit'

Gautam Shakya became 'Buddha' (The Awakened) after having defeated Mara and his host. In Buddhist literature and tradition Mara is the demigod of temptation and evil and therefore of Death. The word is generally accepted as a derivation of the root *mr* 'to die'. This appears to be only folk-etymology as Mara does not strictly conform to the Indian idea of the god or the demon of Death.

Mara is essentially a tempter, and the most powerful of his host are the nymphs that excite passion which is fatal to the meditation of a man on the spiritual path. The most obvious derivation is from the root *smr* 'to remember, to remember longingly, to desire company, to desire lustfully'. 'Mara' therefore comes from an older form *smara* (for the loss of the initial sibilant compare Middle Indo-Aryan 'neha' from *sneba,* and Sanskrit *candra, tayu, tara, pasyati* from historical *scandra, staya, stara, spasyati* respectively) which is a close cognate of Sanskrit *smara* 'sexual love (abstract or personified), god of love'. *Smara* first occurs in *Atharvaveda* where three hymns are devoted to sexual love personified. The first verse of the first of these hymns is quoted below. It shows that 'Smara' of Atharvaveda not only is akin to both 'Mara' of Buddhist literature and 'Smara' of Sanskrit literature but appears to be their source. *ratbajitam rathajiteyinam apsarasam smarab devab pa biouta smaram asan mam anu socatu.*

'This is Sexual Love *(smara)* of the *Ratbajits* (Conquerors of Chariot-riding Warriors, or Fighters Riding Chariots) and of the nymphs belonging to the *Ratbajits.* 0 Gods, send Sexual Love to that man (so that) he would long for me'.

The word mara signifying 'physical love' and 'god of love' is not unknown in Sanskrit literature. The earliest occurrence is in *Harivamsa (vide* Monier-Williams' Dictionary).

or

As conquers of physical love and temptation there is a close agreement between the Buddha and Shiva. Both were the targets of Mara/Smara when engaged in meditation and penance. Gautam Shakya remained unmoved and he ultimately emerged as the vigilant awakened *(Buddha, prabuddha* or *pratibuddha)* conqueror of Mara. Shiva was moved only for a moment and his wrath put Smara to ashes.

It is not unlikely that the two stones are ultimately connected. There is a basic connection between spiritual penance *(tapasya)* and subjugation of passion. At least there is no possibility of the story *of* Shiva having been modelled after the story of the Buddha or *vice versa.*

The story of the destruction of the god of love *(Smara, Madana)* by Shiva ultimately goes back to a Vedic origin. *Satapatha Brabmana* narrates a story which tells us of Rudra's terrible anger "against Prajapati when the latter had contemplated incest with his daughter.

Prajipatir ha vai svam dubitaram abbidadhyan divam vosasam va mitbunyenaya syam the tam sambabhiiva tad van devanam aga asa ya ittbam svam dubitaram esmelam svasaram karotiti, te ba deva ucub yo' yam devab pasunam iste 'trsamdham vayam carat' ya ittbam svam dubitaram asmakam karott vidbyemam its, tam radro 'bbyayatya vruyadba... The creator had desire for his own daughter, Day or Dawn, "I would pair with her", and he paired with her. This appeared as a sin to the gods (who thought,) "He is thus behaving with his own daughter, our sister!" The gods spoke to the god that ruled over the beats, "He is committing an act of transgression as he is behaving thus with his own daughter, and our sister. Do smite him." Rudra charged and smote him.

6

Buddhism in Indian Thought

It is rather striking that the early Pali texts and even later Buddhist Sanskrit texts do not breathe a word about the Upanishads and the Upanishadic philosophers, although there are repeated references to the teachings of the six teachers, Purana Kassapa, Ajita Kesakambalin, Pakudha Kaccayana, Sanjaya Belatthiputta, Makhali Gosala and Nigantha Nataputta. Incidentally in the Pali texts there is also mention of the Vedic *sakhas,* viz., Addhariya, Bahvrija, Chandoka, and Tiatiriya and Vedic seers, Atthaka, Vamaka, Vamadeva, and others who are said to have taught mainly *Brahma-sahavyata* or the attainment of Brahmaloka, supposed to be the highest form of existence.

In the sixty two views envisaged in the *Brabmajalasutta,* there are criticisms of the belief in the existence of a self and of its transmigration from one existence to another. This criticism is elaborated in later Mahayana texts particularly in that of Nagarjuna. In the Pali *Nikayas* there are several discourses of a stereotyped nature discussing the problem whether the soul is identical with the body or not, and the conclusion drawn is that there cannot arise any question of the existence or non-existence of soul, as from the Buddhist point of view it has no more existence than that of the son of a barren woman or that of a flower in the sky. Hence, it is an indeterminable problem *(avyakata)* to be left aside *(thapaniya).*

The fundamental query of almost all the *Upanishads is* the nature of soul and its transmigration from one existence to another. It seems that Buddha deliberately ignored the *Upanishads* as in them the existence of soul is taken for granted while his main thesis was the total denial of the existence of this soul *(anatta)* and through all his philosophical discourses he tried to establish that there could not exist any permanent self unalloyed by worldly impurities. Hence, it is idle to say that Buddhism issued out of the *Upanishads* and was a phase in the evolution of Upanishadic thought.

On the other hand, it may be stated that Buddhism was a revolt against the Upanishadic thought and it was this denial of soul, which undermined the belief in the efficacy of the sacrificial rituals and ceremonies. The three primary conditions which make one a true Buddhist is the elimination of the belief in the existence of a self *(sakkayadittbi)* and in the efficacy of rituals *(silabba-taparamasa),* to which is to be added the implicit faith in the *Triratna* by discarding all doubts *(vicikiccba)* about their excellence. This revolutionary teaching of Buddha instead of frightening away some of the Brahminic teachers and students, opened up a new vista before their eyes and made them not only staunch supporters but the best exponents of the new teaching.

Buddha subscribed to the theories of *karman* and rebirth but in a way completely different from those of the Upanishadas. The Upanishadic view of *karman is* linked up with the permanent and unchangeable self while Buddha's view was that changing *karman* could never be associated with an unchanging substance like the self. He was a strong advocate of *karman* and its effects and he laid the utmost emphasis on it throughout his teachings. He criticised those teachers who denied or minimised the efficacy of *karman* and it is with this purpose that he discussed the doctrines of the six teachers mentioned above and condemned them in no uncertain terms.

The upholders of *Akiriyavada* were destined to hell—this was his repeated assertion. He elaborated his cosmological ideas of heaven and hell mainly with a view to educate his large number of disciples who were not spiritually advanced and to infuse into them the spirit of doing good deeds and avoiding evils in order to assure a better and happier afterlife. Of the six teachers he made an exception of only one, viz., Nigantha Nataputta, whom he regarded as a *kiriyavadin* and passed over the views of the Agnostic teacher Sanjaya Belatthiputta.

T.R.V. Mum writes in his *Central Philosophy of Buddhism.* "The Upanishads and Buddhism belong to the same spiritual genus, they differ as species, and the differentia are the acceptance or rejection of the *atman.*

The doctrinal views of these six teachers are presented in the. Pali texts thus:

- Purana Kassapa seems to be the oldest teacher and held views wavering between antinomianism and fatalism. His doctrine is that soul remains inactive as in Sankhya and it is the body which acts, hence soul remains unaffected by the results of good and bad deeds of the body. A person earns neither merit by pious acts such as gifts, sacrifices, or by abstinence from evil acts nor demerit by killing, stealing, adultery or speaking falsehood. It is rather difficult to find out exactly what was Purana's views from such cryptic statements, It may mean that the body enjoys or suffers according to its deeds but not the soul, a doctrine which cannot reasonably, be refuted by a Sankhya or a Vedanta schoolman. In Buddhism however soul and body are not admitted as two separate entities, not also as identical. Purana's doctrine is grouped in the Pali texts as an *"Akiriyavada"*, i.e. non-existence of *karmaic* effects.
- Makkhali Gosala, the founder of the Ajivika sect, was at first a follower of Parshvanatha, the traditional founder of Jainism. One day he observed a sprout growing up again after it was trampled down. This changed his outlook and he came to the conclusion that beings were subject to reanimation and not death and destruction. He added to it the doctrine that all beings were subject to a fixed series of existence from the lowliest to the highest and this series was unchangeable *(niyati sangatibhava)* and every existence had its own unalterable characteristic as heat is of fire or coldness of ice. He denied the effects of deeds *(karma)* and energy *(virya).* He upheld fatalism of the extreme type. A being when nearing the end of the several

spans of its lives becomes a human being. Its existence as such is divided into six categories, viz., (i) black *(kanba)* as bird catchers, hunters, fishermen, etc., (ii) blue *(nila)* as ascetics observing rigorous practices, including the Buddhists (Sakyaputtiya Samanas), (iii) red *(lohita)* as monks of the Jaina order, (iv) yellow *(balidda)* as lay-devotees of Acelakas and Ajivikas, (v) white *(sukka)* as Ajivika monks like Nanda, Vaccha and Sankicca, and lastly (vi) very white *(paramasukka)* as Ajivika saints. Buddhaghosa has made an attempt to explain in detail the various states of existence envisaged in Makkhali Gosala's doctrines. In the Jaina literature as also in Tamil works like the *Manimekhalai* of the 4th century AD and *Civanana Cittiyar* of the 14th century, the various states of existence distinguished by colour as black, dark, blue, green, red, golden and white have been dealt with in connection with the doctrines of the Ajivikas. The distinctions made by colour, though not now intelligible, must have been a prominent feature of Ajivikism. It is not unlikely that the term *'niyati'* was introduced into Indian thought by the Ajivikas and it cast a definite influence on the Epics particularly the *Mahabharata.* Manu and compiler of *Hitopadesa* tried to disabuse the minds of the people of this faith in fatalism though Bhartrhari extolled it in his *Nitisataka.* The Ajivikas, it seems, attained great popularity in post-Ashokan age. There is a tradition that King Bindusara consulted Pingalavatsa (Janasana in Pali chronicles) an Ajivika monk for ascertaining which of his two sons, Ashoka and Vitasoka would succeed him to the throne. Ashoka's mother was very likely a follower of the Ajivikas. After Ashoka's demise his grandson Dasaratha dedicated a few caves to the Ajivika saints specially, showing thereby that the successors of Ashoka preferred the Ajivikas to the Buddhists. Dr. Basham has collected reliable evidences to show that this sect became popular in South India and was in existence up to the medieval period

- Nigantha Nataputta (fetterless son of the Naya clan) or Mahavira happened to be an older contemporary of

Buddha. Like Buddha he came of a noble family, perhaps the chief of the clan. He led for some time a married life and then renounced the world. He revived the teachings of Parshvanatha, and formed an order of monks who however led a much more austere life than that of a Buddhist monk. His philosophical views are as follows: There are nine substances *(navatattva),* viz., (i) soul *(jiva)* present in all that is conscious including a tree or a fruit, (ii) non-soul *(ajiva)* which serves as the basis for the functioning of soul *(jiva)* as body is of the soul; (iii) merits and dements *(punya, papa)* which are also substances produced by actions *(karman)* of jiva through mind, speech and body, (v) impurities *(asrava)* which flow into the body due to *karmaic* effects; (vi) self-control *(samvara)* which arrests the flow of *karmaic* effects, and also neutralises them; (vii) bondage *(bandha)* of the soul caused by *karmaic* effects transformed into *asrava* and leading to repeated existence *(samsara),* (viii) elimination *(nirjara)* of *karmaic* effects or *asravas* through *samvara* as prescribed for the Jain monks; and lastly (ix) liberation *(moksha)* attained by a monk who has perfected himself in the disciplinary practices and realised the truth as inculcated in Jain philosophy.

In Jain philosophy no definite statement *(syadvada)* can be made about any object, not even about the highest truth. Every object is subject to three momentary states, viz., origin (*utpada),* continuity *(stbiti)* and decay *(vinasa).* The object in its state of continuity may be regarded as the substance *(dravya)* while in the other two states it is subject to change *(paryaya).* According to *anekantavada* an object is permanent from the standpoint of continuity (*nitya),* but it is impermanent *(anitya)* from the other two standpoints. Every object has to be determined from different standpoints, as it has several aspects and so there can be no absolute statement regarding the nature of an object. This is known as the Jain doctrine of *Anekantavada.* In order to have a true knowledge of an object, its examination is necessary from various aspects and it is by this means alone that the perfect knowledge can be attained. For the sake of practical application, the *Anekantavada* has been condensed into seven members *(saptabhangi)* thus:—From seven different standpoints a being is (i) permanent; (ii) impermanent; (iii) both permanent and impermanent; (iv) indescribable; (v) permanent and indescribable; (vi) impermanent and indescribable; (vii) both permanent and impermanent as also indescribable.

This religion with its great emphasis on asceticism and rigorism imposed on monks and nuns has maintained its existence in India up to the present day. Its lay followers however are limited and still observe many hard and fast rules of self-discipline.

- Sanjaya Belatthiputta did not give out any definite views about the ultimates. He is generally described as a sceptic unwilling to give any definite answer to the ultimate problems, which were, according to him, were indeterminable, a view not incompatible with Buddha's declaration that the problems: whether the soul is identical with body or not, whether an emancipated being exists after death or not, and so forth are also indeterminable *(avyakata)* and should be left aside. Sanjaya happened to be the teacher of Sariputta and Moggallana who joined the Buddhist order along with the other disciples of the teacher and who were much impressed by Buddha's theory of causation, which explained that the beings of the world were in a ceaseless state of flux governed by certain causes and conditions.

- Ajita Kesakambalin was a materialist. He denies an afterlife and *so* according to him there is no need of earning merits by good deeds, sacrifices or service to parents. There is no spiritual advancement or perfection in knowledge likewise. There is no demerit if one commits evil deeds. A being is composed of five elements: earth, water, air, fire and space *(akasha).* After death each of these returns to the corresponding miss of great elements while the senses *(indriyas)* pass into spice. A person's earthly existence ends in the funeral pyre. Nothing survives after death *(bhasmibhutasya debasya punaragamanam kutab).*

This doctrine of Ajita is clearly a restatement of the Lokayata or Barhaspatya school of thought. Dhisana, to whom is attributed this type of doctrine in the *Padma Purana,* asserts that there is no God. The variegated world exists by itself. He admits only four elements and not the fifth *akasha*. The combination of the four elements produces consciousness *(chaitanya)* as liquor is produced by the fermentation of rice and molasses. When everything ends in death, there is no sense in performing sacrifices or in seeking heaven. It was an anti-Vedic movement and established chat a being should seek his own happiness by whatever means he can devise, and not perform acts which are supposed to bring fruits in the next life. It identifies soul with body, a doctrine which has been bitterly criticised by Buddha and closed as annihilationism, i.e., the doctrine that a being disappears for ever with the dissolution of the body.

- Pakudha Kaccayana was a pluralist and a semi-materialist Like Ajita he holds that a being is composed of seven elements: earth, water, air, fire, pleasure *(sukha),* pain *(dukkha)* and soul *(jiva).* These seven elements are neither created nor moulded. They are barren and fixed as a rock or a stone-pillar and do not produce anything. They neither move nor change nor hinder one another so as to cause pain or pleasure or indifference. Hence, there is no killer nor instigator of killing, no heater nor preacher, no learner nor teacher. If a sword passes through the body of a being, it does not destroy it but only slips through the interspaces of the elements forming the body. It is a form of atomism without any parallel. It has been criticised by Buddha as a kind of eternalism *(sassatavada)* and grouped with Ajita's teaching of annihilationism *(uccbedavada),* i.e., everything ends with death.

Besides these six renowned teachers there was another class of religious men known as the Paribhajakas or Wanderers. These moved about all over the country either singly or in groups. There were provisions for their residence called *Paribhajakarama* in important villages and towns. This shows that the Paribhajaka form of life was in vogue in ancient India in the 5th century BC or even earlier. The Paribhajakas could be either Brahminic or non-Brahminic. From their nature of discussions with Buddha it seems that they had no confirmed doctrinal views but not without predilections for either a Brahminic or a particular non-Brahminic system. The problems broached by them with Buddha related to soul, *karman,* efficacy of ascetic practices, elimination of mental impurities, attainment of perfect knowledge, soundness of views of Nigantha Nataputta and so forth. A number of Paribhajakas were impressed by Buddha's teachings and became lay-devotees and a few became full-fledged monks. The Paribhajakas were generally in quest of the Truth and tried to find out what was the best teaching which of course they did not necessarily accept. They may be regarded as students of religion and philosophy with a receptive mind, and some of them ultimately joined a particular religious order or reverted to a householder's life. From the discourses specially delivered to them, as embodied in the *Nikayas,* it appears that they formed an important part of the religious and philosophical movement of ancient India. It is also evident that in those days change of doctrinal views was the rule of the day and there was no slur on a person even if he changed his religious affiliation. Had it not been so, Buddha could not have formed his band of disciples, whom he recruited largely from the Brahminic and Sresthi families and *paribhajakas.*

The Paribhajakas or the Sanghas or Ganas of the six heretical teachers formed a very small section of the religion of ancient India. In spite of Buddha's silence about the *Upanishads* it cannot but be taken for granted that the Upanishadic thinkers held the torch of religion, philosophy and culture in pre-Buddha days. There are at least ten Upanishads, viz., Brhadaranyaka and Chandogya, Aitareya and Taittiriya, Isa, Kena and Katha, Prasna, Mundaka and Mandukya, which are attributed to a date much earlier than Buddha's time. These are mostly compilations of dialogues and monologues of Brahminic seers and not systematic expositions of a particular school of thought. In some of them there are traces of *Samkhya, Yoga* and *Mimamsa* schools of thought but the central theme of most of them is the exposition of the monistic philosophy, well known as *Vedanta,* developed with great subtlety in the two principal Upanishads, *Brhadaranyaka* and *Chandogya*. The oneness of Brahmin or the Reality, and the world as a diversified superimposition on the Reality are the keynotes of this philosophy.

The Sankhya school of philosophy, the origin of which is traced in the *Katha* and *Svetasvatara Upanishads* took a modified Vedantic view. It explains that the appearance of worldly objects is due to ignorance *(avidya)* of the separateness of the two teals, *Purusa* and *Prakrit*. It however held that the appearance of phenomenal world is not wholly baseless or a delusion as the primeval cause *(prakriti)* does undergo a change *(parinami)* and the changed object is substantially the *prakrti*, the change being confined to characteristics *(nimitta)* only of the basic cause *(upadana)*. For this reason it is called *'satkarya-vada* or the view that cause exists in its effect. The untenability of the Sankhya view, as argued by the Buddhists, lies in the fact that it admits two reals with different characteristics, which are not logical, viz, one, *Purusa*, as unchangeable and the other *Prakriti* as changeable *(parinami)*.

The latter being real and eternally existing *(nitya)* it is further led to the fallacy that an eternal entity undergoes change. According to the Sankhya view, the evolution of the *Prakriti* takes place thus: Out of *Prakriti* issues *Mahan* or its cosmic aspect or *Buddhi* or psychical aspect. It is the unindividuated cosmic intellect which gives rise to *Ahamkara* (egoism) or individuated intellect, which is also a substance, an active agent. In its *sattvika* (pure) aspect it leads to the origin of *Manas* (mind), the function of which is determinate perception, it is the central organ of the sense-organs and their perceptions. *Ahamkara* also gives rise to five subtle essences *Tanmatra*, which in their turn evolve into five gross elements: earth, water, fire, air and ether. Out of these originate the five sense-organs: eyes, ears, nose,' tongue and body as also the five physical organs: voice, feet, hands, anus and generating organ. The process of evolution as shown in the *Buddhacharita* is a little different. It is as follows: The primal or ultimate cause *(Prakriti)* and its evolutes *(vikara)* constitute a being *(sattva)* with the concomitants: birth, old age, disease and death. The primal cause manifests itself in five great elements *(panchabhuta)* in their minutest states *(tanmatra)*, egoism *(ahamkara)* and unindividuated *(avyakta)* cosmic intellect *(buddhi* or maban*)*. Their evolutes are the sense-organs and their objects, the hands and feet, the voice, the organs of generation and excretion and also the mind. There is the soul (atman) which is conscious of the body. This consciousness or awareness is intellection, which was possessed by saints like Kapila. It is the absence of intellection that produces the world of beings.

Those who develop individuation *(vyakta)* and are unable to go beyond the notion of I-ness get entangled in worldly joys and sufferings while those who discard the notion of I-ness and maintain an unindividuated mind go beyond the world of pain and pleasures, This type of Sankhya teachings, according to the testimony of Ashvaghosha's *Buddhacharita,* was imparted to Prince Siddhartha by his spiritual teachers, Arada Kalama and Rudraka Ramaputra and might have some influence on his mind in his formulation of the law of causation *(paticcasamuppada).*

The Yoga philosophy is similar to that of Sankhya. It has only added the existence of the God. It developed the meditational practices which perhaps were well known to the Upanishadic seers. There is much in common between the Yoga and the Buddhist systems of meditation including the meditational terms.

The Mimamsakas also admit the reality of the world. According to them the souls are eternal, permanent as also the material elements composing the universe. Their universe consists (a) of living bodies, in which the soul reaps the karmaic effects *(bhogayatara),* (b) of sense-organs *(indriya-bhoga-sadhana)* and (c) of sense-objects *(bhoga-visaya).*

The Nyaya-Vaisesikas go a step further and in place of two reals of the Sankhya admit six categories of reality, viz., subtance *(dravye),* quality *(guna),* motion *(karman),* universality *(samanya),* particularity *(visesa)* and inherence *(samavaya).* Their *dravya* consists of the four eternal constituents space *(akasa),* time *(kala),* mind *(manas)* and soul *(atman).* Their viewpoints can also be traced in the Upanisads. They are opposed to mere subjectivity of the Vedantists.

Prince Siddhartha, educated as he was and engaged in search of the truth, must have been acquainted with most of the non-Buddhistic doctrines stated above. He no doubt denied the existence of a permanent soul but he accepted the theory of *karman* and rebirth, which, of course, he had to interpret in a way suited to his non-soul doctrine.

The doctrine of impermanence *(amtyata)* of the phenomenal world must have appealed to him most and led him to give up his princely life and luxuries. He recognised at the same time that the only means to get out of the clutches of *anityata* was spiritual exercises as a recluse. The principle of retirement from worldly joys and pleasures is denoted as pessimism though strictly speaking the under-lying force for retirement is not so much disgust with the world as the attainment of *nityata* (eternality)—an ineffable state surpassing the highest conceivable form of worldly existence, which is unalterably associated with birth, old age, disease and death, the four factors, which according to the Buddhist traditions filled the mind of Prince Siddhartha with consternation not so much for himself as for the humanity in general.

The impetus to the Prince's retirement came from human misery and so the Prince directed his mind to evolve a path that might put an end to that misery and not so much for the unfolding of the eternal Truth, on which was concentrated the attention of the Upanisadic seers. But there can be no connection of the path unless the Truth is known and so the Prince went through a long course of spiritual exercises and succeeded ultimately in visualising the Truth—the truth of oneness which of course was different from the oneness of *Jivatman* and *Paramatman.* It is not known if the Upanisadic teachers had formulated any code of duties or chalked out a course for the guidance of their followers, perhaps it was kept secret and handed down esoterically from teacher to disciple. Buddha made no secret of the path of achieving the goal and so he had bare his scheme of life before one and all who approached him with the sincere desire of exerting to overcome the worldly sufferings.

His ethical teachings and his monastic discipline marked a complete departure from the old ways of attaining perfection in knowledge.

Dakkha (Duhkha): Misery of phenomenal existence had already got hold of the minds of the Upanisadic thinkers. In the *Chandogya* (vii.1.3) it is stated that a wise man, the knower of self, goes beyond the sea of misery *(tarati sokam atmavit)* while in a late text like the *Vedantasara* (31) appears the statement that a person oppressed by death and rebirth, and worldly fire should approach for the true knowledge a learned teacher conversant with Brahman, the Truth. The Sankhya schoolmen spoke of the misery of human existence and analysed it under three heads, viz., internal *(adhyatmika)* due to physical disorder and mental agitation, external *(adhibhautika)* due to injuries caused by men and beasts or by any outside agency, and supernormal *(adhidaivika)* due to supernatural factors, or the great elements *(mahabhutas).*

Thus it is evident that the pessimistic view of life was already in the air and Buddha only picked it up and made it a starting point of his teachings. Buddha told his monks to realise that the tears shed by a being in his innumerable existences if accumulated would exceed the water of a sea. In Pali texts, human misery has been subdivided in a different manner thus: mental and or physical pain *(dukkha-dukkhata),* pleasure turning into pain *(viparinama-dukkhata)* and pain which arises and disappears due to change *(sankhara-dukkhata)* Of the four truths *(cattari ariyasaccani)* the first truth to be realised by the wise is *"dukkha"* pain or suffering concomitant to phenomenal existence. Its popular exposition is the non-fulfilment of one's desire causing resentment or disappointment, separation from the dear ones or association with the undesired causing mental pain.

This *dukkha* is suffered by the commoners and not by the elect *(ariya),* and *so,* strictly speaking, such *dukkha* is not *ariyasacca. Dukkha* in the *eyes* of an advanced monk *(ariya) is* the possession of one's body of five constituents *(upadana-khandhas),* of wealth and property, because of the fact that one's earthly possessions are evanescent and subject to decay *(vayadhamma),* to impermanence, *(aniccata).* Unless and until this nature of *dukkha* is fully comprehended by a monk, the next three "truths, viz., desire as the source of *dukkha,* end of desire as the termination of *dukkha* and eightfold path as leading to the end of *dukkha* remain incomprehensible to him. Realisation of *dukkha* therefore forms the first step in the Buddhist code of spiritual practices and its interpretation is more comprehensive than that of the earlier systems. In almost every school of Indian thought the woes and worries of a living being due to unfulfilled desires are spoken of and there are also suggestions about the means of avoiding the same. The Buddhists however have worked out the problem of *dukkha* in as thorough a manner as possible.

Aniccata (Anityata): There can be no two opinions about the fact that the pessimistic view of life *(dukkha)* is based on impermanence or rather evanescence *(anicrata)* of phenomenal objects. Buddha repeatedly reminded his disciples of this fact by saying *'anicca vata sankhara uppadavayadhammino'* (impermanent are the composites which are subject to origin and decay). Except *Nirvana* and *Akasha* there is nothing unconstituted in this world. Even the infinitesmal atoms of earth, water, air and fire (i.e. *rupa)* contain all the four elements and the four qualities: colour *(varna)*, smell *(gandba)*, taste *(rasa)* and nutritive essence (oja) which cannot be separated, and as such each of the material elements as distinct objects exists in thought only so are the other *khandhas*, viz., feeling *(vedana)*, perception *(sanna)*, impressions *(sankhara)* and knowledge derived through the senses *(vinnana)*. A being therefore is a conceptual entity and has no real existence.

The Buddhist point of view differs substantially from that of the Nyaya-Vaisesikas, according to whom, there are six irreducible categories of reality. The Jain school of thought goes a step further and asserts that matter *(pudgala)* is constituted of atoms *(paramanu) which* are real and eternal while its action *(karma)* is also material *(pandgalika)*. The Sarvastivadins (or the Vaibhasikas or the Abhidhammikas) advocated, according to some scholars, 'radical pluralism erected on the denial of substance (soul) and the acceptance of discreet momentary entities' and 'change as the replacement of one entity by another, it is the cessation of one and emergence of another. The combination (of constituents) is not real over and above the constituents. The components are real *(vastusat)*, the combination is appearance (prajnapti-sat)' The true import of the words *'sarvamasti'* of the Sarvastivadins is something different from what has been said above. It is a fact that the Sarvastivadins offer a list of seventy two *dharmas* under the heads: (i) Matter (Rupa)—11; (ii) Mind (*Citta)*—1; Mental states *(Caitasikas)* —46; and Non-mentals *Citta-viprayuktas)*—14. By "all exists" *(sarvamasti)* the Sarvastivadins mean existence of concepts of past, present and future *(trikalasat)* and not the eternal existence of phenomenal objects or of their minutest elements, which also are impermanent but not as false as a mirage or objects seen in a dream. It is through the realisation of their impermanence and making one's mind completely free from the notion of existence of phenomenal objects that an adept can attain emancipation. Hence, the Sarvastivadins do not really mean that all objects are real and exist eternally. *Khanikatta* (Ksanikatva): The Buddhists qualify impermanence *(anityata)* with momentariness *(ksanika)*, i. e., the phenomenal objects are subject to change every moment, and within one moment take place origin *(utpatti)*, duration *(stbiti)* and decay *(vinasa). As* against this contention of the Buddhists, it is argued that momentariness cannot be directly perceived and further it leads to the admission of the absence of any cause *(abetukatva)* for the origin of the second moment, because the first momentary existence disappears then and there and cannot be effective in producing the second momentary state. The counter-argument of the Buddhists is that momentariness cannot, it is true, be established by direct perception but it should be noted that momentariness is the characteristic nature *(svabhava)* of effectiveness *(arthakriyakaritva)*, By momentary cessation of an object is meant the absence of immediately preceding state *(svadhikarana-samaya-prag-abhava)*. If momentariness as explained above be not admitted, then an object would remain the same for more than one moment, and the object that produces an effect in the present would also produce the same effect in the past and future and would be subject to the fallacy that there could not be an accomplished effect *(krta-karita)* of an object, in other words, the purpose of an object would not be served.

Hence the Buddhists rightly contend that an object is momentary and produces its effect then and there and not in the past or future. It may be argued that an object retains its potentiality which will be effective in future but this argument is also fallacious because of the fact that two opposite characteristics, viz., presentness and pastness, or presentness and futurity cannot exist together. Therefore it should be admitted that the momentariness of an object can only establish the fulfilment of a purpose and this is not possible if an object remains unchanged for more than one moment. The subtlety of the Buddhist interpretation of *ksanika* is rather unique and may be regarded as a contribution to Indian thought. In short, it explains fully the dynamism of worldly objects or ceaseless change that takes place in worldly objects, in nature.

Patrccasamuppada (Pratityasamutpada): The question that arises next is whether this ceaseless change is accidental or predestined or is effected by certain causes (*hetu*) and conditions (*pratyaya*). The Buddhists reject the first two views and accept the last and offer their formula of the law of causation, *Paticcasamuppada*, popularly known as *Dharmacakra* or the ceaseless cycles of existences of a being. The word *"samutpada"* created a confusion in the minds of some who took the word in its literal sense and attempted to interpret the formula as Buddha's conception of the origin of the world of beings. Buddhighosa the great Pali commentator of the 4th century AD, pointed out in his *Visuddhimarga* that the word *samutpida* (origin) was used to counteract the false notion of nihilism *(asat-drsti)* while the other word *pratitya* (dependent) as an antidote to the notion of real existence of worldly object *(satdrsti)*. Buddha repeatedly asserted that his interpretation of the Truth kept clear of the two extreme views of existence *(sat/asti)* and non-existence *(asit/nisti)* of worldly objects, of eternalism *(sasvata)* and annihilationism (*accbeda*), of their limitedness *(antavan)* and unlimitedness (*anantavan*). This is described as the middle path (majjbima *patipada)* developed later by Nagarjuna as *Madhyamika* or *Sunyata* philosophy, and by Asanga as Yogacara or *Vijnaptimatrata*.

In the Abhidhamma texts like the *Patthana* appears an exhaustive, study of the causes *(hetu)* and conditions *(paccaya)*. The formula of causation has been explained both externally in connection with material objects and internally in relation to living beings. The origin of an earthen pot depends on several causes, viz., clay, water, fire, potter, wheel and so forth, while that of a sprout on seed, water, gardener, etc. The origin of a being is due to non-realisation of the Truth *(avidya)*, thirst *(trsna)*, deeds *(karma)* which give a shape to its constituents, organs of sense, and mind. The *Patthana* states that there are in all twenty-four kinds of causes, more than one of which are applicable *to* the origin of an object or a being. Some of these causes, again, mean invariable sequences. In fact, the complete cessation of the previous momentary state cannot produce the succeeding one, and again, there is nothing to pass from the former to the latter. In that case, the law of causation really means only the law of invariable sequence which is observed in nature. The *Lankavatara-sutra* denies causal origin and speaks of sequence of objects, but it also discusses six kinds of causes which are quite different from those of the *Patthana,* Nagarjuna in his *Madhyamakakarika* refers to four out of the twenty-four causes mentioned in the *Patthana.*

The Madhyamikas and the Yogacaras like the Vedantists do not admit the existence of the phenomenal world and so they relegate the law of causation to conventional truths *(samvrtisatya)* and utilise it to establish the relative appearance of objects, e.g., long and short, red and black are mere conventional terms used relatively and have no existence whatsoever. Nagarjuna remarks that as objects that have origination do not exist and *so i*ts existence cannot be established as uncaused, or as caused by itself, or by non-self, or by both self and non-self. The *Lankavatara* states that the ignorant only conceive of objects as originating out of causes and conditions, and for not knowing the true law takes repeated births in the three worlds. In the *Brahmasutra* there is the statement that there can be no origination of an ever existing substance. Thus, there is complete unanimity between the Mahayanists and the Vedantists about the ever existent Real as causeless and conditionless.

The question then arises, why the Mahayanists take the law of causation into their consideration. They state that this law has twofold purpose, first to point out the relative appearance of phenomenals objects and secondly to establish by inference that the Real has nothing to do with cause and condition *(apratityasamatpanna).* This law is needed to initiate the unliberated into the Truth of non-existence of the phenomenal world and thereby into the uncaused Truth Both the Hinayana and Mahayana texts state that one, who comprehend the law of causation, realises the Truth and visualises the Buddha. The law of causation leads to the realisation of the fact that the Reality remains undisturbed by origin and decay and is beyond any description and so the law is called fondly by Candrakirti as the mother of Buddhas of ten powers.

Slightly different is the line of reasoning adopted by the Hinayanists for showing that the law of causation leads to the realisation of the Truth. They have developed a chain of illustrative terms such as ignorance *(avidya)* of past life causing certain impressions *(samskara)*, which in turn produce consciousness that takes rebirth (pratisandhi-vijnana). It is followed by the present life consisting of the five constituents *(nama-rupa)*, six sense-organs and their objects *(sadayatana)*, contact *(sparsa)*, feeling *(vedana)*, thirst *(trsna)*, strong attachment *(upadana)* and lastly, clinging for rebirth *(bhava)*. After this, takes place another existence *(jati)* which ends ultimately in old age and death.

Lest this formula of twelve terms creates the impression that it represents the Buddhist view of the tree of life similar to that of Sankhya, Buddhaghosa pointed out in his *Visuddhimarga* that according to Sankhya school, the first term *Prakrit* is uncaused and is the primeval source of the tree of life whereas *Avidya* is not necessarily the first term in the Buddhist law of causation and also it is not uncaused and hence it cannot be the primeval source. The chain of terms may commence at any link, say, thirst or even birth. *Avidya* has for its cause thirst or wrong views, etc. The terms illustrate only some invariable sequences.

Avidya (Ajnana): Like the Buddhists, Shankara also states that ignorance *(avidya)* cannot be the primeval cause but he argues against the Buddhist contention that *avidya* cannot be the cause of mental impressions *(samskara)* because, logically, negation or absence of something cannot be a productive cause. In reply the Buddhists state that *avidya is* not a mere negation but is something positive—it is the misguided knowledge due to wrong views *(mithya-darsana). It* is impure and acts as a hindrance to knowledge. It is produced by attachment, hatred and delusion *(raga, dvesa, moha)* and belief in a self *(satkayadrsti)* leading to erroneous apprehensions *(viparyasa)*, e.g., evil as good, unhappiness as happiness, impurity as purity, non-soul as soul and so forth. It is due to incorrect mental application *(ayoniso manasikaro)*. It means a clouded and deluded mind. Shankara in his comment on *Brahmasutra* points out that *avidya* means the apprehension of certain qualities superimposed oh the attribute-less Reality, the Pure Soul. The opponents argue that superimposition can take place only upon an object directly perceived and not on an imperceptible pure self. Shankara in reply points out that sky *(akasha)* has no objective existence still the unenlightened men speak of the sky as blue or compare it with cauldron upturned and so forth. He argues further that though the pure self is attributeless still it serves as the basis of the notion of I-ness, hence it is not as non-existent as the sky. The knowledge derived through superimposition on an object and its consequent misapprehension, e.g., nacre as silver, rope as snake, is known as Nescience *(Avidya)* in Vedanta. In his 23 comments on *Brahmasutra;* (II. 1. 14) Shankara offers another exposition of Avidya. He writes that name and form *(nama-rupa)* are manifestations of ignorance (avidya) and as such they are indescribable as existing or non-existing and are included in Ishvara or the God, the creator 2nd are known as Cosmic Nescience *(Maya),* Energy *(Shakti).* Ishwara is different from *nama-rupa* but is its upholder or is circumscribed by namarupa, *i.e., avidya is* similar to space in an earthen jar. He is therefore the moulder of a conscious being From the standpoint of *Avidya,* Ishwara is supreme, omnipotent and omniscient, and from the highest standpoint He is identical with Brahmin, the ultimate Truth. In His subtlest form He is Ishvara, the omniscient and in His grossest form the manifested world in its infinite diversity.

The later Vedantists have given more positive conception of nescience *(Ajnana=Avidya),* saying that it is composed of three qualities, purity *(sattvas),* activity *(rajas)* and impurity *(tamas),* which in turn produce the five subtle elements and so forth as found in the Sankhya *system.* The *Ajnana* of the Vedantists is said to be neither existing nor non-existing because though it does not exist in reality, it has an apparent existence which is indescribable but causes delusion. The Lankavatara uses the term *Bhranti* in place of *Vecaztic 'Ajnana'* and expatiates on it saying that the glow of a circling fire (alatacakra) *is* seen by the wise. It is devoid of both existence and non-existence but at the same time it is in a sense eternal *(bhrantib sassata).* It continues to exist so long as one's knowledge functions but it ceases when one puts at rest all his thought-constructions. In other words, the *Lankavatara* supports the Vedantic concept on of *Ajnana.*

Kanama (Karman): The Buddhists fully recognise the influence of Karman and its effects on a being's repeated existences. Of the twelve terns or Iinas in the chain of causation the second and the tenth, i.e. mental impressions *(samskara)* and desire for re-existence *(bhava)* are regarded as resultants of acts of one's past life and present life respectively. The fact that a being is born with name and form, i.e., mental and material constituents, implies that in its previous existence it had mental obsessions due to lack of true knowledge *(avidya)* and collected the so-called merits and demerits and developed certain mental dispositions *(samskaras)* which produced the consciousness for rebirth *(prati-sandhi-vijnana)*, which in its turn brought about its re-existence and gave it a name and form. After re-existence the being in due course becomes subject to the roots of evils, viz., attachment, hatred and delusion and reaches the end of its life with a desire *(bhava)* for another existence. And so it is said in the *Mahavastu* that the first and the eighth links, nescience and thirst, are the roots of *Karma* leading to rebirth. In Buddhist texts it is repeatedly stated that a being is subject to his deeds, inherits the good or bad effects, and has its origin out of his own past deeds. It is on account of an individual's deeds that one becomes a cultivator, an artist or a King. Deeds are divided into three categories thus: those which produce fruit (i) in this life *(ditthadhammavedaniya)*, (ii) in the next life *(uppajjavedaniya)*, (iii) in a future life *(aparapariya-vedaniya)*. Some of the *Avadanas* and *Jatakas*, particularly the *Vima-navatthu* and *Petavattbu* and *Mahakarmavibhanga* illustrate through stories the effects of good and evil deeds.

It is by the elimination of deeds *(karma)* that a person attains full emancipation. Self-exertion is the only means of Nirvana, said Buddha and by self-exertion he meant the performance of certain deeds, spiritual or otherwise. Hence, the greatest emphasis was laid on one's acts and exertion and non-dependence on 3 superior power or on any ritual and ceremony. *Karma is* inexorable and can only be counteracted by proper exertions as Angulimala got rid of his sins of indiscriminate killing by his spiritual exercises *(sadhana)*. Again, Buddha himself could not escape the effects of his past deeds as is illustrated by the event of his being wounded by a stone chip of a missile thrown by Devadatta. Shankara also admits that man is the architect of his destiny and that his *karma*, past and present, must produce fruits which are to be exhausted by enjoyment or suffering. According to the Vedantists however, *karma* connotes not only meritorious and demeritorious deeds but also fulfilment of duties prescribed for a particular caste *(varna)* and stage of life *(ashrama)*, as well as performance of sacrifices and expiatory ceremonies *(prayascitta)*. Liberation is to be attained, according to Ramanuja, not only by true knowledge *(jnana)* but also by *karma*, by which, he meant, rituals prescribed in the *shastras*. It is also enjoined in the Vedantic texts that *karma* should be free from any desire for reward *(niskama)* and such *karma* can destroy the accumulated effects of one's past life. *Karma is* divided into three categories: (i) deed already commenced *(prarabdha)*, (ii) deed already accumulated *(sancita)*, and (iii) deed that is being accumulated *(sanciyamana)*. Of these three, the first must take its own course while the second can be destroyed, and the third prevented by acquisition of true knowledge.

There is a general agreement between the Vedantic and the Buddhist view of *karman* and its elimination, except that the former relics partially on rituals and ceremonies for neutralising *karmaic* effects—a view wholly unacceptable to the Buddhists.

Soul end Rebirth: As the Buddhists do not admit the existence of a permanent self, they replace the word "transmigration" by "rebirth". The conception of *atman in* the *Upanishads* has given rise to two views: (i) that the self is similar to a spark issuing out of a mass of fire; and (ii) that the self is similar to space within an earthen jar. Shankara gives preference to the second view and describes it as eternal, unchanging, undecaying, immaculate. It is not gross, not eyes, not life-force, not mind, not doer, it is just pure intelligence. It pervades the whole body though it is infinitesmally small. At death it passes out of the eyes, or skull or some other portion of the body.

The living self limited by the adjuncts of the body of an individual, his sense-organs, mind, intelligence and notion of I-ness becomes an empirical self, perceiving pleasant and unpleasant feelings. It is unaware of its true nature and is in the grip of nescience, its power and knowledge become limited and it becomes an agent, an enjoyer of acts, by which it accumulates merits and demerits.

The Buddhists contend that in the ultimate analysis of the constituents of a being there is no trace of a permanent soul, which according to the Vedantists, is unconstituted *(asamskrta)* They argue that the unconstituted, immaculate and permanent substance has nothing to do with the constituted *(samskrta),* and logically also, two objects, having opposite characteristics, can never exist together as light and darkness. Hence, they uphold the doctrine of the non-existence of a real self. They point out that the five constituents forming a being (i.e. *upadana-skandhas)* as distinguished from the mass of elements *(skandharasi)* give rise to the wrong notion of I-ness or *satkayadrsti.* They do not also accept the position taken by the Sammitiya Buddhists that the five constituents on combination produce a sixth constituent called *Pudgala* which lasts as long as the *upadana-skandhas* continue. They deny the existence of empirical self of the Vedantists or of *Pudgala* of the Sammitiyas. Such denial leads to the question as to how the Buddhists explain the transference of *karmaic* effects of an individual from one existence to another.

The Vedantists hold the view that the empirical self serves as the transmitter of *karmaic* effects. It continues after the death of a living being and transmigrates like a caterpillar from one existence to another. It does not give up the old body till it obtains a foothold in another body. In his comments on *Brahmasutra* Shankara states that the living being at the time of his death dreams of his future existence and grows an attachment for it, and so the empirical self extends its creative effort, it is a continuation or extension *(dirghikarana)* and not exactly similar to the movement of a caterpillar. The empirical self carries with it the subtle body *(suksma-sarira = linga-deha)* composed of three vestures or sheaths *(kosa)* This subtle body carries with it all the merits and demerits accumulated in past existences as also nescience *(avidya)* along with the impressions left by past experiences *(purvaprajna janmantariya samskarah),* leaving behind all material elements, gross or subtle. This subtle body remains along with the empirical self till the attainment of liberation.

Regarding the transference of *karmaic* effects, the Buddhist view is wholly different from that of the Vedanta. The Buddhists take their stand on their doctrine of momentariness, and explain that the mental and material constituents *(namarupa)* of a being undergo change, in other words, birth and death, cessation and reappearance, decay and origination, occur at every moment, which has not even an infinitesmal duration. These are as dynamic as nature and are never static even for a moment. Hence, the *karmaic* effects are transmitted every moment. At the time of death the *namarupa* obtains the subtlest form modified by the impressions of past life and develops a will for re-existence *(pratisandhivijnana)* which in turn gives rise in the next existence to the nascent mental state *(bhavanga-citta)* similar to the Yogacara conception of *alayavijnana* or consciousness-receptacle. This *bhavanga-citta* comes out of the womb or the eggshell and develops the ascent sense-organs. Hence, according to the Buddhists, there is rebirth and not transmigration and the reborn *namarupa* carries with them all the *karmaic* effects of past life.

They explain the continuity of a constituted being and its *karmaic* effects as a ceaseless flux like fire passing over dry grass in a field. In the day to day life of an individual, this ceaseless change is perceptible. An individual never remains identically the same from day to day, i.e. from moment to moment. In this unending flux death and rebirth are mere sequences. The flux ceases only when the individual realises the Truth and arrests the flow of *Larmaic* effects or mental dispositions *(samskara).*

The Mahayanists do not admit the existence of the phenomenal world of beings and objects, which according to the Yogacara school, is the mental creation of a being out of desires conserved in a latent form from time immemorial *(anadikalavasana).* It is a conceptual world *(prapanca)* of its own—a world which has no more existence than objects seen in a dream. Hence, the Yogacarins do not speculate about *namarupa* or their momentariness. The Madhyamikas go a step further and do not even admit that the phenomenal world is an extension of mind. They simply state that the origin, continuity and decay of the phenomenal world has no more existence than delusion, dream or city of Gandharvas, or the two Moons seen by jaundiced eyes.

The Buddhists regard that the Vedantic conception of *Jivatman* stands in the way of the removal of the notion of I-ness *(ahankara)* which is the only means for attaining liberation.

The Reality or the Highest Truth: The conception of *Brahmin* or the Absolute varies slightly in the different Upanishads. Shankara has tried to reconcile them to propound his own

Advayavada or Monism. On the basis of statements mainly of the *Chandogya Upanishad,* he says that Brahmin is ever existent and is identical with the universe. It is both infinitely large and infinitesmally small. It is one, real, eternal, non-dual and attributeless. In the *Brhadaranyaka-upanishad* there are references to the two aspects of Brahmin, as *Parabrahma* and *Aparabrahma.* The former represents the Brahmin which is pure, subtle, immortal, undefined, attributeless *(nirupadhi),* transcendent, beyond description with the limited vocabularies of the world. The latter represents Brahmin as superimposed by Nescience *(Ajnana)* when it appears as gross, limited, mortal, determinate, and possessed of certain attributes *(sopadhi).*

These two aspects are expressed in the words *"tat tvarn asi"* (Thou are that)" and compared to a snake and its coils, the snake being the Real self and the coil the individuated self. A simpler simile is unlimited space limited within a jar, the former being *Parabrahma* and the latter *Aparabrahma.* In the *Brhadaranyaka, Chandogya* and *Taittiriya Upanishads,* Brahmin is described as the supreme bliss *(paramananda)* and pure intelligence *(vijnana).* In the *Mandukya-bariha* Brahmin is said to be indeterminate, inexpressible, eternally refulgent and trans-empirical, while in the *Brahmasutra* it is stated that Brahmin can only be referred to by negations of known concepts *(neti neti).* The conceptions about Brahmin in the various *texts m*ay be summed up thus: (i) *Brahmin* is non-dual, inexpressible, trans-empirical and can be spoken of by negative concepts only, (ii) *Brahmin* is immanent in the universe, and (iii) *Brahmin* exists, it is pure intelligence and supreme bliss *(sat-cit-ananda)* and (iv) *Brahmin* may become limited, gross and endowed with attributes from the conventional but not from the highest standpoint.

The Monistic philosophy of Vedanta finds a better exposition in the Buddhist, specially Mahayanic texts, in which the Truth is repeatedly referred to as non-dual and non-divisible *(advayam advaidhi-haram).* In the Pali texts Nirvana is described by negatives only as not born, not diseased, not dying, not happiness, not unhappiness and so forth. It is only in popular phraseology we come across its positive account as tranquil, i.e., undisturbed by origin and decay *(santam), happ, (sukham)* and deathless *(amrtapadam)*. The Mahayanists are emphatic in their statements that the Reality is attributeless *(sunyata)*, oneness and sameness *(tathata)*, the end of phenomenal existences *(bhutakoti)*, the sum-total of all existences *(dharmadhatu)*. It is ever existent, unoriginated and undecaying, and as such it is unchangeable and infinite and can in no circumstances become limited. Thus, it is apparent that the Buddhists were more accurate than the Vedantists in their exposition of the Monistic philosophy.

The first fundamental difference between Vedanta and Buddhism regarding the highest Truth is the former's attempt to offer a positive description of the Reality as existent *(sat)*, pure consciousness (cit) and supreme bliss *(ananda)*. Excepting the attribute *'sat'* and that also used very discreetly, the other attributes are not acceptable to the Buddhists, who contend that any positive description of the transcendental implies its opposites, viz., non-existence, non-consciousness and non-bliss and that any characterisation of the Reality is false representation *(prapanca)*. The only approach to the highest Reality, they state, is possible by negation alone. The Madhyamikas confine themselves therefore to the description of *nirvana* in pure negative terms thus: Nuvana is that which is neither to be eschewed nor to be obtained, which is neither eternal nor subject to extinction, which is beyond origin and decay. But they do not say that Nirvana of Buddha or Tathagata is non-existent. They agree with the Vedantists in holding that the Absolute is not non-existent. They hold that those who attempt to characterise the inexpressible undecaying one get bewildered by characterisation and do not visualise the Tathagata.

The second fundamental difference between Vedanta and Buddhism lies in the Vedantic conception of the Absolute becoming limited temporarily although superficially. The Buddhists are unrelenting in their arguments that the Real must remain the Real for ever and suffer no change even superficially and temporarily because it ran no longer be called Absolute. They have used the terms unreal or conventional *(samvrti)* and real or absolute *(paramartha)* but they regard the former as non-existent as objects seen in a dream. They hold that there is no *via media* between the two, hence, they do not accept the conception of *Aparabrahma*. Even the temporary and superficial association of two with opposite characteristics, viz., purity and impurity, unlimitedness and limitedness, they state, is as illogical as the coexistence of blackness and whiteness, of hotness and coldness.

It is noteworthy that the Vedantic conception of the identity of Brahmin with the universe is fully endorsed by the Madhyamikas who state that there is not the slightest difference between *Nirvana* and the phenomenal world *(Samsara).*

The Yogacarins hold a view midway between the Madhyamikas and the Vedantists in that they qualify the Absolute as not only existent (sat) but also as pure mind or consciousness *(vijnanamatra).* They have also introduced the conception of *Tathagatagarbha* which bears comparison with the Vedantic conception of *Jivatman.* In the *Lankavatara* it is stated that the Teacher spoke of the *Tathagetagarbha,* which is pure and refulgent by inherent nature, dwells in every living being, encased in sense-organs and other constituents forming a being. It is like an invaluable jewel wrapped m a dirty cloth. It is ever existent, unchanging, tranquil and eternal. In the text, care however has been taken to point out that their conception of *Tathagatagarbha* is not identical with the heretical doctrine of the soul-theorists, as they do not admit the existence of the Highest Soul *(Paramatman).*

Duhkha-Satya

The first Noble Truth of Buddhism, *Dukkham anyasaccam, is* generally translated by almost all scholars as "The Noble Truth of Suffering", and it is interpreted to mean that life according to Buddhism is nothing but suffering and pain. This translation and interpretation are highly unsatisfactory and misleading. It is because of this narrow translation and interpretation that many people are misguided to regard Buddhism as pessimistic. First of all, Buddhism is neither pessimistic nor optimistic. It takes a realistic view of life and of the world. It looks at things objectively. It does not falsely lull you to live m a fool's paradise, nor does it frighten and agonise you with all kinds of ideas of imaginary fears and sins. It tells you exactly and objectively *(yathabhutam)* what you are and what the world is, and shows you the right way to perfect freedom, peace, tranquillity and happiness.

It is true that the Pali word *dukkha* or Sanskrit *duhkba* in ordinary usage means "suffering", "pain" or "misery" as opposed to the word *sukha* meaning "happiness", "comfort" or "ease". But the term *dukkha* as the first Noble Truth has a philosophical meaning and connotes an enormously wider sense. It is admitted that the term *dukkha* in the first Noble Truth contains the ordinary meaning of "suffering" or "pain", but in addition to that it includes also deeper ideas such as "imperfection", "impermanence", "emptiness", "unsubstantiality", "conflict". It is difficult therefore to find one word to embrace the whole conception of the term *dukkha* as the first Noble Truth, and so it is better to leave it untranslated than to give an incomplete and wrong idea by conveniently rendering it as "suffering" or "pain".

Buddhism does not deny happiness in life. On the contrary it admits different forms of happiness, both material and spiritual, for laymen as well as for monks. But all that is included in the dukkha. Even the very pure states of *dhyana* attained by the practice of higher meditation, which are free even from a shadow of suffering or pain in the accepted sense of those words and which may be described as unmixed happiness, and also the state of *dhyana* which is free from sensations both pleasant *(sukha)* and unpleasant *(dukkha)* and which is only pure equanimity and awareness—even these extremely high, pure spiritual states are included in the *dukkha*. Not because they are suffering or pain, but because they too are *sankhara*, conditioned, subject to change, impermanent and unsubstantial.

The conception of the dukkha as the first Noble Truth may be viewed from three aspects (i) dukkha as ordinary suffering *(dukkhadukkha)*, (ii) dukkha as change *(viparinama-dukkha)* and (iii) dukkha as conditioned state *(sankhara-dukkha)*.

All kinds of suffering in life like birth, old age, sickness, death, union with unpleasant conditions, separation from beloved ones and agreeable conditions, not getting what one desires, grief, lamentation, distress—all such forms of physical and mental suffering, which are universally accepted as suffering and pain, are included in the dukkha as ordinary suffering *(dukkha-dukkba)*.

A happy feeling, a happy condition in our life is not permanent, not everlasting It changes sooner or later. When it changes it produces an unhappy feeling, an unhappy condition. This vicissitude is included in the dukkha as change *(viparinama-dukkba).*

These two forms of dukkha, namely *dukkba-dukkba* and *viparinama-dukkha,* may be included in the first Noble Truth according to the conventional *(samvrti)* sense. But the third form of dukkha, i.e. dukkha as a conditioned state *(sunkhara-dukkha),* is dukkha in the ultimate sense *(paramarth),* and calls for a little analytical explanation of what we consider as "being", as "individual" or as "I". According to Buddhist philosophy what we call a "being", ' individual" or "I'" is only a combination of everchanging physical and mental energies which may be divided into five aggregates *(panchakkbandha).* The Buddha says: "In short, these five aggregates of attachment are dukkha" *(sankhutena pancupadanak-Lhandha dttkkba).* Here it should be clearly understood that the dukkha and the five aggregates are not two different things, the five aggregates themselves are the *dukkha.* We will understand this point better when we get an idea about the five aggregates.

Now what are these five aggregates which constitute the so-called being?

The first is the aggregate of matter *(rupakkhandha).* In this term "the aggregate of matter" are included the four great elements *(cattari mahabhutani),* namely, the elements of solidity, fluidity, energy and motion, and their derivatives *(upadaya-rupa).* In the "derivatives of four great elements" are included our five material sense organs, i.e. the faculties of eye, ear, nose, tongue and body and their corresponding objects in the external world, i.e. visible form, sound, odour, taste and tangible things and also some ideas or thoughts which are objects of mind. Thus, the whole sphere of matter, both internal and external, is included in the aggregate of matter.

The second is the aggregate of sensations *(vedanakkhandha).* In this group are included all our sensations, pleasant or unpleasant or neither pleasant not unpleasant, experienced through the contact of our sense organs with the external world. That is to say, the sensations experienced through the contact of the eye with visible forms, ear with sounds, nose with odour, tongue with taste, body with tangible objects and mind (which is the sixth faculty in Buddhist philosophy) with mind-objects or thoughts or ideas. All our physical and mental sensations are included in this group.

The third is the aggregate of perceptions *(sannakkhandha)*. Like the sensations, perceptions also are produced through the contact of out serve faculties with the external world.

The fourth is the aggregate of mental formations *(sankharakkhandha)* In this group are included all volitional mental activities, both good and bad, which produce karmic effects, such as attention *(man-asikara)*, will *(chanda)*, determination *(adhimokkha)*, confidence *(saddha)*, concentration *(samadhi)*, intelligence or wisdom *(panna)*, energy *(viriya)*, desire *(raga)*, repugnance or hate *(patigha)*, conceit *(mana)*, idea of self *(sakkaya-ditthi)*, etc. There are 52 such mental activities which constitute the aggregate of mental formations.

The fifth is the aggregate of consciousness *(vinnanakkhandha)*. Consciousness is a reaction or a response which has one of the six sense faculties (eye, ear, nose, tongue, body and mind) as its basis and an external phenomenon as its object. E.g. the visual consciousness has the eye as its basis and a visible form as its object. So is the consciousness connected with other faculties.

Very briefly these are the five aggregates. What we call "being" or "individual' or "I" is only a name or a label given to the combination or these five groups. They are all impermanent. They are in a state of flux of momentary arising and disappearing. One thing disappears conditioning the appearance of the next in a series of cause and effect. There is no substantiality in them. There is nothing behind them that can be called a permanent, unclanging self, individuality or am thing that can be called "I", apart from these five aggregates. Everyone will agree that neither matter, nor sensation, nor perception, nor any one of those mental activities, nor *consciousness* can really be called "I". But when these five physical and mental aggregates, which are interdependent, are working together in combination as a physio-psychological machine we get the idea of "I". But this is only an imaginary idea which is nothing but one of those 52 mental formations of the fourth aggregate, which we have just mentioned. These five aggregates together, which we popularly call a being, are the *duttba* itself *(sribhiri-lubhi)*. There is no other "being" or "I" standing behind these five aggregates who experiences the *dukkba*. There is no unmoving mover behind the movement. It is only movement. In other words, there is no thinker behind the thought. Thought, itself is the thinker. If you remove the thought there is no thinker. Here one cannot fail to notice how this Buddhist view is diametrically opposed to the conception of Cartesna cogito

This is the Noble Truth of Dukkhi. This does not at all make the life of a Buddhist melancholy or sorrowful, as some people wrongly imagined. On the contrary, a true Buddhist is the happiest in the world. He has no fears or anxieties. He is always calm and serene, and cannot be upset or dismayed by changes or calamities, because he sees and takes things as they are. The Buddha was never melancholy or gloomy. He was described by his contemporaries as "ever-smiling" (mrbita-pubbwigama). In Buddhist paintings and sculptures the Buddha is always represented with a face happy, contented and serene. Never a trace of suffering or agon) is to be seen. There are two ancient Buddhist texts called the *Theragatha* and the *Therigatla which* are full of happy and joyful utterances by the Buddha's disciples, both male and female, who found peace and happiness in his teaching. The King of Kosala once told the Buddha that unlike many a disciple of other religious systems who looked haggard, coarse, pale, emaciated and unprepossessing, the disciples of the Buddha were "joyful and elated *(hatthapabattha),* jubilant and exultant *(uddggudagga),* enjoying the religious life *(abhiratarupa),* with senses pleased *(pinitindriya),* free from anxiety *(appossukkha),* serene *(pannaloma),* peaceful *(paradavutta)* and living with a gazelle's mind *(migabhutena cetasa)", i.e.* light hearted. The King added that he believed that this healthy disposition was due to the fact that "these venerable ones had certainly realised the great and full significance of the Blessed one's teaching." Buddhism is quite opposed to melancholic, sorrowful and gloomy attitude of mind which is considered a hindrance to the realisation of Truth. On the other hand, it is interesting to remember that joy *(piti)* is one of the seven essential qualities to be cultivated for the realisation of Nirvana.

Nirodha-Satya

In the Abhidharma all objects (dharma) are classified under two heads, samskrta (constituted) and asamskrta (unconstituted). Objects as are caused or constituted are called 'samskrta' and those which are not caused or constituted, that is to say, which are eternal, are called 'asamskrta'. Asamskrta objects are of three types,— 'dkasa', 'pratisamkhya-nirodha' and 'apratisamkhya-nirodha'. In the present paper we confine ourselves to the study of 'nirodha'. In this connection it should be borne in mind that according to the Sautrantika view, asamskrta objects are denied physical and intellectual existence. The Sautrantika thinks that as all objects are fluxional in character, their physical or intellectual existence is a contradiction in term. It is for this reason that the Sautrantika has not recognised 'nirodha' as physically or intellectually existing (dravyasat) though its existence (as prajnaptisat) is acknowledged in the Shastras. The Vatsiputriyas state that 'nirvana' alone is asamskrta, and therefore they do not also admit its dravyasatta. The Yogacara school does not recognise the dravyasatta of 'nirodha' apart from consciousness. The Madhyamikas also cannot posit 'nirodha' as physically existing. It seems therefore that it is only in the opinion of the Vaibhasika that 'nirodha' possesses dravyasatta, and it will be our endeavour in this article to discuss 'nirodha' as described by the Vaibhasika.

Nirodha is classified under three heads, viz., 'Pratisamkhya-nirodha', 'Apratisamkhya-nirodha' and 'Anityata-nirodha'. It is worthy of notice that in the original Abhidharmakosa we come across two types of nirodha,—Pratisamkhyanirodha and Apratisamkhya-nirodha. But the Anityatanirodha also has been specifically mentioned in the Sphutartha.

It is to be seen that the two terms, 'nirodha' and 'nirodha-satya' have not been used as synonyms. Because the term 'nirodha' has been used to refer to three types of 'nirodha', while the term 'nirodha-satya' denotes only pratisamkhyanirodha and apratisamkhyanirodha. It is for this reason that when the Abhidharmakosa describes 'nirodha-satya' as one of the four 'Arya-satyas', it means pratisamkhya-nirodha and apratisamkhyanirodha only and does not take notice of anityata-nirodha.

The term 'nirodha' is generally used to denote negation The expression 'nirodha of a jar' means the negation or the destruction of a jar. Similarly the sentence 'the current of the stream has been niruddha (stopped)' conveys that the stream which had been flowing on from before has ceased, that is to say, the current is no more and has been destroyed. But in the present article, where we propose to review the nirodha-satya from the Vaibhasika point of view, it cannot be maintained that the term conveys the sense of negation, inasmuch as according to the Vaibhasika, negation is a figment of imagination like the rabbit's horn. Nirodha has been described in Buddha-vacana as an Aryasatya. Further the Vaibhasika includes pratisamkhyanirodha and apratisamkhyanirodha in the list of asamskrta objects. And, as such they are recognised as eternal entities. Hence, pratisamkhyanirodha and apratisamkhyanirodha ace not, in the opinion of the Vaibhasika, of the nature of negation.

Let us now analyse the derivative meaning of the term 'nirodha'. The suffix to imply 'bhava' has not been attached, but it conveys the meaning of the agent (kartr). As such the derivative meaning of the word 'nirodha' is, that which retards or shuts out. It is for this reason Yasomitra has described 'vi-samyoga' or pratisamkhyanirodha as 'a closed door, which shuts out the different klesas'. So the Vaibhasika conceives of the pratisamkhyanirodha and apratisamkhyanirodha as different kinds of 'invincible walls' which are eternal entities. The person striving for Nirvana does not create pratisamkhyanirodha and apratisamkhyanirodha, but he collects those ever-existing *entities* for his own purpose, i.e., for the attainment of Nirvana.

Pratisamkhyanirodha

The Vaibhasika texts have mentioned only two varieties of nirodha-satya, viz., pratisamkhyanirodha and apratisamkhya-nirodha. The term pratisamkhyanirodha may be explained as nirodha, which an individual secures by means of pratisamkhya. It is with the help of the Anantarya-marga' (the 16th ksana of the Nirvedhabhagiya) the individual drives out the klesas, and with the help of the 'Vimukti-marga' (the first fifteen ksanas of the Nirvedhabhagiya) the door of the visamyoga or pratisamkhyanirodha is shut against these different klesas. It is therefore to be understood that the 'nirodha' which the individual attains through the pursuit of vimuktimarga is called pratisamkhyanirodha. But, it should be pointed out that the aforesaid meaning of pratisamkhyanirodha cannot be endorsed in view of the fact that the Yaibhasika texts have laid it down that certain apratisamkhyanirodhas too may be secured with the help of pratisamkhya or vimuktimarga. It is therefore quite in the fitness of things that Vasubandhu has sought to describe or define it in a different way. In his opinion pratisamkhyanirodha is an object which retards contact. The prefix 'vi' in the term visamyoga suggests 'opposition', and as such the term (visamyoga) means 'that which opposes or retards contact'.

It should be mentioned here that though pratisamkhyanirodha means 'what retards contact', still it does not set forth the full connotation of the term. From a critical study of Yasomitra's Sphutartha it appears that pratisamkhyanirodha means those objects which invariably oppose the attainment of contact with 'sasrava' objects. The individual who is fortunate enough to realise pratisamkhyanirodha will no more come in contact with sasrava objects. As the nirodha is obtained through pratisamkhya it is called pratisamkhyanirodha. The 'asravas', such as klesas and others cannot reside in the asamskrta objects as ether and the like, and as such asamskrta objects are not sasravas. Even some samskrta objects, such as marga-satya and others cannot be the locus of the asravas. So margasatya and such others are not sasrava. It is to be seen that the nirodha of those samskrta objects, whether sasrava or anasrava, which may have been born but never come to life (anutpatti-dharma), is not called pratisamkhyanirodha in the Abhidharma text. So the object that invariably retards the attainment of contact with the sasrava objects that are past, born and are in the embryo form, is called the pratisamkhyanirodha.

It is to be carefully noticed that 'samyoga' and 'prapti' are not synonymous, according to the Vaibhasika text. Both 'sattvakhya' and 'asattvakhya' objects may have samyoga, but according to the Vaibhasikas, prapti has been admitted in the case of sattvakhya *objects* only. Those that relate to objects endowed with life, are called sattvakhya. The Vaibhasika admits 'prapti' in the case of pratisamkhya-nirodha, though the latter is not a sattvakhya object. To be precise, what waxes with the waxing of the body and wanes with the waning of the body is called sattvakhya. But pratisamkhyanirodha is an eternal entity and cannot be looked upon as a sattvakhya object, still its prapti has been admitted by the Vaibhasikas.

It has been stated above that pratisamkhyanirodha is an object which invariably retards the attainment of contact with sasrava objects. Now, a question may be raised here, if it were said that pratisamkhya-nirodha is the object invariably retarding the contact with sasrava objects, and not the attainment of contact with them as stated in the description, the description of the pratisamkhyanirodha could have been quite accurate and precise. In answer to this, it may be pointed out that the pratisamkhyanirodha cannot retard the contact with the sasrava objects in general, but it can only oppose the attainment of contact with the sasrava objects. The *raison d'etre* is this that when the individual with the help of the 'anantarya-marga' drives out the klesas, and the pratisamkhyanirodha shuts the door against them, the contact of klesas with the individual ceases; but that does not mean that the klesas cannot have any contact whatsoever with any other things outside the individual. It comes to this therefore, that if pratisamkhyanirodha was described only as the object retarding the contact with sasrava objects, and not as the object retarding the attainment of contact with the sasrava objects, the description would not have been correct and adequate.

Pratisamkhyanirodha has no 'sabhagahetu', because 'sabhagahetu' is possible only for the samskrta objects. According to the Vaibhasikas, the pratisamkhyanirodha has been included in the list of asamskrta objects. So it is an eternal entity. Pratisamkhyanirodha can neither be described as past nor as 'anutpattidharma', but it lives in the present It is for this reason that the pratisamkhyanirodha cannot be retarded by anything else. It should be stated here that pratisamkhyanirodha does not also become the sabhagahetu of any other object. Apratisamkhyanirodha and anityatanirodha are called nirodhas, but there is no similarity between them and the pratisamkhyanirodha. So pratisamkhyanirodha is described as 'a-sabhaga', i.e., having no similarity with others, and it is an eternal entity. Pratisamkhyanirodha is not negation and as such it has no negatum (pratiyogi object).

Vasubandhu opines that pratisamkhyanirodhas are innumerable; and, those are not uniform either. As otherwise, on the attainment of pratisamkhyanirodha as a result of the knowledge of one of the Aryasatyas, such as, 'dharma-jnana with duhkha as its content', the pursuit of other kinds of Aryasatyas, such as, 'dharma-jnana relating to samudaya', etc., would become useless. And, in view of the fact that pratisamkhyanirodha obstructs the way, the Anantaryamarga can no longer drive out the klesas. But if we admit the plurality of pratisamkhyanirodha such anomalies would be obviated. For, the particular pratisamkhyanirodha, which is obtained by 'dharmajnana relating to duhkha', does not obstruct the way through which klesas are driven by 'dharmajnana-ksanti' relating to samudaya-satya and so on.

Apratisamkhyanirodha

Prima facie apratisamkhyanirodha is that which is 'not pratisamkhyanirodha'. But this interpretation is not accurate, as anityatanirodha is also 'not pratisamkhyanirodha'. Vasubandhu defines apratisamkhyanirodha as that form of nirodha which permanently obstructs the creation of objects (vastu), thereby distinguishing it from anityatanirodha. The latter does not obstruct the creation of objects, but it obstructs the existence of the created objects (utpanna-vastu). It is for this reason the Buddhist philosophers believe in the transitoriness or fluxional character of all created objects.

Apratisamkhyanirodha cannot also be explained as the nirodha which is 'not attainable by means of pratisamkhya or vimuktimarga', as in that case also it becomes applicable to anityatanirodha. Moreover such an explanation often proves to be inadequate. As for example, according to the Vaibhasikas, a 'srotapanna' person, (one who is in the stream leading to Nirvana) has no more to suffer from 'apiyagati' (i.e., he is not to be reborn in the preta or tiryak-yoni). The apratisamkhyanirodha form of barrier against his future 'apiyagati' has thus been obtained by means of pratisamkhya. This nirodha cannot be pratisamkhyanirodha as it obstructs apayagati, which is anutpattidharma, whereas the function of pratisamkhyanirodha is to retard the sasrava objects, past, born 01 yet to be born (utpattidharma).

It has also been suggested that apratisamkhyanirodha is obtainable by a form of 'pratyayavaikalya' (absence of the totality of creative elements), which is 'a-pratisamkhya' (not pratisamkhya).

In this definition pratyayavaikalya has been equated with apratisamkhya, and thus it indicates the process of attainment of apratisamkhyanirodha. But, according to the Vaibhasikas, absence or abhava being illusory (alika), absence of the totality of creative elements (pratyayavaikalya) can hardly be accepted as the means of attainment of apratisamkhyanirodha.

Vasubandhu's definition of apratisamkhyanirodha (nirodha which permanently obstructs the origin of dharma or objects) helps us to distinguish it from anityatanirodha and also from pratisamkhyanirodha. The former obstructs the existence of constituted objects and not their origin, while the latter prevents the attainment of contact with sasrava objects and not their existence or origin.

According to the Vaibhasika a person who is 'sattvavasastha' is described as 'Asamjnikasattva'. An asamjnikasattva person during his 'sattvavasa' naturally acquires certain condition or state of spiritual upliftment when he is not baffled by future sasrava objects. During this state of asamjnikata, therefore, the very creation of sasrava objects is obstructed for a specific period. This makes it almost similar to apratisamkhyanirodha, and may be mistaken for the latter. On analysis, however, it will be found that there is a subtle difference between the two. Apratisamkhyanirodha permanently obstructs the creation or origin of all objects, whereas the asamjnikatva prevents the origin of sasrava objects only during the state of asamjnikata, while out of the state of asamjnikata a person may once again be baffled by the sasrava objects.

The Vaibhasikas mention another form of nirodha, viz., Asamjni-kanirodha-samapatti or Nirodha-samapatti. This may be acquired by a person, susceptible to all desires, by means of meditation. On its attainment sasrava objects do not originate in a person, expert in meditation, during the period of his meditation. So during the state of Nirodha-samapatti also the origin of sasrava objects is obstructed temporarily for him. But the expression, 'permanent obstruction' of the origin of objects in respect of apratisamkhyanirodha, will enable *us* to distinguish it from the above-mentioned nirodha-samapatti, which effects a temporary obstruction only.

Apratisamkhyanirodha effectively and permanently retards the origin of Anasrava objects as well. A 'srotapanna' person, free from the two Klesas born of low sight and low thoughts, becomes 'Anagami' (i.e., one who will be born once more only to attain Nirvana). Such persons are generally averse to the acquisition of more and more higher states of existence, and those anagamis who attain nirvana during their 'antaribhava' (the period intervening between the death in one existence and rebirth in another) do not require these higher planes. By means of their knowledge or pratisamkhya they obtain a form of apratisamkhyanirodha which obstructs the origin of future anasrava higher planes for them. Though it is attained by means of pratisamkhya still it retards the origin of anasrava constituted objects.

In summing up it may be observed, therefore, that the existence of all constituted objects, sasrava and anasrava, is obstructed by anityatanirodha, the attainment of contact with sasrava objects, past, born or yet to be born is obstructed by pratisamkhyanirodha; and, the very creation or origin of anutpattidharma objects, sasrava or anasrava, is permanently obstructed by apratisamkhyanirodha. The first strikes at the existence, the second at the attainment, and, the third at the very origin.

The constituted objects are related to anityatanirodha by their own creative elements, as they are created in collaboration with that nirodha. The pratisamkhyanirodha is attainable only by pratisamkhya or vimuktimarga and by no other process. Apratisamkhyanirodha urn, however, be obtained by nature as well as by pratisamkhya. Some even believe that it may be attained by pratyayavaikalya, which is not accepted by the Vaibhasikas.

Pratityasamutpada

Pratityasamutpada is one of the modes of casual relation in Buddhism—the other being Patthananaya. It is 'a mode marked by the simple condition of the happening of a phenomenon on the occurrence of its sole invariable antecedent phenomenon.' It states that things of the world are neither due to one cause (ekahetuka) nor are they causeless (ahetuka). It proves that things are due to manifold causes (nanahetuka).

Buddhaghosa states that pratityasamutpada is one of the four difficult subjects (catvari duskarasthanani) to be expounded. It is to be understood under four different aspects of profundity (catvari gambhirasthanani), *viz.*, meaning (artha), doctrine (dharma), teaching (desana) and penetration (prativeda). It should further be known according to the four different methods as to the meaning (catvara arthanaya) and these are the method of unity (ekatvanaya), of diversity (nanatvanaya), of non-occupation (abyaparanaya) and of the nature of being such (evamdharmatanaya). This formula is characterised as the order of becoming (dharmasthitata), happening of things (dharmaniyamata), suchness (tathata), uncontrariness (avitathata) and tins-conditioned nature (idapratyayata).

Pratitya means after reaching (prapya), or depending on (apeksya), and samutpada means origination. Combining the two we get dependent origination. It establishes that things have only a dependent origination.

We are told that the Buddha, while sitting under the Bodhi tree, determined to acquire enlightenment, realised at the third watch of the night the root cause of all sufferings and sorrows, which is comprised in the second noble truth (samudayasatya), the concatenation of causes and effects, *viz.*, pratityasamutpada (dependent origination) with its 12 nidanas or links They are: (i) avidya (ignorance), (ii) samskara (impression), (iii) vijnana (consciousness), (iv) namarupa (mind and matter), (v) sadayatana (six organs of sense), (vi) sparsa (contact), (vii) vedani (feeling), (viii) trishna (desire), (ix) upadana (attachment), (x) bhava (existence), (xi) jati (birth) and (xii) jaramarana (old age and death). This is the wheel of life revolving day after day from birth to death and death to birth.

Here is given a brief exposition of the terms constituting the formula. Avidya (ignorance) is the non-comprehension of the four Noble Truths (aryasatya), the past (purvanta), the future (aparanta), both the past and the future (purvantaparanta) and pratityasamutpada (dependent origination). It is identified with delusion (moha). Samskara (impression) denotes actions which are (i) meritorious (punyabhi-samskara), (ii) sinful (apunyabhisamskara) and (iii) static (anenjabhi-samskara). Punyabhisamskara appertains to eight kamavacarakusala and five rupavacarakusalacetanas (volitions), apunyabhisamskara to twelve akusalacetanas (volitions) and anenjabhisamskara to four arupakusalacetanas (volitions) only. They are thus wholesome and unwholesome worldly volitions (cetanas). These three together with the three kinds of deeds belonging to the body (kayika), speech (vacasika) and mind (manasika) are the six samskaras (impressions) which are conditioned by ignorance (avidya). Vijnana (consciousness) means here pratisandhivijnana (rebirth consciousness) and pravrttivijnana (a continuous flow of mental states). Pratisandhivijnana is of nineteen kinds while pravrttivijnana is of thirty-two laukika vipakas (resultants). Namarupa (mind and matter) denote pratisandhinama and pravrttinama, and pratisandhirupa and pravrttirupa.

Pratisandhinama means thirty-five cetanas (volitions) associated with nineteen pratisandhis while pravrttinama denotes thirty-five cetanas (volitions) associated with thirty-two laukika cittas. By pratisandhirupa is meant the nineteen kinds of pratisandhi and karmajarupa (form arising out of deeds), and by pravrttirupa is taken the pravrtticittajarupa (form arising out of mind in this life). Sadayatana denotes caksayatana (eye-base), srotrayatana (ear-base), ghranayatana (nose-base), jihvayatana (tongue-base), kaya-yatana (body-base) and manayatana (mind-base). Caksayatana is caksuprasada (sensitivity of eye) and so on while manayatana is thirty-two laukika vipakas (resultants).

Sparsa (contact) is of six kinds corresponding to the six kinds of ayatanas (bases). Cakshusparsa (eye-contact) is contact associated with eye-consciousness (cakshu-vijnana), srotrasparsa (ear-contact) is contact associated with car-consciousness (srotravijnana), and so forth, but manosparsa (mind-contact) is but contact associated with twenty-two laukika vipakas (resultants) Vedana (feeling) is also of six kinds corresponding to six sense-organs Cakshuvedana (feeling born of eye) is feeling associated with eye-consciousness (cakshuvijnana) and so on while manovedana is but feeling associated with thirty-two laukika vipakas (resultants). Trsna (craving) is of six kinds, *viz.*, rupatrsna (craving for form), sabdatrsna (craving for sound), gandhatrsna (craving for smell), rasatrsna (craving for taste), sprstavyatrsna (craving for touch) and dharmatrsna (craving for objects). Rupatrsna is craving for the visible objects Similarly sabdatrsna is craving for the sounds and so forth Upadana (attachment) is of four kinds. Kama, disti, silavrata and atmavada, Kamupadana is mental concomitants rooted in greed (lobha cetasika). Drstupadana is the wrong view that there is no resultant of the gift. Silavratupadana is the belief that ceremonial observances lead to purification. Atmavadupadana is the belief in the existence of one's individuality. Bhava (existence) is of two kinds, karmabhava and utpattibhava. Karmabhava is twenty-nine kusala and akusala cetanas (wholesome and unwholesome volitions) and twenty ways of good conduct and of evil conduct associated with these cetanas (volitions). It represents the active side of life Utpattibhava is the resultant of thirty-two laukika vipakas and thirty-five cetasikas and the material phenomena produced by karma Jati (birth) is the appearance of the five skandhas (aggregates) of a being who is reborn Jara (decay) is the decay of those skandhas Marana (death) is the passing away of those skandhas.

Pratityasamutpada refers to three periods—the past, present and the future. Avidya (ignorance) and samskara (impression) belong to the past, vijnana, namarupa, sadayatana, sparsa, vedana, trsna, upadana and bhava to the present, jati and jaramarana to the future. It has twelve factors (anga) as mentioned above It has also twenty modes (akara). Thus, in the past there are five causes and in the present there are five resultants. Similarly there are five causes in the present and five resultants also in the future. There are four groups (sanksepa) in this formula one casual group in the past, one resultant group in the present, one casual group in the present and one resultant group in the future. It has three connections (sandhi): one between samskara and vijnana, one between vedana and trsna and one between bhava and jati. There are three rounds (vrtta) in it. They are klesavrtta, karmavrtta and vipakavrtta. It has further two roots—avidya and trsna. Lastly, it is taught in four different ways: (i) from the beginning to the end, (ii) from the middle to the end, (iii) from the end to the beginning and (iv) from the middle to the beginning.

Pratityasamutpada (dependent origination) is one of the most fundamental doctrines of Buddhism, as Buddha himself has declared:

'He who realises pratityasamutpada sees dharma (truth) and he who sees dharma (truth) *sees* pratityasamutpada'. It is a very important philosophical doctrine in Mahayana philosophy. Nagarjuna, the founder of the Madhyamika system, has established his whole philosophy on pratityasamutpada. According to this doctrine it is the nature of all things (bhava) to depend on a number of causes and conditions for their origination, and what are so produced cannot be said to have independent origination and are without any reality and nothing can, therefore, be declared of such unreal things. In the invocatory verses at the beginning of his *Madhyamikakarika* Nagarjuna has described pratityasamutpada by eight negatives. He says that there is neither origination nor cessation, neither permanence nor impermanence, neither unity nor diversity, neither coming in nor going out in the principle of pratityasamutpada. Here the negatives describe the unrelatedness of everything produced through this principle and pratityasamutpada is rightly declared as the cessation of phenomena (prapancopasama) and all quiescence (shiva). Elsewhere he has further stated that looked at from the relative standpoint (samvrtisatya) pratityasamutpada means origination of the world-order depending on a concurrence of causes, but from the absolute standpoint (paramartha-satya), it means non-origination at all times and is equated with Nirvana. This is the basic principle of Nagarjuna's philosophy.

Brahmin of Shankara and Sunyata of Madhyamikas

The central point of Shankara's Vedanta is that consciousness absolute is the fundamental reality and Brahmin is that consciousness. It is devoid of all attributes and devoid of any distinct mark. It is one indivisible unit without a second having in itself no difference either arising out of an individuality as a member of a certain class or a difference arising out of an individuality belonging to another class. Each individual is essentially the same as Brahmin but it appears as other than Brahmin because of adjuncts that arise out of nescience.

The world consisting of individuals is there and it has the self-same Brahmin as the cause both material and efficacious. The world emanates from it and subsists in it. Now the question is how can this non-relational Brahmin be linked up with this relational world? Shankara, however, says this is possible. The world, as it is, does not exist at all nor did it ever exist nor will it exist in future. The truly existing being is alone Brahmin and all else is naught. All else is *maya* or *adhyasa,* the principle of individuation or the principle of unifying opposites—unification of the self and not-self, of the ego and not-ego, of the subject and object, of the cause and effect and of Brahmin and the world Opposites can never be reconciled. But unless they are reconciled no experience is possible. In our every day experience we are accustomed to reconcile such opposites. We make an object identified with that which it is not. We take a rope to be a snake. There cannot be an identification between the rope and a snake in any way. Yet they are identified. This is the case also with truth and falsehood. Very often we identify truth with falsehood. In fact, there cannot be any reason for such an identification but such is the case in all human affairs. Such a nature regulates all activities,—a law that makes the world as it is. A man believes as that he is identical with his body and he never explicitly denies that he is his body and never feels detached from his body. The notion of this false identification of the self with the body would never occur to a person who has an experience of himself as the supreme consciousness. It is only one who had realised such a distinction between self and not-self and that he would wonder at this identity.

The identity of self with not-self has the form of the self existing as embodied and not as a conscious body. An individual self means a self feeling itself as embodied. The illusoriness of the embodiment is the illusoriness of the body itself as also the self's identity with it. The idea of an object as distinct from the subject is derived from the notion of this embodiment. This notion again is born in the consciousness of the self and is regarded as false in consideration of its individuality. To be conscious of one's self as an individual as in the case 'I know me' is to be conscious of *me* as illusory and of the subject, that is, I, as truth. The *me is* the prototype of the whole realm of objectivity, a sort of *you*. To feel it to be illusory is to be aware of the possibility of all objects to be illusory. We can never conceive the illusoriness of the world unless we start with the illusoriness of me. The illusoriness of me leads to the feeling that the self can never be identified with not-self. This feeling forms the very background on which Shankara establishes his theory of objective illusion. This objective illusion again calls for its counterpart the subjective illusion, the *avidya* or *maya,* the principle of individuation. It is an illusion primary, through which the self believes in willing and feeling that it is an individual. This principle exists in Brahmin prior to the beginning of actual consciousness of one's self as an individual or prior to the starting of this world as an object of experience. Through it an individual self becomes conditioned and begins to conceive individually about himself and also of his subjective experience. Due to such experience every individual thinks that there are as many individuals as there are beings. This principle of individuation is entirely dependent because nothing can be conceived without being related to pure consciousness which is Brahmin. Absolute Brahmin is independent. It has nothing to do with condition and has no concern with the world.

This world has no ultimate reality and will be perceived as such as long as the ultimate reality is not realised. Even the mental states are not real. But so long this world continues to be perceived and Brahmin is not realised both the internal and the external objects are to be regarded as facts. All these objects have got some value. The world also has got a value so long its knowledge as a world persists but when the knowledge of Brahmin arises the world with its value ceases automatically).

Brahmin is eternal, and has neither positive nor negative attributes It is above all determinations. Words fail to express it. In it there is a total extinction of empirical life along with the relative distinctions of subject and object. The concept of bliss in the *Turiya* state may appear as positive, and although there is absence of all determinate knowledge the self persists as subject to witness this absence itself. In the ecstatic consciousness it breaks through the last vestige of subject-object consciousness and attains an absolute state, it can then truly be said that all melt into one atman,—who knows what? The outstanding mark of this state is the sublation of all determinate knowledge where the soul regains its original purity and self-sufficiency in which there was a temporary lapse owing to its association with the limiting adjuncts of the waking and dreaming life. It is not a goal to be reached or something to be effected but is the self itself. The absolute is not an object to be attained. Freed from all limitations the self attains it *oneness* with Brahmin which is undifferentiated consciousness and bliss.

The cardinal point in the metaphysical speculation of the Madhyamikas is *Sunyata,* that is, non-existence of everything worldly. The world has no independent existence of its own. It is a mere apparition of *Sunyata.* The objects of the world have no existence at all. They are perceived as existing but in essence they are not so. To exist in reality is not the same as to be perceived as existing. *Esse* may be *percipi* but *percipi* is not *esse.* Appearance though exists *per se* subsequently dies out and is discovered later on as never existing. Yet it has got its empirical value—an empirical reality. This empirical reality is derived from the absolute where there is not even a shadow of distinction between within and without. No doubt, absolute thus reached is ineffable and indescribable and may appear as if it were identical with nothing. But this negative has its counterpart in the positive. It is another way of positing a true reality. In truth it is "the very opposite of a mere nothing. For it is fulfilment, attainment, peace, the goal of life, the object of desire, the end of knowledge. It is our finite realm that is the falsity, the mere nothing, the absolute is all truth." Naturally for the Madhyamikas such a reality escapes all conceptual determinations, Intellect is at a miss to conceive how appearance is linked up with reality. To conceive of any relation is to allow a status to both and to a third element. The removal of differences takes away from reality its concreteness and opens it to the character of pseudo-reality. Madhyamikas, therefore, were forced to postulate an indeterminate reality which presupposes instead a determinate universe. But to be determinate and at the same time to transcend constitute a contradiction. To avoid this difficulty the Madhyamikas had to chalk out the principle of *avidya.* It is not clear how and why the absolute becomes determined itself. The only plausible answer to this question is offered in the principle of *avidya* which does justice to the determinate and indeterminate aspects of existence and at the same time avoids the error of either making the indeterminate determinate or installing determinate as reality.

This *avidya* has its *locus* not in *Sunyata* This is not possible, though possible from the point of view of Shankara. *Sunyata* which literally means voidness or emptiness has suffered a great deal of misunderstanding by those who are not well acquainted with the Buddhist phraseology. Madhyamikas imagined *Sunyata* as the highest truth denying the existence of everything conditional as well as unconditional, relative as well as independent. It is a perfect state of consciousness than which nothing can be more excellent. What the Sunyata doctrine positively insists on is the annihilation of the imagination that weaves the dualistic conception of the world. If this could be called nihilism Shankara's intellectual attempt to reach a monistic view of the universe could also be called nihilistic, for it declares as well the untenability of a separate existence of thought and matter-I and not-I. It is called *Sunya* because it transcends all forms of separation and individuation. Even to attribute the notion of *Sunyata* to it is wrong. Language is deficient to express that state exactly. But it is to be expressed. So such terms are used. It is to be designated in a term with which we are familiar. We are accustomed to call such a state as *Sunya.* By abnegating all phenomenal existences we can reach to that state which is the highest. Madhymikas cannot define that state arrived at by such abnegation. They, therefore, had *to* designate it as *Sunya.* Ignorant minds are deeply saturated with wrong affirmations and false judgements. They are accustomed to understand everything in terms of existence and non-existence but it is neither that which is existent nor that which is non-existent nor that which is or is not at once existent or non-existent. It is again, neither unity nor that which is plurality nor that which is or is not at once a unity and plurality. In it there is no origination, no destruction no annihilation, no persistence, no unity In short, it transcends all modes of relativity.

Teachings of Buddha are based on two kinds of truth. One is conventional or empirical and the other is transcendental and real. It is called *Samvrti* because it envelops the real knowledge and also that it helps to uncover which as a matter of fact is enveloped. It is the same as ignorance on account of its completely enveloping the reality. It is characteristic with *avidya* that it superimposes a form on a non-existent and thus creates an obstacle in having a correct view of the reality. It again implies a thing which depends on another for its existence, that is, what is subject to cause and condition. A really self-existent thing requires no cause and condition and does not undergo any kind of transformation such as origin and decay. So whatever is caused and conditioned is *Samvrta. Avidya* also refers to signs and words current in the world. The signs and words form the basis of perception which is accepted by people in general as true. The form, etc. should not be supposed to be really existing. Their existences are substantiated by proofs which are valid from worldly standpoint. If all that is perceived by the senses be true, then a fool's knowledge which is acquired by his senses will also be true. The body of a *paramarthasatya* is beyond the cognisance of *buddhi,* beyond the purview of knowledge, beyond the possibility of detailed description, beyond all possible form of imagination. The only way to explain this ultimate truth to the worldly people is through commonplace terms and illustrations. A person with diseased *eyes* sees a net of hair. He is corrected by another whose *eyes* are healthy. He sees the real nature of things by negating that there is a net of hair. Similarly a person whose right vision is obstructed by ignorance conceives the existence of *dharma, dhatu* etc. as existent which are, in fact, non-existent in their phenomenal forms. Buddha who is like a person having healthy *eyes* knows this truly and cannot help but saying that there are in reality no *skandhas,* no *dhatus,* etc.

One of the essential characteristics of *Sunyata* is that no instruction can be imparted about it. Once is to realise this within himself. He cannot understand it by listening to the instruction of the perfect. Besides *Sunyata* everything is unreal. But the worldly people whose vision is already obscured cannot understand how the objects which they perceive directly by sense organs can be unreal. They fail to realise those abstruse arguments without the help of illustrations with which they are familiar. Accordingly they are taught with the help of illustration of a snake and rope. Due to defects in vision one mistakes a rope for a snake. Due to this mistake there arises some reactions in his mind such as fear in consequence of which he runs away. This false attribution is *samaropa.* That there is a snake in the form of the rope is nothing but a fabrication, is a construction of the mind. The rope which is the locus to which the mentally created or imagined snake is attributed through imagination is true whereas the imagined snake which is attributed is false. That this imagined attribution is false has been termed as *apavada.* The world we see about is supposed to be existent. In reality it is not so. It is false. The only reality is other than this which is supposed to be existent. We attribute existence to this world but this attribution is false. That is only true which is other than this existent and that is *Sunyata* but not an annihilation".

In this way through the polemics of *samaropa* and *apavada* Madhyamikas try to impart their teachings for the realisation of the ultimate truth. The Yogacaras adopt the same method. Shankarites also have done so.

So the Madhyamikas were led to think that there is nothing real in this world. Everything is devoid of its innate or independent nature. It is wrong to suppose that there is anything in its own or innate from. Things we see around are no doubt there but they appear before us only in their imposed forms. Their own form is *Sunyata* which is devoid of any *svabhava*. This is called also *tathata* or the state of such nature. This is not liable to any change and is of permanent existence. It does not come into existence through any agency. It does not depend on anything for its creation. In *Sunyata* there appears nothing nor does anything disappear.

Taking the objects of this world in this light the philosophers of the Madhyamika school declare that anything external or internal that appears to us existing, is in fact unreal and looks like an imaginary town. There is nothing either internal or external. The notion of I and Mine technically known as *satkayadrsti* disappears completely in the ultimate state where there is neither subject nor object. The disappearance of such notion is followed by the disappearance of sanisara, where its root is stuck deep into. The sole aim of Sunyavada is to nullify or to root out the notion of I and Mine. One who realises *Sunyata* has neither likes nor dislikes. He feels attached neither to gain nor pleasure nor does he feel aversion to loss or pain." As there is no *atman* the notion of it will not arise and when the notion of *ātman* ceases to arise the notion of mine will necessarily disappear.

But, when anyone speaks of *nirvana* he imagines the existence of a man and his n*irvana*. Due to imperfect vision he thinks that a man can attain this ultimate state after practising the disciplinary rules. But all these are fancies. It has no concern with the development of *citta,* stage of spiritual progress, fruits of spiritual discipline. On ultimate analysis there is neither a monk nor a *nirvana* to be attained. One should remove all misconceptions about the world and should realise the non-duality of all worldly things.

Brahmin of Shankara has been characterised as *sat, cit,* and *ananda* but these are not determinations being each of them unspeakable, absolute beyond the determinate construction of *sat* and *cit* and *ananda* formulated by our consciousness. An individual has not only to correct his self from the subjective illusion of individuality, not only to wait for objective illusion of individuality to be corrected but also to contemplate all these corrections as false. He has to contemplate *moksha* not as something to be realised or effected or remanifested, not even as an eternal predicament of the self but as the absolute self itself. An individual illusorily thinks that he is not free. So he wants to be free. But he is eternally free. For the dawning of the consciousness that he is always free there is the necessity of *sadhana* or discipline. *Sadhana* prepares the ground for attaining to the sculptures under discussion.

This form of Avalokitesvara is thus described in the *Sadhanamala Tarn sitam rakta-varnam tu padmaraga-sama-dyutim Panca-Buddha-makuta-dharam barsenotphulla-locanam Vamato spardhaya nalam dhrtva sodasa-patrakam Padmam vikasayantam ca brdi daksina-panina Mayuropari madhyastbe nisannam chandra-mandale Sattvaparyankam abhujya sa-smgara-rasotsavam Chaityantastha-mahakarma-kiitagara-vtharmam Bhavayed Vajradharmagryani nityam bodhim avapnuyat* (The worshipper) should meditate on that supreme Vajradharma, who is of reddish white complexion, who has the brilliance of the *padmaraga* gem, who holds on his crown the five Buddhas, whose *eyes* beam with delight, who, while proudly holding in his left hand a lotus-stalk, causes a sixteen-petalled lotus to bloom on his chest with his right hand, who is seated in the centre of a lunar orb on a peacock while enjoying his animal-seat, who is festive with amorous sentiment and who lives in the sanctum inside a *chaitya,* where great performances take place. (The worshipper meditating this form) obtains the *bodhi* eternally.'

The Sanchi sculptures agree in almost all the details with the above description of Vajradharma Lokesvara, except that the right hand is in *varada* and is not placed on the breast in the attitude of causing a lotus to blossom. The *dbyana* does not specify the a*sana* of the deity but the *lalitasana* of the sculptures is not unbecoming a god 'who is festive with amorous sentiment', with which is also consistent the rich ornamentation of the sculptures. As the crown along with the head is broken in both the images we cannot be sure whether it bore the effigies of the five Dhyani Buddhas, as enjoined in the sadhana of Vajradharma Lokesvara.

It may be noted, however, that the images of Vajradharma Lokesvara, truly answering to the description in the *Sadhanamala*, are not unknown. In the gallery of the Indian Museum is exhibited an image of the deity, hailing from Bihar. Richly bejewelled he is seated in *paryankasana* on a *visvapadma* (double-petalled lotus) resting on a throne supported by a pair of peacocks; he opens against his breast petals of a locus, the stalk of which is held by his left hand.

On his *karanda-makuta* are shown five Dhyani Buddhas in three rows of three, one and one each respectively. The oval halo is inscribed with the Buddhist creed and a donative record in characters of *circa* tenth century. In front of the throne is a dwarfish fierce-looking figure with bristling flame-like hair in *pratyalidha* attitude, with his right hand he brandishes a mace *(mudgara)*, while his left hand is shown against his breast with the index finger raised and holding a noose *(tarjanipasa-brdsyastba vamakaram)*. This figure may stand for Krsnayamari as described in one of the *sadhanas* quoted by B. Bhattacharyya in his Indian Buddhist Iconography. The description tallies in most of the details with it except in the matter of the buffalo-mount which is absent here. A second representation of the deity exists in the reserved collection of the said museum. The main deity seated on a *visvapadma* supported by a pair of peacocks is remarkably similar to the preceding, but here he is flanked by two goddesses seated in the same *asana*, the left one of whom holds *vajraghantas* in her both hands. She may be described is the goddess Vajraghanta, one of the four 'guardians of the gates' associated *with* such Vajrayana deities as Lokanatha and Vajratara.

The *sudhanas* describe her as one-faced and two-armed carrying a bell surmounted by *vajra*. The attributes in the hands of the right hand goddess are broken. Above these goddesses are the representations of a *visvavajra* and *ratna* on a stand. On the pedestal is a three-headed six-armed dwarfish deity with terrible appearance, open mouths and bare fangs in *alidha* attitude, in his right hand he carries a sword, a mace and a *padma*, of his left hands, one holds a *pasa*, the second broken and the third is in *katibasta* pose. This deity may stand for another variety of Krsnayamari as described in the *Sadhanamala*. The absence of mounts in both the forms of Krsnayamari, as represented in the pedestal of the two Vajradharma Lokesvara images, may be due to their being attendant deities. On two sides of this figure on the pedestal are two goddesses, the left one of whom standing in *alidha* pose and holding a *kartr* and a *kapala is* equally awe-inspiring and dwarfish, corresponding in her iconographic details to Ekajata, the right one holding a rosary and a *kamandalu* stands in *pratyalidba* attitude. The sculpture, dating from area tenth century, comes from Nalanda.

7

Buddha and Hinduism

Gautam Buddha and his teachings and philosophy have had an enormous impact on not only the evolution of Hinduism, but also the medieval as well as the modern Indian society.

In Hinduism, Buddha is considered the ninth incarnation of Vishnu, the form of Almighty God that preserves life and universe. While Buddhism thrived and prospered in countries outside India as an independent entity, within India, Buddhism does not seem to be a very popular religion, nor is Buddha one of the primary deities in most Hindu temples. It is an irony that is probably the main reason for Buddhism being considered as a totally different religion from Hinduism.

To solve this riddle, one needs to run through a few millennia of history and culture of India. However, even before that, one needs to understand what is meant by Hinduism.

Role of Gautam Buddha in Hinduism

The word Hinduism is not indicative of a particular religion in the way the term religion' is understood in the West as a divine gospel or diktat, that humans can only understand, not contribute to. In ancient India, the equivalent word for religion was DHARMA, meaning duty, wherein the primary focus was on the conduct and the duty of a person in the social context. The divine texts or VEDAs were certainly there, but more important was the conduct of a person. The almighty god was defined as an omnipotent, omnipresent entity, that neither begins nor ends and that is beyond human understanding, though we can feel him in a spiritual way.

The almighty god in Sanatana Dharma (the name by which Hinduism used to be called in ancient times) was worshipped both as a formless entity, and in different forms- mostly human. The three major forms were BRAHMA, the form which is the creator of universe; VISHNU, the preserver; and SHIVA, the form in which Lord destroys the old to make way for the new. Vishnu is said to have come to our world in a mortal form nine times till date, to save the living world, guide the humans, and destroy the evil. The ninth such incarnation was Gautam Buddha.

Here again it is important to appreciate that in ancient India, Dharma had the primary focus on duty and conduct, and since it was not restricted as a divine diktat, several schools of thought and philosophy with subtle differences existed simultaneously, and each one of them was respected, though some of them used to be more popular than others at any given point of time. There was a tradition of debate and discussion, wherein experts from different schools used to come at a platform and prove a point or two. It was in this background that Buddha started preaching his philosophy.

Relevance of Buddha

Gautam Buddha was born as Siddhartha, a prince in a small kingdom in Northern India. After his birth, an astrologer told his father, the King, that the boy will either become a great King or else he will denounce the world and become a great saint. The King did not want his son to become an ascetic, so he attempted to ensure that Siddhartha was always surrounded by worldly pleasures and luxuries. Nothing pitiful, nor anything that would have raised compassion in the mind of the young Prince or encouraged detachment from worldly affairs was ever allowed to come close to him.

Unfortunately, such isolation from pain and suffering only made him extraordinarily sensitive to it. It is said that the grown up Prince once asked his charioteer to take him to the city. On the way, he met a person who was very sick. Siddhartha did not understand what was happening to this person, and was very surprised to know that people fell so sick. Next he saw a person who was very old. The Prince was surprised and asked what disease he suffered. When told that it was not a disease, but the destiny of every person, he was even more deeply perturbed. Finally, he came across a funeral procession, and asked what was happening. When told that a person had died, he enquired about death. He was told that every person dies, and so would all his relatives and friend. Ever since that moment, Siddhartha realised that everything in life is temporary, and started wondering whether it is worth all the suffering that the mankind has to endure.

After he had been married, and blessed with a child, Siddhartha left his palace one night, and went away from his family, to learn more about life and destiny, so as to find a way to redress human suffering. He spent many years in the company of learned saints and philosophers. He also undertook rigorous meditation and yoga on the Himalayas. However, he was not satisfied with what he learnt. Finally, one morning, under the Bodhi tree in the city of Gaya, he attained self-actualisation. Thereafter, he started preaching his understanding. He prescribed the middle path the path between the two extremes of religious fanaticism and totally self-centred materialistic lifestyle. He used to preach in local language, unlike other scholars who used Sanskrit the language of scholars, which unfortunately, most ordinary people did not understood very well. In many other ways too, Buddha differed from the prevalent schools of philosophy in India. He did not give any significance to the class differentiation. He preached non-violence, and giving up all greed, lust and attachments, as a means to attain peace and reduce one's own suffering.

Schools of Philosophy

Buddha devised simple solutions for problem of human suffering. Primary among them was the detachment to all worldly affairs and articles, and leading a simple life with ordinary means. He never declared himself as an incarnation of god, nor did he gave any name to his followers. With time, his followers became almost a sect within Hinduism. Many Kings gave patronage to Buddhist school of philosophy, which was very much a part of Hindu mainstream, even though it differed with some of the tenets of Sanatana Dharma' the traditional faith. One of the most famous example of royal patronage to Buddhism is Emperor Ashoka, often considered the greatest Emperors of ancient India, who gave up all violence under the influence of his Buddhist teacher, and sent his children to Sri Lanka and Myanmar. Incidentally, Ashoka's father Bimbisara was a patron of Sanatana Dharma, the traditional school, while his grandfather Chandragupta Maurya was a patron of Jainism, another popular school of philosophy during those times that still survives in India, but is considered an integral part of Hinduism.

In the first thousand years after Christ, Buddhism and Jainism were the dominant schools of philosophy in India, till the Adi Shankaracharya, a brilliant scholar and proponent of ancient Sanatana Dharma again took the lead and re-established Sanatan dharma and primacy of Vedas in Hinduism as the dominant schools, in eighth century AD. During the period between Buddha and the Shankaracharya, Buddhist schools had been dominant, and had reshaped Hinduism as per their own principles. Notably, in India, Buddhism was never a separate religion from Hinduism. It was, in fact, the dominant school of philosophy within Hinduism. Thus, during this period, non-violence was established deep in the Hindu psyche. Killing and wars were disliked a phenomenon that some claim as a factor for subsequent submission of Indian armies before the foreign invaders.

By tenth century, India had become the primary target of Muslim invaders in the middle ages. It was India's wealth that they wanted, but when they invaded, they destroyed everything related to its religion too. In the process, they destroyed the libraries of Takshashila in the West, and Nalanda in the East, which were the primary reservoirs of all ancient Indian knowledge and scriptures. The last of them in Nalanda were handed over to the Tibetan students by the teachers in Nalanda so that they can be preserved. Thus, more scriptures of Buddhism are probably preserved in Tibet than in India today. Interestingly, some of these ancient scriptures, were subsequently sent to China under the influence of spreading Buddhism, and many such scriptures are hidden even today in the forbidden city of Beijing in the joints and domes of the main buildings.

In India, Buddhism was never identified as a religion separate from Hinduism. Till the eighth century AD it was the dominant school of philosophy within Hinduism. After Shankaracharya established his philosophy, Advaitavad or the philosophy of unitary existence of god and soul in the eighth century AD, Buddhism lost its dominance within Hinduism but its tenets remained an integral part of Hinduism, having become fully merged in it.

In the foreign countries, Buddhist philosophy was taught, and Buddha was treated as god. There, other forms of incarnations like Krishna began to be considered an earlier incarnation of Buddha, instead of being considered as incarnations of Vishnu. Thus, outside India, Buddhism came to have an identity that was considered different from Hinduism, even though there, Buddhism was deeply influenced by different schools of philosophy in Hinduism. With time, the two streams of Buddhism outside India and Hinduism within it began to diverge, being aided by local customs, different languages and changing times. Once power in India was captured by Muslim Emperors, the evolution and further development of Hinduism as well as Buddhism was thwarted. During the next thousand years, Dharma became Hinduism largely as a result of separation of identity from Islam. In this faith called Hinduism, Buddhist philosophies of non-violence, middle path and detachment were deeply embedded, but somewhere along, Buddhist scriptures were lost. So was the emphasis on Buddha as a deity.

8

Buddha's Philosophy

Human Experience

The Wheel

The world we live in is a world of pain. The inexorable process of life and death, the process of becoming and ceasing-to-be, is profoundly bound up with suffering; at the root of it there is an ever-throbbing sense of grief, of deficit and desolation, like a thorn in the flesh. This, in essence, is the 'noble' truth of pain.

Unpleasant Truth

It is obviously not a pleasant truth; by the very nature of things it cannot be a pleasant truth. Yet Gautam took this tragic affirmation as the starting-point of his critique of life. He took it for his starting-point because he was, above all other things, concerned with analysis of the content of human experience, with understanding the elusive pattern of man's subjective universe. His interpretation remains essentially a psychological interpretation. While the metaphysicians of his age, the amateurs as well as the professionals, were wrangling for all they were worth over abstract problems, Gautam seems to have been content with focusing his whole attention on psychological observations. These observations led him to a most disconcerting discovery: the discovery that pain is the most universal, the most significant element in human awareness. The discovery was not, in itself, particularly original; what was original was the emphasis which Gautam placed on it and the comprehensiveness which he gave to it. He made the truth of pain the basis of his doctrine. It has to be accepted in entirety or rejected in entirety; there is no possible middle way. If we reject it, the whole structure of his word crumbles.

It is, of course, possible to reject the truth of pain, to deny its distressing implications. There were many among his own contemporaries who totally rejected his tragic basis. There were the Lokayatikas, or the Worldly-Wise, for instance. These flamboyant philosophers not only denied validity to the 'noble' truth of pain, but they made uproarious fun of the Tathagata. Being worldly-wise, they were impatient of tragic philosophies which might, through slow contagion, undermine their solid certitudes. 'It is absurd,' mocked these hilarious positivists, 'absurd to condemn pleasures because they are mixed with sorrow and dissatisfaction; absurd to throw away rice because the kernel is wrapped in a rough shell.' But their mockery was scarcely a cogent argument; the fact that they thought it to be an adequate answer to Gautam's affirmation was a confession of intellectual confusion. The analogy of rice is misleading.

It does not disprove the truth of pain: it merely begs the question. The implication of Gautam's utterance is not that the wrapping is rough, but that the kernel is bitter. He would probably have agreed that the shell of human experience is both soft and tempting, that so long as one is content with the shell one can afford to be oblivious of the reality of suffering. The actuality of life reveals itself, he would have argued, when one has torn asunder the wrapping, penetrated a little deeper than the shell. It is then that an abyss, an apparently bottomless abyss, opens before one; it is then that one is able to recognise 'the misery in the world as it is' in its stark and terrifying actuality.

Whether the implications of Gautam's affirmation are true or not, is an issue which cannot be decided by means of syllogisms. A statement concerning the nature of human experience is not capable of being logically proved or contradicted. The psychological universe is by no means an Euclidean universe: a psychological critique of life, therefore, falls outside the grasp of 'mere logic.' The crucial experience of suffering, even of purely physical suffering—if such a thing is conceivable—is not logically demonstrable. What is more, it eludes all attempts to bring it within the compass of objective comprehension. Ultimately, an aching stomach and an aching soul are equally beyond the sphere of objective understanding: one can dissect the one, and one can record the symptoms of the other, but the immediate actuality of experience in either case cannot be grasped. Strictly speaking, the world of pain is an impalpable and invisible world.

The proper study of human experience, then, is human experience itself. As such Gautam's truth of pain does not admit of any objective test. We can, of course, view the pattern of human consciousness in a historical perspective; observe the expression which it has found at its highest level. The method is no doubt arbitrary to a degree; but no other approach seems practicable. And one fact emerges abundantly clear from an empirical retrospect of this nature: the fact that, at its most significant, human experience has so far found the tragic expression to be the most adequate representation of its reality. There are the bitter lamentations of a man of the land of Uz, whose name was Job: he feared God, and eschewed evil, and yet had to suffer torments of hell.

There are the biblical Wisdom Books reminding us that human existence is a sore travail. There is Solon—a man-of-the-world and a sagacious lawgiver— courting the disfavour of Croesus, King of Lydia, by observing 'consider the end of everything, and count no man happy till he is dead.' There is the 'Prince of Glory' kneeling in Gethsemane with his 'soul exceeding sorrowful unto death.' There is Kabir: he lived in God as 'fish live in water,' he was never haunted by that excruciating sense of exile from the Deity which drove so balanced a person as Em-pedocles to the verge of madness—and yet even Kabir lived long enough to admit that suffering is the common lot of men, believers and non-believers alike. There is Hamlet helpless against a 'sea of troubles'; Macbeth bearing the corpse of sleep 'to the last syllable of recorded time; Lear 'a poor old man, as full of grief as age'—in tears; and Othello being goaded by a nameless and inscrutable cause into the murder of the thing he loved. There is Baudelaire. There is Dostoievsky...

But one can prolong the tragic testimony indefinitely: it is overwhelming. The tragic, said D. H. Lawrence, is the most holding. It is the most holding, perhaps, because it is the most universal.

Universal, but not Final: The truth of pain represents the point of departure for Gautam's critique of human experience, but it does not constitute the whole. Every truth has its limits: it is limited in its purpose, as also in its sphere of application. Gautam did not regard the truth of pain as the whole truth about life. He clearly defined its sphere, its purpose. 'So long, Monks,' he said, 'as I did not comprehend... the misery in the world as such, so long did I not discern the meaning of being enlightened... But, monks, when I fully comprehended... the misery in the world as such... then did I discern the meaning of being enlightened.' The understanding of 'the misery in the world as such,' is the primary condition of enlightenment. For Socrates the recognition of one's ignorance was the beginning of knowledge; for Gautam, on the other hand, the recognition of one's misery was the beginning of knowledge. But the beginning of knowledge is not the end of knowledge. To comprehend the fact of suffering in its universal implications is to discern the meaning of being enlightened; but the enlightenment itself, which is demonstrably a residual condition, is something-other-than-suffering. The recognition of the tragic motive as being the dominant motive in human psychology leads to an awareness which does not partake of the nature of the process through which it is reached: the ultimate issue of tragedy is something-other-than-tragedy. Some such baffling paradox was vaguely at the root of the classical concept of 'catharsis' as being the purpose of tragedy: such, too, is the paradox underlying Gautam's critique of life.

It is essential to understand this paradox, because failure to grasp it has led to many misinterpretations of Gautam's doctrine. The ignorant charge of morbidity, for instance, which is so often levelled against Gautam, may be directly attributed to a misconception prevailing with regard to his attitude to the problem of suffering. Gautam never claimed that the truth of pain is all-comprehensive; it is only the first of a series of four 'noble' truths he postulated; and he admitted that there are truths more comprehensive than the truth of pain—truths which include and transcend it. For pain itself is a condition, not a finality; a universal and poignantly significant condition, but still a condition. And to every condition, according to Gautam, there is a cause. The world we live in is a world of dependent origination; everything that exists in this world is bound in a chain of causal relationship; and all phenomena proceed from a cause. An infant crying in the night has cause for his complaint. The general phenomenon of 'the misery in the world as such,' also proceeds from a general cause. What is that cause, and is it possible to discover it and understand it 'as it really is?'

Gautam answered the question in the affirmative. We may, or may not, agree with his answer. Perhaps it tends to oversimplify the issue; but, for all its shortcomings, it remains a remarkable explanation—remarkable for its originality no less than for its depth and comprehensiveness. It anticipates—indeed, in some ways, it strikes a note that goes beyond—the modern psychological hypotheses. For Gautam seems to have resolved the problem of human suffering in psychological terms, though it is necessary to add that his analysis is nearer Shakespeare than Freud. His diagnosis does not attempt to postulate a metaphysical and abstract cause for human suffering. It does not attempt to drag in the Deity and appeal to an arbitrary dualism of good and evil after the fashion of theologians. The tormenting sense of sin, which plays so important a partin the pathological philosophy of the Church Fathers and their latter-day devotees, does not enter into it: we do not hear of *'le spectacle ennuyeux de l'immortel peche'* as in Baudelaire, or of the 'doctrine of original sin' which is such a 'real and tremendous thing' to Mr. T. S. Eliot. The critique is kept on a humanistic level: the explanation of human suffering is found in an immediate and intelligible cause. 'By oneself one suffers,' says the Dhammapada: by oneself—not because of Adam's fall from Grace, not because of the sins of our fathers. By oneself one suffers—but why? Because there is a contradiction in one's experience, a contradiction in one's approach to experience, In contemporary phraseology we should describe it as a 'complex,' but contradiction is a more expressive and inclusive term. What is this contradiction which cuts across the whole of one's experience and transforms life into a perpetual agony?

The Fire Sermon hints at an explanation. The title of the sermon itself furnishes a clue to the issue: 'the Conflagration of the Senses' is precisely what constitutes a constant source of irritation and inquietude in the human psyche. We suffer because our hearts, our eyes, and, indeed, all other vehicles of our sense-perceptions are of the nature of a flame. We suffer because 'O monks, the knowledge... the feeling arising from contact with the visible... the audible... the palpable... be it pleasure, be it pain, be it neither pleasure nor pain, this also is in flames.' But how is the conflagration of the senses kindled? By what fire? By the fire of desire, says the Fire Sermon, above all by the fire of desire. The world we live in is a world of suffering because we approach it through the mediacy of desire. And desire is hunger; desire is deficit. And it is a hunger and deficit of a specific kind: it is a hunger for which there can be no satisfaction, a deficit which can in no way be filled. Desire reaches out towards the unattainable: it is, in fact, *soif de l'impossible.*

But why? Why does desire assume an insatiable hunger, an insatiable deficit, and an unquenchable thirst? We have the testimony of Nietzsche—a testimony all the more convincing because it comes from a man who, in his writings, appears to take a position almost diametrically opposed to Gautam. All desire, he says poignantly, yearns for eternity —yearns for deep, deep eternity. Desire, in other words, is not just necessity (what is necessary is, in fact, seldom desirable). Its demands are infinitely more exacting. To desire is inevitably to crave for eternity—for deep, deep eternity. And such a craving is foredoomed to frustration. For the world we live in is a world of transient things—in spite of Plato, in spite of Sankra. Every object which desire can 'grasp,' would like to 'grasp,' contains within it the inherent necessity of decay and dissolution. The 'grasping' mind itself is a component thing and, like the baseless fabric of Prospero's vision, dissolves, leaving not a rack behind. The *Brahmin* of the Vedantic daydream is no more eternal than 'the cloud-capped towers, the gorgeous palaces, the solemn temples, the great globe itself...' The immanent soul of the Platonic fancy is no more immortal than the face that launched a thousand ships. These fantasies are the desperate, touching, and hopelessly inadequate refuges built by the 'grasping' mind to escape the inherent necessity of dissolution.

Noble Truth

Such is the 'noble' truth of the cause of pain. But, even this is not the whole truth. Gautam's critique goes further, postulating the cessation of pain. This may, or may not, satisfy us; but it is well worth some serious consideration. If the misery in the world as such, it argues, proceeds from a cause—from an immediate and intelligible cause—then it is perhaps possible, at least it is conceivable, that the cause can be extirpated. If we know and realise what is the source of irritation in our psyche, then we should try to remove that source of irritation. If we know and realise that we suffer because we approach life through the mediacy of desire, then the only thing to do is to learn not to approach it through the mediacy of desire. There are other ways of approach to life, other modes of experiencing reality, than desire.

For desire itself, according to Gautam's analysis, is not a finality. He never posited it—as Schopenhauer posited his Will—as the Thing-In-Itself. Of the Thing-In-Itself he never pretended to have any definitive knowledge. Indeed, he appears to have believed that the knowledge of such would not be particularly useful even if it were possible; that the only kind of knowledge which is at once relevant to human purpose, and within the compass of human understanding, is the knowledge of relations, of conditions. As such, he represented desire as yet another condition, not the Thing-In-Itself; a deep-rooted condition which, as Nietzsche beautifully put it, 'is deeper yet than heartbreak'—but still a condition. And because it is a condition and not the Thing-In-Itself, it can be changed, it can cease to be.

The change, the cessation, is not only possible; it is even inevitable. Inevitable that the grasping approach should change; inevitable, too, that desire should cease to be. For though it is true that desire 'is deeper yet than heartbreak,' there is also such a thing as a gradual wearying of desire. If the heartbreaks are persistent—and in the very nature of things, they must be persistent—then there is bound to come a moment in the curve of desire when it wearies of itself, ceases to be, through a process of self-exhaustion; a moment, in other words, when the 'grasping' mind has been so deeply annihilated by its successive failures that it automatically abandons its tendency to grasp. The infant crying in the night would, in the absence of the mother, cry itself to a profound silence; even Nietzsche could not pursue the Dionysian ecstasy of desire— desire to 'create something beyond himself'— further than a stupefying and speechless madness.

But, this is not the kind of renunciation that Gautam contemplated. His is an 'Apollonian' rather than 'Dionysian' approach: it demands a conscious and intelligent renunciation of the element of irritation in the human psyche, a conscious and intelligent abandonment of the grasping attitude of mind. It is a renunciation which one has to achieve through one's own strenuous effort: by oneself one suffers, and by oneself one ceases to suffer.

Such is the 'noble' truth of the cessation of pain; leading us to the problem of the Way.

The Way: There is a middle path, O Bhikhsus, avoiding the two extremes, discovered by the Tathagata—a path which opens the eyes, and bestows understanding, which leads to the higher wisdom, to full enlightenment, to Nirvana:

Foundation of the Kingdom of Righteousness

The Way is of the world; and yet it is not a worldly way. The Way demands renunciation of a very ultimate nature; and yet the renunciation it demands is but an acceptance of the order of actuality. The Way sets forth limits to human experience; and yet these limits, when properly realised, become the vehicle of liberation for the consciousness. The Way is not the way of ardent love and desire; and yet it releases a tenderness which is beyond all measure. The Way leads through a wilderness of doubt and despair; and yet the 'wayfarer' in the very process of 'wayfaring' attains to a serenity free from all doubt and despair. The knowledge of The Way is born from the recognition of pain; and yet The Way transcends the condition of pain from which it is born.

The Way is a moral way; and yet it has no use for mere moralities. The Way is based on a concept of normality; and yet the 'Norm' it offers is not a measuring-rod, not just a social convention. The Way involves the working out of a technique of living; and yet the technique it contemplates is not a matter of ceremonious formalities, of codes of outward behaviour, of cultivating masks for presentation in public places. The Way is a way of detachment; and yet it is not the way of egotistic, self-centred indifference, which is merely an intellectual form of self-indulgence. The Way is simple, manifestly reasonable, and within the grasp of the humblest of men; and yet subtle, hard to perceive, hard to know—and harder still to follow. The Way is a paradox.

The Way is of the world because it concerns itself with the most universal, the most immediate problem of life: the problem of grief and tribulation, of ill, sorrow and distraction. It is of the world because the calm, the insight, the enlightenment and Nirvana to which it tends are not esoteric states, and are relevant only in the here and now. And yet it is not a worldly way; and the worldly-wise, both those who seek their land of heart's desire in the here and now, and those who project it into an imaginary hereafter, have always found it unsatisfactory. It is not a worldly way because it does not concern itself with the mere acquisition of sensations, physical or spiritual, positive or negative, of this world or of the *next;* because it avoids the two extremes which have a basic identity of purpose—'that conjoined with the passions, low, vulgar, common, ignoble, and useless, and that conjoined with self-torture, painful, ignoble, and useless.'

The Way demands renunciation, a difficult and irredeemable psychological surrender: the surrender of one of the most deep-rooted habits of the human ego—the habit of grasping. Other religions, other faiths and philosophies have also demanded such a surrender. There is, however, a qualitative difference between their demands and the demand which is implicit in Gautam's conception of The Way. The latter does not make the demand for renunciation conditional upon any arbitrary ethical principles or compensatory promises. It asks for the abandonment of the habit of grasping because it recognises the contradiction inherent in the acquisitive approach; recognises the illusory nature of the human grasp—the illusory nature, indeed, of the very ego that wants to grasp; recognises, in the ultimate analysis, the utter impossibility of grasping anything at all in a universe of sense and succession. It asks for the abandonment of the habit of grasping because it knows 'that it is in the very nature of all things most near and dear to us that we must divide ourselves from them, leave them, sever ourselves from them.' The renunciation which is demanded is thus no more than an objective acceptance of the actual conditions of existence.

These conditions necessarily impose limits on human experience. The periphery of human experience—both in its actuality and its potentiality—is strictly finite, and as such, limited. It is limited in time; it is limited in space. And although these limits are not stationary, but always changing, yet the measure of that change is always finite and subject to limitations. The Way, therefore, admits the essentially limited character of our experience. It goes further: it suggests that the only manner of expanding the horizon of our awareness is by accepting its finiteness, and the finiteness of our vision. Do not look long, it says, and do not look short; in other words, avoid long-sightedness as well as myopia. For, The Way can be perceived only by a normal vision; and the normal vision is a finite vision. It is neither macrocosmic nor microcosmic. It does not concern itself with the infinite or the infinitesimal. Its principal focus is the finite universe—that strangest of all paradoxes which is at once a part of the infinite, and contains an infinity within it. Do not look long, and do not look short. For between the tip of one's nose and the darknesses which stretch beyond the remotest star there are a multitude of finite objects and distances, which our eyes are often apt to overlook, yet which it is imperative not to overlook. It is only by restricting our focus to a finite universe that we can hope to attain to some measure of lucidity and freedom of vision. Freedom, said Engels, is the recognition of necessity. Gautam would have agreed, though he would probably have added that necessity can be apprehended only by a vision that is neither long-sighted nor myopic. Such is the essence of a truly human perspective—it is the essence of The Way also.

The Way is weary of ardent love and desire. And why? Because love and desire cannot be adjusted to necessity, to the conditions of a finite universe. They demand too much or too little; look too far or too near. And why? Because they are, in a more than mere symbolic sense, blind. And blindness separates, creates insuperable barriers. Ardent love and desire separate one from the very object which one so loves and desires. The Way is weary of them also because they are still involved in personality, in the ego: they represent, in fact, one of the most subtle attempts on the part of the ego to save itself—by losing itself in something-other-than itself. And yet, of course, the ego can never really lose itself in the object: it merely subjectifies and appropriates it. Ardent love and desire are insatiably acquisitive, and because they are thus, they stultify that all-pervasive tenderness which is not born of hunger, but of understanding; which, because it is not blind, does not create barriers, but unites. To abandon the way of love and desire, therefore, is to remove barriers, to release a tenderness, which, because it is not involved in the ego's hankering for possession, and is free from the limitations of personality:

> *... Plane sur la vie, et comprend sans effort Le langage des fleurs et des choses muettes!*

However, to arrive at such an all-comprehensive understanding, to realise in one's being such a quality of immediate and effortless sympathy, it is necessary to pass through a desolation of doubt and despair, to know the depths of human suffering in their utter nakedness. For, says Gautam, 'so long, O monks, as I did not comprehend, as it really is, the satisfaction in the world as such, the misery in the world as such, the escape therefrom (i.e. misery) as such, so long did I not discern the meaning of being enlightened... But, monks, when I fully comprehended, as it really is, the satisfaction in the world as such, the misery in the world as such, the escape therefrom as such, then did I discern the meaning of being enlightened in the world. Then did knowledge and insight arise in me...'

The Way is a moral way; and yet Gautam himself repeatedly discouraged those among his followers who wanted to interpret his teachings on a purely ethical level, divorce his precepts from their psychological background, and turn his critique of experience into a mere formula. In the *Brahmajala-sutta* he declares quite frankly that those who praise him on account of his morality praise him for the wrong reason. 'It is in respect only of trifling things,' he says, 'of matters of little value, of mere morality, that an ignorant man, when praising the Tathagata, would speak.' The Eightfold Path of right views, right intention, right speech, right action, right livelihood, right effort, right mindfulness, right concentration, has, therefore, little meaning when considered in isolation from his psychological interpretation of the nature of human experience. It is only when we correlate it with the whole analytical process of his thought that it acquires a vital, highly original significance. For instance, the phrase 'right views,' which forms the basis of the Eightfold Path, is a mere ethical cliche considered by itself. But it ceases to be an ethical cliche when it is realised that Gautam did not use it in its ordinary didactic implication; that by 'right views' he seems to have implied a perspective of life free from such common 'delusions' as belief in an omnipotent Deity, in the permanence of the human ego, in personal immortality and posthumous compensations—a perspective, in other words, which is not distorted by one's more obvious desires and wishes. Thus, The Way is moral only in a very novel sense: it is moral in the sense that, quite independent of any metaphysical and supernatural considerations, it places the responsibility of action upon the individual; that, taking psychological observations as its starting point, it finds 'by oneself is wrong done, by oneself one suffers. By oneself wrong is left undone; by oneself one is purified. Purity and impurity belong to oneself; no one can purify another.'

The Way reduces morality to a function of human intelligence, to a kind of honest self-criticism and censorship. And though the notion of 'right' underlying The Way presupposes a concept of normality, the Norm which is set forth is not just a measuring-rod, not a moral dogma. All that it implies is a concept of centrality in human experience. The Norm is not meant to be a formula nor a code of reference, but a focus—a point of integration for the psyche. Human awareness, one might say, evolves within the spiral of increasing perception; and the Norm is as the centre about which the spiral revolves.

The Way obviously does involve a technique of living, an *ars vivendi.* Equally obvious is the fact that the technique of The Way is not a matter of outward form. Gautam, unlike Comte, never attempted to 'strengthen the feeble altruism of human nature by exalting Humanity as the object of ceremonial worship,' and did not spend his twilight years 'devising for this Religion of Humanity an intricate system of priesthood, sacraments, prayers, and discipline.' Life in the Order during his Ministry seems to have been remarkably free from ceremony and ritual, for such a quasi-religious body.

Yet The Way insists on the need for discipline; not a ritualistic and ceremonious discipline, but a discipline of the whole being. There is nothing esoteric about the discipline of The Way: for Gautam 'preached the truth without making any distinction between exoteric and esoteric doctrine.' The discipline only emphasises 'right mindfulness and right concentration. The purpose of this discipline is not, as in Yoga, the attainment of a subjective state akin to 'deep and dreamless sleep,' or a sense of unity with the Absolute; that peculiar interpretation of The Way, the concept of *'Dhayana'* for instance, is a latter-day innovation; it belongs to men like Bodhidharma who went to China and founded what developed into Zen Buddhism, a cult which for all practical purposes is indistinguishable from Yoga. Actually, both in its method and purpose The Way is so utterly different from the method and purpose of Yoga that it is difficult to understand how Louis de la Vallee Poussin could confuse the two, saying: '*Le Bouddhisme est une certaine forme deyoga ou ascitisme-mysticisme; il est ne de la cristallisation rapide de donnie generalement Indienne sous l'influence de Cakya Muni, "le grand religieux"* '

This confusion results, of course, from a complete misunderstanding of the issue. Yoga aims at achieving oneness with the Supreme, with the Immanent Brahma; and it proceeds by way of subjectification of the object. The Way, on the other hand, if it does not deny the reality of Brahma, at least expresses very grave doubts as to his importance; as such it is not very much concerned with chasing the Absolute. The method of The Way is also almost diametrically opposed to the method of Yoga: it tends to approach 'the world within' from as objective an angle as is humanly possible, to bring the chaotic tendencies of the psyche under some kind of a rational control by cultivating the habit of dispassionate introspection and meditation. The Way seeks tranquillity rather than exultation, the peace which resides in detachment rather than the ecstasy of imaginative identification, which constitutes the *elan* of the mystic.

The whole essence of The Way is expressed in one of Gautam's very last sermons which has been given elsewhere, but which may pertinently be repeated here. 'Herein, O mendicants, let a brother, as he dwells in the body, so regard the body that he, being strenuous, thoughtful, and mindful may, whilst in the world, overcome the grief which arises from bodily craving—while subject to sensations, let him continue so to regard the sensations that he, being strenuous, thoughtful, and mindful, may, whilst in the world, overcome the grief arising from the craving which follows our sensation—and so also as he thinks or reasons or feels let him overcome the grief which arises from the craving due to ideas, or reasoning, or feeling.'

The sermon doubtless sets forth an ideal of detachment. However, the detachment that is demanded should not be confused with the negative ideal of indifference. The distinction between the two ideals may be subtle, but it *is* there: it is to be found in Gautam's emphasis on the necessity of 'being mindful and thoughtful.' The mindfulness and thoughtfulness which are contemplated in The Way assume a high degree of sensitiveness to the world around one; they assume a comprehensive awareness which is ready to admit the fullness of knowledge into itself. For, demonstrably, it is impossible to be constantly 'mindful and thoughtful' when one is indifferent. The detachment of The Way, then, is in reality, sensibility in its most crystallised and awakened form. Such a crystallisation may, or may not, be practicable for humanity *en masse.* Still the fact that Gautam in his own person almost succeeded in realising an awareness of this order, is something over which one may justifiably rejoice.

The Way is profoundly paradoxical in its realisation as well as in its practice. Yet the paradox is one which is by no means beyond the grasp of human intelligence: to resolve it merely requires the use of what Descartes called 'le *bon sens*' and described as being '*la chose du Monde mieux partagee.*' Only, of course, there is the good sense which is an active agency, and the good sense which lies dormant and passive as an unrealised potentiality. Till now, at any rate, active good sense has been conspicuous mostly by its absence from human affairs. That is why The Way is hard to perceive, hard to know—and harder still to follow.

World of Difference

There is always a world of difference between the mere recognition of The Way and its attainment.

The Void: We are such stuff. As dreams are made on, and our little life Is rounded with a sleep... *Prospero in The Tempest*

Man, Schopenhauer was fond of saying, is a metaphysical animal. Schopenhauer, it is well known, was an ardent admirer of Indian philosophy; he had drunk rather deeply of its sad wisdom; and probably he was thinking of the Hindus in particular when he pronounced this acute judgement on the nature of man. For no other people under the sun have been so addicted to metaphysics as the Hindus'; it is their hereditary passion; and there is scarcely anything in their complex culture which is not permeated with it. The Hindu is, in truth, the metaphysical animal *par excellence.* This is not to suggest that he is fundamentally different from the rest of mankind; or even that, because of his metaphysical preoccupations, he in any way neglects the physical side of life. Far from it! He takes the physical ritual of existence as seriously as anybody else; and indeed, if anything, he attends to the mundane processes of eating and evacuating, breathing and procreating with an even greater relish and gusto than an ordinary *homme moyen sensuel.* However, where he differs from the latter is in the peculiar habit he has of giving a transcendental twist to his physical functions.

This transcendentalism may partly be attributed to the quite extraordinary, and often exasperating, vanity of the Hindu mind: a vanity which, at root, is a subtle form of megalomania. It enables the Hindu to surround himself with a cosmic aura, and to invest the most trivial details of his life with a sense of importance for which there would appear to be not the slightest justification. Moreover, metaphysics serves him as a kind of intoxicant: an intoxicant in some ways even more stimulating than the potent essence of Soma, whose magical qualities have been celebrated with such extravagant lyrical abandon in the Sama Veda —more stimulating since it dispenses with the mediacy of the senses and directly attacks the brain. His transcendentalism renders the Hindu almost completely immune from that most universal of human afflictions—*ennui.*

The Hindus of Gautam's days were even more strongly addicted to metaphysics than the Hindus of today. Gautam was one of the very few thinkers of his age who successfully resisted the temptation of abstract beatitudes. It must have required no small amount of courage and strength. In fact, he did more than merely resist the temptation: he actually raised a voice of protest against this spiritual form of indulgence, and pleaded for temperance. For all practical purposes it was a voice in the wilderness, since even those who cared to listen to him did not take the trouble to understand him. Yet the fact that it was raised is in itself pregnant with meaning.

Gautam was not at all a metaphysician. Indeed, he never concealed the fact that he regarded metaphysics as an irrelevance—an intellectual luxury which might be permissible in some happier world, but not in this best of all possible worlds, where the tears shed by all sentient creatures exceed 'the water in the four oceans.' He described the endless wrangles of different schools of metaphysicians as 'the thicket of theorising, the wilderness of theorising, the tangle, the bondage and shackles of theorising.' For himself he had no use whatever for theorising. His method of attack is always direct and concrete; his arguments are lucid and lively, relieved, as they often are, by a gentle irony which some of his contemporaries considered as erring on the side of levity. In an age and a country given to excessive indulgence in abstractions and daydreams, he insisted on the too, too solid world of pain; insisted on the necessity of facing the urgent problem of conduct; insisted on placing first things first. This was his distinctive contribution to the cause of humanism.

Obviously, then, it would be futile to look for anything like a completed system of metaphysics in his critique. The bulk of the Buddhist metaphysics, such as we know it today, is the product of the fertile imagination of the Mahayana School, or the Greater Vehicle, just as the formalised morality and ethics is mostly the creation of the puritanism of the Hinayana School, or the Lesser

Vehicle. Gautam's own attitude to metaphysics was akin to that of Hume and his followers: he mistrusted speculative philosophy because he considered it to be based on insufficient data, to be no more than an infantile pastime of building castles in the air. This does not justify the inference—often too easily drawn by his hostile critics—that his reluctance to commit himself with regard to the metaphysical issue was due to his desire to avoid the mental effort necessary to resolve it, and that his baffling silences were nothing but a confession of his lack of a comprehensive and coherent world-view. In point of fact, during the years between his Renunciation and his Enlightenment Gautam had followed the metaphysical method as far as the most advanced among the metaphysicians of his age—only to realise its hopeless limitations. And he was honest enough to confess them. He had rejected the metaphysical approach for the same reason for which he rejected mysticism: because he did not think it touched the heart of the human problem. His critique outlines a world-view, a remarkably coherent and comprehensive world-view; only it is not a metaphysical world-view. In the last analysis perhaps, metaphysics is an intellectual equivalent of the Myth. And the problem before man, as Gautam conceived of it, was not merely to rationalise the Myth, or find an intellectual substitute for it, but to dispense with its mediacy altogether—to outgrow the Myth-Complex.

Even to refute metaphysics, however, one has to be metaphysical. Nobody disliked abstruse ratiocination more than Gautam; and yet he could not help having endless arguments about precisely those matters which he regarded as 'irrelevant.' In these arguments, naturally, he had to adopt a somewhat negative position: one cannot be expected to be positive about things which one considers as of little importance.

There was the problem of God, for instance. It was in every way a tantalising problem. To begin with, it was a difficult problem to define. Different people interpreted the term in different ways. A most bewildering diversity of views prevailed about God; beliefs ranging from polytheism to atheism, from a rigid and refined monism to the most primitive animism. In their attempts to reach a conclusive and all-embracing definition of the issue many a brilliant intellect had been driven to the verge of insanity. And yet no satisfactory definition had been realised. In the very nature of things, it could not be realised.

Gautam's attitude to God was simple and straightforward. Of God in the teleological sense—that is in the sense of the First Cause, *causa causans*—he frankly admitted he knew nothing. He went even further, saying that he did not particularly want to know who was the ultimate author of this universe, and how and why it had originally come into being. He did not want to know because he did not think it either possible or important to know. He was content to take the universe for granted, to make the best of it as it was, and to understand its internal laws and relations without troubling about the ultimate 'how' and 'why.' It was not a very heroic attitude, but it was the only attitude compatible with common sense. As he said to one of his disciples who had decided to leave because the Tathagata would not reveal 'the beginning of things': 'Whether the beginning of things be revealed or not, the object for which I teach the Norm is this: that it leads to the thorough destruction of ill for the doer thereof.

Of God in the sense of the personal Creator, the Deity ruling over the universe, the Dispenser of the moral law of retribution and reward, Gautam was more than sceptical. There is scarcely anything in his more authentic dialogues which can be suspected of the slightest trace of agnosticism either in the theological or mystical interpretation of the term. On the other hand, there are many categorical statements to show that he found it impossible to believe in a personal Deity as a matter of faith, and that as a matter of experience it never became real to him. There is the evidence of the *Tevigga Sutra,* for example. 'But then, Vasettha, is there a single one of the Brahmins versed in the Three Vedas who has ever seen Brahma face to face?' Gautam asks a young Brahmin. On the latter's replying in the negative, he remarks: 'So that the Brahmins versed in the Three Vedas have forsooth said thus, "What we know not, what we have not seen, to a state of union with *that* we can show the way, and can say: 'this is the straight path, this is the direct way which leads him, who acts according to it, into a state of union with Brahma.' "Now what think you Vasettha? Does it not follow, this being so, that the talk of the Brahmins, versed though they be in the Three Vedas, is foolish talk?'

Further, in the same discourse he says: 'Just, Vasettha, as though a man should make a staircase in the place where four roads cross, to mount up into a mansion. And people should say to him, "Well, good friend, this mansion to mount up into which you are making the staircase, do you know whether it is in the east, or in the south, or in the west, or in the north? Whether it is high or low or of medium size?" And when so asked he should answer "No." And people should say to him, "But then, good friend, you are making a staircase to mount up into something—taking it for a mansion—which all the while you know not, neither have seen." And when so asked he should answer "Yes." Now what think you, Vasettha? Would it not turn out, this being so, that the talk of that man was foolish talk?' The Brahmins are then compared to the man who constructs 'a staircase to mount up into something—taking it for a mansion—which, all the while, he knows not, neither has seen,' and Brahma to the mansion the existence of which is highly problematical.

But, this is not all. Gautam's agnosticism cuts much deeper. There was still one way open to him whereby he could have retained God in his scheme of things—that is, on the ground of expediency and necessity. The eighteenth-century Deists like Voltaire maintained that if there were no God it was necessary to invent Him; they evidently believed this, because otherwise it is impossible to establish any form of moral order in the world. Similarly, modern pragmatists like William James and John Dewey have stood by the Deity because they have found that the concept 'works.' Gautam's position on this issue is in striking contrast to the utilitarian Deists. He did not regard God as a necessity. Gautam regarded the universe-in-manifestation as a self-sufficient actuality that could, and did, function without divine intervention. This position was already implicit in Kapila's dualistic philosophy. But while Kapila had been anxious not to cause offence to the hierarchical authority, and had left the whole matter somewhat equivocal, Gautam restated the problem with absolute clarity. He considered it perfectly possible for man to evolve a scheme of moral sanctions, to develop a sense of individual responsibility, without any reference to an external and omnipotent authority. The purpose and function of human intelligence then, is not so much to attempt the impossible task of explaining the ultimate origin of the universe, as to observe and comprehend the order of its manifestations 'as it really is. This is all that Gautam himself appears to have attempted.

Very closely linked with the question of God, was the question of soul—a permanent and immortal soul. It was in Gautam's days—as it has been ever since—a burning question. Also a difficult question to discuss, since it directly involves human wishes and *amour propre.* And wherever human wishes and *amour propre* are at stake, it is idle to expect any objectivity. Gautam seems to have been one of the very few men who succeeded in discussing the problem with a certain measure of dispassionateness. And because he discussed the problem dispassionately, his analysis once again led to a negation. He denied the existence of a permanent soul, or self, or Atman as the Brahminical metaphysicians described their fanciful creation.

In the *Anatta-lakkhana-sutta,* the second sermon he preached to the five monks in the Deer-park of Isipatana at Banaras, he explicitly declared that there is nothing in all the elements which constitute an individual, that corresponds to the notion of an immanent and immortal soul as conceived by the Vedantists. 'The body, feeling, perception, consciousness, and the aggregates,' he insisted 'are all soulless.' The only sense in which he was prepared to admit the idea of the soul, or the self, was in its empirical sense; in the sense in which the enigmatic Buddhist sage Nagasena was to define it in the course of his famous argument with King Milinda (Greek-Menander) of Bactria—that is, as a component thing which is not at all of the nature of a permanent and unchanging reality underlying our experience, but merely represents the synthesis of the totality of our sensations, perceptions, institutions, bodily and mental reactions at any given moment at any given place. And because the soul of human experience was for him a component thing, he held that it was not an absolute and static reality, but a sequence of kaleidoscopic patterns. In other words, he regarded the self, or the soul, as a mirror; a mirror of a special and unusual kind, a mirror that does not exist apart and independently of what it reflects, but comes into being and exists only by virtue of what it reflects. Thus, on the one hand, Gautam's conception of the soul, or the self, was nearer Heraclitus the Obscure than the Vedantic revivalists like Sankra; on the other, it corresponded more closely to the views held by Democritus and his sadly neglected master Leucippus, than Plato.

This peculiar conception of the soul is so unequivocally expressed by Gautam that there is hardly any room for misunderstanding on the crucial issue. Rhys Davids observes: 'The position is so absolute, so often insisted on, so fundamental to the right understanding of primitive Buddhism, that it is essential there should be no mistake about it. Yet the position is also so original, so fundamentally opposed to what is usually regarded as religious belief, both in India and elsewhere, that there is a great temptation to attempt to find a loophole through which at least a covert or esoteric belief in the soul, and in the future life (that is of course, of the soul) can be recognised, in some sort of way, as part of so widely accepted a religious system. There is no loophole, and the efforts to find one have always met with unswerving opposition, both in the Pitakas themselves and in extra-canonical works.'

In view of Gautam's categorical denial of the permanent nature of the soul, it is difficult to understand how anybody could justifiably credit him with belief in transmigration. Yet from the time of the earliest compilers of the Canon to the present day, it has been the custom to attribute this absurdity to the Tathagata. Even Rhys Davids, after commenting that 'it would not be possible in a more complete and categorical manner to deny that there is any soul—any entity, of any kind, which continues to exist, in any manner, after death,' than was done by Gautam in the *Brahmajala-sutta*, goes on somewhat surprisingly to argue that 'Gautam had not been able to give up the belief in transmigration.' If Gautam had not been able to give up the belief in transmigration, then one can only conclude that he was either so muddle-headed that he did not know what he believed, or was being deliberately dishonest. For the dogma of transmigration in its Brahminical form at least has the saving grace of being a consistent, and up to a point, satisfying, doctrine; but in the form in which it has been retained to support the Buddhist eschatology, it is the most obvious piece of chicanery. Belief in transmigration when combined with belief in a permanent soul still remains very much of a wish-projection and an illusion; but at least it is a logical and consistent illusion. Belief in transmigration without a corresponding belief in an immortal soul is an illusion which is at once illogical and inconsistent.

In all other respects Gautam's world-view is so transparently sound and reasonable, that it is hard to believe, in this particular case, he should suddenly have abandoned his rational outlook, thus annihilating the whole purpose of his philosophy. On the other hand, it seems much more credible, and is indeed highly probable, that the references to the doctrine of transmigration which are to be found in the Buddhist Canon—and they are legion—have been introduced there by the compilers. In the first instance this strange doctrine, which figures in all subsequent developments of Buddhism as a religion, must have been incorporated into the original teaching of Gautam as a concession to, and compromise with, the prevailing popular belief in rebirth, the idea being to render Buddhism acceptable to the masses. Moreover, the Buddhist lawgivers must have perceived that the doctrine in question, however arbitrary it might be, was an excellent device for strengthening their hands in the task of enforcing 'the Good Law' among the faithful.

For, demonstrably, the doctrine that, 'as soon as a sentient being (man, animal, or angel) dies, a new being is produced in a more or less painful and material state of existence, according to the "karma," the desert or merit, of the being who had died, is calculated to exercise a restraining influence over all refractory and rebellious spirits in the flock, as well as to promote social stability. Indeed, in some ways this doctrine is far more effective in realising its moral ends and making the people follow the straight and narrow path than the doctrine of fire and brimstone, and the thundering voice of that 'righteous judge,' Jehovah, who, simply because 'He is angry every day,' ceases after a time to strike terror into the souls of all but the most timid. Finally, it is possible that the concept of survival and rebirth was foisted into Gautam's doctrine by his interpreters, who were anxious to discover some tangible expıanation for his 'ethical insistence.' Even today highly advanced and idealistic writers—men like Sir

Radhakrishnan—seem to experience an insuperable difficulty in conceiving of a moral philosophy devoid of all compensatory motives. It is, therefore, easy to imagine the difficulty experienced in this matter by interpreters of an earlier epoch. For all their good intentions, they could not understand for their own sake the practice of such human qualities as goodness, truth, virtue, and compassion—could not understand, as Spinoza puts it, 'that blessedness is not the reward of virtue, but virtue itself.' Yet, as has already been stressed, it was precisely in this that the originality of Gautam's morality consisted: it was not dictated by any consideration of the hereafter, but by the compelling exigencies of existence in the here and now—a position which Aristotle also takes up in his Ethics. For Gautam, The Way was not something apart from the goal: The Way was the goal.

The Way was not contingent on a knowledge of the 'eternal order' immanent in the pattern of the universe: rather, it was contingent on a proper realisation of the manifest aspects of the pattern. From a narrow philosophical point of view, this position might be interpreted as being tantamount to complete repudiation of philosophy as a mode of arriving at truth. Not unnaturally, certain strict philosophers have been inclined to see in Gautam an early avatar of Sophists like Gorgias and Hippias. To do so, however, is to misrepresent and misunderstand Gautam. His position was fundamentally different from that of the Sophists — in India they were known as 'Eel-wrigglers'—with whom he had little sympathy. His critique of philosophy repudiates a particular approach to philosophy, not philosophy as such.

The difference is important. Indeed, his very negations are pregnant with a definite and positive philosophic purpose. There is his negation of the Vedantic Absolutism, for instance. At the time when it came, it served as a positive and liberating influence. It brought a breath of fresh air into the exhausted philosophic atmosphere of India. For ever since Vyasa fell to the lures of Absolutism and landed in the labyrinthine cul-de-sac of Uttara Mimansa, Indian thought had not been able to find its way back out into the open air. The bulk of Indian thinkers had got so perfectly reconciled to their cul-de-sac after a time, that they regarded any attempt to get away from it as, if not actual heresy, at least something in thoroughly bad taste. Their prolonged preoccupation with what George Santayana aptly calls 'the musty Absolute' had reduced Indian philosophy to the most abject state of anaemia. Gautam's departure from Absolutism was, therefore, highly opportune: it had the effect of galvanising Indian thought into new life.

Equally positive was Gautam's affirmation of the principle of causality, or the doctrine of *Paticcasamupada*—the doctrine, that is to say, 'that all *dharma* [phenomena, mental and physical] are *Paticcasamppana* [happen by way of cause].' This was not an entirely new doctrine. The Chain of Causation is mentioned both in the Yoga and in Samkhya systems. However, it is only in the Great Discourse of Causation *(Mahanidana-sutta)* of *Digha-nikaya* that it first emerges with absolute clarity as the basis of a world-view. 'It is only in the Buddhist Nikaya,' says Rhys Davids, 'that we come up against the actual effort itself of the human mind to get at a more scientific view of the world-order— an effort which is marked with the freshness and vigour of a new fetch of intellectual expansion, and the importance and gravity of which is affirmed with the utmost emphasis, both in the earliest records and in the orthodox literature often centuries later.' Further, the principle of causality in Gautam's world-view is allied with a still more important principle—the principle of flux, of sense and succession, of change and Becoming. His was one of the earliest formulations of a dynamic view of life. He unfolded before the human mind the vision of vast and fluid horizons—the vision of a universe literally without beginning or end. It was like awakening to a new and apparently endless dawn. In formulating his dynamic view of life, however, Gautam did not lose his sober judgement. He seems to have been careful to avoid the pitfalls to which most dynamic philosophies are liable. He never abandoned himself to that sense of irresponsibility which led Heraclitus—in many other respects a wise, and even profound man—to interpret his dialectics of universal flux as a philosophic justification for the ideal of perpetual war and strife, conflict and unrest. On the contrary, paradoxical though it may sound, the fact that we live in a world of flux and movement was, for Gautam, all the more reason for cultivating precisely those habits of mind which the 'Obscure' sage of Ephesus so heartily despised—that is to say, tranquillity, peace, contemplative detachment, stillness and poise. Unlike Bergson, Gautam was never carried away by the inebriating exuberance of his own phraseology: he was far too deeply aware of the inordinate squalor and misery, the unavailing suffering and waste, the unutterable frustrations and shipwrecks of life to offer mere verbal palliatives. His was a compassionate view of life.

'All that we are is the result of what we have thought: it is founded on our thoughts, it is made up of our thoughts'— reads a passage in the Dhammapada. It might almost be interpreted as the idealism which is implicit in the Cartesian proposition of *cogito ergo sum.* But Descartes's proposition is open to one rather facile, but all the same very pertinent, criticism—the criticism which Mr. Aldous Huxley voices through one of the characters in *Eyeless in Gaza. 'Cogito ergo sum,'* ruminates Anthony Beavis (ruminates, let it be added, over a typewriter—apparently for the convenience of posterity), 'But why not *coco ergo sum? Eructo ergo sum?* Or, escaping solipsism, why not *futuo ergo sumus?* Ribald questions. But what is "personality"? ' And after a long and discursive meditation (duly reduced to typescript), he decides that the most valid proof that we exist is that our bodies are *there.* 'In the swamp and welter of this uncertainty,' he concludes with evident satisfaction at having solved the riddle of personality, 'the body stands firm like a Rock of Ages. *Jesu, pro me perforatus, Condar intra tuum latus.*

Even faith hankers for warm caverns of perforated flesh. How much more wildly urgent must be the demands of a scepticism that has ceased to believe even in its own personality! *Condar intra* MEUM *latus!* It is the only place of refuge left to us.'

Condar intra MEUM *latus!* Surprisingly, this also happens to be the refrain of one of Gautam's dialogues. Surprisingly —because usually one does not associate such views with the Tathagata whose very glance, M. Rene Grousset tells us, 'seems to be plunged back into the interior Essence, into the ineffable Buddha-state— a glance which sees into the beyond, a glance that haunts, heavy with all the metaphysical thought of the Mahayana, weighted, in its ardent fixity, with all the virtualities of the cosmic play, and vanishing within into the vacuity of substance.' Indeed, after reading such ecstatic eloquence, one would hardly dare to attribute the dialogue in question to the Buddha, were it not that irreproachable authorities have already done so. For in this discourse, Gautam not only represents the body as 'a Rock of Ages,' but he suggests that it contains within its narrow confines the whole content of this vast universe of sense and succession—its myriad stars, and its empty spaces, and its unfathomable abysses. 'Verily, I declare unto you,' he says, as though forestalling the objections of some unborn Anthony Beavis, 'that with this very body, mortal as it is, and only a fathom high, but conscious and endowed with mind, is the world, and the waxing thereof and the waning thereof and the way that leads to the passing away thereof.' If this is an idealistic position, then Protagoras and Hume must have been idealists.

Gnotki Seauton: Socrates declaims the inscription from the oracle at Delphi for the general enlightenment and edification of mankind. The war about the origin, nature and validity of knowledge which Descartes started with his *'cogito ergo sum'* is still in progress, though mighty heroes like Leibnitz, Locke, Bishop Berkeley, Hume, and Kant fell and were buried long ago. Kant's *Critique of Pure Reason* destroyed all that was left intact of the philosophical Troy; and Helen must now be sought within, not without us. Fichte seriously informs us that 'the world is his idea.' Schopenhauer repeats Fichte's dictum with an even more emphatic shake of his head. But, we are tempted to ask, what does it all mean? And where does the philosophical flight lead to? What is the 'self' which we ought to know about and of which we should take care? What is the thing that cogitates? Where precisely must we look for the seat of Pure Reason? It is all a tremendous question-mark. And the philosophers seldom come to the aid of bewildered Philistines. They evade the issue, or answer in terms which are far too abstruse and vague to be satisfying. It is safer to return to Gautam. With him we at least know where we stand. His answer is straightforward and intelligible. It is not an heroic answer. Some would probably regard it as bordering on frivolity—a weakness not at all becoming in a Tathagata, in a 'Knower of The Way.' But there is serious purpose behind Gautam's frivolity, if frivolity it is. His answer has the great advantage of being intelligible, whereas most other philosophers are obscure; the truth it contains is—in a certain measure— actually verifiable.

Condar intra MEUM *latus.* The whole of man's knowledge and experience begins and ends in what Father Hopkins describes as 'his bone-house, mean house.' This is Kant, minus, fortunately, his 'Transcendental Esthetic and Transcendental Logic. At least we know what 'within us' means. There is no ambiguity in the term: Gautam's words are crystal-clear—'Verily, I declare unto you, that with this very body, mortal as it is, and only a fathom high, but conscious and endowed with mind, is the world, and the waxing thereof and the waning thereof, and the way that leads to the passing away thereof.'

Mrs. Rhys Davids protests that this amounts to 'an irrational denial of the man as man,' it is reducing man 'to his instruments'; it is 'the rejection of divinity in the self, the self himself, the man, the person...' Perhaps it is all these things. But it also means making man the measure of his world.

'In reality,' declared Democritus, more than a hundred years after Gautam's death, 'there are only atoms and the void.' In the ultimate analysis, this is no doubt true. However, the ultimate analysis is so much of a simplification that it bears little recognisable likeness to reality as our eyes are capable of perceiving it. Democritus' ruthlessly analytical vision had failed to perceive a whole world of things. In a sense it had even failed in being properly analytical. It had failed to perceive that atoms are not atomic; that the mustard-seed is a microcosm. 'The atom,' Vasubandhu, a worthy exponent of the *Togacara* system of Mahayana metaphysics, was to point out in the fifth century AD, 'is not proved as such.' He meant, of course, that the atom is notan ultimate unit; that it is not one thing, but many; and that the whole concept of the atomists, in so far as it claims to be the concept of ultimates, is contradictory and absurd.

What then is there in Reality?

Gautam, who preferred not to look long and not to look short, answers that in reality there are only component things. No matter how far and how deep we carry our analysis of reality we still stand face to face with component things capable of still further analysis; no matter whether our eye travels outward, in ever-widening circles, or inward, in ever-narrowing circles, it can see only patterns which are made up of still other patterns. All our knowledge is a knowledge of relations, of conditions—not finalities. This is not a doctrine of *Maya,* or Illusion, as it is so often represented: it is simply a doctrine of relativity. For all relations are by their very nature relative—relative to the conditions which determine them. We are back again at the causal formula.

What are the elements which go to the making of these relations? What lies beyond and behind the conditions? These are tantalising questions. The two chief schools of Buddhist metaphysics which grew up with the Greater Vehicle have each offered their own answers. There is the *Sunyata* doctrine of the Madhyamika School, founded by Nagarjuna, a metaphysician who lived in northern Deccan in the first century of our era. *Sunyata,* literally vacuity, is interpreted in the *Garland of Flowers,* a mystical work written in the second or third century AD, as the Essential Nature of things, the *tathata* in Sanskrit. 'This Essential Nature,' observes M. Grousset, 'will constitute a kind of Divinity appearing in the very bosom of the Nagarjuna vacuity. It will present itself to feeling, if not from the metaphysical point of view, as an equivalent of the Absolute, or, if you like, as an Absolute no longer superior to phenomena, but entirely inherent in them, the Absolute as the actual processes of things. On the surface and in the bosom of the unfathomable vacuity, the bottomless ocean supposed by Nagarjuna, the phenomena are the ocean considered as waves; the Essential Nature is the waves considered as the ocean.' Later on, *Sunyata,* or the Essential Nature, became 'under the name *of Prajna Paramita* or Perfection of Sapience a kind of revelation of truth or, if you like, of the Buddhist holy wisdom, a veritable hypostasis which will be prayed to and invoked, and which will communicate itself to the mind in an ineffable communion.'

The *Yogacara* system attributed to Ashvaghosha, but really developed by men like Vasubandhu, Asanga, Dignaga, and Shilabhadra in the fifth and sixth centuries, evolved the notion of a subconscious substratum of phenomena, called *alqya-vijnana,* literally sensation of the groundwork. The concept had very great influence on Chinese Buddhism thanks to Huen-tsang, who studied under Silabhadra, and on his return from his fruitful pilgrimage, wrote a book on Absolute Idealism in which he expounded the *Yogacara* metaphysics at considerable length.

There are also less ingenious answers. But Gautam himself, who was probably wiser than these Mahayanist metaphysicians and mystics, observed what his biographies describe as 'a noble silence' on the matter. He made no quixotic attempts to pierce the 'sleep' which hangs round our 'little life': to see through some of the dreams which men dream within the dream, was as much as he could hope to do in a lifetime.

The mystics of Ephesus who edited the Johannine Gospel were men of profound insight: they knew the working of the Word. In the heart of the Word there is an irrepressible urge to become flesh. The Buddhist art of India reveals something of the nature of this intricate and universal process: it shows the Word becoming flesh almost with vengeance.

If renunciation in one form or another was the keynote of the original doctrine of Buddhism, then in the Buddhist art of India we witness the world-renouncers returning to the world by devious paths; returning, if not actually in body, at least in imagination. In body, too, sometimes! There is at Ajanta a fresco—not very important from an aesthetic point of view it is true, but nevertheless possessing considerable psychological significance—which depicts a Bhikshu standing expectantly at the palace door. Mr. Laurence Binyon sees in him a spiritual presence, a welcome messenger bringing with him a soft breath of other-worldly peace and serenity into the feverish world of men. He may be right; it is no doubt all a matter of interpretation. But in India we have been accustomed to the world-renouncers sufficiently long to know that their visits to this unsatisfactory world of ours are usually actuated by a purpose other than the mere desire to minister to our spiritual needs. The Bhikshu standing at the palace door may hold the Lotus of the Good Law in his hand. It is evident, however, that he has come not only to preach, but also to beg. In spite of his half-averted, downcast eyes there is, as it were, a certain air of expectancy about the unworldly visitor in the picture; obviously, he expects to be taken in, to be given a meal, since even 'a spiritual presence' has need of 'solid food.' And there is perhaps a still subtler motive to account for the Bhikshu's presence at the gilded threshold of the palace; there is in those eyes a shy desire, a half-conscious, inarticulate desire; and one cannot help feeling that the world-renouncer has come to the palace to have a glimpse of the world he has renounced. For though they could not confess it openly, it seems that these Buddhist monks loved the world; loved its joys and delights, even its pains and griefs.

The art of Ajanta is authentic and genuine; it lives with a life of its own, even though time has dimmed some of its brilliance. From a purely aesthetic angle, the pictorial tradition of Indian art here seems to touch its zenith; already at Ellora, as Dr. Koomaraswamy has observed, the representation begins to lose its living quality and tends to flatness; and ever since, there has been a steady and distressing decline till, in our own days, Indian painting is hardly distinguishable from the inanities of the picture-postcard industry.

But at Ajanta there is vision at work, with the result that even the faintest figure that can still be seen emerging from the colourless clay, has a grace and beauty which belongs to the highest art. Using the simplest colours—lampblack, red ochre, yellow ochre, and lapis-lazuli—the painters of Ajanta succeed in realising delicate and vibrant tones which endow their forms with a movement and animation that is convincingly of the earth and flesh. Their approach to composition is spontaneous, but a spontaneity which points to full awareness of the problem involved, and not carelessness. Their grouping might appear crowded and complex at times, but there is seldom incoherence or chaos. The arrangement of figures, the balance of movement and attitude, partake of a large rhythm such as is inherent in life; and which, though it is not insisted upon by means of theatrical gestures as in the canvases of some of the Renaissance and post-Renaissance painters, is none the less real and palpable. As M. Ivan Stchoukine remarks with keen perception, The abundance of forms is far from producing chaotic designs, opposed to all ideas of unity; used with art, it helps to create well-planned compositions, the unity of which is not impaired by the fact that it is made up of heterogeneous elements.' The perspective, as in the early Italian frescoes, is empirical, but it is never arbitrary, and there are no descents into the grotesque.

On the whole the treatment of subjects is far more refined and urbane than anything we meet in late medieval Christian art.

There is, in fact, a distinct suggestion of depth, of relief even, which is in some ways quite as satisfying as the western tradition of representation that tends to resolve pictorial problems in terms of the plastic, and which has led us to expect statues in paint. At Ajanta, unlike the Sistine Chapel, one is never in doubt that it is the brush, and not the chisel, that has been at work; and if the Bodhisattva Pad-mapani lacks the three-dimensional monumental grandeur of Michael Angelo's Promethean Isaiah, for instance, it has the advantage of being of flesh and blood, and not stone.

These, however, are technical and aesthetic subtleties. The significance of Ajanta derives from the fact that, like all authentic and genuine art, it represents a kind of apocalypse: it reveals in its full urgency a conflict which seems to be fundamental to Buddhism in general, and Buddhist monachism in particular. True, the avowed aim of the monks who painted these frescoes was to illustrate the legends of the Great Life for the edification of the faithful. True, they had no conscious intention of expressing the dichotomy of their own souls, and they would have been extremely shocked if any one had imputed such a profane motive to them. But all art, whether religious or secular, involves, and cannot help involving, some sort of a personal confession on the part of the artist. The artists of Ajanta, for all their attempts at impersonality, actually tell us more about their own state of mind, their own struggles and vacillations, than the experience of the Buddha. That is what gives Ajanta its importance.

Ajanta impresses. Firstly, there is the scene; desolation alternating with luxuriant verdure; and Waghora tumbling into the ravine in a series of seven cascades. The caves are cut into a precipitous rock and arranged in the form of a crescent. Inside the caves there is twilight—a twilight that invites speculation. What, one wonders, were the thoughts which possessed the Buddhist cenobites who dwelt in these caves, unconcerned with the Mundane Dispensation? Did they spend their time contemplating the various stages of the Eightfold Path and the corresponding Beatitudes? Did they meditate upon the meaning of the Four Noble Truths, upon the ineffable joy of arahatship and Nirvana? Were their dreams centred round the Foundation of the Kingdom of Righteousness? Were they always reflecting on the doctrine *of*

Sunyata, which, 'in the theory of a world as will and representation... is the state of a mind free of both representation and will?' Were they preoccupied with the pursuit of the elusive *alaya-vijnana,* or the Universal Subconscious?

From the walls and ceilings of these caves we receive the answer to our questions; but it turns out, alas, to be a negative answer in every instance. The forms which loom out of the twilight of Ajanta leave little room for vague speculations. The spirit of renunciation speaks for itself; and, apparently, it speaks of very different things from those which one is in the habit of associating with it. Above everything, the world-renouncers of Ajanta appear to be obsessed with the mystery of female flesh and its promises of bliss; they crave for its tenderness and comfort with an almost adolescent passion. Fluttering against their mental eyes are visions of dancing girls, of tender-limbed maidens reclining in inviting postures of abandon and nakedness, of voluptuous princesses disporting themselves with their youthful lovers. They dream of brilliant scenes at Court, of pot-bellied householders relishing wine with ribald pleasantries, of the thrilling game of dice. They imagine the ecstasy of the lovers' intimate embraces, and an almost audible sigh of regret escapes their lips; all the Beatitudes of the Path, even Nirvana, seem cold comfort beside the solid certitude of conjugal felicity.

It is easy to choose; difficult to abide by one's choice. And ' there are always regrets. Reassuringly, the Bodhisattva Padmapani twists the Lotus of the Good Law between his beautiful fingers; reassuringly, but he does not succeed in giving comfort. In the faint background there is the tantalising suggestion of flesh; a woman seems abandoning herself to her lover; there are heavenly musicians playing on harps; and finally, as a symbol of the whole mood, there is a peacock crying to its mate.

The Good Law will perhaps never become an adequate substitute for the consolations of flesh, no matter how long those delicate fingers twist the stalk of the chaste lotus they hold. It is difficult to renounce the world; difficult to break away from a thousand subtle psychological ties which bind one to it. One may put on saffron robes; one may take upon oneself the strictest discipline; one may retire into solitude and seclusion. But there is still the imagination. It cannot be put into a monastic uniform; no cloistral walls are thick enough to hold it prisoner; it is impervious to all vows of chastity; it can never be secluded, because it peoples its solitude with creatures of its own making. It is bound only to one thing—desire. And so the world-renouncers invariably return to the world and to the flesh—if not in body, at least in imagination. Such is the unequivocal answer of Ajanta. And it finds an echo across the Himalayas in the grottos of Tun-huang, and at Lung-men, and beyond the coastline of the Middle Kingdom, at Nara, and way down in the Southern Seas—at Borobudur.

Mr. Laurence Binyon, whose views are always illuminating, has observed: To Italian painters of Quattrocento, to Pollaiuolo and Signorelli, and following them the young Michael Angelo, the naked body was a discovered romance.' This seems to be true also of the sculptors of Sanchi and Amravati: for them, too, the naked body was an ecstatiating discovery and revelation. There are, of course, important differences of technique and medium. But when due allowance has been made for these obvious, and ultimately insignificant differences, one has to admit that one experiences in their statuary and reliefs something of the same 'thrill of romantic strangeness in the naked forms of joy' which Mr. Binyon keenly senses in the nudes of Signorelli.

It is true enough that nudity has never been an uncommon sight in India, though even here Mr. Binyon tends somewhat to exaggerate the advantage which the Indian artist is supposed to have had over his western confrere. However, in so far as Buddhist art is concerned, this argument has but little relevance. The Buddhist monks were not normally expected to while away their leisure in loving contemplation of 'the beautiful ways of the human body in its spontaneous gestures and poses.' In fact, ever since Vishakha, the rich and prudish widow of Savatthi, had been shocked by the spectacle of Bhikshuni bathing naked in the river side by side with the unchaste courtezans, and Bhikshus tormented by heat exposing their bodies to rain, both male and female mendicants had been enjoined to observe the utmost circumspection even with regard to their own bodies. Primitive Buddhism, for reasons not difficult to understand, had developed into a strict puritanism; it had set up an impossible ideal of celibacy; and, especially in its monastic form, it had inculcated the same horror of the human body which we find in the Christian monachism. Not only was there no question of the Buddhist monks being allowed to feast their eyes upon 'naked glory,' but they were actually expected to look upon the body as 'a sore with nine openings.' In particular, they were told to avoid all contact with female flesh; the Buddhist elders had gone to the extent of introducing into Gautam's deathbed utterances what seems on the face of it an absurdly irrelevant and spurious conversation: 'How, Lord, are we to conduct ourselves with regard to womankind? Don't see them, Ananda. But if we see them, what are we to do? Abstain from speech. But if they should speak to us what are we to do? Keep wide awake.'

This recoil from, and disgust with, things carnal is not confined to primitive Buddhist monachism. It is present in practically all its subsequent developments, and, indeed, ends by becoming an integral part of the Buddhist psychology. Thus, in the seventh century we get Santideva, whose *Journey towards the Light* enjoyed among fervent Buddhists something of the popularity of Thomas a Kempis's *De Imitatione Christi,* exclaiming (in M. Finot's translation): 'Consider this corpse, dragged hither and thither by greedy vultures. Why does it offer no resistance? Why, O my heart, dost thou watch over this mass, taking it for thy ego?... No doubt this vile body is for men an instrument of action. But thou guardest it in vain, pitiless death will seize it from thee to throw to the vultures. Then what wilt thou do?... When shall I go to the charnel-house, the fit dwelling of the body, to come into the presence of the corpses of others and of my own body destined for corruption?... Behold my body, behold the decay it will become; its odour will drive away even the jackals.

Yet, recoil is merely a form of attraction; disgust a kind of fascination. The Buddhist recoil from, and disgust with, the body has always been counterbalanced by an equally powerful fascination and attraction towards it. Even Santideva could sing in eloquent strophes of the exquisite figures of 'thousands of *apasras'* who welcome the Manjusri to heaven; strophes, which, as M. Grousset remarks, 'might serve as a commentary on the frescoes of Ajanta.'

This element of attraction and fascination is manifest in the statuary and reliefs of Sanchi, Bharut, and Amravati, where we witness the unknown Buddhist masters positively revelling in the naked forms of joy. It was probably the first opportunity they had had of experimenting with the possibilities of the human figure and its nakedness; for prior to the building of these stupas, the rule laid down in the *Cul lavagga*—which restricted the decorative scheme of monasteries and shrines to designs of 'wreaths and creepers, and bone hooks and cupboards' and forbade 'imaginative drawings painted in figures of men and women'—was apparently observed with some strictness'. Thus, to the sculptors of Sanchi, Bharut, and Amravati the 'naked glory' was as much a symbol of emancipation as it was to Pollaiuolo, Signorelli, or the young Michael Angelo. One has only to look at the moulded contours of the *Lay-Worshippers* from Amravati to perceive a measure of the ecstasy which the world-renouncers experienced in the creation of those voluptuous curves. Somewhere in *Jesting Pilate,* Mr. Aldous Huxley writes that Indians will never make good artists, because they are too much interested in metaphysics and ultimate Reality. His generalisation is so completely at variance with fact, that it hardly requires contradiction. It might be pointed out, however, that anything less metaphysical, less concerned with the ultimate Reality, than the back view of the *Yakhshini* from the East Gate of Sanchi, it is difficult to imagine. Greek sculptors are by no means unique in having left behind them lasting monuments to the charms of Kallipygos: there are too the unknown Buddhist masters.

For Baumgarten, aesthetics was 'the science of sensuous knowledge.' For the artists of the classical age of India it was something even more precise. No matter what the Silpa Sashtaras, or the accredited interpreters of Indian art might say, the Indian artists of the classical period regarded aesthetics as the science of sensual knowledge. They might be trying to represent 'the ultimate reality,' but they always had the sense to represent it in a form natural to their medium. Even Mr. Aldous Huxley has had time to correct his early generalisation on this point. Contrasting the almost algebraical airiness of Maya sculpture to 'the suffocating animal heat' of Hindu art, he says in *Beyond the Mexique Bay:* 'From Cape Comorin to the Himalayas, and for the last two thousand years, almost every Hindu artist seems to have been engaged in illustrating the works of Aretino. Even the most sacred persons tend to melt—and at the most solemn moments of their religious life—into suggestive postures... The boneless limbs—dozens of them, very often to a single personage—ooze about the picture-space like voluptuous ectoplasm. The haunches jut to right or left; the waists are tapered as though by a delicious process of suction; even the men seem as though inflated about the chest; and as for women... But language fails.'

The sensual preoccupation which, with mingled feelings of disgust and enchantment, Mr. Huxley notes in Brahminical art, is also present in Buddhist art. Present, but with a difference. Whereas Brahminical art is sensual in a straightforward and direct manner, the sensuality of Buddhist art appears to be invariably regressive. The difference becomes obvious if we compare the Vaishnavite and Shaivite sculptures of Mavalipuram and Elephanta with those of Sanchi and Amravati. They point to two very different forms of sensuality. In the one instance we have sensuality—in the case of the Shaivite art of Elephanta, one might almost say sexuality—stretched to the limit of erotic mysticism; in the other, the sensual obsession has its origin and culmination in a nostalgic desire—a nostalgic desire, which, because it recognises the impossibility of any consummation, trembles on the verge of pathos and languorousness.

The nostalgic quality of Buddhist art emerges even more clearly in the catacombs of Ajanta. For those amorous couples whom we see dallying in shady alcoves behind the Bodhisattva do not strike the almost monstrous note of triumphant phallicism which is of the essence of Shaivite art. They are not sensual even in the sense in which the nudes of Titian and Giorgione, or Rubens and Renoir are sensual. Their sensuality is more that of Gauguin in such pictures as *Nave Nave Moe* and *Noa Noa.* There is about them a strangely elusive quality which can best be described as symbolic. They are not just forms and images taken from the tangible world and presented in terms of pure equivalence: they seem to be symbols—symbols of the nostalgia of the disembodied spirit for the warm assurance of the world and the flesh. And in a sense they are not tangible forms at all, but merely phantoms and spirits, haunting the lovesick imagination.

Great Vehicle

The Mahayana was literally a Great Vehicle. In the course of what is known as 'the Flight of the Mahayana' very unusual things happened. It was, of course, an unusual flight. It led Nagarjuna into the bosom of absolute vacuity. It took Vasubandhu to the edge of the Universal Subconscious. It set up the ideal of an abstract Buddha State, which, according to Asanga, 'is like a shrine of precious stones, great in power.' It made Harsha, the poet King, go into orgies of charity. It sent Bodhidharma from the Coast of Coromandal to Canton. It induced Fa Hien, the Master of The Law Huen-tsang, I-Ching and many other Celestials to undertake hazardous voyages to the Buddhist Holy Land. It created a superb 'Mystic Heaven' of whose lures Santideva has sung in such eloquent terms in his *Journey to the Light* In this flight, M. Rene Grousset tells us, 'the external world had dispersed like a dream. But, perhaps, it is not so easy to disperse the external world from the scheme of things. Li Shang-yin may call the world 'small as a grain of dust'; the Master of the Law may speak airily of the Absolute Idealism; and their best modern interpreter, M. Grousset, may dilate on the infinite potentialities of the *tathata.* But it is not possible to explain away the world in such a summary fashion. Mirage or reality, it cannot be dispersed merely by verbal incantations. Even M. Grousset is aware of the difficulty. After taking us into an 'ocean of clouds,' and solemnly telling us that 'all the rest is only appearance and dream,' he declares rather quizzically 'but the finest dream of all is, that all remains.' All remains because actually nothing had ever been dispersed by the Mahayana metaphysics. It was all a kind of self-hypnosis. For if the testimony of Buddhist art is to be believed—and it is an authentic enough testimony—then the truth seems to be that the flight of the Mahayana had ended before it had begun. It had ended, shall we say, in the Kallipygos of the Dryad of Sanchi.

Who is this mysterious apparition? We do not know her identity, because she appears in different guises in different places. Mr. Havell, whose intuitions are seldom wrong, traces her back to the Garden of Eden. Since his fall, man has had opportunity of knowing her better on earth. For she herself is the earth in all its sensuous warmth and fertility. She is a woman, and she is a tree—numinous and yet palpably of the flesh. Here we see her as the spirit of the forest, the wood nymph of whom the Vedic Hymns speak as Arnayani. And the forest is the primeval forest of desire. Beyond Good and Evil, below Good and Evil, she leans forward from the bough of a mango tree, offering herself with voluptuous gesture. And her breasts are more deliciously succulent than the mangoes hanging from the tree. They play havoc with the spirit of renunciation. In vain does the Bodhisattva Padmapani in those dimly-lit catacombs hold out the blue lotus to the faithful.

Perhaps not altogether in vain. There is also another element in Buddhist art. It cannot be seen in the Buddhist art of India. It is not to be found among the 'Thousand Buddhas' of Tun-huang, with some of whom M. Pelliot and Sir Aurel Stein have made us familiar; nor across the seas in the frescoes which adorn the golden temple of Horyuji at Nara; and still less in Krom's albums of reliefs of Borobudur. Further, this element does not manifest itself very conspicuously even among the works of avowedly Buddhist masters like Ku K'ai-chih and Wu Tao-tzu; these worthy Celestials appear to be more interested in painting the Western Paradise and the Buddhist Purgatory than in understanding the profounder implications of the Buddha's word. Where, then, must we seek for it?

The answer, of course, is—in China. For the whole of Chinese art and poetry of the T'ang and the Sung periods appears to be permeated with it. Its expression in poetry may be judged from the following poem by T'ao Han:

> The pine and the cypress hide the mountain gorge,
> But in the West I discover a narrow path.
>
> The sky opens out, a peak is revealed,
>
> And as though it were born in space, a convent rises up before my eyes.
>
> The building seems to be standing on a terrace of cloud.
>
> Its pavilions soar into the air amidst the rugged rocks.
>
> Night comes; monkeys and birds are silent.

> The sound of the bells and the song of the bonzes penetrate beyond the clouds.
>
> I contemplate the blue peaks and the moon which is mirrored in the waters of the lake.
>
> I listen to the sound of the streams and the wind that tosses the leaves on the banks of the rushing torrent.
>
> My soul has flown up beyond things visible
>
> Wandering and captive at once...

This is not merely verbal mesmerism, it signifies a new quality of vision. And this new quality of vision makes itself felt with equal urgency in the landscapes of Hsia Kuei and Ma Lin. Indeed, it is present to a greater or lesser degree in all the best sketches of the T'ang and the Sung epochs.

What does this new quality of vision imply? Definition in such matters is difficult, generalisation hazardous. But it seems that here we see the world and its phenomena—whether they happen to be precipitous mountains, or solitary hermits in their dark retreats, or boats floating on moonlit waters, or birds sitting on fragile boughs, or reeds agitated by the wind—through a consciousness which is no longer time-haunted and time-weary, because it has understood the very nature of time. Here we are in a universe which is devoid of tension—not because contrarieties and conflicts have ceased to operate, but because they have somehow become intelligible. Here, in the very contemplation of transiency, we receive a measure of eternity. Here the mind manages to realise a stasis within the flux itself, so that even a waterfall—normally symbolising incessant movement—emerges as a symbol of stillness. Here the human soul is at once 'wandering and captive.' Here the wheel turns and does not turn. Here the paradox is no longer a paradox, but rather a luminous certitude. Here we are in the very heart of peace.

Vortex of Change

In this vortex of change and becoming which is our world, even the person of the Buddha—the pivot of the Triple Jewel of Buddhism—could not be expected to remain unchanged. 'The

Diamond Throne of the original enlightenment,' writes Okakura Kakuzo with characteristic oriental floridness, charm, and profundity, 'is now hard indeed to discover, surrounded as it is by the labyrinths of gigantic pillars and elaborate porticoes which successive architects have erected, as each has added his portion to the edifice of faith.' From the earliest times to the present day mythographers of varying degrees of talent and ingenuity have subjected the Tathagata to their well-meant, if somewhat embarrassing, attention. His apotheosis, in spite of his repeated warnings, commenced during his own lifetime. As we have seen, all his logic and reasoning was unable to restrain the enthusiasm of the faithful. They lost no time completing the process of apotheosis at the first available opportunity—that is, almost immediately after the Blessed One had been cremated and his ashes distributed among a number of cantankerous nobles, anxious to make sure of their own salvation by building *dagabas* over his remains. Although Gautam himself professed no knowledge of anything beyond this world, and refused to dogmatise over the first and last things, those who have followed in his wake have taken great pains to work out a richly intricate eschatology for his benefit, which, for the sheer complexity of its invention, would do credit to the imagination of a Dante, or the producer of a modern Grand Guignol.

Out of a spirit of revenge, as it were, he has been installed as the impresario of something like seventeen exquisitely delicious paradisiac spheres on the one hand, and saddled with eight blood-curdling 'principal' hells (to leave the innumerable minor hells out of our reckoning) on the other; and what is more, the authors of this colossal scheme of heavens and hells have crowned their remarkable achievement, so Lord Zetland observes, by finding room for it 'within the categories of space and time.' A self-conscious and unassuming intellectual, the apocalyptic fantasy has transfigured Gautam into 'the Great King of Glory'—a role which he was never fitted to fulfil, and which he would have found extremely distasteful had he been compelled to play it. A tragic philosopher who could be accused of almost anything but harbouring immortal longings, the hagiographers have had no scruples about crediting him with comforting notions of personal survival.

All these and many more ironical developments of historical Buddhism were no doubt inevitable. Two thousand years is a long stretch of time; and it is natural that during this period a formidable and fantastic superstructure of myth and legend should grow round the figure of the Buddha, The process of this growth makes a most fascinating study in religious architectonics, which, however, is beyond the scope of the present book. It is sufficient to observe that the process of Buddhist diffusion, a process which has, to some extent, influenced practically every culture flourishing in the Asiatic world, has been far from an unmixed blessing. Thomas Huxley in his Romanes lecture found some hope in the fact that 'a system which knows no God in the Western sense, which denies a soul to man, which counts the belief in immortality a blunder and the hope of it a sin, which refuses any efficacy to prayer and sacrifice, which bids men to look to nothing but their own efforts for salvation, which in its original purity knew nothing of vows of obedience and never sought the aid of the secular arm: yet spread over a considerable moiety of the old world with marvellous rapidity and is still with whatever base admixture of foreign superstitions, the dominant creed of a large fraction of mankind.' But, in honesty, it has to be admitted that it is not by virtue of any of its more pleasant features that Buddhism managed to 'spread over a considerable moiety of the old world with marvellous rapidity'; rather, it was because of its extreme readiness to welcome into its folds every foreign superstition with which it came in contact. Today 'the Diamond Throne of original enlightenment' accommodates not only the lean Tathagata, but also the vast army of the demons of 'a considerable moiety of the old world'; and the 'edifice of faith' is haunted by ghosts whose presence is a menace to human sanity.

Thus, the mere statistical fact that 'the present total of Buddhists in the world is about five hundred millions, or twice as many as that of the Christians—Roman Catholics and other sects included,' hardly affords any solace. Numbers mean little in themselves. In the present case, indeed, the statistics only serve to bring out a tragic fact. H. J. Massingham in his penetrating essay on Buddhism comes to the conclusion that Buddhism in its development as a world-religion has been a 'tragedy.' And he is right. The growth of Buddhism as a world-religion shows how utterly impossible it is for human beings to accept truth in its objective simplicity; it shows, too, that they cannot be content with the principle of reason alone for any length of time; and finally, it shows that to integrate themselves at all in relation to the bewildering but beautiful universe around them, they must resort to the tragic mediacy of the Myth.

Among many becoming, honorific titles which were bestowed upon Gautam by fervent piety, one which has always enjoyed a very wide currency is 'the Light of the World.' The title has only a pathetic interest: 'the Light of the World' seems to have proved singularly inadequate in dispelling the encircling gloom of human ignorance and stupidity.

9

Contemporary Relevance of Buddha

Gautam is not merely a dim figure silhouetted against the twilight of India's legendary past. He has a contemporary interest. Today, his influence extends far beyond the boundaries of the mystic East. Curiously enough, the insidious smile of the World-Renouncer of Kapilavastu has cast even over the supposedly materialistic Western world an enchantment akin to that of the Saviour of St. Sulpicery fame, who has served as a solace for so many broken hearts. Indeed, as a decorative object pure and simple, the image of the Enlightened One possesses an advantage over that of the tortured Galilean nailed to the Cross: the former is more soothing, more restful. It is, of course, a far cry from the primitive mints of Maues, where according to Dr. Koomaraswamy's researches, the Buddha image, as we know it, made its debut some time in the first century BC, to the highly efficient emblem-manufacturing factories of Birmingham which thrive on the love of the faithful. It was to be expected that in the course of this long journey through space and time, the original image should have undergone radical transformations. It is, however, a matter for gratification that these changes have not meant any loss of its magical appeal. In fact, if anything, they have increased it.

They have increased its appeal by the simple fact of making the image accessible to a far larger mass of people than had been possible at any time before in the history of Buddhism. Evidently, it needed a democratic age to turn out luminous statuettes of the 'Self-Luminous' One in sufficiently large numbers at prices within the reach of his humbler devotees. The Buddhist missionary-artists of the great age of Mahayana could only cherish, as a pious dream, the hope of providing a Buddha for every Buddhist home; they struggled in vain with the hopeless limitations of their technique, which rendered the realisation of their ideal impossible; there are, alas! mountains which even the most ardent faith cannot remove. But the modern image-makers —those invisible feeders of faith—with their wizardry of mass-productior have succeeded in working the miracle; the Face of Silence can at last be seen in practically every curiosity shop east as well as west of Greenwich; serene, detached, slightly cynical and world-weary, it seems to watch the mad rush of this age with a baffling indifference. Realised ideals, however, often bring disillusionment in their trail. In the present case, too, there has been cause for disappointment—indeed, even indignant complaint. Mr. Will Hayes, a writer on diverse religious topics, has recorded some instances of minor tragedies arising from the extensive diffusion of the Buddha image in an industrial age. Not long ago, he tells us, the Buddhists in England had to seek the intervention of the authorities with regard to a 'Buddha Hat-Pin,' and also were compelled 'to ask one of the big bazaars not to sell a sixpenny trinket made in the shape of their Master.' He further speaks of a personal experience. The other day,' he writes feelingly, 'I discovered in a shop window a figure of the Buddha labelled "Buddha Paper Weight." ' Had Gautam himself seen this, perhaps he would have enjoyed the joke. But one cannot be a *Bhakta,* a devotee, without dispensing with one's sense of humour: the author of 'My Buddha,' whose deep attachment to his hero is unquestionable, was naturally chagrined rather than amused. 'I walked straight into the shop,' he continues, 'and gave the young lady in charge a serious little lecture.' The young lady in question was unable to see her transgression until she was asked 'what she would think if she looked in the window across the road and saw "Jesus Pepperpot" for sale.' Quite justifiably indignant, Mr. Hayes wags an admonitory finger at the 'Christians who have to realise that these things are not in good taste.' That these things reflect a deplorable lapse of taste on the part of Christians, is true enough. But although one may sympathise with the British Buddhists in their great tribulation, it has to be recognised that the application of Noble Truths *en masse* was bound to create awkward situations like these. It is not known whether the protests led to the withdrawal of the offending articles from the market.

But on the face, it appears unlikely that mere consideration for the hypersensitive susceptibilities of a few votaries of Buddha would induce the souvenir manufacturers to abandon a very lucrative item on their list. Perhaps before long we shall get used to the idea of Buddha hatpins, of cheap trinkets and decorative paperweights made in the shape of the Great Master. After all, the image of Buddha has been subjected to far worse indignities in some of the Buddhist lands themselves. To take an instance which is familiar history, we might mention the story of the infamous King Bidatsu of Japan. The fact that he had been a devout and practising Buddhist did not prevent him from having the temple at Yamato burned, ordering the Buddhist nuns and monks to be flogged, and having the sixteen feet high image of the Buddha thrown into the canal; all this because the Buddha had failed to deliver his people from a severe epidemic of smallpox which had broken out in his kingdom. Such misfortunes must be regarded as an essential part of the dialectics of apotheosis. Those among men who are raised to the pedestal of godhead must also suffer the fate of gods, who are always in imminent danger of being treated as scapegoats.

Reaching the West

The word of the Buddha first reached the West by the overland route. One of the edicts of Emperor Ashoka, the great patron of Hinayana Buddhism, who has been sometimes compared with Constantine, makes a claim on his behalf that he propagated the Dhamma as far as the kingdoms of the four Kings named Ptolemy, Antiochus, Magas and Alexander, who are now believed to have ruled over Syria, Egypt, Macedonia, Cyrene, and Epirus. The claim is probably based on fact; for after the Alexandrian invasion, contact between India and the West was almost continuous, and trading colonies of Indians are known to have existed at various important centres on the coast of the Mediterranean, the one at

Alexandria being well-known. Some time in 21 AD. Augustus, while on a visit to Athens, received an embassy from India which had come by way of Antioch. According to Strabo, there was attached to it a man named Zamanochegas. Sir Hari Singh Gour suggests that this is possibly a corruption of Saman Achary, and that he was probably a Buddhist Bhikshu. The hypothesis seems credible, and offers an explanation for the extraordinary behaviour of the said Zamanochegas: he provided the Athenians with an unusual sensation, burning himself alive in public. It is not known whether the Athenians were impressed by his self-martyrdom; but there is no doubt that this was probably the first demonstration of the doctrine of renunciation carried to its logical extreme.

Towards the closing years of the second century the name of the Buddha actually appears in the writings of a Church Father, wrongly spelt it is true—but still unmistakably his name: Clement of Alexandria writes of 'those of the Indians that obey the precepts of Boutta, whom through exaggeration of his dignity", they honour as god.' Al Biruni's quotations from *Shaburkan*—a work by Mani, the great heretic of Ecbatana (215-276 AD)—leave little room for doubt as to the fact that Manichaeanism was profoundly influenced by the Buddhist doctrines; indeed, Mani claimed to be in the direct line of Buddha, Zoroaster, and Jesus.

References to Buddha in the *Acts of Archelaus* and St. Jerome have already been mentioned. In the thirteenth century we have Marco Polo representing the Buddha as the son of a King of Ceylon, and sadly reflecting what a pity it was that Sagomani Barcan (Marco Polo calls Gautam by his Mongolian title) was an idol-worshipper and not a Christian, or else he would have made such 'a great saint of our Lord Jesus Christ, so good and pure was the life he led.'

The Anglo-Saxon world first came to know of Buddha through an adventurous sailor Robert Knox (1660) who has something to say about 'a great god, whom they [meaning the Singhalese who had kept him a prisoner for nineteen years] call Bouddou, to whom the Salvation of Souls belongs'; and he goes on to add in *An Historical Relation of Ceylon*, the fruit of his captivity, 'Him they believe once to have come upon the earth. And when he was here, that he did usually sit under a large shady Tree, called Bogahah.'

It was not until the nineteenth century, however, that any attempt was made to obtain real knowledge of the Buddhist sources, though Simon de La Loubere, the representative of Louis XIV at the court of Siam (1687-8), had tried to translate a few passages from Pàli books. The first great discovery of the Buddhist scholarship was made by Alexander Csoma de Koros, a Hungarian scholar; he was trying to establish the origin of his people when he accidentally came upon some Tibetan Buddhist texts at Calcutta. Meanwhile, Brian Houghton Hodgson, for ten years (1833-43) the British Resident in Nepal, had gathered over 400 Sanskrit MSS. The discoveries of Csoma and Hodgson were to form the groundwork of Eugene Burnouf's *Introduction a l'histoire du Buddhisme Indien,* which appeared in 1844. It was a monumental work, but its appearance was somewhat eclipsed by the fact that álmost simultaneously George Turnour had unearthed the Pali sources; for, as was later to be proved, the bulk of Burnouf's sources were much later than the Pali.

During the latter half of the nineteenth century a most impressive structure of Buddhist scholarship grew up through the works of Victor Fausboll, Herman Oldenberg, Thomas William Rhys Davids who founded the Pali Text Society, Spence Hardy, and Senart. This tradition of painstaking scholarship has been maintained in our own times by men like T. Stcherbatsky, Louis de La Vallee Poussin, Suzuki, E. J. Thomas, and E. L. Woodward, to mention only a few.

But the Buddha who has captured the popular imagination of the West is not at all the Buddha who is to be found in the works of Buddhist scholars. Popular imagination likes unanimity; and scholars seldom find it possible wholeheartedly to agree on any subject. Popular imagination wants to believe; and acquaintance with works of Buddhist scholarship still sometimes tends to lead to the scepticism which the Russian scholar Vasiliev expressed, almost a century ago, saying: 'Russian, French, English, and German scholars have in fact written much on the subject. I have read through most of their works, but through them I have not learnt to know Buddhism.' So the popular mind in the West, as in the East, has accepted the Buddha of whom Robert Knox speaks: 'the great god to whom the Salvation of Souls belongs. Him they believe once to have come upon the earth. And when he was here, that he did usually sit under a large shady Tree...' The attraction of the Bodhi-Tree is apparently irresistible; its shadow extends even across scholarly pages.

'During the late nineteenth century,' J. B. S. Haldane writes in his *Fact and Faith,* 'certain oriental religions became temporarily fashionable in "advanced circles." ' That fashion is still with us; and we must attribute to it the curiosity which the Buddha and his doctrine have aroused at varying levels of response, from the highest downwards. The popularity of some of the oriental religions among 'advanced circles' is easy to understand; the popularity of the Buddha and his doctrine, however, raises some difficulty. For the idea of Renunciation at some point in a man's psychological development seems to be essential to any attitude which can legitimately claim kinship with the Buddhist view of life. This idea is, of course, capable of being interpreted in a variety of ways; and the motives leading to it will always reveal the widest divergences. But even taken at its crudest, that is when it is indistinguishable from various other doctrines of compensatory wish-fulfilments in a fantastic hereafter, and is a kind of *quid pro quo* for establishing 'proper connections with the higher powers,' it still remains a puzzling anachronism in a world frantically preoccupied with the adoration of Mammon.

Quoting Renan, who maintained that one could not be polite in a Paris omnibus without breaking the rules of the company, Professor Irving Babbitt in the introduction to *Being Creative,* observed with a quiet wisdom that characterised practically everything he wrote: 'Even so, any one who sets out to be a Buddhist today would find himself in conflict with the underlying assumptions of our civilization.' This is undeniable. And yet, it is also a fact that it was precisely at a moment when these assumptions—which Irving Babbitt recognised as being fundamentally in conflict with the essential Buddhist point of view—were becoming fully crystallised that the popular interest in Buddhism was greatly stimulated. The age which saw the translation of the Sacred Books of the Buddhists, also signalled the emergence of a chauvinistic and shamelessly venal Imperialism; it is now seldom remembered that Max Muller and T. W. Rhys

Davids were contemporaries of Meredith Townsend, Rudyard Kipling, and Cecil Rhodes. Contradictions of this nature have, of course, always existed: there is a ubiquitous incongruity between what human beings admire in the abstract and their actual practice. Julien Benda remarks somewhere that for two thousand years humanity has done evil, but honoured good: his statement perhaps possesses a wider application than he claims for it. Moreover, we always interpret our ideals in such a manner as to make them conform with our desires and interests: religion after all, as William James was to observe, revolves on the interest of the individual in his private personal destiny, and constitutes 'a monumental chapter in the history of human egotism.' This is doubtless quite natural and normal. But it should serve as a warning against that easy optimism which sees in the rise of 'Mahabodhi societies for the study and spread of Dharm...' in the Western world an augury of the birth of a 'Third Vehicle,' and a new awakening of compassion in the human breast. Unfortunately, the world is still not fit for Buddhists to live in, and to try to be one is almost as quixotic as trying today to be a Christian.

It was Nietzsche who said that the last Christian died upon the Cross. A truly Nietzschean exaggeration; but, like most of his exaggerations, it trembles on the verge of a profound truth which no amount of pontifical pomp and eloquence can alter. Similarly we might say that the last Buddhist died of dysentery at Kushinara. Meanwhile, those who like, can console themselves with the pathetic spectacle of saffron-robed Buddhist monks crossing perilous seas and taking their stand in the dazzling glare of modern publicity alongside many other professionals, in the vain hope of establishing the Sangha (Brotherhood) in the West; of charming Buddhist nuns whose feet have 'even trod Piccadilly.

The Buddha is a protean character. 'In Earth and Heavens and Hells incomparable,' he appears in different shapes, in different places. He has already appeared on the Indian screen; and Hollywood might yet go one better. M. Axel Raoul Wachtmeister has put him into the operatic repertoire; and though it is unlikely that we shall ever see his Opera-Oratorio at Covent Garden, there is every likelihood that the Buddha may yet appear at the Albert Hall. That the Buddha, has pictorial possibilities is proved not only by the art of Ajanta, Borobudur, Lung-men, and Hadda, but the 'Dictionnaire Infernal' of M. Collin de Plancy: an exhaustive compendium of 'all matters relating to devils, fairies, magic, astrology, etc...'— 'There he appears,' says Rhys Davids, 'in a curious woodcut as "Sakimuni, genie ou dieu," in the character of the Man in the Moon; or rather of the Hare in the Moon.'

All these roles of the Tathagata are easy to understand. But what is surprising is that he appears also in the Roman Calendar. Marco Polo's wish has, in fact, come true: 'Sagomani Barcan' has actually become a Christian saint. Somewhat surreptitiously it is true, but unmistakably he has found his way into the rather exclusive hierarchy of the Holy Apostolic Church. He appears there under the incognito of Josaphat, and has a Church dedicated to him as far west as Palermo. Joseph Jacobs collected the many variations which exist of 'the profitable story brought to the Holy City from the farther part of Ethiopia called India, by John the Monk (probably St. John of Damascus), an honourable and virtuous man of the monastery St. Sabas, containing the life of Barlaam and Josaphat, famous and blessed men both.' The story enjoyed the reputation of a Church best-seller during the middle ages. It is to be found in Vincent de Beauvais's *Speculum Historiale,* Jacques de Voragine's *Golden Legend,* and was sung by the Troubadour poet, Guy de Cambrai. It was so popular that it was translated into practically every European language—even Icelandic.

In the eighteenth century 'a Reverend Divine' of London published at the price of 2d., *The power of Almighty God, set forth in heathen's conversion shewing the whole life of Prince Jehosapkat, the son of King Avenerio of Burma in India in seven parts; how he was converted and made a Christian which was the conversion of his father and the whole land.* But it was Max Muller who first drew attention in his essay on the 'Migration of Fables' to the fact that 'all that is human and personal in the life of St. Josaphat is taken from *Lalita Vistara.*' In other words, he argued that St. Josaphat was none other than the Buddha of the Sanskrit Canon in his initial role of a Bodhisattva. 'Thus the Sage of Kapilavastu,' he observed, 'has received the highest honour that the Christian Church can bestow.' If this argument were admitted, November 27th, which is assigned to Barlaam and Josaphat in the Roman Martyrologium, should really be known as St. Gautam's day.

Official representatives of the Church, however, take a different view of the matter. Vicarious atonement may be permissible, but they are not prepared readily to admit the validity of vicarious canonisation. Their attitude on this point has evoked a spirited protest from Mr. Will Hayes. 'Ignorance of religious history...' he complains bitterly, 'is one of the average Christian's great failings. In lectures on comparative religion I have frequently mentioned the fact that the Buddha is a saint both in the Roman Catholic and Greek sections of the Christian Church. And I know quite well that every time I have said this my reputation for veracity has gone down several points.' But saint or not, on the whole it seems that the orthodoxy 'which would fain narrow the limit of the divine government of the world to the history of the Jewish and Christian nations' has treated Gautam with an indulgence altogether absent from its treatment of other 'false and heathenish prophets.' 'One hardly trusts one's eyes,' wrote Max Muller, 'on seeing Catholic and Protestant missionaries vie with each other in their praises of the Buddha... Indeed, no better authority can be brought forward in this respect than that of a still living Bishop of the Roman Catholic Church...' The Bishop in question, Bishop Bigandet, is no longer living, but his example has not been lost, and the agnostic of Kapilavastu continues to elicit frequent episcopal tributes.

Now, it need not be denied that some of these tributes are genuinely inspired and disinterested; and they indicate, as in the case of the late Bishop Gore and the present Bishop of Birmingham, the growth of a healthier outlook among the Christians. But the motives for praise are not always disinterested. Certain dignitaries of the Church seem to admire Buddhism because they find that in some of its forms, it has constituted itself into a notoriously rigid sacerdotal institution which bears a striking resemblance to Christian orthodoxy. The ceremonials of Lhasa are probably the nearest approach to the glory of the Vatican to be found east of Suez; the chief Temple of the holy city has something of the solidity of St. Peter, if not its formal beauty; and the person of the Dalai Lama is as near the haloed pontifical figure as one can hope to find more than twenty thousand feet above sea-level. 'Lamaism, indeed, with its shaven priests,' writes Rhys Davids, 'its bells and rosaries, its images, and holy water, and gorgeous dresses; its service with double choirs, and processions, and creeds, and mystic rites, and incense, in which the laity are spectators only; its abbots and monks, and nuns of many grades; its worship of the double Virgin, and of the saints and angels; its fasts, confessions, and purgatory; its images, its idols, and its pictures; its huge monasteries, and its gorgeous cathedrals, its powerful hierarchy, its cardinals, its Pope, bears outwardly at least a strong resemblance to Romanism, in spite of the essential difference of its teachings, and of its mode of thought.

Tastes differ: Some Christians, on the other hand, have admired the simplicity of the Buddhist faith. Thus, Bishop Bigandet, though himself a dignitary of the Roman Catholic Church, admired Burmese Buddhism because 'philosophy, which during its often erratic rambles in search of truth, changes, corrects, improves, destroys, and in numberless ways modifies all that it meets, never flourished in these parts,' and as such had no chance of tainting 'the religious institutions, which have remained to this day nearly the same as they were when first imported.'

Finally, there is the all-important missionary interest of Christendom in gleanings from the Buddha's fields. Since the days of the Justinian Code and the Crusades, the Holy Inquisition, and the extirpation of the Albigensian heretics, Torquemada and the gangs of conquistadors, the Faith Militant has learnt better. There are less drastic ways of saving the souls of infidels and heretics than burning, or stretching them on the rack. At the meeting of the International Missionary Council held in Jerusalem in 1928, discussing ways and means of propagating the true faith among the Japanese, Mr. K. J. Saunders made some revealing suggestions. He advocated that Christian workers there should cooperate with the free-thinking Buddhists because 'many in this group are as truly Christian already as most Christians; and others are very near the Kingdom. He added: 'The problem here is how organised Christianity in Japan can definitely win over those non-Church Christians or semi-Christians and then through them reach the other groups.' After all, there is some purpose behind all this eloquence from the pulpit in praise of the Buddha: it may be an olive branch to 'those non-church Christians or semi-Christians' who are very near the Kingdom, and through whom it may be possible to do something for the tormented souls of the unchristian millions dwelling in Buddhist lands. Whether this ingenious plan is likely to save the tragic multitudes of China and Japan and the Far-East, it is hard to say. One cannot help feeling, however, that the aspects of Buddhism which ecclesiastical circles, for one reason or another, find so admirable, have about as little, or as much, to do with Gautam as the Completed Doctrine with Jesus.

Gautam and Jesus

The Buddha and the Christ! Comparisons of this kind seldom serve any useful purpose; they generally involve too much simplification of human character; and they are at times even odious. But in the present case the comparison has *so* often been insisted upon that today it is almost impossible to avoid. To mention only the more familiar instances, the comparison is implicit in Edwin Arnold's *Light of Asia,* which purports to be 'the Scripture of the Saviour of the World'; Thoreau himself 'named the Buddha beside Christ,' though he was aware that in so doing he was laying himself open to the censure of devout Christians; and a contemporary French writer has called Gautam 'le frere aine du Jesus Christ.'

The problem, however, needs some clear definition. In fact, it is not one problem: there are two. Firstly, there is the question whether there are any points of similarity between the Buddhist and the Christian legend. To this question the answer seems to be in the affirmative. The parallels established by Seydel, Van den Bergh van Eysinga, Pischel, A. J. Edmunds, M. Aneski, and others are unmistakable. Some of them—for instance, the story of Simeon, the Temptation, Peter walking on the sea, and the Miracle of the loaves and fishes, which Garbe regards as obvious examples of borrowing by the writers of the Gospel from the Buddhist legend—are so striking that they cannot be explained purely as cases of accidental coincidence in religious legends. Even if there were no direct contact between India and Palestine in the first century AD, the possibility of indirect contact through the Persians was very considerable; and there is no reason why Evangelists should not have known the Buddhist legend in some of its Near-Eastern variations. Actually there has been far more diffusion and interpenetration of legends both secular and religious, current in different parts of the world than is admitted by most people who seem to take a proprietary interest even in legends.

The second question is whether the personalities of Gautam and Jesus, after they have been divested of their obviously legendary and mythological attributes, have anything in common; whether, that is to say, there is any measure of identity between their respective world-views. This is a very complicated question. For it is difficult to obtain any agreement as to which parts of the Buddhist and the Christian stories are historical, and which are not; what pronouncements can be attributed to Gautam and Jesus, and what is to be regarded as the improvisation of later commentators. M. Loisy has caused considerable embarrassment among Biblical critics by suggesting that 'the Sermon on the Mount.. was never preached *(prononce)*.' A similar, possibly even more devastating case could be made with regard to Gautam's first sermon, 'the Sutra of Turning the Wheel of Doctrine'; indeed, the argument is implicit in the Sun-Myth theory of Senart and Kern. Such being the uncertainty, it is necessary to narrow down the issue. The question that we should ask ourselves is whether the integral personality which emerges from a critical analysis of the Pali Canon, on the one hand, and from the Synoptic Gospel, on the other, point to any common basis of experience, or resultant attitude.

To this question one can only return a negative answer. Gautam and Jesus were as different from one another as it is possible for any two human beings to be. The difference is not merely, as Canon Streeter has it, 'that the Christ was a carpenter, the Buddha was a Prince; they experienced life from different angles. The Buddha was a philosopher; Jesus had the mind of a poet.' This is unduly simplifying the issue. It is by no means certain that Gautam was a Prince, though it is true his people were comfortably off. On the other hand, though there is no doubt as to where Jesus' own heart lay, it remains open to question—in spite of Kautsky—whether he personally had any intimate knowledge of poverty; Dean Inge, for instance, rejects the whole notion which makes Christ '*le bon sans-culotte*,' and even goes to the opposite extreme, suggesting that 'Christ and his apostles belonged to the prosperous peasantry of Galilee, a well-educated and comfortable middle class.' And the difference between a poet and a philosopher is, to say the least, rather difficult to define.

A somewhat novel interpretation of the contrast between the personalities of Gautam and Jesus has lately been put forward by those who, presumably, subscribe to what Papini calls 'the exhausting mercantile superstition of our day.' With varying degrees of refinement, they enlarge on Mr. Bruce Barton's conception of Christ as 'a precursor of the modern man of business, an apostle of outer action and even as a go-getter. Against this they assess the Buddha as a typical oriental, a passive dreamer of dreams. The querulous Buddhist, of course, could protest that, as far as action goes, his catechism insists on 'strenuousness' and 'effort' with such vehemence that it might serve as an excellent text for the modern men of action, whose exploits are normally limited to meditations on Stock Exchange reports, and who are wise enough to have their work done for them by paid slaves. Further—since by their deeds shall ye know them!—they might point to the prodigious achievements of their Japanese conferrers who, even Mr. Bruce Barton would admit, have been anything but dreamy and passive in recent years. To see the difference between two men in this light is to miss the significance of what seems most central in their world-views.

The range of our knowledge about them is limited, but one thing may confidently be asserted: that Gautam was as far from being a lotus-eater as Jesus from our glorified slave-drivers of Big Business and High Finance. Dr. Reichelt, a German missionary of very wide sympathies, who founded 'The Society of Religious Friends' in China, informs us that in his conversation with 'really religious Buddhists' he was able to extract from them the admission that 'in the story of Calvary the Bodhisattva doctrine has reached its perfection.' This must have been due to some misapprehension on the part of our 'really religious Buddhists.'

For one thing, the Bodhisattva is nowhere represented as bearing his cross through crowded streets. And the reason why he is not so represented is, partly at least, because Gautam was above all a prudent man, like Confucius, and lived the kind of life which could by no stretch of imagination on the part of his followers be interpreted as martyrdom. He scrupulously avoided getting into trouble with the temporal powers, who would doubtless have given him 'short shrift,' as did Pontius Pilate to the 'Messianic agitator' from Galilee. His concession with regard to the admission of runaway slaves, domestic servants, soldiers, etc., may be mentioned as one example of his desire not to get himself involved in any struggle with Law and Order. Because of this prudence on his part, Buddhism has remained lacking in 'the tremendous fact' which forms the nucleus of the Gospel Passion Play—the fact of a supreme martyrdom. But, on the other hand, for this very reason Buddhists have been spared from having their bowels of compassion moved to the point of excruciation by subtle stabs of remorse.

On the whole, Gautam seems to have had more consideration for his votaries: they are not reminded of the man who died and suffered for them every time they visit their shrines; nor do their temples everlastingly echo the silent but agonising refrain of, 'is it nothing to ye, is it nothing to ye, all ye that pass by?' The idea of dying and suffering for others in the Christian sense is, broadly speaking, alien to practically every form of Buddhism. It was certainly alien to Gautam's teaching; he quite frankly told his Brethren that they must not expect that ultimate self-sacrifice of him: for 'by oneself is evil done, by oneself one suffers. By oneself is evil left undone; by oneself is one purified. Purity and impurity belong to oneself; no one can purify another.' There is no vicarious atonement available to a Buddhist; but then, on the other side, he is spared those painful stigmata which were the lot of 'Christ's Poor Little One,' St. Francis of Assisi. It would be futile to compute whose is the greater felicity, the Christian's or the Buddhist's!

Environmental Differences: It is true, account for the divergences in their public careers up to a point. Gautam was able to avoid a useless martyrdom partly, at any rate, because both his upbringing and the conditions under which he lived were very different from those of Jesus. Given the circumstances with which Jesus was faced, given also his peculiar conditioning, it is arguable that Gautam, too, might (though not necessarily) have ended on the Cross. Fortunately for him, however, India in the sixth century BC presented a very different picture to that of the Holy Land in 27 AD. This is a plain historical fact which is too often overlooked. It is not necessary here to go into details of the social and psychological characteristics of the world of Gautam; it will be sufficient to emphasise the more obvious features of the milieu in which he found himself. It is certain that it was altogether more peaceful, less overwrought, than the one in which Jesus rose to prominence.

'Christianity,' observes Oldenberg, 'founded its kingdom in times of the keenest suffering, amid the death struggle of a collapsing world. India lived in more settled peace.' Here the horizon was not overcast with grim forebodings of the Great Event which was to destroy the existing order and usher in a new era. It was precisely such anticipations, at once morbid and exultant, which made it possible for the Prince of Peace to appear on the scene with his highly explosive message; indeed, it may be suggested that they forced the issue for Jesus and left him with no choice.

At the time of the Buddha in India, too, there was a great deal of intellectual and spiritual ferment. But it was something quite different from the 'Messianic ferment' brewing in the lands bordering on 'the Great Sea.' The distinction is important to recognise. People in Buddhist India were interested in attaining salvation, release from the turmoils of earthly existence, and heaven, as people always and everywhere have been interested in their destiny beyond the grave, and in making proper arrangements for an uncertain, and hence terrifying, future which is perpetually glaring man in the face. But with them it was a leisurely, and, comparatively speaking, normal pursuit. There was hardly any touch of hysterical violence about it. God was being sought after by mortals in a variety of ways, but the technique of this hopeless quest was almost scientific in so far as they proceeded by the method of trial and error in the laboratory of personal experience rather than mob frenzy in the market place. There was no attempt to force God to come down to earth and found his kingdom.

Indians have always been a patient people; that has been their principal virtue as well as their major vice. The men of the age of Gautam could afford to wait for their salvation. They stood on their heads if they so desired, or calmly contemplated the tips of their noses with a fixed, unmoving gaze; followed the straight and narrow path of the true Brahminical faith, or quietly deviated into the fascinating byways of heresy; practised strictest austerities or indulged in the most sensational ritualistic orgies. Not so in Judaea of the time of 'Our Lord.' If the whole of Asia Minor, the Peloponnesian peninsula, and shores of the Adriatic and the Aegean constituted a spiritual, as well as political, powder-magazine, the fuse was being laid in Jerusalem. Successive sanguinary wars had left behind them a trail of death, disease, and misery. In this delirium of suffering, the problem of 'future,' the problem of God, had assumed overwhelming proportions, had become an obsession. Miracles were in the air; the atmosphere was tense with expectations of a cataclysmic end 'coming from the East and shining to the West.' Prophecy had risen to a culminating pitch of morbidity and exultation; people were literally being stampeded into the penitentiary. 'The time is fulfilled,' the resonant voice of the oracle in flesh and blood came echoing through the darkness of an apocalyptic hallucination, 'and the kingdom of God is at hand: repent ye, and believe the gospel.'

A veritable panic was precipitated in the Holy City when a young visionary from Nazareth arrived on the stage. This strange young man had already beguiled a small group of followers by promising that he would make them fishers of men. The authorities, however, were not having any sedition put across under the guise of a new mysticism, and they had little difficulty in effectively suppressing the Messiah. In Golgotha, prophecy was put to a severe and ultimate test; as could have been foretold, it failed miserably, and the forces of Law and Order emerged triumphant. Tragically the twilight fell on the last, perhaps the greatest of prophets, and the first among the martyrs. The whole episode was a short one, like a meteor rending the darkening sky with its incandescent pain for a brief moment, then as quickly vanishing.

Gautam's course, on the other hand, ran through a long, steady, and uneventful groove: it was unspectacular to the point of being mediocre and pedestrian. He lived to a respectable old age; and though the doctrine he preached was, in its own way, quite as revolutionary as that of Jesus, he was discreet enough to adopt methods of propaganda and argument which were not likely to bring him into conflict with the temporal power or the hierarchical authority. He ridiculed the superior pretensions of priests and patriarchs alike, but he did so with a grace and gentle irony which seldom aroused needless antagonisms. As far as possible, he avoided making angry scenes; and that sense of almost physical exhilaration, which El Greco's Christ seems to derive from driving the money-changers from the Temple, was not known to him. He made no quixotic promises, disappointed no eager hopes; he coveted no kingdoms and suffered no crucifixion.

These contrasts are obvious enough. Underlying them there were, of course, subtler differences of tradition, of the background of civilization in each case. Behind Gautam there were the pantheistic lyricism of the Vedic hymns, the diffuse speculations of Upanishads and the Brahminical abstractions; contemporaneous with him were the more metaphysical, though as yet probably unsystematised philosophies of several groups of dialecticians. His predilection was towards intellectuality; his training had been that of an intellectual; and though he clearly saw the limitations of intellect, he did not reject it totally, remaining an intellectual to the end. Jesus, on the contrary, had been nurtured in the highly inflammable tradition of Judaism; a tradition which had produced such eminent prophets as Isaiah, Jeremiah, Ezekiel, and Job; a tradition which, as Canon Streeter admits, had no interest in metaphysics whatever. This was to give his passionate nature an even more passional turn. It accounts for what Sir Charles Eliot calls 'the element of the tragic' in his life; it accounts for his 'nervous irritability'; it accounts for his sorrow tinged with occasional fits of self-pity. 'Christ,' observes Sir Charles Eliot, 'is at conflict with what he calls the world. He is angry with it because it will not hear him. He declares that it hates him. The little towns of Galilee are worse in his eyes than the wicked cities of antiquity because they are not impressed by his miracles... But the Buddha was not angry with the world. He thought of it as unsatisfactory and transitory rather than wicked, as ignorant rather than rebellious... He troubled little about people who would not listen to him.'

Jesus took an altogether more emotional view of life than Gautam. It is impossible to conceive of him as saying: 'All that we are is the result of our thought; it is founded on our thoughts, it is made up of our thoughts'; as impossible as to imagine Gautam supplicating in some Indian Gethsemane, 'Abba Father, all things are possible unto Thee; take away this cup from me: nevertheless not what I will, but what Thou wilt,' or crying, 'My God, My God, why hast Thou forsaken me?' The idea of filial devotion to the Deity, of forsaking and being forsaken, of abject betrayals with a kiss would have appeared rather absurd to the sceptical and matter-of-fact mind of the Tathagata.

The two ways diverge fundamentally. Dr. Reichelt's 'really religious Buddhists' could not have read their Scriptures: Christians, after all, are not the only people to betray ignorance of their religious history. The Bodhisattva doctrine is not the doctrine of Gautam, but it has no connection with Calvary. 'Even the modern developments of Buddhism, writes Sir Charles Eliot, who understood the spirit of Buddhism better than most western writers on the subject, 'which represent the Buddha Amida as a saviour do not contain the idea that he gives up his life for his followers.' Renan was equally near the mark when he pointed out that what distinguishes Buddhism from Christianity, and in fact from practically every other known religion, is that it has its roots in 'la *pensee pure.*' Its basic doctrine, the doctrine of Gautam which Whitehead chooses to describe as 'a tremendous doctrine,' is not, strictly speaking, a religion at all. It does not contain any sense of The Holy—that, which according to Dr. Otto, is 'the "beyond" of the mystic... the kernel of religion.' It offers no consolations and no compensations; it is devoid of faith, and consequently of miracle, which is but faith-in-manifestation. Its central point is an act of mental apprehension and not an ecstasy; as such the emphasis is on Understanding, not on Mystery. The pattern that is projected is cerebral rather than emotional.

Gautam and Jesus stand for two distinct modes of apprehending reality. The resultant world-views have nothing or little in common. They can be reconciled to one another only at the cost of distorting both. For Jesus, Love and the *elan* of Love—an *elan,* let it be recognised, which, though transcendental to a degree, in the end involved an almost physiological rapture, a tingling of the corpuscles of the blood, a nervous transport electrically kindling the very cells of the being—was an absolute value. It needed no external sanction, no outside justification. It was for him the last word on the nature of reality. He was what we in India call *Bkakta.* To this ecstatic attitude, Gautam would have found it very difficult to subscribe. His was the cool, sceptical, and dispassionate disposition of a man of sense. Love, he would almost certainly have reasoned, is far from being the last word about anything. It is not sufficient to go through life; not sufficient to bring life's chaotic tendencies into some kind of an order. It leaves out far too much. Most important of all things, it leaves out its own fulfilment. For it is in the very nature of Love that it shall remain for ever frustrate; it is in the very nature of a craving that it can never be satisfied. These arguments, of course, could hardly have convinced the man of faith. For faith is love; and love is blind. To Gautam's dry, clear-cut intellectual expostulations, Jesus might very well have retorted in the words of Hamlet: 'There are more things in heaven and earth, Horatio, than are dreamt of in your philosophy.' And, for him, no doubt there were. But for him alone; and in the last resort, even for him they turned out to be very different to what he had dreamed.

There is little similarity between the dramas of these two lives. They are enacted on entirely different planes. The one is conceived on a Promethean scale, poignant with great joy and titanic despair. Like a feverish vision, it is vivid with fleeting transparencies and nightmare shadows of an agony 'darker than death or night.' The other theme moves through soft modulations, wistful but satisfying. Like a sober tone-poem, it seldom rises beyond a quiet meditative mood, at once diffuse and precise in its meaning. Perhaps, in the last analysis, both are tragic dramas, tragic in different ways. In one case we are given an act of faith, an act of love, leading to its inevitable, perhaps predestined conclusion in an abject betrayal. In the other, we feel something of the ache of what might almost be described as disembodied thought: a disembodied thought which, having explored the heights and abysses of the universe, discovers that it is like an eternal phantom-pantomime, a process of endless cycles of dissolution and evolution, of change and becoming; that in the end we must part from everything that is 'most near and dear to us'—even our precious thought. So different are these two most significant figures that one cannot even approach them from the same angle, or apply to them the same standards of criticism. One can accept or reject Gautam purely on intellectual grounds. But one cannot hope to treat Jesus in the same dispassionate manner. One gets emotionally involved in him. One must either love him, or struggle against him. And in struggling against him one gets as deeply involved in him as in loving him; we have only to remember the convulsions of antichrists like Nietzsche and D. H. Lawrence, who, for all their fulminations against the Cross, have stigmata written over all their pages. It is, indeed, best either not to think of the strange Galilean at all; or to accept him without reserve, without demanding any explanations, in fullness of heart.

In an article in the *Hibbert Journal* two years ago, Sir Radhakrishnan observed that the wisdom of the Buddha 'has a singular attraction for free and enquiring minds of today.' The reason for this attraction, partly at any rate, is the desire to find in the wisdom of the Buddha a justification for their own beliefs and attitudes. It is quite a natural desire. The tendency to interpret another's experience to justify one's own is not at all reprehensible; up to a point, it is not only excusable, but perfectly legitimate, because inevitable. 'La *verite est,'* Anatole France writes, *'que l'on ne sort jamais de soi-meme.'* This is profoundly true. One always sees, cannot help seeing, reality from the prison-window of one's own experience. No matter how detached, how objective, how dispassionate we may try to be the bars through which we look out upon the world of transient things are always present, casting their grotesquely enlarged shadow over our field of vision. We are so inexorably conditioned by our own experience that it is inevitable we should project our immediate anxieties and fears, doubts, and hesitations on everything with which we come into contact. Complete objectivity is an ideal impossible of achievement. But there are limits to which the process of self-projection may be carried. It is one thing to see the shadow of prison-bars across the horizon, and quite another to see nothing but the prison-bars; one thing to observe a dim reflection of one's own time in other times, and quite another to see in such times nothing but the reflection of one's own time. To disregard these limits is to land oneself in hopeless anachronisms.

Thus the fact that social conflicts have today assumed an overbearing importance has induced some writers to invest the age of the Buddha with a parallel social background; to see in Buddhism something very much akin to a mass-movement of revolt; and to picture Gautam as the leader of a political revolution on the one hand, and a religious reformation on the other. He has even been labelled 'the Divine Socialist' by a writer bearing the name of Sophia Egoroff. Other writers, with less charming names, but more serious purpose, have taken a cue from Carl Kaut-sky's interpretation of primitive Christianity, and tried to interpret primitive Buddhism in purely politico-economic terms. This misplaced emphasis seems to obscure rather than clarify the meaning of primitive Buddhism in general and the Buddhism of Gautam in particular.

M. Jean Przyluski, in a monograph on Buddhism, for instance, comes to a conclusion which is original rather than justifiable. *'Le Bouddhisme..'* he maintains, *'est a l'origine, une doctrine qui s'appuie sur les classes inferieures de la societe Indienne... a cet egard il semble dirige contre le systeme des castes.'* But, as a matter of fact, there is no evidence to show that, originally, Buddhism was a proletarian movement, aiming at the emancipation of the poor and downtrodden strata of Indian society. To attribute to it any such laudable motives is to give it credit which it hardly deserves. M. Przyluski himself seems to feel that his position is untenable; for in the very next paragraph, he admits: *'Le Bouddhisme n'est pas dirige contre les castes en sens etroit. Il ne pretende pas davantage abolir les grandes classes sociales, ni mettre le sujet au niveau du souverain...'* It is reasonable to enquire that if it is not directed against the caste system in any direct and overt sense, if it does not attempt to abolish the major social divisions, and if further it does not contemplate raising the subject to the level of the Sovereign—in what earthly sense then is Buddhism revolutionary?

M. Przyluski has no satisfactory answer; perhaps there can be no satisfactory answer so long as we restrict the word 'revolutionary' to its modern politico-economic sense. Gautam was not a revolutionary in our specialised meaning of the word; at that particular stage of social organisation, it would have been nothing short of a miracle had a revolutionary of this type suddenly appeared on the scene. It would be a complete falsification of facts to proclaim him as an early avatar of Lenin, or even Luther. It is unfortunate that he did not take the line of a revolutionary; had he done so, he might have emerged a more heroic and praiseworthy figure. But evidence on this point leaves little room for such illusions.

However, the fact that Gautam was not a political revolutionary, that the movement he founded had no overt political aims, does not mean that he was simply a 'holy man' who saw the problem as one mainly pivoted on mysticism and religion. August Thalheimer's contention that Gautam sought a solution within the framework of 'religious truths' only proves how difficult it is for even the best of our dialecticians to see anything objectively.

Gautam not only sought no solution within the boundaries of religious dogma, or Mystery, but was probably one of the first men of whom we know, who really saw through religious phenomena and concluded that they afforded no solution. Certainly we do not find in him any violent recoil from religion. He is not the prototype of Marlowe's Faustus. His was not the hopeless, emotional revolt of one who is so inextricably wedded to the religious myth that he would go and sell his soul to the devil to experience the presence of God in its most diabolical and absolute form—as an everlasting absence; who is so attached to the idea of the Good that he deliberately practises evil to assert the existence of its opposite; or who is willing to court eternal damnation to demonstrate to himself the reality of eternal Grace. To deny God one indeed must love him passionately, ecstatically. Gautam's attitude on all these issues was, on the other hand, that of a truly philosophic and scientific spirit; one who is 'above the battle' in the proper sense of the phrase. 'Therefore, O Ananda,' we hear him saying, 'be ye lamps unto yourselves. Be ye refuge to yourselves. Take yourselves to no external refuge. Hold fast to the truth as a lamp.' This cannot by any stretch of imagination be mistaken for the stern voice of religious authority: no religion could foster so open and honest an attitude of enquiry without seriously endangering its own foundations. Still less is this the tortured but adoring litany of a disciple of the Son of Morning. It reflects merely the calm certainty of a reasonable but somewhat uninspiring person who has come to regard the paraphernalia of religious Mystery as irrelevancy rather than falsehood—as something unnecessary.

For Gautam, the only way of resolving life's endless tangles and complications lay through understanding. It was a question of adjustment of mental habits and ways of thought; a question, in the widest interpretation, of psychology. Thus, his objection to the Brahminical tradition based itself neither on moral nor on political grounds. He did not take exception to it because it tended to set up the Brahminical oligarchy as an absolute dictatorship. It is, indeed, open to question whether at any time in Indian history Brahmins have enjoyed the supremacy so often attributed to them. At least, it is certain that at the time of the Buddha, when the caste system was still in the process of formation, they could not have done so. True, they exercised arbitration and prerogative in matters concerning the other world; and they could probably manipulate heavenly wrath at their will. But the temporal power resided entirely with the second caste in the Hindu social tetrachotomy; no matter what the Vedas said, the merchants and nobles could pay the piper and call the tune. As in feudal Europe so in classical India, the priests, while they might conjure horrifying visions of fire and brimstone for the lesser fry, maintained an attitude of obsequious indulgence towards the rich and powerful, and indeed were quite reconciled to the idea of picking the juicy bones and crumbs from the lordly tables.

Thus, if Gautam had wished to lead a political revolution, it would have been altogether more meet to have incited the people against his own caste. But he did not entertain any such intentions. His quarrel with the existing social order was not that it was unjust, but that it was stupid, and unjust because of its stupidity. He objected to Brahmins not because they were tyrants but because they were imbeciles; not because they were showing the wrong path to heaven but because they were raising hopes which could never be fulfilled, since there was no such thing as heaven. He saw in life a conflict, not between good and evil, between caste and caste, between rich and poor, but between ignorance and knowledge. Man's viciousness, his callousness to others, and in the end to himself, his failures and frustrations, he traced back not to a Fall from Grace at some remote date in antiquity but to a much more immediate cause—his failure to think properly, his failure, in fact, to think at all. Jesus said of those who struck him: 'they know not what they do.' In the context in which this was uttered, it might have meant a number of things. But taken literally it comes nearer to Gautam's point of view than any other pronouncement of Jesus.

They know not what they do.' What is more, they *think* not of what they do. That sums up Gautam's criticism of the Brahmins as well as the non-Brahmins of his time— and of all times. As he saw it, the chief task therefore was to impart knowledge to people, to make them think. For if they knew, if they thought, their acts would be different. His was an attempt at a psychological revolution, if we can conceive of such a thing; not a change of heart only—he was inclined to be sceptical about the value and even possibility of a change of heart, and seems to have been one of the few men who have ever cared to give that overrated organ a 'socratic treatment'—but a re-orientation of men's mental horizon and habits of thought. Rightly or wrongly, he believed this to be the only change worth attempting. Rightly or wrongly, he believed, too, that if it were achieved the rest would follow naturally, inevitably.

How far was this belief justified? How far was it an evasion and wish-fulfilment—an 'ideal and fantastic victory' over a world otherwise too difficult to cope with? These are questions upon which it would be better to reserve judgement in the present state of our knowledge. So far Gautam's method has not been given a fair trial; perhaps, by its very nature, it cannot be given a fair trial. But it does present a choice of the most crucial importance; a choice not between moral right and wrong, but between truth and error. It was Goethe who remarked that the fascination of error derives from the almost complete absence of checks from its vast domain, and that what makes human beings fight shy of truth is the limitation it imposes. But perhaps one ought to add that error also has its limitations—limitations far more hopeless than any set by truth; and that, though the sphere of error be vast, its vastness is that of a huge cul-de-sac, and not of sunlit skies. The distinction between truth and error is hard to perceive; the light we possess is always uncertain and wavering, and the darkness immense. Yet the choice is there; and sooner or later mankind will have to face it. And with that choice is linked up the larger issue of humanism; of our belief in human standards, which, though not absolute in the sense in which some of the agelong aberrations of human fancy have been regarded as absolute, represent a residual wisdom, and as such not only lend dignity and meaning to human effort, but form a measure of worth with a more than personal sanction.

Humanism is not a new issue. For over two thousand years sensitive individuals seem to have been aware of the problem, or have been struggling to define it for themselves. There are several methods of approach, but finally they fall into two broad categories. On the one hand, the romantic approach—romantic, that is, not in any derogatory sense, but simply in the sense that it seeks abolition of all limitations which beset human life. Its most outspoken expression is to be found in Rousseau who said: *'J'adore la liberte; j'abhorre la gene, la peine, l'assujettissement, l'injustice.'* A subtler, more tragic manifestation of this attitude is seen in Marlowe; for at root, Faustus' Promethean craving for 'knowledge infinite' and his hopeless attempt to capture immortality in a single kiss, represents a humanistic struggle. But the way of a Rousseau or a Marlowe, though no doubt heroic to a degree, raises more difficulties than it solves. Clearly, it is not simply a question of being passionately attached to the idea of liberty, and revolting against tyranny. As far as freedom goes Rousseau was by no means original in his fervent longings: we all yearn for freedom infinite, and would like to be absolved of the coils which hamper us from every direction. But what we all seem unwilling to admit is that a certain amount of bondage is implicit in the very condition of our existence, is inseparable from it. For instance, although we may burn down all the Bastilles in the world, put every tyrant against the wall, and stamp out all the counter-revolutionary spiders upon whom we can lay hands, death is probably still inevitable. There is death for the tyrant and the tyrannised, for Hitlers as well as Stalins, for Baldwins no less than for Lenins. Death: it is almost a comforting thought.

But there is also the quest of knowledge infinite; of consummation in the ecstasy of love. It is a brave and noble quest. Brave and noble—but, unhappily, foredoomed to failure. Take 'knowledge infinite.' In the nature of things, alas! no such condition can exist. All knowledge to which we have access is, by definition, finite and limited; one of the principal functions of awareness is to demarcate boundaries. True, these boundaries do not remain always the same; they are ever changing; yet some kind of boundaries still remain. To know a thing is also to be conscious of the deficiency of one's knowledge of it, which is always approximate, never final. Knowledge infinite, then, is a mental chimera, a will-o'-the-wisp beyond all human grasp. So, too, the love infinite. The pity of a passion so exhausting and reckless as that of Faustus is that it demands far too much of the object of the heart's desire. Demonstrably, Helen even if she were to grant us far greater favours than a niggardly kiss, could not be expected to transubstantiate our mortal stuff into immortality. Death is no respecter of persons: Helen too is mortal. 'Whereas anything whatever born, brought into being, and organised contains within itself the inherent necessity of dissolution,' so in time all the Helens of the world once 'fairer than the evening air clad in the beauty of a thousand stars, must grow old and weary, and slowly be devoured by the germ of decay. Such is the order of all component things.

Humanism, therefore, so long as it is involved in the mere assertion of human will seems bound to lead to a tragic culmination. Human will, whether collective or individual, cannot accomplish the impossible, cannot bring us the moon of unattainable freedom, and cannot make it possible for us to satisfy all our desires. Wisdom perhaps consists in making an effort to understand the true nature and extent of our bondage, of our deficit. For truly to understand our chains might lead us to the discovery that some at least of them are imaginary, and there are a few others which we can shake off if we work diligently.

So we have the way of Gautam. Less heroic, less spectacular by far, it possesses at least one clear advantage: it spares us the painful switchback experience of high hopes doomed to be disappointed. It makes no desperate gesture to transcend all limits; rather it is content to discover such limits as there are, and to accept them. It is not the way of Will. It does not yield to the inebriation caused by the fleeting moods of the human will in its moments of uncertain triumphs, but is aware of the abysses of dejection that open before us at every step. It sees, in brief, not only the significance of man, but his insignificance. It thus offers a humanism which is not incompatible with reason, discretion, and humility; it contains also a truly human Norm.

But there is a chorus of disapproving voices. The Buddha, if he has had crowds of admiring votaries, has not lacked critics. A typical instance comes from the New World: the case of Ralph Waldo Emerson, a direct descendant of the energetic and industrious Pilgrim Fathers. 'Always motor-minded,' his sympathetic biographer, Frederick Ives Carpenter, writes, 'he hated quietism. And as he associated quietism especially with Buddhism, he often criticised that religion. We have already noticed that he described Buddhism as being literally the tenet of "Fate." ' Ralph Waldo was, indeed, so terribly motor-minded, so anxious to step on the accelerator as it were, that he would not even pause to make sure of his facts, and talked the most disarming nonsense about Buddhism that has ever been heard on either side of the Atlantic. 'He called the *Bhagavat Gita,*' Mr. Carpenter himself adds for our information, ' "the much-renowned book of Buddhism" and so showed his ignorance.' To this comment let us add, that he confessed his ignorance no less blatantly when he confused Buddhism with fatalism; for the Doctrine of Gautam, in so far as it is a doctrine at all, is as far from being a tenet of 'Fate' as the *Bhagavat Gita* from being 'the much-renowned book of Buddhism.' Moreover, if the whole argument against Gautam bases itself on his disapproval of loud-speaking, self-proclaiming, and hysterically go-getting philosophies, then there is something to be said for his quietism.

The Rev. Bruce, in his Gifford Lectures delivered towards the end of the last century, however, levels a more serious and even more typical charge against the Tathagata. Not satisfied with dismissing his doctrine as 'fantastic and morbid,' the learned divine goes on disdainfully to say: The well-being of the race demanded warriors brave in the field of battle against evil, not monks immured in cloister and passing their time in poverty, wearing the yellow robe of a mendicant order.' This gentleman's contempt for the Buddhist attitude should not surprise us. A view of life which does not visualise the world as one great Armageddon, naturally takes away all vestige of justification from the big battalions of Christian soldiers who have proved their mettle worthily in many much wider arenas than the narrow range of the spiritual-symbolic battleground. The impecunious, cloistral life-mode of the Buddhist monks could not possibly have commended itself to this reverend gentleman who, evidently, believed in deriving the fullest secular benefits from the revenues of a flourishing State Church. But one may justifiably wonder if a doctrine, the efficacy of which entirely depends on the existence of evil in the world, and a faith whose very *raison d'etre* is bound up with the consciousness of the all-pervading nature of sin, is not more obviously open to the charge of 'morbidity' than a doctrine which, whatever its drawbacks and shortcomings, at least makes an attempt to resolve human problems by reference to an intelligible causal chain, and is not based on an obsession of the dreadful, everlasting combat between good and evil.

A more sophisticated objection to Gautam's doctrine is to be found in Mr. Paul Elmer More. Until recently an eminently catholic and stimulating writer, Prof. More seems to have decided to recant his early agnostic indiscretions. He has come to the conclusion that there is no consummation to be achieved outside the embrace of a 'personal deity'; and as a result, he has thrown Aristotle overboard and joined the already teeming ranks of Lord Lorders. And like most contrite souls, ever since his appearance in sackcloth, he has turned his battery of recrimination against the company which he cultivated only yesterday. He has some unkind words to say even of the Buddha, whom in a recent essay he has compared to 'a man who has raised a stately flight of stairs that leads nowhere.'

This is perhaps poetic justice. Gautam had used a very similar argument against the Brahmins of his time. However, Gautam had a different context: he had argued that if you lead people up a flight of stairs then you must know where you are leading them. As far as he himself was concerned he was content to remain on the ground level. This takes away the point from Prof. More's analogy. Professor More is so anxious to belled somewhere that he does not mind whether he is landed into the cloud cuckoo-land of theological Heaven or down into the dream torture-chamber of ecclesiastical Inferno. Lead thou me on— *n'importe ou dehors du monde.* It is his own choice.

The foregoing arguments are indicative of the main tenor of Gautam's depreciatory critics. Drawn from many quarters, they include in their fold people holding the most divergent opinions, rankest materialists as well as exultant idealists, ferocious theists and even more ferocious atheists. But all have this much in common. They subscribe to positive beliefs of some sort; they affirm, each in his own way, a staunch and unshakable faith either in this world, or the next, or sometimes as it happens, wisely, in both; and they share with one another that most horrible of all horrors to which man is subject—the *horror nihili.* It certainly seems strange that these titans of faith, armed as they are with all the impregnable virtues of a self-righteous positivism, should see in what they denounce as 'the ineffectual pessimism of the Buddhists,' a serious menace to their firm convictions, and think it fit to lash at it with an earnest fury worthy of the frantic Knight of La Mancha, It is, in fact, revealing. It reveals the weakness inherent in all uncritical positivism, whether of the idealistic or materialistic brand. What Rochester so aptly called 'balloons of philosophy,' no matter of what variety and colour, are all liable to burst at first contact with the actualities of human experience. It seems, however, that the balloon of *positive* philosophy is made of still more flimsy substance. It is not even a proper balloon, perhaps: it is more of a bubble.

It would serve no purpose to enter into the fruitless though popular controversy as to whether Gautam was a nihilist, and if so, to what extent are we justified in regarding his doctrine as of a purely negative character. But this much must be emphasised: the misapprehensions on this point arise chiefly from certain incorrigible mental fixations which have been passed on to us by the 'romantic Indianists' like the Schlegels who, on their own admission, went to Indian thought in search of 'the supremely romantic.' And to them, the supremely romantic definitely meant the supremely desperate, as also the supremely despondent. Not for nothing had they read the Sorrows of Young Werther; not for nothing had they imbibed the education of *La Nouvelle Heloise.* De Musset was voicing a sentiment more characteristically Germanic than Latin when he wrote:

Les plus desesperes sont les chants les plus beaux Etj'en sais d'immortelles qui sont des purs sanglots. It was under the influence of Frederick Schlegel's *The Language and Wisdom of the Hindus* that Schopenhauer was first drawn to Buddhism, and later came to look upon the Buddha as so much of a kindred spirit that he is known to have kept the image of Shakya Muni in his bedroom. And ever since, in many western minds, Gautam has been associated with Schopenhauer. I do not know if this association has been instrumental in bringing us better appreciation of the German philosopher, but as far as the Indian sage is concerned, it has proved extremely unfortunate. It is this misalliance which is principally responsible for our twisting Gautam, one of the most lively as well as sympathetic of men, into the role of a lachrymose and embittered misanthrope. It is true that there is a certain measure of parallelism between the two world-views at the outset; both starting with the recognition of the tragic element in life. But there is a very important qualification to be made. In one case the anguish begins and ends within the confines of an egotistic personality, compensation for this being found in an expansive Will that is, ultimately, self-destructive; in the other, the sense of grief leads to a realisation of the all-embracing problem of suffering, thus releasing unsuspected springs of compassion. There is here a fundamental contrast: the contrast between an adolescent and adult view of life.

Whatever the nature of Buddha's 'nihilism,' and whether it is pessimistic or not, one thing is certain: it does not need apologies. To apologise effectively for Gautam would require an understanding equal to his; and there is no reason to believe that either his admirers, or his critics, possess that degree of comprehension and comprehensiveness. On the contrary, there could be no more convincing proof of the complete bankruptcy of our spiritual criteria than the fact that we know people not by the intrinsic worth of their deeds, but by the slogans they shout, the banners they wave; and that we judge an attitude not by the vitality of experience which sanctions it, but by the arbitrary labels attached to it.

In the year 819, the Tang Emperor, Hsien Tsung, came to hear that the Fa-men monastery in Shen-si housed a bone of the Buddha which was known to exhibit miraculous powers every thirty years. As these miraculous manifestations were expected in that very year, the Emperor gave instructions that the prodigious relic should be brought to the capital, kept for a while in the Imperial Palace, and then sent on a circular tour of the monasteries in the city. This was more than Han-Yu, a statesman and writer of unusual gifts, could tolerate. He worded a petition to the Emperor denouncing the Buddha and Buddhism, and protesting against the policy of allowing an outlandish and barbaric faith to contaminate the ancient civilization of the Middle Kingdom. 'Your Servant is well aware,' wrote the Celestial, at once indignant and apprehensive, 'that your Majesty does not do this in the vain hope of deriving advantage therefrom, but that in the fullness of our present plenty there is a desire to comply with the wishes of the people in the celebration at the capital of this delusive mummery... For Buddha was a barbarian. His language was not the language of China. His clothes were of an alien cut. He did not utter the maxims of our ancient rulers nor conform to the customs which they handed down. He did not appreciate the bond between Prince and minister, the tie between father and son...'

History has a way of emphasising itself in repetition. Han-Yu's bitter complaint is echoed by a living British academician. Professor Berrie-dale Keith, who manages to achieve in his manysided personality a happy combination of expert knowledge of British constitutional history and an equally impressive erudition in Sanskrit literature, does not adopt the Chinese patriot's straightforward manner of invective. Both by training and preference, he is inclined to speak in a subtle and oblique fashion. After suggesting that the Buddha was the child of a barbarous or semi-barbarous age, he leaves us to draw the all too obvious conclusion. He has some particularly scathing remarks to make about the western criticism, which, 'ruthless in probing the claims of its own sacred scriptures, has treated the Pali canon with a respect so profound as to regard with open hostility any attempt to apply to these sources of information the same dispassionate scrutiny which is demanded from the researches into the history of Christianity.'

The justification for this sound and timely corrective is not for us to question. On all Indian matters, one feels strongly, the judgement of our accepted professional interpreters has always been warped by an ignorance which manifests itself either in the form of an excessive enthusiasm, or an ill-concealed prejudice. From every point of view it would be eminently desirable if the treatment of Indian subjects, from religion and philosophy down to cookery and beauty-culture, were informed by a more critical spirit than has hitherto been in evidence. We might further grant Prof. Keith that it is not possible that early in Buddhist thought we encounter 'fully appreciated ideas which have slowly and laboriously been elaborated in Europe and are normally regarded as the particular achievement of modern philosophy.' But when he goes on to say that, given the psychological conditions of his times, it would have been a miracle had Buddha been capable of the rationalism imputed to him, he stretches the argument to make a point which it does not seem reasonably to warrant.

This is historical determinism served with a vengeance, such as one would not expect from the most ardent novitiate of the Marx-Engels Institute. If its implications were accepted, one could similarly throw doubts on the 'wisdom' which it is customary to attribute to Socrates; for the psychological (and even the politico-economic) conditions under which he lived were not so very different to those experienced by Gautam. If the rise of Buddha was contemporaneous with the triumph of the great gods *Shiva* and *Vishnu,* at the time of the enactment of Socratic drama, the glorious days of the Olympian patriarchal family—of Zeus and Hera, and the vast number of their progeny born both within and without the confines of the originally incestuous wedlock—were by no means over. Socrates himself, if the version given in the Apology is to be believed, received instructions of his life's mission from the god of Delphi. And even while the Sun of Hellenism was approaching its zenith, the popular soul of Greece continued to luxuriate in its deep slumber, enveloped by the soft and soothing mist of what Dr. Preuss appropriately designates as 'primal stupidity' (*Urdummheit).*

The Eleusinian Mysteries, with their promise of magic and miracle, their richly entertaining sacramentalism and still more entrancing demonology, claimed an incomparably larger number of votaries than all the academies of the Eleatics put together. Both Zeno and Plato reserve bitter comment for the esoteric cults and secret doctrines that were in vogue in their days, and to which the Pythagoreans had added the alluring oriental fantasy of metempsychosis (Marion Bloom's 'Meet him Pike Hoses'); and from this it may be inferred that their appeal to the mass mind was far more potent than that of the sober, philosophic reflections of the early gnostics, one of whom at least was made to drink the cup of hemlock for the pains he took to teach his fellow citizens 'to care for their souls'—an example of intolerance for which, incidentally, Gautam's India, despite all its 'barbarism,' has no recorded parallel. The old Bacchic wine in the course of its transference into new Orphic bottles had lost none of its delightful orgiastic flavour: the superstitious ritualism, which was the legacy of Greece's 'dark ages,' continued to flourish in an unbroken tradition till it was absorbed almost in entirety by the Mystery of the newly-born Christian Church. Human sacrifice had more or less disappeared, but Sparta had discovered a satisfying substitute for it in the gruesome, but enthralling, practice of flagellating tender youths as a means of inducing spiritual frenzy. Such was the glory that was Greece. We have been too much in the habit of seeing the Greek view of life through monumental marbles. These dignified museum exhibits tell only a part of the story; and perhaps there is another side which is not quite so edifying. Even the great luminaries of the Periclean age seemed less inspiring to their own contemporaries than they appear to us. Plato may call Socrates 'the wisest, the justest, and the best of all men'; but to Aristophanes he appeared a comic figure swearing by 'Chaos, Respiration, and air in his Thinking-Shop.' Pericles considered purely as a lover of the muses is a sympathetic person; but as the lover of Aspasia he was an object of ridicule to the Athenians who, we are told, 'had occasion to execrate the memory of a man who by his example corrupted the purity and innocence of their morals, and who made licentiousness respectable, and the indulgence of every impure desire the qualification of the soldier as well as the senator.' Sophocles' authorship of 120 tragedies points to a more than Shakespearian industry; but his private life, according to Athenaeus, was far less circumspect than that of the Bard of Avon. The somewhat later figure of Diogenes walking through the streets of Athens with a tub on his head, telling Alexander to get out of his light, is a supreme example of philosophic detachment; but the Cynic of Sinope, before his apprenticeship to Antisthenes, was known to have been banished from his country for coining false money. All these are no doubt minor matters when we consider what we owe to these eminent Greeks, but it is well to remember them when acknowledging the legacy of Greece.

It is equally important not to forget that the pursuit of the arts, letters, and sciences by a small minority was rendered possible only because of the slavery which formed the basis of Athenian prosperity. Lost in a loving contemplation of the delicately moulded curves purposefully concealed under the flowing draperies of the Caryatid of the Erechtheum, or pondering the voluptuous possibilities revealed by the proud surrender of Niobid in her semi-nudity, our elderly professorate of 'Humanities' is a little apt to forget that the balanced repose, the harmony, the ideality, the naturalism, and all the other 'lamps' of the art which transports them into a state of such pulsating excitement, rested on a broad base of human misery.

Indeed, if one wanted to condemn Socrates merely on the score of the moral depravity and the intellectual confusion which characterised the milieu in which he lived, it would be possible to make a much more devastating case than could be made against Gautam on similar grounds. But to reason in this manner would be manifestly unfair. The 'miracle' that Prof. Keith does not regard as possible has been happening throughout the ages. Sanity has been known to exist in the midst of rampant lunacy; wisdom has flowered again and again despite ubiquitous human folly. This merciful contradiction runs through the whole of human history; and to it we owe the small measure of civilization which has entered into human intercourse. After all, the world in which we live today—a world which periodically indulges in blood-baths, and subjects vast populations to the most terrible privations in the midst of unparalleled plenty—has not much to distinguish it from a madhouse. Yet it would be taking an unnecessarily pessimistic view to suggest that our age is completely devoid of reason and normality; side by side with our sabre-rattlers and Shylocks there are still men like Professor Keith.

Dean Inge says 'the spirit of man does not live only on tradition; it can draw direct from the fountainhead.' What he says is true to this extent, that there is a residue of human sanity from which gifted individuals can hope to draw wisdom at all times. And although it is true that Gautam did not have the advantage of being conversant with 'the conceptions of rationalism, of psychology without a soul, of Kant, of Schopenhauer, Von Hartmann, Bertrand Russell, Bergson *et hoc genus omne'*—an advantage which Professor Keith undoubtedly possesses—it remains nevertheless possible that, working on his own experience, he arrived at an equally reasonable view of life.

Yet, Professor Keith's argument raises a problem of considerable importance. How far can we regard Gautam as a typical product of his historical background, and how far can he be said to stand outside it? Goethe suggests that the excellencies of an individual are his own; his defects, of the age. In suggesting this arbitrary method he was merely echoing a current fallacy which gave to the individual an altogether undue importance in the scheme of things. No individual, however great, is entirely above his age. But, on the other hand, no truly gifted person is merely a symptom of his times: We may, up to a point, agree with Lytton Strachey that human beings have 'a value which is independent of any temporal processes.' The crucial test of genius is not only the extent to which it participates in the peculiar idiosyncrasies of the soil upon which it grows, but also, and perhaps even more, the extent to which it rises above them and expresses itself in a new and individual form. Seeing Gautam in this light, we find that, while he doubtless shared the virtues and failings of his environment, he had also crystallised in his person a certain synthesis which was of his own individuality. He lived fully the life of his own period, but he also went far beyond it. And the quality of vision which is needed to see beyond one's times, is even more significant than the quality needed to observe the minutiae of one's immediate horizon. For while it is possible to point to a number of characteristically 'period' figures among Gautam's contemporaries, hardly any one of them leaves the impression of being in possession of anything approaching his universality. As such, in considering him, we must not only consider him as a part of his background, but also as apart from it.

ILy avait une fois La Realite, says Aragon cryptically. This too applies to the Buddha: there probably was some reality before the mythographers got busy weaving the intricate webs of their fancy. Divested of these layers of excrescence, the kernel that remains seems to be a profoundly human fact. In passing I have attempted to place this fact in some kind of an intelligible relation to other facts of a similar order, both in the past and the present. The purpose of my argument has been to suggest not only that in Gautam we have a very sensitive individual, a representative figure who sums up in himself the effort of a distant epoch to synthesise the ecstasy and delirium of a nascent self-consciousness, but that in him we have an example of truly humane and civilized sensibility; and I find myself in complete agreement with Irving

Babbitt when he expresses the view that the urbanity resulting from Gautam's influence in India was perhaps the nearest approach that that very unhumanistic land has made to humanism.

The synthesis which Gautam realised in his person is at once a disturbing and saddening example. It is disturbing not because we believe that Gautam belongs to a species of supermen for whom Schweitzer has invented the hyperbolic concept of 'Immeasurably Great.' Fortunately perhaps, 'Immeasurably Great' men do not exist outside the enchanted world of fairy tale and daydream. If Gautam, like Schweitzer's Jesus, were an Immeasurably Great man, then he would be of little value to us. The effective worth of a man, even of a hero among men, can be determined only in terms of his humanity. And it is precisely this essential humanity of the man that is so disturbing about Gautam. He points to a quality of awareness, a way of life, which is not at all an abstraction, but appears to be something tangibly within human reach. And yet for some obscure reason it has so far eluded the grasp of men. They have either been afraid of it, or they have rejected it without caring to examine its meaning; and where they have tried to realise it, their first act seems to have been to distort its vision of light and order into a nightmare of confusion. That is the sadness, the unutterable pity of it.

The nature of this Way, as also the process through which it was reached, I have tried to set forth—at least as a tentative outline. In order not to create a wrong impression, it is perhaps necessary once again to say that I do not look upon Gautam's Way as an *Open Sesame* to the Land of Heart's Desire. Unhappily, there is no such magical formula; for there is no such Land. What Gautam offers one is merely a way of understanding. Therefore, those who are after talismanic effects are likely to be left with a keen sense of disappointment in the last analysis. For it seems to be a way, which, contrary to the current belief, does not lead to the ideal realms of endless bliss: it only brings one to an observation post whence one can take a broader, more comprehensive, and calmer view of the outstretching expanse of life's desert territory, on the fringe of which mirage after mirage rises in quick succession, dances its brief turn, and disappears. Gautam does not pretend to heal the lepers: he merely says that lepers too can, if they make the effort, see their sores for what they are, probe to the root of their disease.

I confess that this is hardly a comforting ministration for an afflicted, long-suffering humanity. But in the long run it seems to me that the real remedy, if there is one at all, lies in discovering the cause rather than fostering hopes of imaginary cures. 'It is the cause, it is the cause, my soul,' cries Othello. It is with the cause that Gautam, too, concerns himself. He does not deal in anodynes: he merely affirms that in the measure in which pain understands its own nature, and ceases to be the blind agony of an embryo — in that measure it also surpasses itself.

It would be romantic to suggest that his is the last word. No word represents finality: it is always the shadow of a thing and not the thing itself. But in the antelucan world of shadows, through which the spirit of man has all this time been trying to feel its way to light, it appears to come as near grasping the sense as well as the mystery of things as any other word uttered before or since.

Now this, O bhikhsus, is the noble truth concerning the way which leads to the destruction of sorrow. Verily! it is this noble eightfold path; that is to say:

Right views; right aspirations; right speech; right behaviour; right livelihood; right effort; right thoughts; and right contemplation.

This, then, O bhikhsus, is the noble truth concerning the destruction of sorrow. "By the practice of loving kindness I have attained liberation of heart, and thus I am assured that I shall never return in renewed births. I have even now attained Nirvana."

Third Sermon at Varanasi

(Buddha teachings' Sermon at Banaras Four Noble Truths and Noble Eightfold Path)

One day, whilst sitting under a great, spreading, Bo tree Siddhartha Gautam felt that he was somehow undergoing profound, and extensive, alterations of realisation and awakening. Siddhartha remained for seven days under the great tree. It is from this times that Siddhartha began to be referred to as the Buddha, a name implying his being Awake and Enlightened. These few day's spent under the Bo tree are considered to have been the time of his Enlightenment.

Buddha is said to have "attained Nirvana" — to have achieved a state where suffering is eliminated through the abandonment of desires — desires being the cause of suffering. Such attainmentment is held to bring release from an otherwise endless succession of reincarnations or rebirths. The term Nirvana has suggestive associations with a verb indicating cooling, or possibly, extinguishment!

Considering himself to have made significant Spiritual Progress and that he now had some Buddha teachings that he thought important to share with others Siddhartha journeyed on foot over one hundred miles to Banaras.

Buddha's Enlightenment was experienced whilst living a life that was neither overly luxurious nor overly austere. His teachings were subsequently framed against an idea of a "Middle Way" that avoided such extremes. In a deer park he delivered the celebrated "The Sermon at Banaras" in which are included two of the more

10

Buddhism in South-East Asia

According to a tradition preserved in the Ceylonese Chronicles. Buddhism was preached in Suvarnabhumi by the missionaries of Ashoka. Though the location of Suvarnabhumi is uncertain, some having identified it with Burma, others with Siam (Thailand), there is no doubt that it refers to some part of Indo-China. But the authenticity of the tradition itself is open to question, as no early and reliable evidence has been obtained so far in support of it. Nor can we accept the view that the first two disciples of the Buddha named Trapusa and Bhallika, who built a sanctuary over his relics in their native land, belonged to Burma, for the Utkala country, which is referred to in the canonical texts as their native land, is certainly to be identified with Orissa.

There is, however, no doubt that Buddhism obtained a definite footing in South-east Asia during the early centuries of the Christian era. This is proved by the discovery of the images of Buddha of the Amaravati style in Thailand (Siam), Annam (Champa), Sumatra, Java and Celebes. The representation of the Buddha by a symbol, such as *dharmacakra* (wheel of law), rather than a human figure, in some of the sculptures in Thailand, also support the introduction of Buddhism in this region at an early date.

Thailand

The early sculptures discovered in Thailand prove conclusively that Buddhism was introduced in this region at the beginning of the Christian era. A Wheel of Law, associated with figures of crouching deer, was dug up at Pra Pathom. Another early site, Pong Tuk, has yielded bronze Buddha images of the Amaravari style, which may be dated in the second century AD Buddhist images of the Gupta style, both of earlier and later type, have also been discovered. As the inscriptions, engraved on the latter, may be referred to the fifth and sixth centuries AD, those of the earlier type probably belong to the fourth century AD.

From this early period we may trace the uninterrupted progress of Hinayana Buddhism in this country. The Thai conquest of the land in the thirteenth century AD gave a great impetus to this religion.

The That rulers were ardent followers of Hinayana Buddhism. We learn from the inscription of Ram Kamheng, that this famous King was an ardent follower of Hinayana Buddhism and decorated his capital Sukhodaya with temples, monasteries and images of Buddha at the close of the thirteenth century AD. The Hinayana Buddhism of the Thais was sustained and influenced by Burma and the island of Ceylon. The intercourse between Mons of Lower Burma and Thailand were of long standing. A That King sent a messenger to Ceylon in AD 1361 who brought back with him a senior monk who reformed the religion. The Hinayana Buddhism with its Pali canon flourishes even now in Thailand, Burma and Ceylon, and it is not therefore necessary to discuss its history in great detail.

Cambodia

Buddhism made its influence felt in Cambodia as early as the fifth century AD, for King Jaya-varman of Fu-nan, who ruled towards the close of that century, sent an embassy to China in AD 503, with presents including an image of Buddha. An inscription of his son Rudravarman begins with an invocation to Buddha. From this time onward the prevalence of Buddhism is proved by inscriptions. But it had a set-back in the 7th century, and the epigraphic records indicate that Shaivism, not Buddhism, was the dominant religion of Cambodia. It is curious, in view of the present state of things, that very few Kings of Cambodia, of whom we possess any epigraphic record, were followers of Buddhism. Suryvarman I (11th century A.D) was a Buddhist, for he had the posthumous title *Nirvana-pada. But* his inscription on a temple at Prah Khan begins with an invocation to Shiva in the first verse, and to the Buddha in the second. Several inscriptions on the temple known as Prasat Ta Keo, in honour of Yogishwara Pandita, the gurn of King Suryavarman, begin with invocations to Shiva and Vishnu, and refer to donations made to these gods. Jayavarman VII, perhaps the greatest King of Kambuja, was a Buddhist and his Ta Prohm Inscription, dated AD 1186, gives a detailed list of his magnificent donations to this temple. The merit of these pious works was to accrue to the King's mother so that she might obtain the state of Buddha. In addition to the Kings mentioned above, high dignitaries like Kavindianmathana and Kirtipandita, both belonging to the tenth century AD, were ardent Buddhists, and the latter claimed to have lighted again the torch of the true law which the sins of the world had extinguished. The form of Buddhism referred to is clearly Mahayana.

But, if we take the epigraphic data as a whole, there remains no doubt that Buddhism was never a dominant religion in Kambuja till the time of Jayavarman VII. But even the patronage of this great Emperor did not establish Buddhism as a state religion, as it is now. It is interesting to note that during the reign of King Srindra-varmadeva, a later King, we find an inscription, dated AD 1308, written in Pali and referring to Hinayana form of Buddhism. The next two Kings, Srindra-Jayavarman and Jayavarma-Paramesvara were followers respectively of Vishnu and Shiva.

The state of religion in Cambodia is described by Cheu Ta-kuan who visited the country in AD 1296. It appears that Hinayana Buddhism was in a flourishing state at this time. Yet the older inscriptions mostly refer to Mahayana doctrine. Taking everything into consideration, we ate forced to the conclusion that it was the influence of Thailand (Siam) that gradually introduced a great change in the religion of Kambuja. On the whole Brahminical religion, specially Shaivism, was dominant in Kambuja, though Mahayana Buddhism was also a powerful sect, up to the end of the thirteenth century AD. But the political dominance of the Thais (of Siam) in Cambodia established the supremacy of Hinayana Buddhism which is now the only religion of the people.

Champa

The ancient Hindu colony of Champa corresponds, roughly, to the southern part of Annam. The early introduction of Buddhism in this region is indicated by an image of Buddha of the Amaravati style at Dong-Duong.

Buddhism before the 9th Century AD: The Bakul Soodae Inscription, dated AD 829, refers to the construction of two temples and two monastics for Jina and Shankara. Jina may denote either the Buddha or Malm-Ira, but as there is no evidence for the existence of Jainism in South-east Asia, Jina may be taken to denote Buddha. The long inscription on the four faces of a stelae found at Dong-Duong records the installation of an image of Buddha in AD 875, and the foundation of a Buddhist temple and a monastery by the Buddhist King India-varman. The remains of a Buddhist temple at this place, far greater in dimensions than the largest Brahminical temple in Champa, prove that Dong-Duong (ancient Amaravati) in the province of Quang Nam was an important stronghold of Buddhism in Champa.

Many later Kings patronised Buddhism, and monasteries and temples were built in different pates of the kingdom. Many Buddhist images have also been found in different parts of Champa. I-tsing refers to the prevalence of Buddhism in Champa and remarks that the "Buddhists generally belong to the Aryasammitiya-nikaya and there are also a few followers of the Sarvastivadamkaya." Thus, Hinayana prevailed at the end of the seventh century AD. But the inscriptions and images leave no doubt that the Mahayana soon occupied the dominant position in Champa. Particular reference may be made to An-Thai Stelae Inscription dated 824 Shaka (=AD 902) which records the erection of a statue of Lokanatha by *sthavira* Nagapuspi, the abbot of the monastery of Pramudita-Lokesvata, and refers to Vajradhatu, Padmadhatu and Cakradhatu, Amitabha and Varocana.

It is interesting to note that Buddhist and Shaiva temples and monasteries were often erected side by side, by the same donor, that the epithet Damaresvara (lord of the *Bhutas)*, originally belonging to Sna, was applied to Buddha, and that figures of Shiva decorated the Buddhist temples of Dong-Duong.

Malay Peninsula

The well-known Buddhist formula *'ye dharma hetuprabhava,* etc. followed by another verse beginning with *Ajnanac = ciyate karma,* is engraved on a slab of stone found amid the ruins of an ancient brick building at Keddah. The second verse alone is engraved on a piece of stone, probably a part of an old shrine, in the northern part of province Wellesley. Both these inscriptions have been referred to the fourth or fifth century AD. Three Sanskrit verses are inscribed on a clay tablet found near Keddah. They inculcate Mahayana philosophical doctrines of Madhyamika school, and have been traced to a text entitled *Sagaramati-pariprccha,* which is known only from a Chinese translation."

The inscriptions mentioned above also prove that Buddhist temples, both of brick and stone, were built in Wellesley Province and Keddah in the fourth or fifth century AD. The great *stupa* of Nakhon Sri Dhammarat and a number of temples surrounding it indicate the existence of a flourishing Buddhist colony in this region. A number of terracotta votive tablets found in neighbouring caves also show that a large number of Buddhist monks resided therein.

Indonesia

Buddhism did not obtain a secure footing in Indonesia till after the fourth century AD. At the time when Fa-hien visited Java there was very little trace of Buddhism in that island. But Gunavarman, who belonged to the royal family of Kipin (Kashmir or Afghanistan) but had taken to religion, preached Buddhism in Java early in the fifth century AD, and it soon took deep root in the soil. As Gunavarman translated a text of the Dharmagupta sect, he must have belonged to the Mulasarvastivada school, and it was evidently due to his influence that this sect became dominant in Java and the neighbouring islands.

The neighbouring island of Bali also came under the influence of Buddhism about the same time. For according to the *History of the Liang Dynasty* (AD 502-556), the earliest Chinese historical annals that give an account of this island, the King of Bah claimed that the wife of Suddhodana was a daughter of his country.

By the seventh century AD. Buddhism flourished all over Indonesia, and Sri-Vijaya in Sumatra became a stronghold of this religion We possess an inscription, dated Shaka 606 (AD 684), of a Buddhist King of this country named Jayanasa. There was a regular trade and maritime intercourse between Sri-Vijaya and India. On his way to India the Chinese pilgrim I-tsing halted at Sri-Vijaya for six months, and he again visited the place, after his return to China, 111 order to copy and translate the voluminous Buddhist texts which he had brought with him from India.

It is evident from I-tsing's statement that although Hinayana was dominant in these regions there were in Sri-Vijaya a few who followed the Mahayana form of Buddhism. This is also proved by the inscription of Jayanasa referred to above. It not only contains definite reference to the Mahayana doctrine, but the use of the word *vajra-sarna* further indicates that this Mahayana was of the Tantuk form known as Vajrayana, Mantrayana or Tantrayana.

Indonesia was visited by eminent Buddhist scholars from India such as Dharmapala, a Professor of Nalanda in the seventh century AD and Vajrabodhi, a South Indian monk. The latter and his disciple Amoghavajra, who accompanied him, were teachers of Tantrik cult and are credited with its introduction to China. Both of them halted at Sri-Vijaya for five months on their way from Ceylon to China, early m the eighth century AD.

Towards the close of this century the Mahayana cult acquired great predominance owing to the patronage of the Shailendras who ruled over the greater part of Indonesia. Two inscriptions, dated AD 778 and 782, refer to the construction of a temple of Tata at Kalasan, and setting up of an image of Manjusri at Kelurak by the Shailendra Emperors. The latter was inspired by their *guru Kumataghosa,* an inhabitant of Gauda. The Shailendra Emperors were in close touch with the Pala Emperor Devapala of Bengal, and the Cola Emperor Rajaraja, both of whom endowed the monasteries built by the Shailendras, respectively at Nalanda and Negapatam.

The Mahayana form of Buddhism has left permanent memorials in Java in the famous *stupa* of Barabudur and a number of other magnificent temples erected during the Shailendra rule. The Javanese literature and the Buddhist images found in Java clearly indicate that all the essential features of Mahayana, even of its last phases, were fully developed in that island. As in India, a number of Hindu gods were adopted in the Buddhist pantheon, though they were relegated to an inferior position. New divinities were introduced, some of which, like Trailokyavijaya, Hevajra, Bhanava and Heruka, were of monstrous or terrifying appearance. The Tantrayana, including Kala-cakratantra, prevailed both in Java and Sumatra. The famous King Krtanagara of Java was a devout follower of the Tantrayana or Vajrayana, and his drinking bout is approved in a Javanese historical text on the ground that he scrupulously followed the prescriptions of religion. King Adityvaraman of Malayu in Sumatra, who was ruling as a vassal of Krtanagara in AD 1286, seems to have been a follower of the Bhairava cult.

As in India, there was a gradual rapprochement between Mahayana and Brahminical religion. This was more clearly indicated in Indonesia by the fact that gradually Shiva, Vishnu and Buddha were regarded as identical and so were their Shaktis. A definite Shiva-Buddha cult existed in Java, and in modern Balinese theology Buddha is regarded as a younger brother of Shiva.

There are two Buddhist texts in Java which give an interesting insight into the developed form of Mahayana. The first, *Sang byang Kamabayanikan* is a free Javanese version of a Sanskrit original, interspersed with a number of original Sanskrit verses. It was probably composed in the Shailendra period (8th century AD), but was modified, about a century or two later, in a manner which has been regarded as a Hinduised or Sarva version of a Buddhist original. It contains an exposition of the leading principles of Mahayana and gives an account of its theology according to the Yogacara system. It brings the Hindu Trinity in organic relation with the Buddhist pantheon. The picture of Mahayana in Java which it unfolds shows a close resemblance with, but also minor differences from, the form of religion current in India.

The second text *Kamabayanan Mantranaya* contains forty-one Sanskrit verses with Javanese commentaries. It contains an exposition of the Tantrayana or Vajrayana both in its theoretical and practical aspects. The five kinds of sensual enjoyments (*panca-ma-kara)* are clearly prescribed, and the devotee is forbidden to communicate the secrets of *vajra, ghanta* and *mudra* to those who do not belong to the *Mandala.*

... His concession with regard
... domestic servants, soldiers,
... ample of his desire not to ...
... ith Law and Order. Because
... ism has remained lacking in
... the nucleus of the Gospel
... martyrdom. But, on the other
... have been spared from having
... the point of excruciating
... have had three consolation
... dea of the man was dead and

11

Buddha's Sermons

Buddha's First Sutra or First Sermon

(Dhammachakkappavattana Sutra Setting the Wheel of Dhamma in Motion)

There are these two extremes that are not to be indulged in by one who has gone forth. Which two? That which is devoted to sensual pleasure with reference to sensual objects: base, vulgar, common, ignoble, unprofitable; and that which is devoted to self-affliction: painful, ignoble, unprofitable. Avoiding both of these extremes, the middle way realised by the Tathagata — producing vision, producing knowledge — leads to calm, to direct knowledge, to self-awakening, to Unbinding.

And what is the middle way realised by the Tathagata that — producing vision, producing knowledge — leads to calm, to direct knowledge, to self-awakening, to Unbinding? Precisely this Noble Eightfold Path: right view, right resolve, right speech, right action, right livelihood, right effort, right mindfulness, right concentration. This is the middle way realised by the Tathagata that — producing vision, producing knowledge — leads to calm, to direct knowledge, to self-awakening, to Unbinding.

Now this, monks, is the noble truth of stress: Birth is stressful, aging is stressful, death is stressful; sorrow, lamentation, pain, distress, and despair are stressful; association with the unbeloved is stressful, separation from the loved is stressful, not getting what is wanted is stressful. In short, the five clinging-aggregates are stressful.

And this, monks, is the noble truth of the origination of stress: the craving that makes for further becoming—accompanied by passion and delight, relishing now here and now there—i.e., craving for sensual pleasure, craving for becoming, craving for non-becoming.

And this, monks, is the noble truth of the cessation of stress: the remainderless fading and cessation, renunciation, relinquishment, release, and letting go of that very craving.

And this, monks, is the noble truth of the way of practice leading to the cessation of stress: precisely this Noble Eightfold Path — right view, right resolve, right speech, right action, right livelihood, right effort, right mindfulness, right concentration.

Vision arose, insight arose, discernment arose, knowledge arose, illumination arose within me with regard to things never heard before: 'This is the noble truth of stress'... 'This noble truth of stress is to be comprehended'... 'This noble truth of stress has been comprehended.'

Vision arose, insight arose, discernment arose, knowledge arose, illumination arose within me with regard to things never heard before: 'This is the noble truth of the origination of stress'... 'This noble truth of the origination of stress is to be abandoned' ... 'This noble truth of the origination of stress has been abandoned.'

Vision arose, insight arose, discernment arose, knowledge arose, illumination arose within me with regard to things never heard before: 'This is the noble truth of the cessation of stress'... 'This noble truth of the cessation of stress is to be directly experienced'... 'This noble truth of the cessation of stress has been directly experienced.'

Vision arose, insight arose, discernment arose, knowledge arose, illumination arose within me with regard to things never heard before: 'This is the noble truth of the way of practice leading to the cessation of stress'... 'This noble truth of the way of practice leading to the cessation of stress is to be developed'... 'This noble truth of the way of practice leading to the cessation of stress has been developed.'

And, monks, as long as this knowledge and vision of mine — with its three rounds and twelve permutations concerning these four noble truths as they actually are present — was not pure, I did not claim to have directly awakened to the right self-awakening unexcelled in the cosmos with its devas, Maras, and Brahmas, with its contemplatives and priests, its royalty and commonfolk. But as soon as this knowledge and vision of mine — with its three rounds and twelve permutations concerning these four noble truths as they actually are present — was truly pure, then I did claim to have directly awakened to the right self-awakening unexcelled in the cosmos with its devas, Maras and Brahmas, with its contemplatives and priests, its royalty and commonfolk. Knowledge and vision arose in me: 'Unprovoked is my release. This is the last birth. There is now no further becoming.'

Four Realities of the Noble Ones

(Dhammacakkappavattana Sutra The Discourse on the Setting in Motion of the Wheel (of Vision) of the Basic Pattern)

And what, bhikhsus, is that middle way awakened to by the One Who Moves in Reality which gives rise to vision, which gives rise to knowledge, which leads to peace, to higher knowledge, to full awakening, to Nirvana? It is just this Noble Eight-factored Path, that is to say, right view, right resolve, right speech, right action, right livelihood, right effort, right mindfulness, right mental unification. This, bhikhsus, is that middle way awakened to by the One Who Moves in Reality, which gives rise to vision, which gives rise to knowledge, which leads to peace, to higher knowledge, to full awakening, to Nirvana.

Now *this*, bhikhsus, for the Noble One(s), is the reality which is pain: birth is painful, aging is painful, illness is painful, death is painful; sorrow, lamentation, physical pain, unhappiness and distress are painful; union with what is disliked is painful; separation from what is liked is painful; not to get what one wants is painful; in brief, the five bundles of grasping-fuel are painful.

Now *this,* bhikhsus, for the Noble One(s), is the pain-originating reality. It is this craving which leads to renewed existence, accompanied by delight and attachment, seeking delight now here now there; that is, craving for sense-pleasures, craving for existence, craving for extermination (of what is not liked).

Now *this,* bhikhsus, for the Noble One(s), is the pain-ceasing reality. It is the remainderless fading away and cessation of that same craving, the giving up and relinquishing of it, freedom from it, non-reliance on it.

Now *this,* bhikhsus, for the Noble One(s), is the reality which is the way leading to the cessation of pain. It is this Noble Eight-factored Path, that is to say, right view, right resolve, right speech, right action, right livelihood, right effort, right mindfulness, right mental unification.

'This for the Noble One(s) is the reality of pain': in me, bhikhsus, in regard to things unheard before, there arose vision, knowledge, wisdom, true knowledge, and light.

Now on this, 'This, for the Noble One(s) the reality of pain, is to be fully understood': in me, bhikhsus, in regard to things unheard before, there arose vision, knowledge, wisdom, true knowledge, and light.

Now on this, 'This, for the Noble One(s) the reality of pain, has been fully understood': in me, bhikhsus, in regard to things unheard before, there arose vision, knowledge, wisdom, true knowledge, and light.

(Likewise,) in me, bhikhsus, in regard to things unheard before, there arose vision, knowledge, wisdom, true knowledge and light, with respect to: 'This for the Noble One(s) is the pain-originating reality,' 'This, for the Noble One(s) the pain-originating reality, is to be abandoned,' and 'This, for the Noble One(s) the pain-originating reality, has been abandoned.'

(Likewise,) in me, bhikhsus, in regard to things unheard before, there arose vision, knowledge, wisdom, true knowledge and light, with respect to: 'This for the Noble One(s) is the pain-ceasing reality,' 'This, for the Noble One(s) the pain-ceasing reality, is to be personally experienced' and 'This, for the Noble One(s) the pain-ceasing reality, has been personally experienced.'

(Likewise,) in me, bhikhsus, in regard to things unheard before, there arose vision, knowledge, wisdom, true knowledge and light, with respect to: 'This for the Noble One(s) is the way leading to the cessation of pain,' 'This, for the Noble One(s) the way leading to the cessation of pain, is to be developed,' and 'This, for the Noble One(s) the way leading to the cessation of pain, has been developed.'

So long, bhikhsus, as my knowledge and seeing of these Four Realities of the Noble One(s), as they really are in their three phases (each) and twelve modes (altogether) was not thoroughly purified in this way, then so long, in the world with its devas, mras and brahms, in this population with its renunciants and Brahmins, its devas and humans, I did not claim to be fully awakened to the unsurpassed perfect awakening. But when, bhikhsus, my knowledge and vision of these Four Realities of the Noble One(s), as they really are in their three phases and twelve modes was thoroughly purified in this way, then, in the world with its devas, mras and brahms, in this population with its renunciants and Brahmins, its devas and humans, I claimed to be fully awakened to the unsurpassed perfect awakening. Indeed, knowledge and seeing arose in me: 'Unshakeable is the liberation of my mind; this is my last birth: now there is no more renewed existence.'

Second Sermon at Varanasi

The Tathagata, does not seek salvation in austerities, but neither does he for that reason indulge in worldly pleasures, nor live in abundance. The Tathagata has found the middle path.

There are two extremes, O bhikhsus, which the man who has given up the world ought not to follow-the habitual practice, on the one hand, of self-indulgence which is unworthy, vain and fit only for the worldly-minded and the habitual practice, on the other hand, of self-mortification, which is painful, useless and unprofitable.

Neither abstinence from fish or flesh, nor going naked, nor shaving the head, nor wearing matted hair, nor dressing in a rough garment, nor covering oneself with dirt, nor sacrificing to Agni, will cleanse a man who is not free from delusions.

Reading the Vedas, making offerings to priests, or sacrifices to the gods, self-mortification by heat or cold, and many such penances performed for the sake of immortality, these do not cleanse the man who is not free from delusions.

Anger, drunkenness, obstinacy, bigotry, deception, envy, self-praise, disparaging others, superciliousness and evil intentions constitute uncleanness; not verily the eating of flesh.

A middle path, O bhikhsus, avoiding the two extremes, has been discovered by the Tathagata-a path which opens the eyes, and bestows understanding, which leads to peace of mind, to the higher wisdom, to full enlightenment, to Nirvana!

What is that middle path, O bhikhsus, avoiding these two extremes, discovered by the Tathagata — that path which opens the eyes, and bestows understanding, which leads to peace of mind, to the higher wisdom, to full enlightenment, to Nirvana?

Let me teach you, O bhikhsus, the middle path, which keeps aloof from both extremes. By suffering, the emaciated devotee produces confusion and sickly thoughts in his mind. Mortification is not conducive even to worldly knowledge; how much less to a triumph over the senses!

He who fills his lamp with water will not dispel the darkness, and he who tries to light a fire with rotten wood will fail. And how can anyone be free from self by leading a wretched life, if he does not succeed in quenching the fires of lust, if he still hankers after either worldly or heavenly- pleasures. But he in whom self has become extinct is free from lust: he will desire neither worldly nor heavenly pleasures, and the satisfaction of his natural wants will not defile him. However, let him be moderate, let him eat and drink according to the needs of the body.

Sensuality is enervating: the "self-indulgent" man is a slave to pleasure to his passions, and pleasure seeking is degrading and vulgar.

But to satisfy the necessities of life is not evil. To keep the body in good health is a duty for otherwise we shall not be able to trim the lamp of wisdom, and keep our mind strong and clear. Water surrounds the lotus-flower, but does not wet its petals.

This is the middle path, O bhikhsus that keeps aloof from both extremes.

The spokes of the wheel are the rules of pure conduct: justice is the uniformity of their length, wisdom is the tire; modesty and thoughtfulness are the hub in which the immovable axle of truth is fixed.

He who recognises the existence of suffering, its cause, its remedy, and its cessation has fathomed the four noble truths. He will walk in the right path.

Right views will be the torch to light his way. Right aspirations will be his guide. Right speech will be his dwelling-place on the road his gait will be straight, for it is right behaviour. His refreshments will be the right way of earning his livelihood right efforts will be his steps right thoughts his breath; and right contemplation will give him the peace that follows in his footprints.

Now, this, O bhikhsus, is the noble truth concerning suffering:

Birth is attended with pain, decay is painful, disease is painful, death is painful. Union, with the unpleasant is painful, painful is separation from the pleasant, and any craving that is unsatisfied, that too is painful. In brief, bodily conditions which spring from attachment are painful.

This, then, O bhiksus, is the noble truth concerning suffering.

Now this, O bhikhsus, is the noble truth concerning the origin of suffering:

Verily, it is that craving which causes the renewal of existence, accompanied by sensual delight, seeking satisfaction now here, now there, the craving for the gratification of the passions, the craving for a future life, and the craving for happiness in this life.

This, then, O bhikhsus, is the noble truth concerning the origin of suffering-

Now this, O bhikhsus, is the noble truth concerning the destruction of suffering:

Verily, it is the destruction, in which no passion remains, of this very thirst; it is the laying aside of, the being free from, the dwelling no longer upon this thirst.

This then, O bhikhsus, is the noble truth concerning the destruction of suffering:

Now this, O bhikhsus, is the noble truth concerning the way which leads to the destruction of sorrow. Verily! it is this noble eightfold path: that is to say:

Right views; right aspirations; right speech; right behaviour; right livelihood, right effort; right thoughts; and right contemplation.

This, then, O bhikhsus, is the noble truth concerning the destruction of sorrow. "By the practice of lovingkindness I have attained liberation of heart, and thus I am assured that I shall never return in renewed births. I have even now attained Nirvana."

Third Sermon at Varanasi

(Buddha teachings' Sermon at Banaras Four Noble Truths and Noble Eightfold Path)

One day, whilst sitting under a great, spreading, Bo tree Siddhartha Gautam felt that he was somehow undergoing profound, and extensive, alterations of realisation and awakening. Siddhartha remained for seven days under the great tree. It is from this times that Siddhartha began to be referred to as the Buddha, a name implying his being Awake and Enlightened. These few day's spent under the Bo tree are considered to have been the time of his Enlightenment.

Buddha is said to have "attained Nirvana" — to have achieved a state where suffering is eliminated through the abandonment of desires — desires being the cause of suffering. Such attainmentment is held to bring release from an otherwise endless succession of reincarnations or rebirths. The term Nirvana has suggestive associations with a verb indicating cooling, or possibly, extinguishment!

Considering himself to have made significant Spiritual Progress and that he now had some Buddha teachings that he thought important to share with others Siddhartha journeyed on foot over one hundred miles to Banaras.

Buddha's Enlightenment was experienced whilst living a life that was neither overly luxurious nor overly austere. His teachings were subsequently framed against an idea of a "Middle Way" that avoided such extremes. In a deer park he delivered the celebrated "The Sermon at Banaras" in which are included two of the more central Buddha teachings, i.e. the "Four Noble Truths" and the "Noble Eightfold Path".

The First Noble Truth is that old age, illness, and death are all forms of human suffering, and that there are many other other ways in which people suffer. The Buddha accepted the Vedic idea of endlessly successive reincarnations where life followed upon life, with much suffering inevitably attending in each of these lives. The idea of Karma further suggesting that in each existence a person's good or bad deeds would respectively impact positively or negatively on their store of "merit". It was this Karma-merit that would underpin the advantageous, or pitiful, state into which individual reincarnations would occur.

The Second Noble Truth is that suffering is closely linked to desire, a desire for being which leads from birth to death and involve ageing, illness, and mortality. There are also various desires for pleasures and for powers which, frustratingly, may not be realised.

The Third Noble Truth is that suffering can be dispelled by the abandonment of all desires.

The last of the Four Noble Truths holds that such abandonment of desires can be achieved by following the Noble Eightfold Path

[The Noble Eightfold Path Right Belief (in the Truth)]

Right Intent (to do good rather than evil)

Right Speech (avoidance of untruth, slander and swearing)

Right Behaviour (avoid blameworthy behaviours)

Right Livelihood (some occupations, e.g. butcher, publican, were disparaged!!!)

Right Effort (towards the good)

Right Contemplation (of the Truth)

Right Concentration (will result from following the Noble Eightfold Path)

Sermon before Five Monks

[The Five Components of Existence and the Doctrine of No-Self (anatta)]

The bodily form (*rupa*), monks, is not the self. If the body, monks, were the self, the body would not tend towards destruction, and we should be able to say: Let my body be this way, let my body not be that way. But since the body, monks, is not the self, therefore the body tends towards destruction, and we are not able to say, Let my body be such and such a one, let my body not be such and such a one.

Sensation (*vedana*), monks, is not the self. If sensations, monks, were the self, the sensations would not tend towards destruction, and we should be able to say: Let my sensations be this way, let my sensations not be that way. But since the sensations, monks, are not the self, therefore the sensations do tend towards destruction, and we are not able to say, Let my sensations be this way, let my sensations not be that way.

Perception (*sanna*) is not the self. If the perceptions, monks, were the self, the perceptions would not tend towards destruction, and we should be able to say: Let my perceptions be this way, let my perceptions not be that way. But since the perceptions, monks, are not the self, therefore the perceptions do tend towards destruction, and we are not able to say, Let my perception be this way, let my perceptions not be that way.

Psychic constructions (*samkhara*) are not the self. If the psychic constructions, monks, were the self, they would not tend towards destruction, and we should be able to say: Let my psychic constructions be this way, let my psychic constructions not be that way. But since the psychic constructions, monks, are not the self, therefore the psychic constructions do tend towards destruction, and we are not able to say, Let my psychic constructions be this way, let my psychic constructions not be that way.

Consciousness (*vinnana*) is not the self. If consciousness, monks, was the self, consciousness would not tend towards destruction, and we should be able to say: Let my consciousness be this way, let consciousness not be that way. But since the consciousness, monks, are not the self, therefore consciousness does tend towards destruction, and we are not able to say, Let my consciousness be this way, let my consciousness not be that way.

Now what do you think, monks, is the bodily form permanent or perishable?

(It is perishable, Lord).

And that which is perishable, does that cause pain or joy?

(It causes pain, Lord).

And that which is perishable, painful, subject to change, is it possible to regard that in this way? This is mine, this am I, this is my self?

That is impossible, Lord.

Now what do you think, monks, are the sensations permanent or perishable?

(They are perishable, Lord).

And that which is perishable, does that cause pain or joy?

(It causes pain, Lord).

And that which is perishable, painful, subject to change, is it possible to regard that in this way? This is mine, this am I, this is my self?

(That is impossible, Lord).

Now what do you think, monks, are the perceptions permanent or perishable?

(They are perishable, Lord).

And that which is perishable, does that cause pain or joy?

(It causes pain, Lord).

And that which is perishable, painful, subject to change, is it possible to regard that in this way? This is mine, this am I, this is my self?

(That is impossible, Lord).

Now what do you think, monks, are the psychic constructions permanent or perishable?

(They are perishable, Lord).

And that which is perishable, does that cause pain or joy?

(It causes pain, Lord).

And that which is perishable, painful, subject to change, is it possible to regard that in this way? This is mine, this am I, this is my self?

(That is impossible, Lord).

Now what do you think, monks, is consciousness permanent or perishable?

(It is perishable, Lord).

And that which is perishable, does that cause pain or joy?

(It causes pain, Lord).

And that which is perishable, painful, subject to change, is it possible to regard that in this way? This is mine, this am I, this is my self?

(That is impossible, Lord).

Therefore, monks, whatever bodily form has been, will be, and is now, belonging or not belonging to sentient beings, gross or subtle, inferior or superior, distant or near, all that bodily form is not mine, is not me, not my self; thus it should be considered by right knowledge according to the truth.

Therefore, monks, whatever sensations have been, will be, and are now, belonging or not belonging to sentient beings, gross or subtle, inferior or superior, distant or near, all those sensations are not mine, are not me, not my self; thus it should be considered by right knowledge according to the truth.

Therefore, monks, whatever perceptions form have been, will be, and are now, belonging or not belonging to sentient beings, gross or subtle, inferior or superior, distant or near, all those perception are not mine, are not me, not my self; thus it should be considered by right knowledge according to the truth.

Therefore, monks, whatever psychic constructions have been, will be, and are now, belonging or not belonging to sentient beings, gross or subtle, inferior or superior, distant or near, all those psychic constructions are not mine, are not me, not my self; thus it should be considered by right knowledge according to the truth.

Therefore, monks, whatever consciousness has been, will be, and is now, belonging or not belonging to sentient beings, gross or subtle, inferior or superior, distant or near, all that consciousness is not mine, is not me, not my self; thus it should be considered by right knowledge according to the truth.

Considering this, monks, the wise and noble disciple turns away from the body, turns away from sensation, turns away from perception, turns away from psychic constructions, turns away from body and mind.

Turning away he loses passion, losing passion he is liberated, in being liberated the knowledge comes to him: "I am liberated," and he knows rebirth is exhausted, the holy life is completed, duty is fulfilled; there is no more living in these conditions.

[*Thus the Blessed One spoke. The five monks were delighted and rejoiced at the words of the Blessed One. And when this exposition had been propounded, the minds of the five monks became free from attachment to the world, and were released from depravities. At that time there were six arhats in the world*].

12

Sacred Words of Buddha

- Never in this world can hatred be stilled by hatred; it will be stilled only by non-hatred — this is the law of eternal.
- Let go of anger. Let go of pride. When you are bound by nothing You go beyond sorrow.
- An unreflecting mind is a poor roof. Passion, like the rain, floods the house. But if the roof is strong, there is shelter. Whoever follows impure thoughts Suffers in this world and the next. In both worlds he suffers And how greatly.
- The Buddhas do but tell the way; it is for you to swelter at the task.
- Thousands of candles can be lighted from a single candle, and the life of the candle will not be shortened. Happiness never decreases by being shared.
- Holding on to anger is like grasping a hot coal with the intent of throwing it at someone else; you are the one getting burned.
- When a man makes utensils out of a metal which has been thoroughly cleansed of dross, the utensils will be excellent. You monks, who wish to follow the Way, make your own hearts clean from the dirt of evil passion, and your conduct will be unimpeachable.

- Few cross over the river. Most are stranded on this side. On the riverbank they run up and down. But the wise man, following the way, Crosses over, beyond the reach of death. He leaves the dark way For the way of light.
- Death is not to be feared so much by one who has lived wisely.
- Those who are pure in heart and single in purpose are able to understand the most supreme Way. It is like polishing a mirror, which becomes bright when the dust is removed. Remove your passions, and have no hankering.
- If a man who has committed many a misdemeanour does not repent and cleanse his heart of the evil, retribution will come upon his person as sure as the streams run into the ocean which becomes ever deeper and wider. If a man who has committed a misdemeanour come to the knowledge of it, reform himself, and practise goodness, the force of retribution will gradually exhaust itself as a disease gradually loses its baneful influence when the patient perspires.
- Wakefulness is the way to life. The fool sleeps As if he were already dead, But the master is awake And he lives forever.
- Endurance is one of the most difficult disciplines, but it is to the one who endures that the final victory comes.
- Hatred does not cease through hatred at any time. Hatred ceases through love. This is an unalterable law.
- The secret of health for both mind and body is not to mourn for the past, not to worry about the future, or not to anticipate troubles, but to live in the present moment wisely and earnestly.
- You cannot travel on the path until you become the path itself.
- Let the wise guard their thoughts, which are difficult to perceive, extremely subtle, and wander at will. Thought, which is well guarded is the bearer of happiness.
- The way is not in the sky. The way is in the heart.

- It is better to conquer yourself than to win a thousand battles. Then the victory is yours. It cannot be taken from you, not by angels or by demons, heaven or hell.
- A great gift — a gift of Dharma conquers all gifts.
- When an evil-doer, seeing you practise goodness, comes and maliciously insults you, you should patiently endure it and not feel angry with him, for the evil-doer is insulting himself by trying to insult you.
- Evil-doers who denounce the wise resemble a person who spits against the sky; the spittle will never reach the sky, but comes down on himself. Evil-doers again resemble a man who stirs the dust against the wind; the dust is never raised without doing him injury. Thus, the wise will never be hurt, but the curse is sure to destroy the evil-doers themselves.
- Moved by their selfish desires, people seek after fame and glory. But when they have acquired it, they are already stricken in years. If you hanker after worldly fame and practise not the Way, your labours are wrongfully applied and your energy is wasted. It is like unto burning an incense stick. However, much its pleasing odour be admired, the fire that consumes is steadily burning up the stick.
- "You can search throughout the entire universe for someone who is more deserving of your love and affection than you are yourself, and that person is not to be found anywhere. You, yourself, as much as anybody in the entire universe, deserve your love and affection."
- "Thousands of candles can be lit from a single candle, and the life of the candle will not be shortened. Happiness never decreases by being shared."
- "An idea that is developed and put into action is more important than an idea that exists only as an idea."
- "An insincere and evil friend is more to be feared than a wild beast; a wild beast may wound your body, but an evil friend will wound your mind."

- "Three things cannot be long hidden: the sun, the moon, and the truth."
- "All that we are is the result of what we have thought. The mind is everything. What we think we become."
- "Peace comes from within. Do not seek it without."
- "To understand everything is to forgive everything"
- "You will not be punished for your anger, you will be punished by your anger."
- "A dog is not considered a good dog because he is a good barker. A man is not considered a good man because he is a good talker."
- "Those who are free of resentful thoughts surely find peace."
- "However many holy words you read, However many you speak, What good will they do you If you do not act on upon them?"
- "We are shaped by our thoughts; we become what we think. When the mind is pure, joy follows like a shadow that never leaves."
- "You cannot travel the path until you have become the path itself"
- "An idea that is developed and put into action is more important than an idea that exists only as an idea."
- "When you realise how perfect everything is you will tilt your head back and laugh at the sky"
- "A jug fills drop by drop."
- "The only real failure in life is not to be true to the best one knows."
- "Believe nothing, no matter where you read it, or who said it, no matter if I have said it, unless it agrees with your own reason and your own common sense."
- "Even death is not to be feared by one who has lived wisely."
- "There is nothing more dreadful than the habit of doubt. Doubt separates people. It is a poison that disintegrates

friendships and breaks up pleasant relations. It is a thorn that irritates and hurts; it is a sword that kills."

- "The way is not in the sky. The way is in the heart."
- "Have compassion for all beings, rich and poor alike; each has their suffering. Some suffer too much, others too little."
- "Teach this triple truth to all: A generous heart, kind speech, and a life of service and compassion are the things which renew humanity."
- "The whole secret of existence is to have no fear. Never fear what will become of you, depend on no one. Only the moment you reject all help are you freed."
- "No one saves us but ourselves. No one can and no one may. We ourselves must walk the path."
- "There are only two mistakes one can make along the road to truth; not going all the way, and not starting."
- "Virtue is persecuted more by the wicked than it is loved by the good."
- "To be idle is a short road to death and to be diligent is a way of life; foolish people are idle, wise people are diligent."
- "The secret of health for both mind and body is not to mourn for the past, worry about the future, or anticipate troubles, but to live in the present moment wisely and earnestly."
- "Your work is to discover your work and then with all your heart to give yourself to it."
- "Work out your own salvation. Do not depend on others."
- "Do not believe in anything simply because you have heard it. Do not believe in anything simply because it is spoken and rumoured by many. Do not believe in anything simply because it is found written in your religious books. Do not believe in anything merely on the authority of your teachers and elders. Do not believe in traditions because they have been handed down for many generations. But after observation and analysis, when you

find that anything agrees with reason and is conducive to the good and benefit of one and all, then accept it and live up to it."

- "To conquer oneself is a greater task than conquering others"
- "Better than a thousand hollow words, is one word that brings peace."
- "He who loves 50 people has 50 woes; he who loves no one has no woes."
- "To keep the body in good health is a duty...otherwise we shall not be able to keep our mind strong and clear."
- "There has to be evil so that good can prove its purity above it."
- "Life is suffering."
- "Hatred does not cease through hatred at any time. Hatred ceases through love. This is an unalterable law."
- "Whatever words we utter should be chosen with care for people will hear them and be influenced by them for good or ill."
- "Every human being is the author of his own health or disease."
- "All things appear and disappear because of the concurrence of causes and conditions. Nothing ever exists entirely alone; everything is in relation to everything else."
- "All wrong-doing arises because of mind. If mind is transformed can wrong-doing remain?"
- "Ambition is like love, impatient both of delays and rivals."
- "Better than a thousand hollow words, is one word that brings peace."
- "Chaos is inherent in all compounded things. Strive on with diligence."
- "The tongue like a sharp knife... Kills without drawing blood."

- "Do not dwell in the past, do not dream of the future, concentrate the mind on the present moment."
- "Do not overrate what you have received, nor envy others. He who envies others does not obtain peace of mind."
- "Every human being is the author of his own health or disease."
- "Hatred does not cease by hatred, but only by love; this is the eternal rule."
- "He is able who thinks he is able"
- "He who experiences the unity of life sees his own Self in all beings, and all beings in his own Self, and looks on everything with an impartial eye."
- "Health is the greatest gift, contentment the greatest wealth, faithfulness the best relationship."
- "Holding on to anger is like grasping a hot coal with the intent of throwing it at someone else; you are the one who gets burned."
- "I do not believe in a fate that falls on men however they act; but I do believe in a fate that falls on them unless they act."
- "I never see what has been done; I only see what remains to be done."
- "In a controversy the instant we feel anger we have already ceased striving for the truth, and have begun striving for ourselves."
- "In the sky, there is no distinction of east and west; people create distinctions out of their own minds and then believe them to be true."
- "It is a man's own mind, not his enemy or foe, that lures him to evil ways."
- "Just as treasures are uncovered from the earth, so virtue appears from good deeds, and wisdom appears from a pure and peaceful mind. To walk safely through the maze of human life, one needs the light of wisdom and the guidance of virtue."

- "On life's journey faith is nourishment, virtuous deeds are a shelter, wisdom is the light by day and right mindfulness is the protection by night. If a man lives a pure life, nothing can destroy him."
- "Teach this triple truth to all: A generous heart, kind speech, and a life of service and compassion are the things which renew humanity."
- "The foot feels the foot when it feels the ground."
- "The only real failure in life is not to be true to the best one knows."
- "The wise ones fashioned speech with their thought, sifting it as grain is sifted through a sieve."
- "Unity can only be manifested by the Binary. Unity itself and the idea of Unity are already two."
- "We are formed and moulded by our thoughts. Those whose minds are shaped by selfless thoughts give joy when they speak or act. Joy follows them like a shadow that never leaves them."

13

Great Life at a Glance

563 BC: Siddhartha Gautam, was born in Lumbini, in Nepal.

534 BC: Gautam left his inheritance and became an ascetic.

528 BC: Gautam attained Enlightenment, became the Buddha, and began his ministry.

Abt. 500 BC: Classical Sanskrit replaced Vedic Language.

Abt. 483 BC: Shakyamuni Buddha died at Kushinara (now called Kushinagar).

383 BC: The Second Buddhist Council was convened by King Kalasoka and held at Vaishali.

300s BC: Oldest Brahmi script (the ancestor of Indic languages) dated from this period.

Abt. 250 BC: Third Buddhist Council convened by Ashoka and chaired by Moggaliputta Tissa, compiled the Kathavatthu to refute the heretical views and theories held by some Buddhist sects. Ashoka erected a number of edicts (Edicts of Ashoka) about the kingdom in support of Buddhism.

200s BC: Sanskrit and Prakrit languages emerged in northern India.

Abt. 220 BC: Theravada Buddhism was officially introduced in Sri Lanka by the Venerable Mahindra, the son of the Emperor Ashoka during the reign of King Devanampriya Tissa.

185 BC: Brahmin general Pusyamitra Sunga overthrew the Mauryan dynasty and established the Sunga Empire, starting of wave of persecution against Buddhism.

180 BC: Greco-Bactrian King Demetrius invaded India as far as Pataliputra, and established the Indo-Greek kingdom (180-10 BC), under which Buddhism flourished.

Abt. 150 BC: Indo-Greek King Menander I converted to Buddhism under the sage Nagasena, according to the account of the Milinda Panha.

120 BC: The Chinese Emperor Han Wudi (156-87 BC) received two golden statues of the Buddha, according to inscriptions in the Mogao Caves, Dunhuang.

1st century BC: The Indo-Greek governor Theodorus enshrined relics of the Buddha, dedicating them to "Lord Shakyamuni".

Bibliography

A.K. Narain and D.C. Ahir: *Dr. Ambedkar, Buddhism and Social Change*, Buddhist World Press, 2010.

Ananda, K. Coomaraswamy: *Buddha and the Gospel of Buddhism*, Munshiram Manoharlal, 2003.

Arthur, Lillie: *Buddha and Buddhism*, AES, 2000.

Arvind Kumar Singh: *Buddhism in Far East Asia*, MD Pub., 2009.

Asim, Kumar Chatterjee: *A Comprehensive History of Indian Buddhism*, Punthi Pustak, 2005.

B. C. Sinha and Rakesh Sharma: *Buddhism and Symbol Worship*, Satyam Publication, 2005.

B.L. Mungekar: *Dr. Ambedkar's Approach to Buddhism : Towards A Socio-Cultural and Democratic Revolution*, Northern Book Centre, 2000.

Bechert, Heinz and Richard Gombrich: *The World of Buddhism*, Thames & Hudson, 1984.

Bechert, Heinz: *When Did the Buddha Live? The Controversy on the Dating of the Historical Buddha*, Sri Satguru, Delhi, 1996.

Biswanath, Banerjee and Sukomal Chaudhuri: *Buddha and Buddhism*, The Asiatic Society, 2005.

Bodo, Balsys: *Ahimsa : Buddhism and the Vegetarian Ideal*, Munshiram Manoharlal Pub, 2004.

Buswell, Robert E.: *Encyclopedia of Buddhism*, MacMillan Reference Books, 2003.

Charles S. Prebish: *Buddhism : A Modern Perspective*, Satguru, 1995.

Chitrarekha, V. Kher: *Buddhism as Presented by the Brahmanical Systems*, 1992.

Conze, Edward: *Buddhist Scriptures*, Penguin Books, London, 1959.

Coogan, Michael D.: *The Illustrated Guide to World Religions*, Oxford University Press, 2003.

Coomeraswamy, Ananda K.: *Buddha and the Gospel of Buddhism*, London, 1928.

D. R. Jatava: *Buddhism in Modern World*, ABD Publication, 2007.

D.C. Ahir: *A Panorama of Indian Buddhism : Selections from the Maha Bodhi Journal (1892-1992)*, Satguru, 1995.

Damien, Keown: *Buddhism : A Very Short Introduction*, Oxford University, 2005.

Davidson, Ronald M.: *Indian Esoteric Buddhism: A Social History of the Tantric Movement*, Columbia University Press, New York, 2003.

Edward, Conze: *Buddhism: Its Essence and Development*, Rupa, 2005.

Ernest, J. Eitel: *Buddhism : Its Historical Theoretical and Popular Aspects*, AES, 1993.

G. Kamalakar: *Buddhism : Art, Architecture, Literature and Philosophy (2 Vols-Set)*, Sharada Pub, 2005.

Gethin, Rupert: *Foundations of Buddhism*, Oxford University Press, 1998.

Gombrich, Richard F.: *Theravâda Buddhism: A Social History from Ancient Benares to Modern Colombo*, Routledge, London, 1988.

Gunaratana, Bhante Henepola: *Mindfulness in Plain English*, Wisdom Publications, 2002.

Gunnar, Gallmo: *A Few Facts About Buddhism*, D K Printworld, 1998.

Gyatso, Geshe Kelsang: *Introduction to Buddhism: An Explanation of the Buddhist Way of Life*, Tharpa Publications, US 2008.

H.B.M. Ilangasinha: *Buddhism in Medieval Sri Lanka*, Satguru, 1992.

Harischandra, Lal Singh: *Buddhism in Nepal : A Brief Historical Introduction*, Ratna Pustak Bhandar, 2004.

Harvey, Peter: *An Introduction to Buddhism: Teachings, History and Practices*, Cambridge University Press, 1990.

Iqbal Singh, S. Radhakrishnan, Arvind Sharma: *The Buddhism Omnibus : Gautama Buddha ; The Dhammapada ; The Philosophy of Religion : A Buddhist Perspective*, Oxford Univerity Press, 2004.

Iran, Harris: *Buddhism, Power and Political Order*, Manohar, 2007.

Ito, Shinjo: *Shinjo:Reflections*, Somerset Hall Press,2009.

J.G. Da Cunha: *Memoir on the History of the Tooth-Relic of Ceylon with a Preliminary Essay on the Life and System of Gautama Buddha*, AES, 2001.

Jacob, N Kinnard: *Emergence of Buddhism*, Pentagon Press, 2008.

Juergensmeyer, Mark: *The Oxford Handbook of Global Religions*, Oxford University Press, Oxford, 2006.

Juliane: *Sacred Biography in the Buddhist Traditions of South and Southeast Asia*, Motilal Banarsidass, 2002.

Kadambari, Kaul: *Gautama Buddha : A Noble Life*, Rupa & Co, 2003.

Kashi, Nath Upadhyaya: *Early Buddhism and The Bhagavadgita*, Motilal Banarsidass, 1998.

Kohn, Michael H.: *The Shambhala Dictionary of Buddhism and Zen*, Shambhala, 1991.

Lal, Moti Pandit: *Buddhism: A Religion of Salvation*, Munshiram Manoharlal, 2004.

Lamotte, Etienne: *Teaching of Vimalakirti*, Pali Text Society, London, 1976.

Lowenstein, Tom: *The Vision of the Buddha*, Duncan Baird Publishers, 1996.

Malati J. Shendge: *Buddhahood in this Body : Japanese Esoteric Buddhism (Shin-gon) in Context*, Pratibha Prakashan, 2009.

Manan, Sharma: *Buddhism*, Diamond Pocket Books, 2002.

Maurice, Walshe: *The Long Discourses of the Buddha: A Translation of the Dîgha Nikaya*, Wisdom Publications, Boston, 1995.

Mitchell, Robert Allen: *The Buddha*, New York, 1989.

Morgan, Kenneth W.: *The Path of the Buddha: Buddhism Interpreted by Buddhists*, Ronald Press, New York, 1956.

Moti, Lal Pandit: *Encounter with Buddhism : A Study of the Evolution of Buddhist Thought*, Munshiram Manoharlal, 2005.

Nalinaksha, Dutt: *Early History of the Spread of Buddhism and the Buddhist Schools*, Cosmo, 2005.

Narendra, K. Dash: *Buddhism in Indian Literature*, Aryan Books International, 2007.

Pushpesh, Pant: *Buddhism*, Roli, 2000.

R N Salve: *Buddhism and Education*, Shruti Publication, 2008.

R. Spence Hardy: *A Manual of Buddhism in its Modern Development*, Munshiram, 1995.

Rahula, Walpola: *What the Buddha Taught*, Grove Press, 1974.

Ram, Nandan Singh: *Buddhism from Genesis to Decline*, New Bharatiya Book Corporation, 2007.

Rhys, Davids: *A Manual of Buddhism : For Advanced Students*, Low Price, 2000.

Richard King: *Early Advaita Vedanta and Buddhism: The Mahayana Context of the Gaudapadiya-karika*, Satguru, 1997.

Richard, Gombrich: *Theravada Buddhism: A Social History from Ancient Benares to Modern Colombo*, Routledge and Kegan Paul, 1988.

Richard, Gombrich: *Theravada Buddhism: A Social History from Ancient Benares to Modern Colombo*, Routledge and Kegan Paul, 1988.

Robinson, Richard H. and Willard L. Johnson: *The Buddhist Religion: A Historical Introduction*, Belmont, Wadsworth Publishing, California, 1970.

Romila, Thapar: *The Penguin History of Early India: From Origins to AD 1300*, Penguin Books, 2002.

S. Jafar Mahmud: *Buddhism : Religion and Meditation*, A.P.H., 1998.

S. K. Ramachandra Rao: *Encyclopaedia of Indian Iconography: Hinduism-Buddhism-Jainism,* Satguru, 2003.

S. M. Haldhar: *Buddhism in Myanmar and Thailand,* Om Pub, 2005.

S.R. Bakshi and Sangh Mittra: *Gautama Buddha : Saints of India,* Criterion Pub, 2002.

Sameer, Das Gupta: *Buddhism, Reflection on Religious Conversion,* Cyber Tech Pub., 2010.

Sangharakshita: *Ambedkar and Buddhism,* Motilal Banarsidass, 2006.

Sanghasen, Singh: *Buddhism in Comparative Light,* Indo-Asian, 1999.

Sathe, Shriram: *Dates of the Buddha,* Bharatiya Itihasa Sankalana Samiti, Hyderabad, 1987.

Sir M. Monier Williams: *Buddhism : Connexion with Brahmanism, Hinduism and Contrast with Christianity,* Bharatiya Kala Prakashan, 2007.

Sital, Prasad: *A Comparative Study of Jainism and Buddhism,* Satguru, 2003.

Skilton, Andrew: *A Concise History of Buddhism,* Windhorse Publications, 1997.

Smith, Huston and Phillip Novak: *Buddhism: A Concise Introduction,* HarperSanFrancisco, 2003.

Sristidhar, Dutta and Byomakesh Tripathy: *Buddhism in North-East India,* Indus Pub, 2006.

Sue Hamilton: *Early Buddhism: A New Approach,* Routledge, 2000.

Sukumar, Dutt: *Buddhism in East Asia: An Outline of Buddhism in the History and Culture of the Peoples of East Asia,* Originals, 2004.

Suman, Chaterjee: *Buddhism : The Way to Wisdom,* Cyber Tech Publication, 2009.

Suraj, Vashishth: *A Handbook of Buddhism: Art, Architecture, Literature and Philosophy,* Cyber Tech Pub, 2009.

Susan, Roth: *Buddha,* Delacorte Press, New York, 1994.

Sushil, K. Naidu: *Buddhism in Nepal,* Kalinga, 2008.

Sushma, Kulshreshtha: *Amitabha-Buddha-Srih : Gems of Buddhism,* Eastern Book Link, 1996.

T.W. Rhys Davids: *Buddhism : Its History and Literature*, Orient, 1998.

Tansen, Sen: *Buddhism, Diplomacy and Trade : The Realignment of Sino-Indian Relations, 600-1400*, Manohar, 2004.

Thanissaro, Bhikkhu: *Refuge: An Introduction to the Buddha, Dhamma, & Sangha*, 2001.

Thich, Nhat Hanh: *The Heart of the Buddha's Teaching*, Broadway Books, 1974.

Thomas, Edward J.: *The Life of Buddha*, London, 1949.

Thurman, Robert A. F.: *Holy Teaching of Vimalakirti: Mahayana Scripture*, Pennsylvania State University Press, 1976.

Vidhushekhara, Bhattacharya: *Basic Conception of Buddhism*, Universal Voice, 2007.

Vidyotma, Singh: *Buddhism : History, Philosophy and Practices*, Vista International, 2009.

Vishwanath Prasad Varma: *Early Buddhism and its Origins*, Munshiram Manoharlal, 1973.

White, Kenneth: *The Role of Bodhicitta in Buddhist Enlightenment Including a Translation into English of Bodhicitta-sastra, Benkemmitsu-nikyoron, and Sammaya-kaijo*, The Edwin Mellen Press, 2005.

Williams, Paul: *Buddhism: Critical Concepts in Religious Studies*, Routledge, London 2005.

Y. Sudershan Rao and G Bhadru Naik: *Buddhism and Modern Society*, Deep and Deep, 2008.

Yamamoto, Kosho: *The Mahayana Mahaparinirvana Sutra*, Nirvana Publications, London, 2000.

Yin Shun, Yeung H. Wing: *The Way to Buddhahood: Instructions from a Modern Chinese Master*, Wisdom Publications, 1998.

Index

C

D

E

F

G

H

I

J

K

L

M

N

P

Q

R

S

T

U

V

W

Y

❑❑❑